THE PURSUIT OF GREA...

ROBERT HOLLAND

was educated at Southend High School and Jesus College, Oxford. After working for a finance house in the City, he returned to Oxford, where he carried out research at St Antony's College in the field of the history of the British Empire and held the appointment of Beit Junior Lecturer in Imperial and Commonwealth History. Since 1977 he has been a lecturer at the Institute of Commonwealth Studies in London University. He is the author of *Britain and the Commonwealth Alliance, 1918–39, European Decolonization, 1918–81: An Introductory Survey* and numerous articles chiefly concerned with economic and political aspects of British and imperial questions during the twentieth century. He is currently writing a general history of the revolt against British rule in Cyprus during the 1950s.

FONTANA HISTORY OF ENGLAND

Edited by G. R. Elton
Regius Professor of Modern History at the
University of Cambridge

The aim of the series is to reinterpret familiar and unfamiliar
aspects of English history. There will be a pair of volumes on
each chronological period (except the first) which will throw
new light on the age in question by discussing it in relation to
contrasting themes.

ALREADY PUBLISHED

Robert Holland

THE PURSUIT OF GREATNESS

BRITAIN AND THE WORLD ROLE, 1900–1970

FontanaPress

An Imprint of HarperCollinsPublishers

First published in Great Britain in 1991 by Fontana Press,
an imprint of HarperCollins Publishers,
77–85 Fulham Palace Road,
Hammersmith, London W6 8JB

9   8   7   6   5   4   3   2   1

BRITISH LIBRARY CATALOGUING IN PUBLICATION DATA
Holland, R. F.
The pursuit of greatness: 1900–1970.
1. Great Britain, history, 1901–1970.
I. Title
941.082

ISBN 0 00 686110 5

Printed and bound in Great Britain by
HarperCollins Book Manufacturing, Glasgow

TO
REGINALD DOVETON HOLLAND
'MINE HOST'

Contents

Prologue

This fresh instalment of the *Fontana History of England* is a protracted essay on the United Kingdom's foreign policy and imperial entanglements during the twentieth century. The initial problem facing the author of any such enterprise is where, precisely, to begin and what exact juncture should be fixed upon as the destination of the narrative. Our analysis will start with the Anglo-Boer War under way in South Africa right at the end of the nineteenth century, since that conflict was the touchstone of those anxieties and premonitions which not only characterized the ensuing Edwardian era, but cast a shadow over much British history to follow. More problematical is the question of where to end. The broad argument which will be propounded in the following pages, however, makes 1970 an appropriate cut-off point. It was, in sum, the great sterling crisis of November 1967 and its aftermath which finally delivered the *coup de grâce* to those ideas and ideals of British greatness (by then, admittedly, mostly residual) which lie at the heart of this book. This is not to say that certain continuities did not survive into a still later period. Mrs Thatcher's Britain continued to be preponderantly orientated, in foreign policy terms, towards the United States; whilst the Falklands War of 1982 evoked much of the old John Bull emotion, even if the driving force behind the British campaign in the South Atlantic was much more redolent of the narrow English nationalism of the 1980s than of its grander variants which had gone before. Nevertheless, our assumption here will be that the politics which took shape in the United Kingdom after 1970 – with its internal foci, its preoccupations with questions of economic management and consequent social divisiveness – were of a fundamentally different nature than the Great Power, One Nation norms which had impregnated English political discourse for so long.

Books which cover this ground are scarcely in short supply. Their collective theme is invariably that of Britain's progressive decline since *circa* 1900. 'The Weary Titan staggers under the too vast orb of its fate', Joseph Chamberlain roundly declared at the Colonial Conference of 1902; certainly students of recent British history stagger under the weight of tomes which interpret events backwards in terms of Chamberlain's celebrated dictum. As a consequence, Britain during the era we shall be discussing is usually pictured as engaged in a struggle for survival forced upon her by changing, and all too often hostile, forces elsewhere in the world; constantly battling amidst recurrent crises threatening first one vulnerable flank of British interests, and then another; until the herculean effort proved too much and responsibilities had to be matched more carefully with capacity, and mounting liabilities reluctantly set off against rapidly diminishing assets. A veritable declinology has emerged along these lines, the most elegant exponent of which, Paul Kennedy, has distilled from British experience a theory of imperial 'overstretch' which applies to all dominating powers in modern history, including the contemporary United States.[1] There is certainly much in this view which is persuasive. A slippery aspect of these analyses, nevertheless, is the way in which the contentions of participants in the events themselves have subsequently been elevated by scholars into comprehensive historical explanations. In this manner Kennedy, in an earlier work, took up the original theses of the pioneer of modern geo-politics, Halford Mackinder, writing at the turn of the century to the effect that the United Kingdom, as an island race, was destined to lose power and status to the great continental heartlands of Russia and America, and proceeded to incorporate these insights into a framework for interpreting the following decades.[2] This particular analysis, it may be said, was more credible at its inception than it seems today, when an emerging global power for the twenty-first century is also an island community with even greater physical disadvantages, and certainly fewer natural resources, than the United Kingdom – to wit, Japan. Such geographical factors apart, however, it is an obvious truism to assert that the central theme in British affairs during the present century – and hence the organizing principle of any study of those affairs – is what Robert Blake in a similar survey to the present one has called 'The Decline of Power'.[3]

It would be intellectually churlish to seek to part company with these conventions altogether. Transparently, Britain *has* declined in relation to the United States; equally clearly, Britain had come to 'count' for less in the world at the end of the period than she had done at the beginning. Yet Edwardian critics of Joseph Chamberlain's sustained pessimism considered it to be overblown, and a degree of scepticism of the same sort is, perhaps, appropriate in the context of latter-day historiographical controversy also. Has Britain really declined against India, say, or any number of other countries – including the Soviet Union, destined, as some experts now predict, to disappear altogether as an organic power before the millennium is out? Decline may appear as a satisfyingly concrete phenomenon to Foreign Office clerks, or their paler brethren in the groves of Academe, but becomes much more elusive, shaded and even evanescent when considered in relation to British society as a whole. Furthermore, not only is there the issue of decline as measured against specific competitors, but there is also a difficulty posed by an assumed fall from a peak of grandeur which is itself wrapped in hypothetical clouds. The phrase 'Splendid Isolation', coined to describe the United Kingdom's condition and posture at the very end of the Victorian Age, and to which our opening chapter shall revert, was intended by its overseas creator to have a jocular ring; later commentators have frequently taken it at face value, and thereby missed the joke. For those who believe that Britain's rulers were once capable of mediating the destiny of Europe, the subsequent decline of power seems awesome in its extent; but if it is recognized that such claims were always vestigial – that it was Blücher, not Wellington, for example, who had earlier swung the balance at Waterloo – the fall of British *imperium* assumes a less catastrophic, even theatrical, air, reminiscent of Shakespeare's Duke of Gloucester stumbling over the putative chalk-cliff at Dover only to find that all his limbs remained amazingly unharmed.[4] What needs explaining quite as much as the causes and course of British decline as a world force, therefore, is why and how an inflated conception of national prestige and 'reach' – a conception over and beyond the more discriminating orthodoxies of Victorian England – came to predominate at the highest levels of British statecraft after 1900, and why it was able to remain in place for so long.

One reason for this longevity is to be found in the moral compulsions surrounding the United Kingdom's 'world role' – as it eventually came to be summarized – and which were such a distinctive part of the trappings of British political culture. A comparison may be made here with France. In the nineteenth century it was the French, with their revolutionary credentials, who sought to define their political purposes in moral terms, whilst their British neighbours and inveterate rivals prided themselves on their practicality and common sense. In 1940, however, France had all the moral stuffing knocked out of her; afterwards she espoused a peculiarly crystalline, almost consciously amoral, form of expediency in which a pragmatic settlement with Germany featured prominently. Conversely, it was the United Kingdom whose leaderships frequently, if not invariably, came to view the world through a particular kind of moral lens, and for whom the events of 1940 extrapolated, rather than exploded, this tendency. The moral component in British greatness was such that not only is it true to say that the United Kingdom was subject after 1900 to successive challenges from one quarter or another – be it from an upstart Hohenzollern prince, an Austrian corporal made good as Reich Chancellor, 'the Red menace', or, in the seminal Suez crisis of 1956, from an impudent Egyptian Colonel – but that there was displayed at the same time an in-built *susceptibility* to identify threats with which to engage, since the very engagement solidified a political hierarchy for which greatness overseas, and the preservation of the so-called 'Balance of Power' at large, had become essential cement. It is this complicated link between ideals and values as they pertained to a distressingly unstable and unreliable outside world, and matching ideals and values as they pertained to a social order at home which also exhibited periodic signs of stress, which will be an important – if not always explicit – element in the development of our overall argument.

British political morality, and its prefectural instincts, was, of course, closely bound up with the possession of a great Empire. The hey-day of that Empire is usually considered to be part and parcel of the mid-Victorian climax, and yet the Victorians always retained a healthy scepticism when it came to equating 'red on the map' with real power; success at bringing more and more Hottentots under the sway of the Union Jack was not taken as proof that the British Government had the capacity to play a determining role in the resolution of the Schleswig-Holstein Question. Paradoxically, the orchestration of imperial power and its attendant morality played a far more prominent role in British life, and profoundly affected Britons' views of themselves, *after* 1900, when the structure began to heave, than it had done before. It was then that the fact of empire, and the ideology to which it gave rise, was used to undergird a vision of national greatness on which the legitimacy of the status quo had come to depend. Our thesis will be, in part, that the process which thus evolved was one in which the ability to distinguish the secular interests of the British home islands, in fact the notion of 'nationhood' itself, became blurred by its confusion with a far wider, disparate and ultimately unworkable association. When the empire fell apart, the British, in a very real sense, had to rediscover themselves as a distinct community, and this was to prove – especially as it coincided with grave internal difficulties – far from easy to achieve amidst a welter of regional, social and economic divisions.

Any discussion of empire and imperialism as a phenomenon is complicated by the necessity to distinguish between their formal and informal manifestations. This is particularly relevant to the themes we shall discuss in so far as British overseas power was constantly shifting its axis from extensive formal obligations which were increasingly unsustainable to areas where informal domination appeared to remain a viable mode. Above all, this expressed itself in a relegation of Asia in general, and India especially, within the pecking-order of British interests, and the promotion of the Middle East and the Eastern Mediterranean. From at least the Great War of 1914–18 onwards it was Egypt, not India, which was the bastion around which the United Kingdom tried to construct a new, leaner system of prestige and influence. When British attempts to establish a role as a great Continental land power repeatedly came to grief, as they did in both world wars, it was to the 'soft underbelly' of an extended Middle Eastern region that first Lloyd George, and later Winston Churchill, looked for compensation. This new geographical bias will feature largely in our account. Retrospectively the British – not unnaturally – were far more ready to congratulate themselves on their relatively graceful demission of power in India in 1947 than they were to acknowledge the effects which flowed from their simultaneous efforts to exploit fresh opportunities elsewhere. Britain was not, for the most part, hated by Indians in the period of our study, but she did come to be so regarded at certain points by Cypriots, Maltese, Egyptians, Syrians, Jews as well as Arabs in Palestine, Persians and Iraqis. Attempts to delineate the course of British policies which do not account for this pattern of discontents, intruding powerfully as they do into our own day, surely gloss over matters of some import.

The rhythm of British policy outside Europe was, as we have already implied, closely connected with her erratic Continental fortunes. In reacting against the Victorian establishment, one of the striking traits of much Edwardian thinking was the goal of an increased leverage over the direction of European affairs. This was reflected at many levels: where Queen Victoria, for example, had styled herself Empress of India, her successor, Edward VII, veered towards an alternative emphasis on the British monarchy's status as a great European dynasty, so that almost his first act of Household policy was to command the eviction of his mother's much-resented Indian servitors from their lodgings within Windsor Castle.[5] Before long this tendency was tendency was to attain its critical medium through the making of a diplomatic, and soon afterwards a military, tie with France. It was a policy and an ambition which was to endure many ups and downs in the future, and which came to form – as in a sense it still does today – a principal dividing line in British politics. United Kingdom attitudes towards Europe, however, always swung ponderously between two opposite poles: between, on the one hand, a commitment to the leadership of a Continental coalition, and on the other hand, a desire to have as little to do with the adjoining mainland as possible. What those who supported British engagement in the struggle for mastery in Europe, and those who found such commotions alien to a clinical understanding of British interests, essentially shared was a distaste for negotiation, a feeling that amidst the wheeler-dealing of the Continental chancellories the British voice was always liable to be shouted down or reduced to a squeaking chorus from the sidelines. A certain dignified acceptance of the proper role to be played by Britain in the nineteenth-century Concert of Europe, and a recognition of its limits, was replaced by a nagging uncertainty and nervousness which led to alternate bouts of braggadocio – climaxing in the view widely expressed in Whitehall after 1940 that many of the smaller European nations would have no option in the future but to become British Dominions[6] – or of the kind of isolationism which later became such a tangible part of British attitudes in the 1950s. Whilst these issues were not wholly resolved by 1970, and after 1972 were to some extent only brought *within* the ambit of the European Community, they were at least reduced to something much more resembling the scales of reality.

British sensibilities towards Europe, of course, were above all a matter of the sensibilities aroused with respect to Germany and German power. Again, at the outset of our period it was suggestive that Kaiser Wilhelm II's grief at the death-bed of his grandmother, Queen Victoria, was regarded by the British courtiers at Osborne House as embarrassing and unwanted.[7] This episode was the symbol of a fast-fading amity between the leaders and peoples of the two countries. 'Painting the German devil on the wall' was within a few years to become the leading motif of British diplomacy; it was one way, for example, that the Foreign Office – otherwise much prone to criticism for being 'soft' on foreigners – could cultivate an appearance of toughness in line with 'manly' Edwardian imagery; Germanophobia also had the utility of providing an essentially aristocratic organ of government[8] with populist credentials that were otherwise hard to come by. The roots of this national prejudice, as it undoubtedly became, was as much cultural as bureaucratic, and to that extent firmly embedded in British life: the growth of German dominance in Europe became fatally entwined with the United Kingdom's sense of its own resilience and status as a nation. Against this background we shall contend that the controversy over Appeasement in the 1930s was the most powerful and determining episode for British politics during the century. The problem was that any system of alliances and expedients which sought to redirect the natural flow of power in central and eastern Europe could never be truly lasting. As such, it was the very artificiality and contrivance of post-1945 Cold War divisions which made that order of things for British Governments the best of all possible worlds. From this situation flowed the eventual irony that it was the United Kingdom – much more so, for instance, than the United States or even France – who showed evident signs of being nonplussed when one effect of the European revolutions in *Mitteleuropa* during the autumn of 1989 was to trigger a forced march towards German reunification. Since that remarkable sequence of events it has been commonly declared that all the history books need to be rewritten, and although this is clearly hyperbolic it can be more soberly said that the revisonist implications for the British experience are more pronounced than for most of the other affected countries.

It was, suggestively, on the rebound from successive near-fatal blows in Europe, first in the great German offensive of March 1918 and much more definitively with Hitler's *blitzkrieg* in Western Europe during the spring of 1940, that the British were to be propelled willy-nilly into a much closer alliance with the United States, and the course of Anglo-American relations will necessarily constitute a feature of our narrative.

For Lloyd George, as we shall see, this dependence was alien and curiously demeaning; for Churchill – whose aristocratic background meant that he was well-attuned to the ploy of tapping into American cash – it evoked no such reluctance. Looking back on the course of the 'Special Relationship' between London and Washington during the twentieth century, however, perhaps what is most striking is the extent to which its existence was so overwhelmingly mediated at the rarefied level of President and Prime Minister, with its trio of magnetic pairings: Winston Churchill-Franklin Roosevelt, Harold Macmillan-John Kennedy and (to go slightly beyond the scope of this study) Margaret Thatcher-Ronald Reagan. Its meanings and affections became more unstable the lower down the hierarchy, and the further out into the country, one went; British politicians generally may have admired, and above all needed, America in the years after 1940, but they did not love her as, for example, one British Foreign Secretary in the 1920s, Austen Chamberlain, claimed to love France. This was natural enough, since it is always difficult to love one's superiors, and whereas in constructing bilateral ties between 1900 and 1940 the United Kingdom could usually play the part of principal, afterwards in the most important bilateral tie of all she was transparently junior. 'Why can't we have our own foreign policy?' remonstrated Anthony Eden in 1943, for whom this subordination cut especially deeply[9], and one of the critical tensions underlying the second half of this work – a joker, as it were, in the pack – is the fact that a British polity which had come to be founded on the primacy of foreign policy discovered to its consternation that events had conspired to undermine even this consolation. In establishing external goals over and above the capacity of British power and influence to secure, the United Kingdom was forced into an unusual degree of intimacy with a nation more powerful than she was, and such a position – whatever compensating links of language and culture there may be – is inevitably full of ambiguities and occasional discomforts. The painful 'writing down' of the United Kingdom's world position finally confronted from the mid-1960s onwards, therefore, went hand-in-hand with a reduction in the transatlantic commitment, and it was part of the same logic that the most 'pro-European' politicians in Britain were also those with a pronounced tendency to depreciate the 'Special Relationship' with America; under Edward Heath's premiership between 1970 and 1974, indeed, that relationship not only ceased to be special, but became cooler than at any time since Eden's unavailing 'dash' for his own, untrammelled foreign policy in 1956.

These various diplomatic orientations derived much of their more subterranean significance for Britain from the manner in which they impinged upon the uneasy relationship between civilian and power-political ideals in national affairs. The rivalry between *Aussenpolitik* and *Innenpolitik*, between the discrete imperatives of economics and military strength, has been much written about in German historical science, but the model is useful in understanding the British case as well. Thus whereas the Victorians had admired and generally awarded the palm to essentially domestic statesmen, for whom the presentation of an acclaimed Budget was the acme of greatness, during most of the twentieth century such talents were mostly left to wither on the vine, or rather were accorded a purely subordinate place within the hierarchy of the state. Britain remained too rich and diverse a society, its civic impulses too continuous, for domestic currents to be kept permanently at bay, and during interludes of tranquillity they always rose powerfully to the surface, as they did after 1919 (and more fitfully after 1945). David Low's famous cartoons of 'Colonel Blimp' during the era of Appeasement encapsulated just such a reaction against the caste values which continued to be powerfully entrenched in Britain. Successive national crises, nevertheless, served to give the 'Old World', as Churchill liked to summarize his political ideal, a fresh lease of life. 'Today, a new generation of [British] subalterns, with the approval or by the orders of County Officers', a confidential American survey of the United Kingdom Armed Forces observed during the Second World War, 'have gone back to the polished cross-straps, swagger canes, long haircuts and Mayfair moustaches of the traditional "military gentleman". Superficial as these physical changes seem, they have brought to the commissioned ranks a renewed emphasis on privilege and social precedence.'[10] Nor was this precedence, in slightly amended form at least, without legitimacy across a surprisingly broad spectrum of British life and institutions; as one astute journalistic observer of post-war England has put it, with his tongue not wholly in his cheek, the Labour Government which entered office in July 1945, with its 'fitness to govern' still to prove, subsequently presided over 'the greatest restoration of traditional social values since the return of the monarchy in 1660'.[11] In this regard the first key to any understanding of the country's alleged economic 'failure' in modern times, which has become such a bone of contention among economists and historians, is that whilst the traces of an expanding and capitalist society were never entirely obscured from view, for long periods the United Kingdom was converted into a kind of qualified *ancien régime* for whom success was measured – as in all such regimes – by its achievements in war and diplomacy rather than by more complex and material criteria.

Finally, a recurrent concern of the following pages will be the evolution of the national consensus on which this shaky edifice rested. From the trade-offs of 'New Liberalism' and Edwardian Conservatism on the eve of 1914, through to the Beveridge-style collectivism of the 1940s, a deal emerged in which the Right was given a lien on Greatness abroad whilst the Left was accorded a legacy of publicly-administered Welfare at home. These were the inflexible parameters within which British affairs were guided and within which, too, the machine of government became not only peculiarly susceptible to inflation, but in fact inoperable without it. The resulting structure of interests and groups held together so long as the twin burdens of Greatness and Welfare could be financed without too visibly curtailing the aspirations of large numbers of people, and in particular the needs of the middling classes of society. This was, indeed, the point reached after 1960 when a combination of fiscal-cum-currency crisis and a newly-enlarged, more marginal and therefore more assertive middle class at last burst the bounds of the existing framework; and since few things are so revealing of any generation as its jokes, we may remark that the true successor of the social and political critique of 'Colonel Blimp' was the fierce new television satire of the early and middle sixties, with its scarcely-concealed contempt for an entity which had belatedly been identified as The Establishment. The ensuing devaluation of sterling, the retreat from the Persian Gulf, and the long-delayed move towards joining the European Community during the latter part of the decade was simply part of a wider *re-embourgeoisement* of British politics whose ramifications were to continue throughout the seventies and eighties. In this process we have a key to explaining the paradox that it was in the end a renegade Toryism, rather than some Labour variant, which ultimately elbowed itself free from the old order and proceeded to bury it. Whether the British political order which by the final phases of the century had emerged from this thorough-going, if not uniformly triumphant, reform was any better, or any more at ease with itself, than the one it had displaced must be left to the judgement of the reader.

1

Greatness and the Edwardians

When Queen Victoria died on 22 January 1901, the United Kingdom was engaged in a tiresome and unexpectedly prolonged war against the Afrikaner republics of the Transvaal and the Orange Free State in South Africa. The debate over the causes of this 'big little' conflict has never lost its controversial quality. In recent decades, when material and *marxisant* explanations have been predominant, it has become common to consider the major figures on the British side – above all Joseph Chamberlain, the Colonial Secretary in the incumbent Unionist ministry led by the third Lord Salisbury, and Sir Alfred Milner, the zealous United Kingdom High Commissioner in South Africa – as, in varying degrees, the agents of the gold-mine owners bent on sweeping aside the allegedly decrepit and obstructive Boer regime in the Transvaal.[1] More recently, a renewed emphasis has been given by some commentators to the fact that, however impetuous and bellicose was the role played by certain individuals, the decision to go to war in October 1899 was ultimately taken by a united Cabinet in London, compelled not by economic considerations but by the necessity to show that in South Africa 'we not the Dutch are boss'.[2] In the light of later British history it is this evocation of the diplomatic and military priorities within the metropolitan official mind which is perhaps the most persuasive.

Whatever the causes of the South African War may have been, the fortunes which awaited the British Army were not brilliant.[3] The successive defeats incurred in 'Black Week' (9–16 December 1899) constituted a heavy blow to Britain's martial repute. The British Government tided over the crisis by framing

21

the Commander-in-Chief of the Imperial forces, General Sir Redvers Buller, as a scapegoat, and instituting the dual command of Lords Roberts and Kitchener, backed by large reinforcements of men and money. It still proved, however, a long haul to victory; even after Pretoria had finally been occupied by British troops in June 1900, the struggle assumed a haphazard pattern in which the mobile Dutch commandos raided up and down the veldt, and even into the Cape itself, as Kitchener unavailingly sought to starve and harass his elusive opponents into submission. When peace was finally stumbled into at the Vereeniging talks in May 1902, famine and disease gripped much of South Africa, and the resulting sufferings visited upon the Boers (including a new strategic invention called a 'concentration camp') bonded this intractable people into a more resolute and solidified entity than had been the case before the conflict began. The British were, perhaps, unlucky to be the first in the modern century to come up against the messy and invariably insoluble problems of guerilla combat; the lessons were to be badly learned by others as well as themselves. Nevertheless, it was of the highest moment that the Edwardian era opened in the United Kingdom amidst such shadows and was touched by triumph only of a highly ambiguous kind.

Nevertheless, with British mastery restored in the region, Lord Milner – now not only High Commissioner, but Governor of the Transvaal and Orange River colonies – set about the reconstruction of the war-torn provinces, sketching the ideal of a new South African Dominion, the infusing principle of which was to be an ultra-imperial patriotism. He proceeded to gather about him a select band of athletic and well-bred young gentlemen (the famous 'Kindergarten') dedicated to an administrative and social revolution. Driven by the exhilaration, as one observer remarked, of 'men who have a great new country given into their hands like a lump of clay to be modelled'[4], they laboured at Anglicizing the education system, unlocking adequate supplies of African labour and reforming land tenure. Yet their enthusiasms, whilst undeniably scintillating, struck some as bogus. 'The day of the cads is at hand', Raymond Asquith, the flower of a liberal

generation bound for the killing-ground of the Somme, remarked
of the kindergarten phenomenon, 'I always knew it would come
to this if we let ourselves in for an empire'.[5] In fact the clay of
South Africa soon showed a tendency to resist, in defeat as in war,
any modelling from the outside. Yet the difference, so powerfully
evoked by events in that country, between rival values in English
statecraft was to underlie much of the passion in British politics
during the years ahead.

What, then, were the essential instincts and characteristics
of the *religio Milneriana*, as one commentator has called it[6],
which cut a wide swathe through British upper-class thought
and feeling in the *fin-de-siècle* era? By temperament 'thorough',
and with a strict training in logic from the University of
Heidelberg, Milner frankly hated the liberal Victorian state
and the social climate which sustained it. He was impervious
to the achievements of the Gladstonian polity, and scathing
towards its delicate accommodations. 'Lord Milner,' it has
been written of this acidulous figure, 'could only see the
tactics, and the evasions, and the faults of the system he
loathed'.[7] The mystic appeal of 'Constructive and Imperial
Ideals' for many Britons lay precisely in the antithesis they
supposedly presented to what was stigmatized as a rampant
and negative individualism. Nobody expressed this militant
tendency more pungently and pitilessly than the poetic darling
of Edwardian England, Rudyard Kipling. With the breath
of India still clinging to him, he pronounced England to
be 'a stuffy little place, mentally, morally and physically'.[8]
Made rank and odiferous by its narrow preoccupation with
commerce, and its stultifying penchant for the quiet life,
according to Kipling's aesthetic theory England's only hope
lay in the ventilation afforded by the flexing of imperial
strength. Comparing Japan and the United Kingdom, for
example, he remarked that the former, for all her immense
range in arts and crafts

> has been denied the last touch of firmness in her
> character which would enable her to play with the

whole round world. We possess that – we, the nation
of the glass flower shade, the pink worsted mat, the
red and green china puppy-dog, and the poisonous
Brussels carpet. It is our compensation.[9]

In sentences such as these Kipling both reflected and shaped an
important strain in modern English life which excoriated 'pale'
intellectual values and elevated bulldog philistinism into an arch
virtue. At the heart of this system of values lay a veneration
of bracing strength, and a contempt for the relaxing effects of
prosperity (though, as we shall see, not foregoing resentment
when the latter quality was increasingly possessed by other
nations). There was one feature of this putative schema,
furthermore, which was particularly to influence the English
political idyll during coming decades. This was the supposition
that what the British did best – what was best, indeed, *about*
the British – lay in their actions outside, not inside, the Home
nation. No other lines of verse had an equivalent resonance
in British public life to Kipling's much-quoted couplet 'What
do they know of England/Who only England know'. Thus
inspired, many Britons began to deprecate any form of national
patriotism which confined and defined itself within the perimeter of what was often described as a small, cramped and
petty island off the mainland of Europe. By such processes
the wider imperial idea was interwoven with those sources of
social *Angst* which marked the transition to the post-Victorian
age.

A principal touchstone of anxiety amongst the Edwardian
political classes was the apparent passing of Britain's pre-
eminence as the 'workshop of the world'. Ever since the
Merchandise Marks Act of 1887, decreeing that the country
of origin of imports had to be displayed on articles, a handle
had been given to propagandists who latched on to the theme
of the demise of English economic supremacy. Ernest Williams's
Made in Germany painted the classic picture in which German
machines, tools, household goods and toys were portrayed as
flooding into the country; the book was to have many imitators in

which countries other than Germany sometimes appeared as the chief culprit (though the efficiency, often described as 'sedulous', of the latter remained the most popular bugaboo). That what yet remained the greatest commercial nation in the world should have a taste for imports, and should even for long stretches run a trade deficit, should, perhaps, have surprised nobody; and the Free Traders who looked askance on the thesis of national decay were not slow to point out that the constant and increasing flow of imports was a natural measure of Britain's wealth and success over a long period. Yet the debate which raged rather inexpertly around crude aggregates of the nation's foreign trade was not really about economics at all. 'My opponents seem to me intellectually shortsighted', Joseph Chamberlain revealingly complained at one point. 'Throughout this controversy they have failed to seize what I believe is the essential thing to keep in mind – namely, that the greatness of a nation is not to be measured by a comparison with its own past, but by its relative position in the councils of the world'.[10] Here was the true source of the despondency which characterized many of the Edwardian cadres, and which Chamberlain especially sought to mould into a 'constructive' political force: not that the United Kingdom was getting poorer (since it was self-evidently getting richer very quickly) but that suddenly other nations, too, were prospering at an equivalent or even faster rate; and that the closing of this material gap necessarily implied an erosion of her leading place in the 'councils of the world'. At heart, then, the problem which the Edwardian elite felt itself to be confronted by was inherently political, rather than economic, and as such required political answers.

The 'controversy' to which Chamberlain referred in the quotation above was one he had himself inaugurated on 15 May 1903 when, having recently returned from a trip to South Africa, he gave an address in Birmingham Town Hall in which he attacked the insipid dogma of Free Trade and called for an Imperial *Zollverein*. This proved a formative moment for many rising Conservative politicians. The young Leopold Amery may be taken as an illustration. After a period as a military correspondent in South Africa, Amery had returned to a Fellowship at All Souls College, Oxford, where he worked in a desultory way on a history of the war commissioned by *The Times*. Jobs and opportunities at this time were scarce; All Souls Fellowships do not on their own satisfy the ambitious; and for Amery the future looked, if not exactly bleak, then definitely uncertain. In short, he was a model of the talented, aspiring but less than gilded middle-class male for whom much of Chamberlain's rhetoric was designed. In his memoirs Amery fondly recalled the morning in his College room when he sat reading, with mounting excitement, the newspaper report of Chamberlain's Birmingham address on Tariff Reform. 'The door opened and in rushed Leo Maxse,' he wrote many years later. 'For a moment or two we danced round hand in hand before we could unloose our tongues'.[11] As one reads Chamberlain's text today, with its ponderous and exclamatory periods, it seems incongruous that it should have wrought such lyrical effects. Nevertheless, Amery's sentiments were sincere, and he never afterwards departed from the faith he thus imbibed. From a podium in his native city Chamberlain had tossed a huge boulder into the still waters of the English political world; and there were many young aspirants, just like Amery and Maxse, who watched, fascinated, as its ripples spread, and saw themselves moving with it into the future. Unless account is taken of this emotional and generational *élan* the sheer ebullience of the movement towards Imperial Protection within early twentieth century English Conservatism, and its subsequent longevity despite the transparent practical difficulties of the proposal, are impossible to appreciate.

In terms of national policy, however, Chamberlain's demand for Tariff Reform simply marked a new episode in the long-simmering fiscal crisis which the South African war had accentuated. To cautious financiers such as Sir Michael Hicks-Beach, who presided as Chancellor of the Exchequer between 1895 and 1902, the most worrying aspect of this problem was not the extraordinary levies associated with the recent hostilities, unwelcome though these had been, but the fact that the *ordinary* spending of the British Government had over a long period outpaced available revenue. To a much greater extent than in the past, the United Kingdom authorities were now committed to funding services – as in the field of education – with an automatic tendency to escalate; whilst the 'votes' for the Army and the Royal Navy always more than kept pace with these increases. By the time he left the Exchequer, Hicks-Beach was convinced of the need to rein in all forms of expenditure in order to restore the harmonious balance of economy and society on which Britain's nineteenth-century successes had been based. In countering these assumptions, Chamberlain's fundamental point was that the problem thus conjured up did not, in fact, exist, since the overall tax burden remained modest compared to that which had been sustained at the outset of the nineteenth century. Hicks-Beach was not swayed by the analogy. 'It is true that our present burthens are light, considering the increase of population and wealth, compared with those borne by our ancestors one hundred years ago,' the Chancellor retorted, 'but they were then engaged in a life-and-death struggle with France; we, on my assumption, will not be at war; the cases do not admit of comparison'.[12] Yet the cases *did* admit of comparison for those who felt that the nation was heading into the midst of a new life-and-death struggle, and whose assumptions were not so pacific as those of Sir Michael Hicks-Beach. What made this polemic so intense – like all the great controversies in British affairs during the twentieth century, cutting across purely party divides – was the fact that inherent in it were two opposed ideals of the political nation, and divergent conceptions of the sort of future which lay ahead.

To some contemporaries the widespread agonizing over the United Kingdom's allegedly vulnerable situation seemed absurdly overdone. The Liberal peer, Lord Courtney, commented:

> We have been doing well [in Britain] and shall continue to do well, but this last truth must be coupled with an acknowledgement that though we are still absolutely

going forward we are losing and must lose first place.
Our national vainglory will not easily acquiesce in
being second; and any quack who proffers to have
a remedy against this loss of supremacy will attract
the support of a great many and it might be in a
bad season of a majority of electors. It seems to me
wise not to conceal the unpalatable truth but to try
to bring our countrymen to realize it as a fact which
tariffs cannot alter.[13]

Such prudentialism appears, from the vantage-point of the end
of the century, wholly valid; indeed the essential failure of the
British governmental system thereafter, it may be contended,
lay in a chronic inability to digest the sort of 'unpalatable
truth' to which Lord Courtney referred. Nevertheless, for any
party to frame an electoral programme on the basis of such an
insight would have been rashly courageous. Arthur Balfour,
who succeeded his uncle, Lord Salisbury, as Conservative
leader and Prime Minister in July 1902, was certainly not
noted for any proclivity to go to the heart of the matter.
The question of Tariff Reform threatened to split his party
wide open, just as it had been splintered by Corn Law
repeal half a century before; under these circumstances it was
characteristic of the new premier that he sought to contain the
pressure by cleaving rigidly to a *via media* between the Free
Fooders on the one hand and the Tariff Reformers, with their
fixed notions of competitive national power, on the other. He
achieved a working, albeit unstable, compromise in September
1903 by dropping the extremists from his cabinet, including
Chamberlain (shortly to be laid low by a stroke), and by
subsequently espousing a policy of 'Retaliation', which meant
what anybody wanted it to mean whilst giving the 'foreigner' a
metaphorical punch on the nose.[14] In fact the controversy over
Tariffs was before long overshadowed by other commotions,
principally over Ireland and successive foreign policy crises,
but it was long to retain a place on the British political
agenda.

Late Victorian fiscal orthodoxy naturally had matching instincts in the field of diplomacy. These foreign policy assumptions, especially as they were reflected in the preferences of Lord Salisbury, have often been taken to be encapsulated in the phrase 'Splendid Isolation'. In fact Salisbury did not habitually employ this usage, and he certainly did not invent it (it was coined by a Canadian journalist to convey, with a touch of sarcasm, Britain's friendlessness in Europe following the Jameson Raid on the Transvaal in 1895).[15] Salisbury's bias towards isolation arose not from its splendour, but from the fact that it was, in the context of British interests, both utilitarian and necessary. In no branch of policy was this more the case than naval affairs. Other great powers might envy and grumble about British pre-eminence on the seas; many of them had the financial and industrial muscle to challenge this primacy if they chose; *but they would not do so*, in Salisbury's view, so long as the United Kingdom's policy remained international and neutral, not continental and partisan. The acceptability of British power, its most supple quality, would be destroyed if the United Kingdom allowed itself to be absorbed into any of the contending systems of alliance which had begun to take shape after 1890, with France and Russia on one side, and the Triple Alliance of Germany, Austria and Italy on the other. England's principal diplomatic task was to modulate these antagonisms, whilst remaining unsullied by them. This was a policy of isolation from the Europe of alliances, but not from Europe itself. 'We are part of the Community of Europe,' Salisbury declared on one occasion, 'and we must do our duty as such'.[16] At the time this led him to oppose those of his colleagues (Chamberlain among them) who favoured aligning Britain alongside Germany against France. The same principle, it may be surmised, would have led him, once diplomatic fashions had undergone a somersault, to resist the opposite formulation. By this point, however, Salisbury, like his Queen, had departed from the English political scene.

Salisbury had none the less been conscious towards the end of his premiership of fundamental alterations in world politics, an awareness perhaps intensified by his long final illness. 'It may be a misconception,' he wrote to the Viceroy of India, Lord Curzon, in August 1902, 'but I cannot resist the impression that we are near some great change in public affairs – in which the forces which contend for mastery among us will be differently arranged and balanced. The large aggregations of human force which lie around our empire seem to draw more closely together, and to assume almost unconsciously a more and more aggressive aspect'.[17] His own instinct was against meeting such forces head on, but to draw in the imperial flanks and to offer a compact resistance to inimical elements. Here, in part at least, was the origin of the so-called Diplomatic Revolution under way at the time of his demise. The essence of this change was to reduce the United Kingdom's vulnerability to a war on her imperial circumference, and to free resources to meet ostensible threats closer to home. To this end the British Government negotiated an agreement with the United States, with whom relations had been prickly ever since the differences between the two countries at the time of the civil war in America, in which the Royal Navy's claim to a leading role within American home waters was repudiated. More important than this departure, however, was the Treaty signed with Japan in January 1902, which allowed the strength of the China Station to be reduced and warships redeployed in the Mediterranean and the English Channel.[18] In brief, the historic conception of British power as a pan-oceanic and inherently dispersed phenomenon, whilst very far from being dissolved, was qualified by a tendency to concentrate to a greater extent on resisting those 'aggregations of human force' which oppressed Salisbury's mind as he drew to the end of his life.

Along with these changing strategic proclivities went a shift in the criteria by which likely future threats were evaluated. The notion of 'concentration', for example, underpinned a bias towards locating an appropriate enemy in the vicinity of the Home island. Here were at least some of the roots of that *morbus Germanicus* which came to form a central feature of English political feeling in the first decade of the century. But why did the refurbishment of the Imperial German Navy under the Laws of 1894, 1898 and 1900 have such profound repercussions in the United Kingdom? After all, whilst the efficiency of the *Kaiserflotten* was evident in their spotless hulls and neat ratings, this force was clearly never going to rival the Royal Navy in numbers or firepower. Britain's own fleet modernization after the 1889 Naval Defence Act had been aimed at the Franco-Russian challenge, not at Germany, and this remained the ostensible theory of the Two-Power Standard (the principle, that is, whereby the Royal Navy should always be equal to the combined strengths of the second and third nations in the maritime league) into the new century. These assumed rankings, however, became subject to alteration in response to the 'risk fleet' theory of Admiral von Tirpitz. According to this insight, Germany had only to equip herself with a medium-sized, but well-armed, navy in order to gain a disproportionate leverage over those rivals whose strengths were dissipated across wide stretches of ocean.[19] Here was a novel concept of deterrence in which Germany would never have to go to war at all, but only to arm up to certain prescribed levels, and so alter permanently the facts on which power was based. This, from the British vantage-point, was the fundamental difference between France and Germany by *circa* 1900. France could bluster and threaten, but in the end she was not capable of changing facts; hence – as during the Fashoda crisis of 1898 – she could in the last resort be faced down. Germany, assisted by her central geo-political location and integrated railway connections, had it in the grasp of her industrialists, bankers, craftsmen and strategists to recast the numbers from which power flowed in contemporary Europe. It was the consequent sense of imminent displacement which led foreign auditors to react in nervous fashion to the Kaiser's loose talk of gaining for his country 'a place in the sun'. In fact he meant little more by this phrase than gratifying his own penchant for dramatic visitations to the Mediterranean littoral which marked his career. '[He] simply formulated a principle of proportionality,' Eric Hobsbawm has written of Kaiser Wilhelm in this connection, '. . . the more powerful a country's economy, the larger its population, the greater the international position of its nation-state.' By this commonplace logic of human affairs post-Bismarckian Germany unwisely, but largely accidentally, lent itself as the measure of other people's dreads, not least in the United Kingdom.[20]

These dreads gave a powerful stimulus to an important *fin-de-siècle* trait within British society: the rise of a new breed of military professional. This phenomenon was especially to the fore in the British Army. In an age when the epitome of the modern militarist was Count von Moltke, the hero of the Franco-Prussian struggle of 1870–1, rather than Horatio Nelson, the English officer class evinced a fresh determination to lift itself out of the rut of the purely supporting role which had been its rather dull lot during the hey-day of the blue-water doctrine of *Pax Britannica*. This cadre's aspirations had received a bad jolt when a respectably-sized war had at last come its way in South Africa, and an unholy mess had resulted, with revelations of crass incompetence in the field and organizational chaos (even peculation) in the War Office itself. The great drive to Army 'reform' in the aftermath of that conflict, and the evolution of the beau ideal of the 'thinking soldier', received their momentum from the need to snatch some sort of advantage from the jaws of humiliation. Haig, French, Hamilton, Callwell, Wilson, Grierson (names later to be entwined with the Great War of 1914–18) were prominent amongst the South African veterans who subsequently evoked these new nostrums. A perceptive scholar has written the following of Haig and his peers at this formative juncture in their careers:

> These were the men who [after 1900] read and studied and constructed appreciations of what that new [military] professionalism should constitute. From the beginning they looked to some form of attachment to France. They visited the frontiers, attended the manoeuvres of the great Continental armies, built their military organizations on similar patterns, and endeavoured at every turn to imitate their European paragons. To many of them seapower meant nothing.

They became obsessed with the military basis of power in Europe.[21]

Chasing Boer farmers across the veldt, or come to that pursuing Pathan marauders up and down the Hindu Kush, was not the stuff of which this new-mint Army professionalism was made. The force of the attraction behind the burgeoning relationship with France, so recently close to rupture over a barren tract of the Nile Basin, derived not least from the disdain for such tasks felt by Haig's generation and tendency. There was a certain logic, therefore, in the fact that the negotiations leading to the Entente Cordiale between London and Paris in April 1904 were ostensibly concerned with reconciling long-standing differences in Africa. Yet what was, superficially, a surprising rapprochement was driven from the start by larger considerations than such preliminary subject matter might indicate. Above all, by forging a link with France the United Kingdom could indeed hope to inject itself into the 'military basis of power in Europe'; and it was because the British Army's claims and identity as an institution came to hinge crucially on seeing this policy through that years later it was to stoutly resist any curtailment of its operations on the Western Front.

Meanwhile, however, the strategic flux after 1900 also involved a challenge to the Royal Navy's status as the 'Senior Service'; and it is ironic that Admiral Mahan's epic tract, *The Significance of Seapower in History*, should have appeared just when its British exemplar was faced with a crisis of confidence. 'Jacky' Fisher's remedy for this situation as First Sea Lord after October 1904 was to shift the emphasis towards a 'fighting Navy', and away from the pusillanimous and outdated tasks of chastising Arab slavers and Chinese pirates (a conception of modernity bearing obvious resemblances to the bent we have already detected in the Army). Thus Fisher uprooted many traditional practices and 'dead wood' in the Fleet, alienating many of his colleagues as he did so.[22] Furthermore, his definition of the Mediterranean as 'the vital strategic Centre of Britain's position' was suggestive of a bias in British defence thinking which will feature prominently in our future narrative.[23] But Fisher's most concrete innovation at this time was his support for the super-battleship, coded Dreadnought, which in its scale, glamour and gunweight summed up his ideal future for the Royal Navy. This was a Navy measured not by its flexible capacity to clear up petty nuisances on the ocean wave, but by the width of the orange flashes emitted from its armoured turrets. Super-battleships, however, needed a super-enemy to justify their huge expense, and it was by such arcane processes that the assumed threat from Imperial Germany was refracted through inter-service rivalries within the United Kingdom. In fact the containment of these spiralling disputes, principally over access to the public purse, was the chief purpose behind the establishment of the Committee of Imperial Defence in 1904, which Balfour afterwards considered the most lasting achievement of his premiership. It was, however, an achievement which could all too easily boomerang, as one insider recognized when commenting that the CID thereafter became 'a dangerous weapon . . . in the hands of the services to bully the Cabinet'.[24]

During the autumn of 1905 these tendencies coincided with a change of government in the United Kingdom. His ministry acutely sapped by internal differences, Balfour sought to make a virtue of necessity and in December resigned from office instead of dissolving Parliament, hoping that even a brief period of responsibility would reveal his Liberal opponents to be even more divided among themselves. So fragmented, indeed, had the Liberals become ever since the retirement of Gladstone in 1894 that latterly it had even been doubted whether they were capable of forming a ministry. The main fissure lay between the Radical wing of the party, still intellectually and morally attached to the Gladstonian legacy, and a younger breed of Liberal Imperialists whose mentor, Lord Rosebery, had experimented with a heady mix of Free Trade economics and forceful imperial diplomacy. Right up until the last moment it was unsure whether Henry Campbell-Bannerman, who had succeeded Rosebery as leader and was himself of a Radical persuasion, would accept the chalice offered him by Balfour. When he eventually did so, it was at the cost of a ministerial compromise in which the 'Imperialist' faction obtained a virtual monopoly of those portfolios concerned with overseas policy: thus Lord Grey became Foreign Secretary, Lord Haldane went to the War Office, whilst Herbert Asquith, swiftly emerging as the connecting-rod between the disparate elements in the party, became Chancellor of the Exchequer.

The intrinsic significance of this sequence is that it set a pattern which was followed thereafter whenever a British administration was formed 'from the Left': the more conservative elements clustered swiftly around the levers of foreign and military policy, seeking to establish the main thrust of affairs from a commanding height. In 1905, as in later instances of this manifestation, it was felt that the sooner such a lead was given, the better. Thus whilst the Liberal Government was being constituted, Haldane stressed in private that the *beginning* of the ministry would be absolutely vital. 'A decided lead in the right direction is what is essential', he advised. 'The necessity for it will probably arise before the new administration is many days old'.[25] Against this background we may understand why two initiatives of first-rate importance were taken in the brief interregnum between the Liberal Cabinet's appointment and the general election which was held in the middle of January 1906. The first of these was the acceleration of the Dreadnought construction programme. Even more telling as a pointer to the future, however, was the authorization of talks between British and French military staffs designed to put a 'spine' into the Entente Cordiale. This latter incident had a picturesque angle: Haldane, spurred on by his War Office officials, proceeded to track the Foreign Secretary down to his Northumbrian constituency, and there in a shrouded horse-drawn carriage on the edge of a public meeting he persuaded Grey to agree to the French request for an *entente militaire* which had been lodged, not accidentally, at this critical juncture.[26] When the great crisis of August 1914 arrived it was, paradoxically, the secret military obligation of 1905, hastily assumed by Liberal ministers in the very early stages of their long occupation of office, rather than the vaguer but more considered diplomatic agreement of 1904 negotiated by its Unionist predecessor, which constrained the decision-making process. Such an outcome, of course, was hardly anticipated at the outset. Nevertheless, the fact that the entente commitment, in an explicitly military sense, was from the start part and parcel of the delicate compromises within the Liberal ministry after 1905 helps to explain not only the subsequent choices that government made in the sphere of foreign policy, but ultimately its political fate.

Given that the Liberal leadership had thus signalled its willingness to co-operate in the need – as the patrician Conservative statesman, Lord Lansdowne, put it – to 'lift' questions of foreign policy above party politics and put them on 'a higher and different plane'[27], it was ironical that the election of 1906 proved one of the most bitter ever contested in Britain. These passions turned on the controversial Education Act of 1902 (which had horrified Non-Conformists by putting Anglican schools 'on the rates'), Milner's use and abuse of Chinese indentured labour ('Chinese Slavery') in South Africa, and tariffs (or 'stomach taxes', as the Liberals pilloried them). The last electoral contest in Britain to be explicitly marked by religious and ethical principle, its outcome confirmed the Liberal Government in office with an overwhelming majority of 124 seats (and well over 300 if the Irish Nationalists were counted). Yet if the parliamentary allocation of power had thus been determined, the degree to which the *substance* of authority had altered was more problematical. Thus Balfour greeted the Liberal victory with the stern injunction that 'the great Unionist Party should still control, whether in power or in opposition, the destinies of this great Empire'.[28] The principle here enunciated was not one known to Walter Bagehot, the great Victorian analyst of the English constitution. It did, however, reflect the common apprehension in Edwardian society that political civilization at home and abroad was being measured in the balance. Questions of empire entered so powerfully into political discourse precisely because they provided a convenient and readily understood test as to where individuals and groups stood in relation to what was anticipated as a coming schism. Whilst in the end, therefore, it was on the rock of the Balance of Power in Europe that British Liberalism was finally to break

up, for the first few years after 1905 its characteristic dilemmas
derived from more exotic climes.

Predictably, in the light of recent events, it was South Africa
which provided the key test for the Liberal Government's
resolve to mark itself off, in some phases of public policy
at least, from the previous administration. The controversial
Milner had retired from his post in April 1905, but his successor
as High Commissioner, Lord Selborne, was a defender of his
legacy; nor was it merely by chance that, whilst the reins of
government were changing hands in London, a fresh consignment
of imported Chinese coolies for employment in the reconstruction
of the Transvaal mines was hurriedly authorized. This presented
Campbell-Bannerman with a painful dilemma. To leave 'Chinese
Slavery' untouched was impossible without risking an explosion
on the Government's own back benches; to cancel all indentures
forthwith, and allow production in the mines to sag, would give
the Unionists an opportunity to recommence their traditional
refrain in Opposition that the Liberals, through an implied
mixture of stupidity and cowardice, were allowing the nation's
patrimony to slip through their fingers. In the end the new
government in London banned any future contracts of the
kind being negotiated, whilst allowing those presently existing
to run their course. To this equivocation was added a symbol
of overt ideological distaste in a Motion of Censure on Milner –
arising from his earlier concurrence in the imposition of illegal
physical punishments on oriental labourers – passed in the
House of Commons amid scenes of considerable disorder and
resentment. 'It [the debate] was the harbinger', one historian
has noted, 'of that extreme bitterness in English politics which
distinguished the years 1908–1914. For it represented in the
minds of contemporaries two different ways of dealing with the
crisis of the nation and the Empire as they entered the twentieth
century'.[29]
   The most decisive act of the Liberal Government regarding
South African affairs, however, and the departure which more

than any other fixed its reputation in the history books, was the concession of responsible self-government to the Transvaal in November 1906 (a similar grant being made to the Orange River Colony the following year). This initiative was portrayed by its architects as a 'Magnanimous Gesture', although like many such acts it has more recently been ascribed to a cynical calculation of self-interest. Thus one historian has explained that in yielding control of the Transvaal, the Liberal Government expected the English-speaking elements in the territory to triumph at the elections of January 1907, only to find that the chief organ of Afrikaner protest, Het Volk, won in a landslide.[30] In the confused conditions prevailing locally such a metropolitan miscalculation was certainly feasible, though given the intense bitterness among the Dutch population at British pacification it is hard to credit that the imperial authorities were wholly taken aback at the outcome. Whatever the degree of surprise, the Imperial Government showed no hesitation in assisting the newly-elected authorities in the Transvaal with loans and even with troops to help police the unruly gold-diggings. Undoubtedly, a critical factor in these changes was the determination of Campbell-Bannerman, ailing and disillusioned, to bring off a Radical flourish on the question which mattered more to him than any other.[31] The fact that he was able to convince his colleagues of the wisdom of such a critical change of direction implies that more fundamental forces were at work in effecting the stabilization of Anglo-Transvaal relations. Nothing quite so nicely conjured up the desire for a restoration of 'normality', indeed, than the fact that when the Colonial Conference met in London during the summer of 1907, the British representatives were quick to compare favourably the smooth and pliable manners of the old Boer leader, Louis Botha, to the gauche stubbornness of the visitors from Australia.

During the course of this reconciliation the ideological and political frenzy so much to the fore over the preceding fifteen years drained out of Anglo-South African affairs. This explains why the subsequent run-up to the unification of the South African colonies – a fundamental aim of British Governments for some four decades – proved such an anti-climax. The distinctive aspect of this approach to regional amalgamation was that it was inspired and executed by local, rather than imperial, agencies. Indeed, the Government in London had almost nothing substantially to do with what was, at bottom, a home-made process; as Lord Loreburn, the Lord Chancellor, remarked, the role of the metropolis was simply to encourage the various participants from the sidelines so that 'the different sections [could] find their own level and shape their own destiny'[32], which they duly did at a series of Inter-Colonial Conferences before the South Africa Act passed formally through the Westminster Parliament in September 1909, receiving the Royal Assent in the following year.

Amidst all this finding of levels and shaping of destinies, the natives got inexorably pushed to the bottom of the pile. Furthermore, in sloughing-off responsibility for the welfare of indigenous inhabitants in a British territory, the Liberal Government (led by Herbert Asquith following the death of Campbell-Bannerman in April 1908) effectively diluted its commitment to traditional liberal shibboleths in the imperial field, just as it was doing in other areas of policy. The evasion, even abandonment, of 'Native Rights' has been taken by much latter-day scholarship to give the lie to the interpretation of the South Africa Act as the beneficent culmination of a theory of colonial self-rule which for many years served (somewhat self-preeningly) as the orthodox version.[33] In this harsher light that legislation becomes, instead, the reflection of an efficient interlocking of local and metropolitan capitalisms whose interests had at last become fully congruent with each other.[34] There is a good deal of validity in this latter account. Still, the most tangible, and therefore the most powerful, motive of the Liberal politicians in London was not concerned with grand economic vistas, but rather related to a more mundane political desire to get themselves off the hook of 'British Supremacy' which over a long period their opponents had succeeded in making into a principal touchstone of British affairs. After 1910 South Africa was to occupy a distinguished place in the pantheon of British overseas interests, but it was never again to evoke the same resonances in imperial developments that it had at the end of the nineteenth century. At bottom, it had not been the lure of gold which elevated the South African provinces in this way, but their utility as a dividing-line in British politics; and during the century ahead other markers were to appear intrinsically better equipped to play this role.

In its characteristic search for malleable local partners to reduce the pressures and embarrassments of overseas rule, the Liberal Government was less lucky in Egypt than in South Africa. The former country possessed a special meaning for the party of Gladstone, since it was his second administration which in 1882 had spectacularly occupied the Ottoman province. The Liberal conscience had been salved on that occasion by the promise that British troops would be evacuated once Egyptian disorders were corrected. Time (and disorder) passed, but the British did not. Under the proconsular tutelage of Lord Cromer, Egypt indubitably benefited from the huge increase in irrigated land and the consequent boost to cotton production.[35] Simultaneously, however, the pharaonic lure impressed itself on the career classes of the metropole; they read Milner's proselytizing tract *England in Egypt*; and the message that jobs were going quickly circulated. Hence the light and flexible methods of the early Occupation gave way to an angular, dense and increasingly Anglicized bureaucracy. What was still, in theory, a Turkish dominion thus became subject to the banality of English imperialism, so that the *Oxford Magazine* noted in 1905 the demand of the Egyptian and Sudanese administrations for the 'good all round man' who 'without being a pure athlete, has distinguished himself in College life'.[36] This was a warning sign, and all the indications of Lord Cromer's conduct towards the end of his stewardship in Cairo, as one scholar has remarked, pointed to the fact that he had turned his back on any return to Egyptian self-government, and was groping towards a more overt form of British intervention.[37] Evidently this tendency did not go unnoticed amongst the Egyptians themselves, since when Cromer's much-delayed retirement finally arrived he had to be driven to the railway station in the dead of night lest his departure be the cause of celebratory riots in the city.

In selecting Sir Eldon Gorst as successor to Cromer, the authorities in London chose an officer who knew the Egyptian ropes intimately from long service, but who also shared the belief that British purposes might be pursued with success in less heavy-handed ways than were currently being employed. 'Lord Cromer created Egypt', an astute observer remarked, 'his successor has to produce good Egyptians'.[38] He attempted to find them, and so establish a working model of 'Native Agency', by acting through the Khedive, his ministers and the notabilia clustered around the Palace. At the same time Gorst attenuated European control of the judiciary, refused to dole out compensation to expatriate speculators caught in the cotton crash of 1907, and excised dead wood from among the British sinecurists in the Egyptian civil service. There was necessarily a whiff of corruption which attached itself to a system of administration operating in tandem with the Egyptian monarchy, not noted for its fastidiousness in financial matters, but Gorst's formula had at least an intelligent hope that an essentially imperial Occupation could be softened and diluted into a subtle but effective presence.

What killed this hope was not so much the dearth of Britons prepared to retire to Cheltenham, but the fact that there were not enough 'good Egyptians' to go round. The mosques in particular were hostile to an experiment which gave salience to secular politicians and institutions, including that quintessentially Egyptian phenomenon, a sham-parliament. The turning point came with the assassination of Gorst's Coptic premier, Butros Ghali, in February 1910. After that the High Commissioner himself admitted that stability was only possible if the British 'came [once] more into the open'.[39] They proceeded to do so, and when Gorst, broken in health, retired in 1911, his policy was already transparently bankrupt. His place was taken by Lord Kitchener, for whom 'Native Agency' had little meaning. We shall see in the next chapter that it was the Great War of 1914–18 which heightened the Middle East in general, and Egypt in particular, as major benchmarks of British power and prestige overseas. Nevertheless, the fact that in the preceding phase a quasi-autonomist solution had been tried and found wanting was suggestive of the dilemmas the United Kingdom faced in what was to become its prime imperial haunt in the twentieth century.

If Edwardian Liberalism wilted in the Egyptian climate, it was not surprising that in India, too, its bloom was distinctly pale. In 1905, it is true, the Secretaryship of State for India had been given to John Morley, the senior member of the Government most closely associated with Gladstonian radicalism. Yet this appointment had largely been determined by the need to keep Morley (and his Home Rule beliefs) out of the Irish Office, which he coveted; as Stephen Koss has expressed it, in assuming responsibility for the Sub-Continent the appointee was well aware that 'neither he nor his doctrines had any place else to go'.[40] Morley instinctively disliked the Indian National Congress, and never saw that body – as he saw, for example, the Catholic Nationalism of Dillon and Redmond in Ireland – as a respectable and workable vehicle for Home Rule principles. In his view, Irish Nationalists, for all their occasional waywardness, genuinely represented The People; Indian Nationalists represented nobody but a narrow circle of self-interested Bengali wire-pullers. As the responsible minister, therefore, he set out little disposed to reverse the Partition of Bengal which Curzon had implemented as Viceroy some years before, and which had in the interim stimulated a surge of nationalist feeling. Morley's predilections in this regard had little to do with the niceties of Indian social geography, but, as he defined his own motives, because 'it [the partition] has become the test, and by that test I mean to abide'.[41]

The overarching 'test' implicit in Indian administration after 1905 was that of the Liberal Government's willingness to raise the stick of coercion in defence of Law and Order. This naturally put Morley at a disadvantage whenever the authorities in one Indian province or another pulled hard on the lever of 'Native Unrest'. 'No I can't stand that', he shouted at his Permanent Secretary when the Punjab Government demanded a fresh set of repressive powers following a crowd disturbance, 'I will not have that'[42], but he did. The Secretary of State sought to off-set this authoritarian bias by an innovation which has gone down in history as the Morley-Minto Reforms of 1909. Given Morley's assumptions, the criticism which has often been levelled at this package – that it had little to do with Indian self-government – is mostly beside the point. What it *did* do was to marginally readjust the balance between expatriate rule and Indian opinion which the purple viceroyalty of Curzon had upset. Morley's principal contribution to this goal, in fact, came late in the day, and had little to do with constitutional tinkering: it lay in his adamant refusal to grant Kitchener the viceroyalty when Lord Minto retired in 1910 – such an appointment, he argued, would be 'to plant our Indian system on a military basis, and would be the symbol to India that this is what we mean'.[43] That for all the pressures sporadically but powerfully pointing in the other direction, the British Raj remained essentially civilian in spirit, is something that can be partly credited to Morley. Nevertheless, the conduct of British policy after 1906 proved that there could be no such thing as a distinctively Liberal philosophy when it came to presiding over what was one of the world's great autocracies. To this extent, Balfour's earlier assertion that, whether in power or in opposition, the great Unionist party retained a prescriptive right to mould the destiny of the Empire was shown, in India as elsewhere, to have a certain practical legitimacy.

Whilst this imperial logic was unfolding, in the field of foreign policy the Diplomatic Revolution already afoot when the Liberals first came to office also gathered momentum. It transpired, for example, that one effect of Russia's defeat at the hands of Japan in 1904–5 was to foreclose the great Asian enterprise of the Tsars, and to reorient the perspectives of St Petersburg back towards the West. The traditional anxiety concerning a Russian threat to India (the credibility of which had always been doubted by radical sceptics) disappeared almost overnight, and the exotic industry of the 'Great Game' played by intrepid agents from Peshawar to Kabul became redundant. Amidst the backwash of this development British and Russian interests suddenly converged, propelled partly by a common link to France, and partly by a shared focus on the forestalling of German power. 'An entente between Russia, France and ourselves', Lord Grey speculated on such a tie-up, 'would be absolutely secure. If it is necessary to check Germany it could then be done'.[44] The Anglo-Russian accord signed in August 1907 raised just such a prospect. In the unstable triangular relationship between Britain, France and Germany it had for some time been inevitable, as a leading journalist put it at the time, that the United Kingdom would topple over on one side or the other of the razor's edge[45]; the link with Russia dictated on which side the toppling would be done.

The new strategic calculus manifested itself on sea as well as on land. There was a paradox here, since the sinking of the main Russian battle-fleet by Japan in 1905 had fortuitously made the United Kingdom's maritime superiority more secure than at any time since the days of Trafalgar. This apparent easement, however, was soon vitiated by a new arms race in which the traditional bogey of *Franco-Russe* was definitively replaced by that of Wilhelmine Germany. Thus when a Naval Law was announced in Berlin during 1908, including the construction of four new battleships, the British Admiralty immediately lodged a demand for eight new Dreadnoughts of its own. The resulting controversy brought to a head the latent tensions between the 'Imperialist' wing within the Liberal Cabinet and those ministers whose watchword remained the old Radical cry of 'Economy'. Prominent amongst the latter were David Lloyd George and Winston Churchill, respectively Chancellor of the Exchequer and President of the Board of Trade. These two ministers, having failed in their earlier bid to block Haldane's Army reforms (incorporating the principle of 'expansion' to meet a hypothetical emergency), now set themselves to oppose the extravagance of Dreadnoughts. By the spring of 1909 they had failed. 'Eight, eight, we won't wait' the jingo-mob had chanted in Leicester Square, and before long they got most, if not quite all, of their desires. Amidst this heat and noise a shift of the highest importance came about, summed up in Paul Kennedy's observation that, whilst in 1900 a war between Britain and Germany was inconceivable, by the end of the first decade of the century such an event was already predictable.[46]

One effect of the battle over Dreadnought construction was to convince Lloyd George and Churchill that spending, rather than economizing, constituted the wave of the future. The implications of this were soon expressed in the Chancellor's 'People's Budget' of 1909 which constituted the founding-charter of a modern and considerably expanded fiscal polity. Implicit in this Budget, furthermore, was the message that those who wished to see spending on arms progressively increased would have to pay for the privilege through an augmented income-tax. This, unsurprisingly, was not at all what the patriotic cadres had in mind. The Conservative peers in the House of Lords rejected the Finance Bill; two general elections then followed in quick succession, from which the Liberal Government emerged dependent on the votes of Irish Nationalists in the House of Commons. The price of this latter support was, naturally, Home Rule, and when, amidst great commotions, a way for such a Bill was cleared by legislation curtailing the 'blocking' powers of the upper chamber, the Government's Irish measure finally began its stormy passage through Parliament in April 1912. The complex interaction which ensued between the constitutional crisis and fierce passions over Ireland, intensified by ultra-loyalist reaction in Protestant Ulster, go beyond the scope of this study. Along the way, however, the United Kingdom was to hover perilously close to the brink of civil war. When the Liberal Government, and the nation as a whole, came to embrace a conflict in August 1914 which had fortuitously broken out on foreign (not domestic) soil, it was with an almost audible sigh of relief.

Such internal polarization – in which industrial riots and the Suffragette movement also played their part – has dominated most reconstructions of British affairs in the run-up to 1914, notably in George Dangerfield's influential book *The Strange Death of Liberal England*. Yet parallel with these fissures went another (ultimately more powerful) tendency, whereby the leading politicians began to cast anxiously about for ways to shut down the pressures making for disintegration. In this vein it is striking that Lloyd George began talking about the merits of Coalition almost as soon as the constitutional crisis erupted[47]; whilst Churchill greeted the passing of the Parliament Act in June 1911, for example, with the hope that it might mark '. . . a new era in our politics – an era not of strife but of settlement'.[48] These tentative feelers assume a heightened meaning when viewed in relation to the attempts then being made in all the great European states to heal their internal wounds. Of this general process Norman Stone has written:

> After 1911, the atmosphere was of arms race. Oddly enough, this served, in most countries, to solve the problem of taxation which had bedevilled parliamentary affairs since the early 1890s. The right would vote for graduated income taxes, provided they were spent on arms; and the left would accept arms, provided that they came with graduated income taxes. By 1912, that problem had been sorted out almost everywhere, and large armies went together with large taxes; although the details of the process caused endless trouble and the . . . upsetting of endless governments. By 1913, all of Europe was committed to an arms race; and after 1911 the war had already broken out in people's minds.[49]

As a short-hand summary of the causes of the Great War this will do as well as any. In Britain, therefore, where the old-fashioned Hicks-Beach had once envisaged that the path to stability could only be found through a reduction of social and military expenditure, events showed that it was easier in the modern age to bring off the trick by winding both sides of the account *up*. Militarists and social collectivists discovered, as a consequence, that their interests, far from being diametrically opposed, were actually complementary. Lloyd George, the critical figure in this British evolution, was quick to spread his canvas to catch the breeze. Proof of this came during the Agadir crisis during July 1911, when France and Germany appeared on the verge of going to war with each other over rival claims in Morocco. Interrupting his annual speech as Chancellor at the Mansion Hall, where his auditors had gathered expecting to hear of the course of sound finance, the Chancellor delivered his celebrated 'warning shot' to Germany. 'I believe it is essential in the higher interests, not merely of this country, but of the world', he somewhat portentously declared, 'that Britain should at all hazards maintain her place and prestige among the Great Powers of the world'.[50] From this statement the government in Berlin made the rational deduction that the United Kingdom had irreversibly hitched its wagon to that of France. In the British political world, however, it had the wider import that 'prestige', not 'economy', had become the key word in the vocabulary of public affairs.

Agadir had a practical as well as a symbolic effect on British politics and strategy. At the height of the crisis it transpired that the Admiralty had not seen fit to draw up any plans for the ferrying of a large expeditionary force across the Channel, a scenario which scarcely fitted with its own blue-water ideal of British warfare. When the Admiralty's evasions of Entente orthodoxy were thus revealed, acrimony broke out among the relevant Cabinet ministers. Reginald McKenna, the First Lord of the offending department, put the crux of the matter when he asserted that the United Kingdom would never be the beneficiary of any decision to concentrate its resources on land in order, as he scathingly put it, to make France the most powerful nation in Europe.[51] This dissent was enough to lose McKenna his job, and he was replaced by Churchill, who in a remarkably brief span of time had emerged as the chief *condottiere* in British politics. The latter's subsequent remit was to whip the Admiralty into expeditionary shape, which he proceeded to do with such aplomb that it was reported that those naval officers who were out of sympathy with the conception discovered their office luggage stuck out on the pavement even before official notifications of dismissal had been received.[52] Suggestively, when Asquith tried to placate McKenna over his exile to the Home Office by offering the assurance that, as Prime Minister, he remained as certain as ever that the United Kingdom would always draw back from entering a great European war, he received the sharp response that 'he [Asquith] might be rushed into it by [the] situation being developed by the War Office'.[53] In short, if by 1910 it was fairly clear that sooner or later Britain and Germany would be at war, the Agadir affair predetermined how the British would choose to fight.

After 1911, then, the tramlines were set; we may hurry over them. Relations between Britain and Germany, superficially at least, showed at first some signs of improvement. As late as June 1914 the two countries settled their long-standing dispute over the Baghdad Railway. Meanwhile, through the early summer of that year, Ireland continued to dominate British horizons. When Lord Grey, following a stressful session on a possible compromise in the latter province, thus attempted to read out in Cabinet on 24 July the terms of Austria's communication to Serbia following the assassination of the Archduke Ferdinand in Sarajevo, with its burden that the great Continental systems of alliance were about to fall violently upon each other, he did not readily find a hearing. Churchill's account of this moment goes as follows:

> He [Grey] had been reading or speaking for several minutes before I could disengage my mind from the tedious and bewildering debate which had just closed. We were all very tired, but gradually as the phrases and sentences followed one another, impressions of a wholly different character began to form in my mind. This note was clearly an ultimatum; but it was an ultimatum such as had never been penned in modern times . . . The parishes of Fermanagh and Tyrone faded back into the mists and squalls of Ireland, and a strange light began immediately, but by perceptible gradations, to fall and grow upon the map of Europe.[54]

This pictorial rendering is not entirely disingenuous, but it evokes the essential truth that the Liberal Government was propelled towards war in Europe 'on the rebound' from the insoluble dilemmas of Ireland. Compared to the latter, the challenge in Europe looked clear-cut, less divisive of the political nation and susceptible – in a way Ireland was not – to the arbitrament of force. As such, arguments *against* intervention were apt to be glossed over. Thus John Morley, giving voice to the dying echoes of Gladstonianism, warned dourly that belligerence on Britain's part 'would break down the whole system of credit with London as its centre, how it would cut up commerce and manufacture . . . how it would hit labour and wages and prices, and when the winter came, would inevitably produce violence and tumult'[55], only to find that such emphases on the material depredations of large-scale warfare were not welcome to his colleagues. Admittedly, at one critical moment Lloyd George – who, after all, was still Chancellor of the Exchequer – showed signs of wobbling, but he was quickly swayed by a note tossed to him across the table by Churchill, pointing out that not only would the war be cheap, but there would be enough left over in the kitty of emergency taxation to provide compensatory benefits for the masses.[56] Touches such as this indicated how the *hubris* of the modern British state – one which could prove itself by participating in a major land war, whilst simultaneously modulating the struggle between the classes at home – helped to shape the decision of the Liberal Government.

What fundamental consideration, then, may be said to have pushed the Liberal Government into war in the summer of 1914? Was it a concern with the security of the British islands themselves? This is not really tenable. Every professional assessment in recent times had concluded that, given proper precautions, the United Kingdom was invulnerable to invasion (a point which underlay the observation afterwards made by some that, of all the major participants in the Great War of 1914–18, Britain was the only one which actually *volunteered*). Was it, then, the existence of a guarantee (dating back to 1839) to defend the integrity of Belgium, eventually violated by the movement of German troops in their advance on the French flank? Here, too, scepticism is in order: a senior Foreign Office official had foretold years before that whether or not the British authorities would hold such an infraction to be a *casus belli* would depend on who was doing the infracting at the time.[57] As one historian has depicted the situation, once the decision to intervene was taken in London, there remained the problem of the grounds on which it should be *advertised*[58]; and it was as such an advertisement – held up throughout Lord Grey's clinching speech in the House of Commons on Monday 13 August – that the matter of Belgium loomed large.

At the heart of the Liberal Government's decision lay, rather, a vague but powerfully obsessive fear of isolation. This anxiety was inherent in one of Lord Grey's essential theses: that Britain would suffer no more by going *into* the conflagration than she would by staying *out*. 'Should the war come, and England stand aside', the Foreign Secretary put the case at one point, 'one of two things will happen: (a) Either Germany and Austria will win, crush France, and humiliate Russia . . . What will be the position of a friendless England? . . . (b) Or France and Russia will win. What will then be their attitude towards England? What about India and the Mediterranean?'.[59] This curious conflation – whereby the entire edifice of Britain's world interests was held to depend on a localized outcome in Europe – was to feature in foreign policy debates for much of the century ahead.[60] More immediately, during the years leading up to 1914 the 'soundness' of the British polity itself, and above all its hopes of fending off the threat of decadence which weighed so heavily on Edwardian minds, came to be measured by its putative standing in 'the councils of the world'; and this standing in turn was defined in terms of a capacity to deliver military support to Continental allies. In this context, recent research has emphasized the major contribution made to cutting away what ground remained beneath the feet of advocates of non-intervention by the announcement of the Conservative leaders (principally Andrew Bonar Law, who had replaced Balfour, and Lord Lansdowne) that they would support the Government in the crisis of the hour *providing that it stood by its obligations to France and Russia*.[61] Ultimately, therefore, the United Kingdom entered a landlubbing war in 1914 to prove her worth, not to herself, but to other people, since greatness, like beauty, was held to reside in the eye of the beholder. 'We pulled a lever', was how Lloyd George summed up the spirit of the exercise, 'which might land us on a star or lead us into chaos'.[62] Our narrative will endeavour to determine which of these fates was to supervene.

2

The Knock-Out War

It was commonly remarked towards the end of the Great War that the 'truth' about the cataclysm could never be told, by which was meant that the scale and complexity of the story itself would defy accurate reconstruction. So, despite an endless stream of narratives and monographs, it has largely proved, as is inevitably the case with any great conflict marked by ambiguity, dissimulation and the covering of tracks all round.[1] British understanding of the First World War has also been distorted by the conventional assumption that in the end 'victory' was achieved, and with it the purposes for which the United Kingdom entered the contest in the first place. Naturally, genuflections have been made to the human cost represented by the 'lost generation' which became such an article of post-War belief, and the economic cost of a hugely enlarged National Debt, liquidated investments and lost export markets. The common British conviction remained, nevertheless, that on balance things turned out right in the end: the Kaiser was deposed, Belgium restored, Anglo-French honour vindicated and a good bag of territorial spoils acquired into the bargain. Indeed, the British experience between 1914 and 1918 has even received back-handed compliments as the emancipator of women, catalyst of social reform and generator of technological innovation.[2] So deeply has this version influenced the stock of the United Kingdom's modern myths that the latter-day debate focusing on the causes of Britain's decline in the century after 1880 has a curious tendency to skip over the First World War as some kind of neutral episode, so that it has become almost a convention to emphasize instead the nature of Britain's educational institutions for almost a century after 1870 as a drag anchor on her national performance.[3] The argument in these pages will be somewhat different: to wit, that whereas in 1914 the United Kingdom was still fundamentally well equipped to succeed under twentieth-century conditions, by 1918 she had incurred handicaps which, unlike some other belligerents, she was never able to fully shake off.

An essential risk inherent in the British decision of August 1914 surfaced right at the start: the country's strategic independence was forfeited to the French High Command. The episode which highlighted this tendency was itself highly dramatic. Thus the weight of the initial German thrust through Belgium led to the long Allied retreat towards Paris. Amidst a crisis of such magnitude General Joffre, the French Commander-in-Chief, understandably looked upon the British Expeditionary Force (BEF) as a reserve to be used up whilst his main forces were consolidated. Since this fate was not what the British Army had anticipated, however, its leader in the field, General Sir John French, moved to disengage his troops from the collapsing front, and even, according to rumours, prepared to make a dash for the Channel ports.[4] As soon as these rumblings reached London the freshly-appointed Secretary of State for War, Lord Kitchener, was dispatched post-haste to the BEF's Headquarters, where he instructed French under all circumstances to keep his Army's place in the line. During the stiff fighting which followed, the German advance was finally held along the River Marne, and the shooting became interspersed with digging, until the trenches ran from the Channel to the Swiss frontier. Once meshed into this system there could be no escape – although, just to make sure, the French military command afterwards insisted that their British ally invariably occupy positions well away from the coast, lest the lure of home should threaten once more to become overwhelming (a precaution, it might be said, which the events of 1940 were retrospectively to justify).[5]

The remarkable resilience of the British authorities in the face of these early reverses arose not least from the surge of confidence associated with the 'New Armies' being assembled under Lord Kitchener's watchful eye. As the rush to the recruiting stations got under way there were not enough rifles, bedding or sanitary ware to go round. Voluntaryism, in fact, was the key to the Liberal Cabinet's thinking about the probable course of events thereafter. According to this scenario, the main combatants in Europe with their great conscript peasant armies were bound rapidly to exhaust their wealth and manpower in the struggle. Furthermore, because Britain's expeditionary commitment was so much smaller to begin with, she would be able to mobilize a progressively increasing percentage of adult males, and thus become stronger precisely when others (friends as well as foes) were becoming weaker. Thus it was the unique flexibility of the United Kingdom's machinery for war which would allow her to secure a preponderant position when the time came to make peace, and permit Lord Grey to bestride the ensuing Conference as Lord Castlereagh had dominated that held in Paris in 1815. It was because the French were alert to these ideals that their suspicions of British motives were never entirely dissipated, and towards the end of the war were powerfully to revive. They need not have worried; events were to ensure that when it came to a new Paris Conference in 1919 the position of the British representatives was to be more fragile than that enjoyed by Castlereagh. Meanwhile through the drizzly autumn of 1914 the razzamatazz which accompanied the peculiarly British form of recruiting played an important part in suppressing any doubts to which the initial setbacks in France might otherwise have given rise.

The proconsular figure of Lord Kitchener provided a powerful inspiration for this recruitment drive; his critics were to cherish the joke that the best thing about him was that he made a great poster.[6] Kitchener, indeed, played what was arguably the central role in the British effort until his tragic death when, en route to Russia, HMS *Hampshire* foundered off the Orkneys in June 1916. Few reputations in British history have been more contested. His admirers always believed him to be the architect of victory.[7] Others regarded him as a grand but flawed personality, called upon by the Liberal Government to lend it the glamour of his name, but whose ineptitude as an administrator became all too evident in the glare of responsibility. More important than any summary of Kitchener's pros and cons as wartime overlord, however, is to consider why he emerged as such a lightning-rod for the growing tensions in British politics. The key lies in the fact that he was essentially a great Victorian soldier who felt increasingly troubled and hesitant once the trenches had been laid down on the Western Front. It is true that when war was first declared Kitchener exhibited the acid pleasure felt throughout the Army at the cornering of effete civilian values. Thus he delighted in telling visitors to the War Office that he found England a detestable place, and yearned to go back to the 'true' and manly Orient. 'We must make the English people understand that we are at war', he said on one occasion, 'and that war is not pap'.[8] Yet at the same time Kitchener was sufficiently grounded in the instincts of the old order to believe that the essence of British belligerency was that it must be kept cheap in money and lives. The acclaimed brilliance of his own colonial campaigns – above all the reconquest of the Sudan in 1897–8 – had lain precisely in their economical logistics; it followed naturally that Kitchener's ideal conception of British force was a collage of Maxim fire, light railways and naval supremacy. The traces of this philosophy did not disappear when accident thrust upon him responsibility for Britain's part in a major European conflict. Once it emerged that the latter bore no relationship to these traditional preconceptions, his equivocations became evident: 'I don't know what is to be done', he agonized at one point. 'This isn't war'.[9] There were many, however, who felt that the war on the Western Front was not pap, and that Kitchener – and the nation – had to be made to understand its compulsions.

Kitchener's residual appreciation of the *limits* of British warfare made him a natural partner for Asquith as Prime Minister. There were many, deeply-held differences between them, not least over Ireland; but none was so basic that it could not be suspended for the duration. On the key question of war-management (how far and how fast) the two men were attuned to each other's vibrations. It was their mutual empathy, and the diverse support they were capable of pooling, which made the combination so powerful; and without the accident of Kitchener's death at sea it is conceivable that Asquith might have retained the premiership through to the end of the war, an eventuality which would have dramatically changed British history thereafter. Herein lies a key to the irony that Kitchener – the greatest imperial military figure in his generation – became anathema to so many Unionists and senior Army officers. It was, in short, his mantle which gave rise to the possibility that the hated 'Squiff' (as Asquith was nicknamed by his opponents), having survived the pre-war traps of the Constitution and Ulster, might yet succeed in surviving the greatest trap of all.

By early 1915 these incipient divisions came to revolve around a putative shortage of shells. The roots of this controversy lay in Kitchener's policy at the War Office of restricting munitions production within the long-established ring of armaments firms. This limitation was wholly rational, since to distribute orders with grand largesse threatened to dislocate the industrial structure, reduce overall efficiency and stimulate inflation. Yet such arguments did not recommend themselves to those industrial and commercial interests without a place on the gravy-train. Nor did they pacify the apprehensions of General Headquarters in France (GHQ), where the War Minister was suspected of rationing shells as a covert method of controlling operations. The reverberations this set off can only be fully understood against the background of the evolution of GHQ – replete, as Winston Churchill subsequently found, with 'a fine chateau, bath[s], champagne and all the conveniences'[10] – into a separate and independent estate of the realm. So bitter was GHQ's resentment towards what it regarded as the pusillanimous authorities at home, and so entangled in partisan rivalries, that in May 1915 Sir John French resorted to blatant subterfuge, planting an article in *The Times* claiming that the BEF was being put at risk by a shell famine originating in bumbling incompetence (or worse) at the War Office.[11] In so far as Kitchener did attempt to use the supply of shells as a means of leashing the military machine, experience may be said to have proved his wisdom; when the British Army came to be newly-stuffed with shells as well as youths, the result was scarcely the defeat of the enemy. Under the circumstances, however, the placement of such a well-judged journalistic device triggered a political explosion which helped to cripple the Liberal Government, and forced Asquith into a coalition the making of which he later described as the most uncongenial moment of his career.[12]

Nevertheless, the Liberal Government might well have survived the 'shell scandal' had not the call for a Coalition government been simultaneously facilitated by the failed naval attack on the Dardanelles. Although Turkey had entered the war alongside Germany and Austria in November 1914, and afforded Britain a welcome opportunity to at last annex Egypt as a formal Protectorate, there seemed no reason to expect that large-scale hostilities would spread to the Near East. That they did so was largely due to Churchill at the Admiralty, whose brainchild the Dardanelles campaign was. Much of the trouble stemmed from the bad start to the war enjoyed by the adventurous First Lord. The German raider, the *Graf Spee*, made havoc in the Atlantic; there were losses in the Channel, made worse by a clumsy attempt at concealing the news; whilst embarrassing operational blunders allowed two enemy cruisers, the *Breslau* and the *Goeben*, to slip into the Bosphorus and confirm Germany's preponderant influence at Constantinople.[13] Yet what counted against Churchill at this time more than anything else was his impetuous behaviour during the vain attempt to reinforce Antwerp. He had dramatically rushed off to that besieged city, taking with him a scratch force of untrained Worcestershire Yeomanry, many of them teenagers. It did not escape the notice of his critics that he got himself much photographed, but did not succeed in saving Antwerp. Much impartial opinion, indeed, was aghast at the way that ill-equipped and unprepared levies had been gratuitously risked against crack German troops, giving credence to the suspicions which had long lingered as to the soundness of the First Lord's judgement.[14] Thus it was that the Liberal Government's need for a diversion from the stalemate of the Western Front, and Churchill's personal need for a coup to restore his battered reputation, met during early 1915 at the Turkish intersection.

It has always been a puzzle, none the less, why the British Cabinet authorized an assault on the Dardanelles when every pre-war evaluation had concluded that it was impossible for the Royal Navy to force the Straits. If it had been held to be unfeasible in 1908, the last time such a conclusion had been arrived at, why should it have become practicable in 1915, when the Turks had additionally reinforced the batteries overlooking those grey, inhospitable waters? The answer to this conundrum is that pure practicality had ceased to be the point. 'As always when the Dardanelles were under discussion', Churchill's official biographer has written, 'the minds of ministers wandered off into the territorial sphere. No one felt that they were in the shadow of a great naval disaster. They eagerly devised schemes of partition and control which presupposed victory'.[15] In short, the war in the East began to glisten with the prospect of successes which were clearly not obtainable in the West. When Churchill promised to deliver the Golden Horn into the hands of his Cabinet colleagues, therefore, they were disposed to listen. The operation was decided upon, and on 19 February 1915 the British Mediterranean Fleet did as it was ordered and flung itself into the breach.

The attack was a dismal and bloody failure, and the scapegoating began almost before the firing had died away. Churchill alleged ever afterwards that the British warships had been withdrawn just when the Turkish forts had run out of ammunition, an argument which combined the merits of not easily being proved false with heaping the blame on the responsible Commander-in-Chief, Admiral de Robeck.[16] Whilst personal animosities flared, however, the position of the ministry was parlous, since it was one thing not to enjoy immediate triumphs against 'the Hun', but quite another to fall back before the insipid and incompetent Turk. In these circumstances the temptation was not to confess failure, but rather to press on towards the original objective, albeit at greater cost. Thus, although the initial plans for a naval assault had explicitly ruled out any attempt to sustain the campaign by landing troops on the adjacent Gallipoli

Peninsula, this disclaimer, too, was now reversed, and very soon British, Australian, New Zealand and some French units began their nightmarish vigil, clinging to insecure beachheads against superior Turkish forces entrenched on the surrounding heights. Churchill therefore found himself closely associated with a great combined operation on sea and land whose strategic merits he had espoused ever since 1911. At the same time, he encountered the fierce opposition of his own First Sea Lord, the redoubtable 'Jacky' Fisher, and it was the latter's actions which precipitated the climax of the political crisis at home that brought down the Liberal ministry and, coincidentally, consigned Churchill's career to the first of its wildernesses.

Fisher, mercurial and septuagenarian, had been called back to his old Admiralty job (having retired in 1910) shortly after the outbreak of the war, following the hounding from office of Prince Louis of Battenberg on account of his German name. True to form, he indulged in the most blowsy Nelsonian rhetoric, claiming that he would smash, annihilate, crush (verbs on which he lavished thick red underlinings in his official correspondence) the Kaiser's upstart fleet. It did not happen. The great brooding battleships lay wrapped in their North Sea anchorages, and soon the British public, who had been led to believe in the Dreadnought era that the age of stirring victories afloat was not dead, began to wonder what its vaunted sailors were doing whilst the soldiers fought so valiantly in France.[17] However unfair and superficial such criticisms were, they soon led to a bitter reaction in naval circles against the purely subsidiary role which appeared to be their lot in the present conflict. Thus in the summer of 1914 the Senior Service had merely been a 'carrier' for the BEF across the Channel; in the early summer of 1915 it was set to play the same fetching role for another Expeditionary Force to Turkey. This was, to put it mildly, not the ideal war of Fisher's imagination, nor of his fellow Admirals. As the resentment boiled over, its main force came to be directed against their political boss, whom Fisher had always considered unsound in the strategical sphere. 'Nothing will stop him [Churchill]', Fisher vented his spleen. 'His heart is ashore, not afloat! The joy of his life is to be fifty yards from a German trench'.[18] More distracted by the hour, the First Sea Lord eventually deserted his post. At this point some felt that Fisher had finally given way to the nervous breakdown which always threatened his volcanic and unstable personality. If so his madness was nicely executed, since a British Government unable to trace the professional head of its Navy in time of war (he was, in fact, holed up in the Charing Cross Hotel in the Strand) scarcely constitutes a good bet for survival. Bonar Law had only to threaten to raise the question of Fisher's *de facto* resignation in the House of Commons to force the entry of his party into government for the first time since 1906. In some ways it is indeed incongruous that a Liberal Government that had surmounted one storm after another for so many years should have eventually fallen in such bizarre circumstances, but this is to ignore the peculiar chemistry of High Navalism and High Toryism when these forces cut across each other in wartime. We shall see later on, indeed, how in the comparable circumstances of 1940 the ability of the same combination to wreak powerful effects in the British senate was undiminished, though the effect on Churchill's personal position was then to be markedly different.[19]

The new Coalition Government, of which Asquith remained premier, was scarcely better fitted to survive than its predecessor. '[It was] a Coalition that never coalesced' was the retrospective judgement of the influential Cabinet Secretary, Maurice Hankey.[20] It did not coalesce largely because it was never meant to. The commitment of Bonar Law to its permanence was indicated by the fact that for himself he claimed nothing more than the post of Colonial Secretary; one does not jostle overmuch in an ailing vessel, which starts out low in the water, its crew already divided into sullen and competing factions. The one absolute demand on which Law insisted during these negotiations was the purely negative one that Churchill should not be given a post. Amidst such an inchoate situation, the initiative naturally gravitated towards the one figure with the skills and suppleness to play interlocutor between the discrete elements within the Government. The essence of Lloyd George's success in the years prior to 1915 had been to make himself the 'Indispensable Man' in the divided world of Liberal politics, an indispensability arising from his ability at making himself the cross-over point between the various intellectual and factional currents within the party. This was a faculty which was to prove even more apposite within the different setting of the wartime Coalition.

The central fact about Lloyd George's career was that he was a wholly self-made politician from whom the public had over the years come to expect a 'splash'. Whatever initial doubts he may have harboured about the wisdom of British participation, the Great War was from the start the biggest splash of all, which Lloyd George's rhetoric and personality were peculiarly adapted to exploiting. For the Chancellor, as for most politicians, his personal Rubicon in this respect came not in Parliament, but with his first major recruiting speech outside the chamber. His secretary and mistress, Frances Stevenson, testified to the racking nervousness which went into the composition of this speech; and as he left his home bound for the Queen's Hall on 10 September 1914 he said he felt he 'was about to be executed'.[21] Yet the occasion, with its pulling of the Belgian heart-strings, and its numerous images of sacrifice, turned out to be a huge success, from which Lloyd George never looked back. After May 1915, furthermore, it is true to say that – as the natural bridgehead between the more war-minded Liberals and the Unionists – no Cabinet could easily have been formed without him. His main task as chief of the newly-created Ministry of Munitions was to blunt the influence of Kitchener at the War Office, and to give the Army their shells. In fact this challenge was less forbidding than it seemed. Kitchener by this time was already an exhausted volcano, and no match for the most mentally agile of all leading British politicians in the twentieth century. As for solving the immediate problem of shells, this, too, was not difficult, once the mind was made up to ignore both the costs involved and the disruption caused to other forms of production. Lloyd George, assisted by the crush of businessmen that he was the first to draw into government, simply doled out contracts to any manufacturer willing to take them on to their books; given the fat profit margins, there were few who refused. Along with these bulging orders went a business and industrial 'interest' in the conflict which was not likely to be easily budged afterwards. In sum, the munitions poured out, commercial profits soared and Lloyd George's star rose in the political firmament. All the Minister had to do was sign the chits.

It was logical, nevertheless, that parallel with this tendency there developed the first groundswell of anxiety as to the economic consequences of the sort of war that was now being pursued. The chief figure here was Lloyd George's successor at the Exchequer, Reginald McKenna, whose earlier obstreperousness we have noted.[22] McKenna disappeared so completely from political view after the watershed of December 1916 that it is easy to underestimate his considerable significance up to that point. His only biographer (and relative) has written with respect to the overall impact of the Great War on the United Kingdom as follows:

> Eleven thousand millions [of sterling] in four years; the achievement of raising it would have been prodigious if nothing more had been added, if no more than the original six divisions had ever been put into the field, if the Fleet had been restricted to the policing of the seas and blockading the coasts of Germany and if the rest of Great Britain's contribution to the common cause had been to make munitions for her partners. In fact, she found herself required to be not only the bank and arsenal, but also the dockyard and recruiting station for all the belligerent world that was arrayed against the Central Powers and for all the neutral world that was sheltering behind the ships and guns of the allies.
>
> The task, when the final account came to be rendered, was seen to have been more than any single power could carry out. Her savings exhausted, her foreign securities sold, the debts owing to her unpaid, Great Britain was unable to go on settling in gold her debts to a creditor [the United States] who

> excluded her other exports. *Even in 1915 it could be seen by a few to be a task that should never have been attempted* [Italics added].[23]

These lines were composed in the 1930s, and gained additional emotion and meaning in that context; whether during his time at the Treasury McKenna's doubts and disillusionment with the conduct of the war went quite as far as his biographer implies must remain obscure. What is certain is that at the Treasury Board he sought to restore those financial restraints which his predecessor had happily abjured. Thus 'responsibility' became his keynote, which in the circumstances meant financing the war by taxing existing wealth rather than by appropriating the resources of posterity through an exclusive reliance on loans. In this vein the 'McKenna Duties' featuring in his first budget became a landmark in modern British fiscal history by restoring taxes on food to the customs tariff. Technicalities apart, the infusing principle of McKenna's Chancellorship was that the British war effort should never be pushed beyond the point where the orthodox commercial system was irreparably damaged. Just where this prudential boundary might be said to lie was a question which in 1915–16 came to be defined in terms of manpower rather than of money. McKenna's conclusion was that a seventy-division army was the maximum that Britain should seek to maintain in the field, on the common-sense grounds that the same man could not be down a mine, sowing grain, manufacturing ammunition and firing a rifle all at once. This was the hard truth which the Chancellor purveyed in the salons of the First Coalition as time went on. It brought down many an anathema on his head. 'He [McKenna] really is the most noxious creature' Clementine Churchill wrote to her husband – currently doing the rounds at GHQ by way of political rehabilitation – after one social gathering at which the object of her dislike had emphasized the seventy-division ceiling as a vital British interest.[24]

The increasingly visceral disputes surrounding the Coalition reflected, and were reinforced by, the swelling instability lower down the social scale. As the drive for manpower intensified to replace the drafts wiped out at the Battle of Loos during the summer of 1915, the complex social accommodations of the early phases of the war began to buckle. Once the young, the unmarried and the unskilled had been 'combed out', more senior workers – sporting the badge of a 'reserved occupation', and who had hitherto reckoned themselves out of reach of the recruiting-sergeant – began to feel the pressure. Industrial tension rose; strikes proliferated; and the Trade Union bosses, for whom the war was a heaven-sent leg-up into the penumbra of the establishment, found themselves challenged by the upstart Shop Stewards' Movement, with its heartland along the banks of the Clyde. Voluntaryism was clearly not going to be enough. Ironically, one effect of this was to temporarily strengthen Asquith's hand, since it was widely recognized that only he had the authority in the country – if only because of the longevity of his leadership – to put conscription on to the statute-book without raising the shadow of popular disturbances. This the Prime Minister eventually succeeded in doing with the Military Service Act in January 1916. It was the climax of his war career, although it is also tempting to conclude that he had outlived his usefulness to the coteries that were by this time running, to all intents and purposes, the British administrative machine. Such imponderables apart, it was in the aftermath of this legislative triumph that Asquith's position as Prime Minister was critically undermined by the combined effects of Kitchener's death at sea and the dramatic events in Ireland.

At the outbreak of the war, the Irish Question had been put 'on ice' through the curious technique of first enacting a Home Rule statute as a Catholic sop, and then promptly suspending its operation as an Ulster (and Unionist) sop. Unfortunately the hope that Ireland might be thus screened off from the complicating and distorting effects of a great war was always delusory. British belligerency automatically boosted the brasher forms of Protestant ascendancy in John Bull's other island. Thus the sons of good Protestant families were handed out commissions in bucketfuls; Catholic recruits were herded into the 'other ranks'. Ulster (Protestant) Volunteers were allowed to fly the Red Hand;

the Irish (Catholic) Volunteers were banned from displaying the Green Harp.[25] More conducive to volatile emotions than these (scarcely novel) discriminations, however, was the appointment of Edward Carson, the Ulster patriot hero, to the Coalition Cabinet in May 1915. In short, the curious compromise between Home Rule and Protestant Supremacy which had eased the United Kingdom's path into the war in Europe progressively disintegrated thereafter. One consequence of this was the historic crumbling of moderate Nationalism in Irish life, and the passing of the initiative to revolutionary elements. At Easter-time the following year a group seized the Dublin Post Office and for two days warded off British troops. After the Rising had been crushed, the British Officer Commanding, General Sir John Maxwell, exacted a summary revenge: the executions went on for days, one leader of the rebellion, already dying from his wounds, having to be strapped to his chair for the efficient conduct of the firing party. This was a fatal moment in the modern alienation of British and Irish civilizations. 'Just as the purpose of seizing the Post Office was to house a provisional government', an Irish historian has observed, 'so the purpose of the rising was not to make a protest in arms but formally to declare the existence of an independent Irish republic. In political terms, indeed, this was the principal achievement of the insurrection, the point of departure . . . for all subsequent Irish history.'[26]

If the Easter Rising was a departure for Irish nationalism, it could not but be a point of departure for English Liberalism as well, given the symbiosis that had long existed between the two. Asquith had rushed to Dublin in an attempt to pick up the pieces, but had come back, as it was dismissively observed, 'with nothing but a few relics of the rebellion'.[27] Thereafter he was exposed to his enemies. From the early summer of 1916 onwards a whispering campaign concerning the Prime Minister's personal laxity got under way. The damning anecdotes multiplied: how Bonar Law, for example, visited Asquith unannounced on urgent business at his Surrey home, only to find him engaged in a bridge party with three elderly ladies, and unwilling to break up the entertainment – and this whilst the Battle of the Somme was raging.[28] The impression of culpable indolence has been heightened by what has subsequently come to light concerning Asquith's obsession with the young, but not especially virtuous, Venetia Stanley.[29] The explanation for this erratic behaviour is no doubt partly to be found in the shattering loss of the Prime Minister's eldest son, Raymond, on active service in France; though later on, it must be said, Bonar Law was to prove no more, and probably less, capable of devotion to his official tasks when similar griefs came to be his lot. Yet Asquith's conduct of his office may bear a wider reflection. The Prime Minister knew all too well by the middle of 1916 that control over the war effort had slid out of his hands. Instead of pretending to a spurious efficiency, he relapsed into booze, bridge and (if that was all it amounted to) an epistolary passion for a female acquaintance. Whilst not in itself, perhaps, constituting a moral ideal of leadership in time of grave national crisis, it probably made not a ha'p'orth of difference in the realm of public policy. Nor were these realities to change when Asquith's relaxed style was replaced by the 'man of push and go' himself, so that it is questionable whether Lloyd George, for all his undoubted energy, came any nearer to running the war – at least, that is, the war on the Western Front – than did his predecessor.

Of the Battle of the Somme it has been said that it marked the point at which the British learned what modern war was really about. In fact from an early phase in the conflict the summer of 1916 had been designated as the likely juncture at which the United Kingdom should be able to make its weight tell. The massive offensive on the British sector of the Western Front which commenced on 1 July was launched, therefore, in a spirit of hubris. Unfortunately, when the attack finally petered out on the 13 November, British casualties amounted to well over 400,000, without the objectives initially established for the first day having been attained. This did not stop Sir Douglas Haig (who had replaced French as Commander-in-Chief during 1915), or his later apologists, from claiming that a considerable triumph had been achieved by British arms. 'Within the terms of the 1914–18 War', one military historian has felt able to conclude, '[The Battle of the Somme] was an unquestioned Allied victory'.[30] The terms referred to were those of the theory of attrition which during the Somme offensive necessarily emerged as the guiding principle of Haig's strategy. As a doctrine, this was an extreme variant of the original emphasis on the United Kingdom's supposed manpower advantages, upholding that if the Allies pushed their attacks to the hilt, refusing to be deflected by false sentimentality or cowardly politicians, victory was ultimately assured. In the context of the Western Front this had the in-built advantage that high casualty rates could always be justified on the grounds that the enemy must have lost more. It is tempting to attribute such a philosophy to the crassness of those who invented it; certainly the eminent military controversialist, Basil Liddell Hart, later remarked how after the war he often met men who had enjoyed high staff rank under Haig, and whom as a young subaltern he had regarded with awe, only to be amazed at their incorrigible obtuseness.[31] Yet intelligence was never really the point. After the Somme, the evolution of 'attrition' was the only way that the British Army's role in France could be legitimated. Hence, as at the Dardanelles, one went forward because one could not go back. By the autumn of 1916, it was inevitable that 'going forward' on a basis of attrition was bound sooner or later to require a political reconstruction back in England.

This latter political and strategic logic was itself related to the effects which the losses of the Somme had on British opinion, and the consequent repercussions within the governing Coalition. Thus as the official, dull-grey envelopes slipped through the letter-boxes of British homes with their grim news, a blight fell across large tracts of the Home Front. There was, furthermore, something special about the 1916 class of war dead. Unlike the cadres of 1914 and 1915, they were conscripts, not volunteers, and this gave an extra poignancy to the sadness they left behind, unsmoothed by the rhetorical glow of purely voluntary sacrifice. The summer of 1916, therefore, also witnessed the rising murmurs of a 'peace party' in Britain. The components of this movement were diverse and still inchoate: motives inevitably being mixed, they included some who feared the draft, some who had failed to get their share of war profits, some who grieved, some who reckoned that the war could never be won and that there was therefore no point in fighting it, in addition to the philosophical and religious dissidents who had opposed it from the start. With the democratic apparatus of elections suspended for the duration, the crystallization of such opinions could only come about gradually. After all, not every hearth was kept burning for the absent – on Bank Holidays during the war the queues at Liverpool Street Station for tickets to the Essex riviera were said to dwarf those of pre-war days. Nevertheless, the latent strength of peace-sentiment by the autumn of 1916 was graphically illustrated by the fact that it had even penetrated to the parts most difficult to reach: the principal convert was none other than Lord Lansdowne, senior Cabinet Minister and the most distinguished (and patrician) Unionist statesman alive.

Lansdowne in August 1914 had played what was arguably the most vital role in swinging his party behind the Liberal Government's decision to intervene in the war. Having previously filled a galaxy of ministerial and administrative positions (including those of Foreign Secretary and Viceroy of India), and as one of the greatest landlords in England, he was indisputably the doyen of traditional Toryism; and without his imprimatur it is doubtful whether the more ardent interventionists among his party colleagues would have got their way. In October 1914, however, Lansdowne's youngest son was killed on active service in France and, according to his sole biographer and close friend, the blow never afterwards left him.[32] The gradual shift in his attitude to the war was none the less also due, if not to deeper, then to wider considerations than this. The nub of Lansdowne's career had been to sustain the old regime, in which he felt the true greatness of England to lie. By 1916 it was clear to him that the war was subversive of this aim. Revealingly, on one occasion, whilst recuperating on his Bowood estate, Lansdowne spread a map of the locality before an acquaintance, pointed to the big green patches denoting the Great Houses with their surrounding estates, and warned that the growing burden of war taxation would ensure their liquidation.[33] By 1916, indeed, the observation that one side-effect of the present conflict was the destruction of aristocratic England – economically, socially, morally – had become something of a commonplace (it was, for example, a theme which Arnold Bennett portrayed in his novel, *The Pretty Lady*, published during the course of that year). Nor were such prognostications wholly unfounded: the massive shake-out of agricultural property which followed almost as soon as the war ended was to permanently truncate rural England as a social and political force.

This is not to say, of course, that Lansdowne's concerns in 1916 were exclusively those of social privilege. His traditionalism was also of the sort which, in its foreign policy and military aspect, conceived of British interests as pre-eminently naval, Indian and colonial; over and above a modest continental stake, represented by the six divisions of the original BEF, he had not anticipated a war in which the main British battle-fleet kept to its home ports, whilst the flower of the nation's manhood spent itself on European soil. When Herbert Asquith – prompted by the offer of the United States President, Woodrow Wilson, to act as mediator in the struggle – solicited written advice from his Cabinet colleagues as to how to respond, it was Lansdowne who thus produced a memorandum in November 1916 calling for a radical stocktaking of the United Kingdom's economic capacity to sustain its current burdens, and (not least importantly) for Sir Douglas Haig to be bluntly quizzed as to whether or not a resolution to the stalemate in France was imminent. Since these were precisely the issues which could not be raised without acute political controversy resulting, it followed that Lansdowne's paper soon became what one inside observer described as the *causa causans* of the crisis which finally destroyed the First Coalition[34], and put in its place a new formation led by 'the man of push and go', Lloyd George.

Much the same sort of considerations which coloured Lord Lansdowne's changed stance towards the continuance of the war helps in part to explain why Lloyd George's tendency lay in the opposite direction. He had found, for example, that his reputation as a social radical, and in particular as the scourge of the ducal classes, came to fit very neatly with the advocacy of 'total' war. 'Our war aim is war' as the Welshman put it in a famous interview with the American press agencies in September 1916, hoping thereby to kill two birds with one stone – that is, warning the Americans off from an attempted mediation, whilst putting down a marker against stocktaking at home. Much ink has been spilt on describing the complex intrigues during December 1916. Lloyd George always asserted that he never wished to be Prime Minister. What he had demanded, he later claimed in his war memoirs, was merely for the actual running of the war to be put into his discharge; only Asquith's stubborn refusal to agree to such a compromise, the argument went, left him no option but to become party to the dislodgement of his old chief. All that need be said about such a disclaimer is that Asquith could not possibly have agreed to any formula which stripped him of what little effective authority he still had over the administration of military affairs, whilst retaining the burden of full constitutional responsibility for them. Rights and wrongs aside, the outcome was a Cabinet reconstruction in which not only Asquith, Lansdowne and McKenna were purged, but so was Lord Grey, to whose liability of an increasingly poor eyesight had been added in preceding months a distinctly enigmatic relationship to the war itself.[35] Amongst their replacements were such proconsular figures as Curzon and Milner, 'strong men' whose time had come again (Cromer, though offered a position in the new dispensation, turned it down, ostensibly on health grounds). The motif of this new regime, dedicated to securing a 'knock-out blow' against the enemy, was the clenched fist, representations of which appeared on walls and shopfronts throughout the country after the New Year of 1917.

Ironically, just when the United Kingdom thus pronounced itself determined to go on with the conflict, and to pursue it with even greater vigour, her principal opponents showed signs of wishing to enter into preliminary negotiations (the phenomena not being unrelated). The Austrians, especially, evinced such tendencies, and from early 1917 onwards various 'peace feelers' emanated from Vienna. In his memoirs Lloyd George stated that he carefully considered the merits of such talks, but discarded the option on the grounds that no viable basis for a settlement existed. After the war he was to be criticized for missing a 'window of opportunity', and this feeling lingers in some scholarly assessments. Yet it was inherent in the very formation of the new Coalition that the British Army in France should have 'another bite at the cherry' in the form of a grand offensive. One of the most evocative portraits painted by Lloyd George in his autobiographical account is of the day in February 1917 when Haig visited Downing Street to outline his plan for a new 'push', an index finger sporadically stabbed towards a map of Flanders unfurled on his knees, blandly explaining how the Germans would be pushed this way and that, and their lines finally stoved through.[36] The most striking thing about this description, however, is what it misses out; in particular, there is no indication that the Prime Minister – a man justly famed for his ruthlessly incisive inquisition of bankers, businessmen and trade unionists when the occasion demanded it – tried in any serious way to probe the practicalities behind his Commander-in-Chief's gorgeous vision. It is, indeed, only by grasping how skewed were the relations between the civilian and military authorities at the outset of Lloyd George's premiership that it is possible to fully explain the eruptions on the part of the latter when the canny Welshman subsequently tried (with only qualified success) to regather the threads of control into his own hands.

Before then, however, the flaws in Haig's plans for the summer of 1917 had become all too obvious. 'You have two enemies', Marshal Pétain had unavailingly tried to forewarn his British counterpart, 'the *Boche* and the *Boue* [mud]. You may defeat the *Boche*, but the *Boue* will defeat you.'[37] In truth the British Army probably had little chance against either of these awkward foes. The Germans, by withdrawing into the Hindenburg Line, were now encased in a powerful redoubt with compact supply lines. To launch a massive infantry drive against such a hardened object across sodden terrain, the latter having been ploughed up by a cannonade whose effect otherwise on the opponent was simply to alert him to what was coming, and then to expect the *coup de grâce* to be delivered by British cavalry dashing across the surrealist landscape, was to court disaster on the heroic scale. So it proved. If the Battle of the Somme had begun the martyrdom of the United Kingdom's conscript army, the Battle of Passchendaele brought it to a climax. Between 31 July and 15 November the British incurred losses in excess of 300,000 men, and in return occupied two villages and a hamlet. Here, it may be argued, was the *reductio ad absurdum* of the modern British aspiration to be a great land power on the continent of Europe. The lessons deduced from it were to be deeply imbibed in many (if not all) quarters of British political life; so profoundly was the thinking of a younger generation of Army commanders to be influenced, furthermore, that some two decades later, in another great war, they were to refuse to be sacrificed in quite the same way again.[38] Even those historians who have seen the Somme as a British 'victory' have not quite been able to write of Passchendaele in the same apologetic vein.

Apart from the blunting of the British attack in Flanders, 1917 was a year marked by one great setback for the Allies and one bonus. The setback was the February Revolution in Russia, which confirmed the Russians' *de facto* disappearance from the war (though only later events, the Bolshevik take-over in the following October and finally the Treaty of Brest Litovsk in March 1918, were to make it *de jure*). With the significance of this departure in world history we are not concerned here. Nevertheless, it was stressed earlier how central the entente with Russia had been to the United Kingdom's calculations before 1914; following its disintegration, not only did those calculations become susceptible to revision, but the original entente with France automatically lost some of its lustre. The mutinies within the French armies at this juncture only added to the effect, so that before long it was respectable again in official circles in London to venture discreet asides that it was France, with her evidently hegemonic ambitions in Europe, not Germany, who represented the biggest long-term threat to British interests.[39] Against this background Lord Lansdowne, who had unsuccessfully hawked his putative 'Peace Letter' from one newspaper proprietor to another ever since his departure from government, finally had his controversial missive published in the *Daily Telegraph* during November 1917.[40] With these continuously shifting public and private moods, a ministry which had come to power in Britain based on the principle that 'Our war aim is war' began, in the wake of Passchendaele, surreptitiously to scout out ways of getting itself off the hook.

Meanwhile the ostensible bonus which obtained during the course of 1917 was the entry of the United States into the war, a decision forced on the Americans by recognition of the fact that it was necessary to become a belligerent if their voice was to be heard at all when a settlement was finally made.[41] Even here, however, the nuances had a sombre tinge. Hence the Wilson Administration, in joining the fray, was careful to describe itself as an 'Associate' of Britain and France rather than a fully-fledged ally. The equivocal sentiments were not all on one side. A major attraction of the old entente with Russia had been that it was Britain, as the paymaster, who could contrive (not always with the success it wished) to pull the strings. In the case of this new transatlantic association, patently the United States was the paymaster. In the light of later history this may appear (and indeed in some sense it was) the beginning of a 'Special Relationship' between the Anglo-Saxon cousins; at the time it did not feel like it to the British political and official cadres. Lloyd George, in particular, was typical of his generation in having, as an observer once remarked, no sense of, or liking for, 'the power of modern America'.[42] Concern, however vague, as to just how tangible and constraining such alien power might become was another consideration prompting the British premier to look for ways, not yet to negotiate peace outright, since this remained impracticable, but to move the focus of the war away from the Western Front where the costs were fast becoming unsustainable.

Lloyd George's first choice for an alternative focus to the Western Front was Italy. With this in mind his first trip abroad after becoming premier had been to Rome, where he tried to persuade the Italians to play host to a massive build-up of Allied troops, leading to expanded operations on their northern frontiers against the vulnerable Austrians. Italy, however, had initially had to be bribed into war in 1915, and after that (quite sensibly) sought to have as quiet a time as circumstances allowed; hence the last thing she wished for was a great influx of foreign troops encamped on her soil, if only because getting rid of them afterwards might not prove so easy – a suspicion earlier Italian history went some way to justifying. Lloyd George's efforts in Rome were thus unavailing; and although following the great Austrian victory at Caporetto in November 1917 British reinforcements did eventually find their way to the reluctant peninsula, it was all too clear that the war was not going to end with John Bull arriving (via the Tyrolean passes) at the gates of Vienna. By the end of 1917, nevertheless, Lloyd George *had* discovered a theatre which proved pliable in British hands, and which presented the opportunity of those spoils without which peace could never be made in the requisite blaze of glory. This ideal theatre was the Middle East, where the Turks proved to be that elusive enemy – one that could be beaten, and *seen* to be beaten. To Haig and his compeers at GHQ in France this was not much use, since their quintessential aims and prestige hinged on success on the Continent, not in distant Araby; the argument over the respective merits of an 'Eastern' or a 'Western' strategy was soon to bring to a high pitch the rivalry between the British civil and military authorities which marked the final phases of the Great War. Before dwelling on the conflict in the Middle East, however, we shall first say something about the British Empire at large.

One of the prominent features of the United Kingdom's entry into the Great War had been the remarkable display of imperial unity which attended it. 'Touch one of us and you touch us all' as the prominent Australian politician, Edmund Barton, had once expressed the position.[43] Admittedly, the motives involved were less a matter of unalloyed sentiment than they might appear.

All of the old colonies of British settlement had their eyes on German colonies within their own regions – South Africa, in overrunning German South West Africa in 1915, was just lucky in getting hold of her desired booty early on, whereas Australia and New Zealand had to wait to secure their desiderata in the Pacific. Pure self-interest apart, the sense of a common British nationality remained sufficiently powerful to ensure that the various self-governing Dominions did not wait in August 1914 (as some of them were to wait in September 1939) for votes in local parliaments before confirming their belligerent status. The ideal of a united and militant Empire cherished by so many Edwardian minds thus appeared to be validated by subsequent events; in this vein the Western Front, with a galaxy of Imperial troops among the Allied ranks, was widely typified as 'the Empire made flesh', living proof that its peoples could be welded together into an organic entity if only the politicians could be made to live up to the challenge of the times. It was a mode of thought (hinging on the primacy of 'will') that was to prove of great significance in metropolitan political culture during the decades ahead.

The wartime boom in the significance of Empire for the United Kingdom was particularly marked after Lloyd George became Prime Minister. This was logical, since an imperial bias went hand-in-hand with the commitment after December 1916 to a 'knock-out' war. Mobilizing 'Daughter Nations' and other dependencies was, in short, one of Lloyd George's answers to McKenna's earlier strictures that for Britain to run for any length of time a war effort beyond its own productive resources would prove a fatal error. Hence it was during 1917 that a plethora of committees and boards bearing grandiloquent titles (the Imperial Development Board, to give just one instance) were set up, many of them given birth to by the Imperial War Conference to which Dominion leaders were summoned in April of that year.[44] Even an Imperial War *Cabinet* was now introduced, though this was largely a cosmetic exercise designed to enable Dominion statesmen to reassure their publics that the bloody sacrifice of Armageddon had indeed won them a place in 'the Counsels of the Empire'.[45] From a purely British vantage-point, the chief importance of these developments was that, whilst there was nothing inherently novel about the equation of the United Kingdom's power and status with its possession of an overseas realm, the wartime experience was to inscribe this formula as a vital national principle. As such, for decades thereafter British society was to have great difficulty in conceiving of its own welfare in ways that did not relate to the ideal of Empire.

According to metropolitan criteria, however, some parts of this Empire performed rather better than others between 1914 and 1918. Hence the Western Front may have witnessed the Empire-made-flesh, but most of that flesh was noticed to be white. Whilst the Canadians were therefore lionized for their courage on Vimy Ridge, and the Australians for numerous feats of courage and steadfastness during the Somme offensive, Indian troops were conventionally the subject of at best grudging praise, and at worst rank slurs of cowardice and disloyalty.[46] Events such as the mutiny in Singapore of the Indian Army's Fifth Light Infantry during 1915 egged on this prejudice.[47] Such tendencies masked a wider evolution whereby India's position as the 'Jewel in the Crown' of the British Empire became tarnished. Amongst the war leadership in London it became habitual to accuse the government in Delhi – British-led bureaucracy though it was – of stubbornly refusing to apply itself wholeheartedly to the war in hand.[48] What that hard-pressed institution had most immediately in hand, of course, was the awkward task of holding down a Sub-Continent with a minimum of force, but this did not deflect the critics. The latter became particularly raucous after the only campaign wholly sponsored by the Indian authorities – that in Mesopotamia – had come to grief when General Townshend's army surrendered to the Turks at Kut in April 1916.[49] Indeed, the manner in which British-Indian administration was hauled over the coals during the Commission of Enquiry into the débâcle of the Mesopotamian campaign inaugurated a certain disenchantment with the utility and glamour of India in British minds which the rise of local nationalism (also a facet of these years) only served later to accentuate.

The tacit demotion of India within the imperial pecking order was to run parallel with the promotion of the British stake in the Middle East. Suggestively, the very term 'the Middle East' was invented by the British after 1914 as essentially a strategic concept[50] – it has, after all, no meaningful geographical or cultural content to speak of. The pivot on which this expansive phenomenon hinged was Egypt. After the British Government had declared a formal Protectorate over that country in late 1914, the Army proceeded to dig itself in with a view to permanence; not for nothing was the overlord of the British war effort, Lord Kitchener, at heart an Egyptian soldier. The Suez Base – the most extensive and formidable of all the great military imperial bases to come – rose above the effluence of the Nile. One writer has described the departure as follows:

> The effort to protect the seventy-mile artery was unprecedented in the sheer magnitude of its logistics, involving water-supply, metalled roadways in the sand, floating bridges on the Canal itself, and entrenchment and wiring on an enormous scale. Until nearly halfway through the war, the barricaded encampment in Egypt represented a bottomless sinkhole for imperial resources and manpower . . . [E]xaggerated concern for the defence of Suez warped British diplomacy no less than British strategy. The promises made to the Jews and Arabs, the provisions extracted in secret and occasionally acrimonious negotiations with allies, all reflected a Suez-fixation which, in its political consequences, was destined to be significantly more far-reaching than the actual or potential military danger to the Canal itself'.[51]

This Suez-fixation, with its central political underpinning, would have been much less pronounced had it not been for setbacks elsewhere in the region. The final withdrawal from Gallipoli in January 1916 (mercifully without the massacre on the beaches which many anticipated) and the defeat in Mesopotamia had the natural effect of investing the British hold on Egypt with a heightened importance. Nevertheless, as long as the Western Front was assumed to hold the key to victory, the Egyptian Expeditionary Force (EEF) was kept on a tight ration of manpower and ammunition, its remit merely to keep the marauding Turks away from the Canal. In these dog days of the war in the East the officer caste took to hanging about Shepheard's Hotel – hence a legendary watering-hole entered British imperial annals; the rank-and-file took to hanging around the seedier establishments of Port Said – hence one of the great venereal epidemics of the century.[52] Meanwhile, too, the swarm of British gentlemen and soldiers (many Members of Parliament among them) who had gone out to Cairo during 1914 and 1915 in expectation of hectic events not only found themselves disappointed, but cruelly subject to the allegation that their itinerary had been drawn up to avoid a less exotic sojourn in France. The children of Mark Sykes, a prominent British Arabophile and proponent of an 'active' war against the Turks, for example, had to be removed from Ampleforth School because their classmates fell to vindictive ridicule of this kind.[53] Against this background the mounting frustration to be found in the higher echelons of 'British' Cairo was wholly understandable, especially when it was combined after a while with anxiety that absence from home meant losing out on the patronage and promotions which all wars bring in their path.[54]

This strain for stirring service was especially to the fore amongst the young intelligence officers gathered together in the so-called Arab Bureau in Cairo, and the first wedge into the stagnant status quo was their stimulation of an anti-Turkish revolt in the Hejaz led by the Sherif Hussein of Mecca, a development lubricated by a good deal of secret-service gold distributed liberally off schooners as they cruised along the Red Sea coast. In the long-term this investment in the Hejazi Arabs was to prove misplaced, since the future in the area lay with their arch-foes, the Saudis; in the short term, however, it provided a suitably pictorial outlet for pent-up energies. The Bureau, indeed, was before long to provide the most compelling British legend of the entire war: Lawrence of Arabia. Much later Lawrence was to come in for a good deal of debunking, focusing on the self-aggrandisement and factual errors of his epic tract, *The Seven Pillars of Wisdom*.[55] These attacks hinged, in part, on the thesis that since the Damascus-to-Medina railway, the object of many of his exploits, was always a net liability to the Turks, the raids made upon it were irrelevant; in effect, hacking at the trunk of a crippled man. Contrarily, others have argued that the Hejaz Rebellion pinned down large numbers of Turkish troops, and thus directed enemy resources away from the Sinai lines, about to become the launch-pad for one of the most successful British military offensives in history. This controversy can never be resolved, and therein lay Lawrence's triumph: he converted something that was always close to boy's own adventure into myth, and myth into rich (albeit sometimes over-rich) literature. What is most striking is that it was Lawrence in his romantic costume, rather than some more pedestrian veteran of the Western Front, who in the 1920s was placed on the pedestal of stardom. If Lawrence had not created himself, Britain's war propagandists would have had to invent him.

The climax of Lawrence's raiding career was the capture of Aqaba in July 1917, which shut off the Turks from the Red Sea. After that the Hejaz relapsed into its accustomed drowsiness, and Lawrence's 'Arab Horsemen' (as Lloyd George classically called them) became merely the outlying flank of the EEF as it lay poised over Gaza. The latter, meanwhile, had been put under the command of General Allenby (known familiarly as 'The Bull') at the personal behest of the Prime Minister. Allenby's instructions had the virtue of clarity: they were to stuff Jerusalem into the British stocking in time for Christmas.[56] As the offensive unfolded after October 1917, the overstretched lines of communication, the parched troops, and the plotted course of dead camels and horses driven beyond the limits of endurance were testimony to Allenby's – and Lloyd George's – impatience. The effort climaxed in the fall of the Holy City on 9 December. Allenby, recalling that the Kaiser had once entered its portals on a white charger, did so more modestly on foot, deliriously welcomed by the Arab populace as a saviour from Turkish oppression and (though the future might be said to belie this) a harbinger of Palestinian renaissance. Whilst these shouts echoed around the Dome, the bells of Westminster Abbey hailed what was the first unequivocal British victory gained on land since the war began.

The acquisition of Jerusalem was the symbolic inauguration of an enlarged *imperium* in the Eastern Mediterranean world which was to be a touchstone of British history in the twentieth century. As such, Lloyd George had a very precise idea of 'where he wanted his armies to be [in the Middle East] when the shooting stopped'[57], and according to this formula Allenby's accelerated advance subsequently swept through the Jordan valley, and went on to take Damascus, Baghdad and Aleppo, before the Levant finally fell quiet. As British aims in the region were thus inflated, however, they soon clashed with arrangements that in an earlier phase of the war had been made both with Arab notables (who claimed that they had been promised a prescriptive right to Palestine) and with the French (who under the rubric of the Sykes-Picot Agreement of early 1916 felt themselves entitled to something called Greater Syria). A vast and often polemical scholarship has been erected around these multilateral exchanges: the only sensible conclusion to be drawn is that everybody lied to everybody else, and none with more aplomb, given their ambitions, than the British themselves. In striking out after the summer of 1917 for preponderance in the Middle East, it was characteristic of Lloyd George's supple imagination that he sought to identify proxies who might prove (as the Arabs and the French patently would not) reliable partners in the future. The Balfour Declaration of 2 November 1917[58], in which the Zionists were promised a National Home for Jews in Palestine, forged such a link between Whitehall and what promised to be a vigorous settler community. The British premier, however, put almost an equivalent value on nurturing an affinity with the Greeks, whose own settler aspirations lay in Macedonia and along the fringe of Anatolia. Neither of these ties, from a British point of view, was to prosper mightily in the longer term, though if anything the Greeks were to prove more volatile than the Zionists, helping to bring about Lloyd George's own fall from power in 1922. Yet these traumas lay ahead. By the summer of 1918 the campaign in the Levant ensured that, when the Great War ground to a halt, there was at least one major theatre of operations the success of which, from a British perspective, could not be gainsaid.

That the war in the Orient ended well for Britain was indeed all the more important given the ambivalences which attended the conclusion of war in the West. The advent of 1918 had found the British war machine deeply at odds with itself. The Army leadership, both in France and in Horse Guards Parade, fiercely resented the diversion of effort to the East at the behest of the politicians. To this grievance had been added Lloyd George's championing of the proposal for a Supreme Allied Command on the Western Front.[59] Such a suggestion might sound sensible enough, since it offered the prospect of a better use of reserves and more flexible co-ordination in a crisis. A Supreme Command on French soil, however, would necessarily have to have at its head a French soldier, so that the British Army appeared destined to end the war under foreign control. No fate of this kind, it went without saying, would ever have been contemplated for the Royal Navy, whose tight blockade of Germany now allowed it to regain its lost kudos as the senior British armed service. This apprehension of demotion set Haig, and even more the Chief of the Imperial General Staff, Sir William Robertson, against the Prime Minister – the author, as they saw it, of their impending humiliation. The resulting resentment – amounting, in Robertson's case, even to hatred – was to feed into a campaign against Lloyd George's 'mismanagement' very much along the same lines, and incorporating the same arguments, as had once been used against Asquith; its climax was the 'Maurice' debate in the House of Commons on 9 May 1918 (so named after the officer who leaked what purported to be incriminating data concerning the 'famine' of drafts on the Western Front). By then, however, the situation had been transformed by a trauma which put even these intra-British commotions in the shade: on 21 March 1918 the German military overlord, Field Marshal Erich von Ludendorff, ordered into action the great German spring offensive.

The distinguishing characteristic of this massed attack, its scale apart, was that it was aimed overwhelmingly against the

British lines. Furthermore, after years of holding steady, the latter now broke, and for a while Haig's Army was in headlong retreat.[60] Just as the crucial junction of Amiens seemed about to fall into German hands, however, the attack stalled; Allied reinforcements arrived to stabilize the situation; and on 8 August the counter-offensive began which eventually culminated in early October when a provisional German Government sued for an Armistice on the basis of President Wilson's Fourteen Points, enunciated earlier in the year. Such a précis elides certain crucial developments. Most significantly, during the dark days of March Haig had been forced to plead with his French counterpart, Marshal Foch, for help to save his disintegrating army from outright disaster. Foch had agreed to this at a conference at Doullens on 26 March, but only on conditions which included the recognition of his position as Supreme Commander. It was thus a French military hero who indeed presided like a Titan over the final phases of the Great War on the Western Front; and although the British Army recovered sufficiently to play a prominent part in these operations, its role was distinctly subordinate. As a token of this result, when Generalissimo Foch received the formal surrender of the German military authorities in a railway-carriage in the forest of Compiègne on 5 November, whilst a representative of the British Admiralty was invited to be present, an officer of the British Army was not. Ludendorff's spring offensive may thus have brought Germany ultimately to defeat, but it also succeeded in delivering a hammer-blow to that obsession with 'the military basis of power in Europe' which had been an icon of the British military establishment since the early years of the century. To this extent the Kaiser's advice in 1911 to a high-ranking British officer – 'Excuse my saying so, but the few divisions you can put into the field can make no appreciable difference' – was not altogether belied by events.

Of only slightly lesser import for Britain was another off-shoot of the spring crisis: when the news of Haig's discomfiture reached Downing Street, Lloyd George had no option but to send an urgent telegram to President Wilson requesting an immediate acceleration of American troop shipments to Europe. This was an historic message, as those who helped in its composition well knew[61], since it effectively (and permanently) altered the balance of power between the two Anglo-Saxon democracies. By September 1918 United States' forces were arriving in Europe at the rate of 125,000 men *per month*. The off-shore entity which thus succeeded in tilting the odds of the Continental struggle was not an island close at hand, but another continent stretching its fantastic muscle – industrial as much as human – across three thousand miles of ocean. In this context, too, therefore, assumptions in August 1914 as to the projection of British influence and prestige – assumptions which had been backed up by such a vast investment of blood and treasure thereafter – were shown to be a mirage.

Back in London the effect of this hectic end-game was to generate instant nostalgia for that pre-war orthodoxy which once had been so despised. 'I care not', wrote the Cabinet Secretary, Hankey, despite having penned countless memoranda in the opposite sense, 'if we [now] sink to third place among our military allies'.[62] Reorienting the Army to its traditional role of guarding an overseas Empire, and reviving some suitably modified form of a *Pax Britannica* afloat, became the hallmark of much British defence thinking during the 1920s and 1930s. Yet putting the clock back was easier said than done. The war had awakened 'Big Navyism' in such incipient giants as the United States and Japan; neither of these was to be disposed to tolerate any longer the claims, based insecurely on custom, of the White Ensign. Above all, John Morley's prognostications in August 1914 as to the effects of intervention on the United Kingdom's economic prospects had come home to roost. In the words of McKenna's biographer:

> Four and a quarter years of destroying and not replacing, of consuming and not producing, of borrowing and not repaying, four and a quarter years of spending, lending, mortgaging, 'pegging', requisitioning, inflating! What did anyone think would happen when the pegs were removed, the

> dams broken, the waters left to find their level, the
> 'laws' of economics allowed to take their course? Did
> anyone think at all?[63]

The asperity of this description evokes the tenaciousness with
which many in the British political world subsequently dedicated
themselves to clawing a way back to 'normalcy', by which was
usually meant the lost verities of the late Victorian order. Yet it
was of the highest moment to the later course of British history
that this by no means constituted a national consensus. Hence
if there were many who longed for the sort of normality their
father's (and grandfather's) generation would have recognized,
there were others for whom recent events had underscored,
rather than undermined, Edwardian reactions against the style
and assumptions of an older Victorian establishment. Indeed,
most ordinary citizens, in a roughly comprehending sort of
way, were probably subject to both sets of contrary impulses,
pulled first one way, and then the other, by the rival visions
on offer. Such divergences and pressures came to be rooted
not least in the contrasting emotions which memories of the
Great War were to continue to conjure up. Thus not all – as
the latter-day ethic of 'Remembrance' might lead us to assume –
looked back upon the war of 1914–18 with unrelievedly gloomy
thoughts. Harold (later Lord) Alexander, Winston Churchill's
favourite commander in the Second World War, for example,
hugely enjoyed his career between 1914 and 1918 and, according
to his biographer, afterwards 'was not ashamed to admit it'; he
was not alone.[64] Indeed, behind all the mutations of British
politics and policies in the ensuing era there may be said to
have lain one subliminal distinction: between those who had
detested the last war, and those who had not. In this regard
it was entirely appropriate that ultimately Neville Chamberlain
(for whom 1914–18 was so bitter a void that he could barely
bring himself to talk about it) and Winston Churchill (who began
writing about what he had once described as 'this golden delicious
war' as soon as it was over) were to be at the opposite ends of
the pole of Appeasement diplomacy during the 1930s.[65] Before

arriving at that crossroads, however, we must first deal with the immediate terrain which lay beyond the Armistice concluded in November 1918.

The Policeman of the World?

The dominating political question in Britain when the shooting finally stopped was whether the existing Coalition should stay together and seek a mandate at the election which immediately loomed, or whether the old parties should reconstitute themselves as independent and competing units. In fact Liberal disunity had become so endemic in the backwash of the December 1916 split that such a development was highly unlikely – the bitterness between Asquithians and Lloyd Georgians was, indeed, to prove more or less permanent. The Unionists could conceivably have seceded from the Coalition, triumphed at a patriotic election and restored the Victorian party constitution. Why did they not take the chance? 'I am perfectly certain', their leader, Bonar Law, tellingly remarked, '. . . that our party on the old lines will never have any future again in this country.'[1] That British Conservatism started out after the Great War in such a pessimistic frame of mind throws some light on its recurrent weakness as a governing organ thereafter. Yet Law's confession suggested something more profound still: an uneasy sense on the part of the political class as a whole that the war had undermined the legitimacy of its authority. The Lloyd George Coalition, therefore, fundamentally stuck together because none of its parts dared to forgo the protective cover it continued to provide.

The most powerful evocation of this period, and above all of the Paris Peace Conference which convened in January 1919, is that classic of English political literature, John Maynard Keynes's *The Economic Consequences of the Peace*. This visceral critique, featuring Lloyd George and the French premier, Georges Clemenceau, as arch-culprits, has been said by his most recent biographer to reflect Keynes's own sense of guilt at having helped arrange the financial levers of a war in which he had never really believed.[2] Certainly there was a strong hint of moral convenience in attributing the rank chauvinism of the British hustings during December 1918 solely to the evil genius of Lloyd George. In fact the Coalition's leaders did try to talk idealistically about social reconstruction and domestic improvement. They quickly found, however, that what went down best with the honest citizenry was undiluted Germanophobia, and especially the plank that 'the Hun' should pay the *whole* cost of the war. This happy euphoria peaked in that repository of cool English objectivity, the constituency of Cambridge. 'The Germans, if this Government is returned', declared the First Lord of the Admiralty, Sir Eric Geddes, at a meeting in the town, 'are going to pay every penny; they are going to be squeezed as a lemon is squeezed. My only doubt is not whether we can squeeze hard enough, but whether there is enough juice.'[3] Perhaps it was inevitable that a regime which had based itself on the principle of a knock-out war should also find itself propelled along by the imperatives of a knock-out peace.

The mechanism of this logic, however, requires further consideration. After all, the British people had sincerely welcomed the end of hostilities; nor was their history habitually stained by arrogance or contempt towards defeated foes, at least not towards those of a like race and culture. The very scale of the Great War, and the burdens it had involved, made a vital difference here. It was a neutral and therefore impartial expert, Gerard Vissering, the leading Dutch banker of his generation, who in 1920 delineated the locust harvest of war finance. One historian has compressed his analysis as follows:

Governments [had] floated loans and sold bonds to their citizens, giving in return only an acknowledgement of debt. The patriotic subscribers accepted and considered these claims on their governments as assets, a notion the governments encouraged. Subscribers understood that they would receive their money back

with interest. It therefore came as a rude shock after
the war when many finally discovered that "they
had . . . accepted as an asset something that eventually
for each of them proved to be part of their own
liabilities". The people owed themselves massive sums
which could be received [only] through confiscatory
levels of taxation or by making Germany pay.[4]

The psychology of bond-holding and Germanophobia ran
throughout Allied Europe, but it marked some countries more
than others. In France, for example, the capital-owning classes
had donated their sons to *la gloire*, but not, for the most part,
their treasure, if only because so much of the latter was in land.
Afterwards their hatreds were not primarily financial. It was in
Britain that was to be found the largest middle-class sitting on a
pile of war certificates. The determination to see that these assets
were not devalued ('make Germany pay') therefore dominated
the 1918 general election, and packed Lloyd George off to Paris
imprisoned within his own mandate.

The dominating aspect of the Paris Peace Conference was
thus the co-operation of Lloyd George and Clemenceau in
bending the pliable moralism of President Woodrow Wilson.[5]
Along the way the latter's Fourteen Points of January 1918,
on which the Germans understood the Armistice to have been
based, were progressively discarded; as Clemenceau said at one
point, even God only needed ten to secure His purposes. Why,
then, did Lloyd George not try harder to wriggle off the hook of
revanche, and instead ended up becoming bound to what even
some of his own Cabinet colleagues referred to scathingly as a
'French document'?[6] In fact he had little choice. The British
looked to France for diplomatic support on a range of vital
matters – support not likely to emanate from other quarters.
Hence in the naval sphere there was at first the question of
the destiny of the German Fleet; and although this matter
was soon pre-empted when the latter scuttled itself on a cold
night in Scapa Flow, there remained the traditionally envenomed
controversy with the United States over 'maritime rights'. In

addition to these considerations there were many decisions to be taken on territorial matters outside Europe in which Britain had a vital interest, not least in the Middle East, where the authorities in London were banking on French willingness to be fobbed off with the small change of a truncated Syria and its Lebanese outhouse. If France was to help Britain achieve her aims in matters such as these, the latter had no choice but to continue to assist its old partner in gaining the Continental primacy on which she appeared to be bent. This did not mean that the British premier never clashed heatedly with his French counterpart when differences arose during the Conference, but the fact remained that when Clemenceau cracked his whip, Lloyd George invariably surrendered. In the making of peace, as in the conduct of war, the entente principle was one which favoured landlubbers over the island race.

The outcome was a Carthaginian peace which enshrined the necessity, in Winston Churchill's words, that 'France has got to win and know that she has won, and Germany has got to be beat and know that she is beaten'.[7] A Reparations Commission was set up to establish Germany's total liability for war damage, its remit expanded at the last moment by British insistence that payment for war pensions be included in the arithmetic. Germany's colonies were forfeited and parcelled out among new occupiers under the fictional cover of 'mandates' – as Leopold Amery remarked, the label 'makes no difference as long as we actually get our flag up'.[8] The Saar Region passed under the supervision of a new international body, the League of Nations, its coal output leased to France for fifteen years, after which a plebiscite was to be held. In the west, Alsace-Lorraine returned to France; in the east, vast tracts were lopped off East Prussia to facilitate the restoration of an independent Poland. It was true that many of these terms represented a watered-down version of Clemenceau's initial demands, not least owing to Lloyd George's pressure; the Rhineland, for example, was not hived off into a French puppet-state, though it was demilitarized. Nevertheless, Marshall Foch, for one, did not allow such petty detractions to obscure the essential message. Visiting London for an Allied military feast in 1920, he spoke of the Versailles settlement and declared 'Germany is ended! There is no Germany now! There are Germans, but no Germany. It is finished!'[9] This was vulgar nonsense, and always likely to evoke an even more vulgar – and more powerful – response before too long had passed. It was, furthermore, a nonsense to which the British remained organically linked.

The triumphalism of Marshal Foch was especially related to the settlement in East-Central Europe, and here the pattern was set not least by the separate peace treaties negotiated by the victors with the fragments of the disintegrated Austro-Hungarian Empire following the abdication of Emperor Charles I on 11 November 1918: principally with Austria at St Germain in September 1919, and with Hungary at Trianon in June 1920. The selective application of the principle of ethnic self-determination (selective in that it operated to keep Germans apart rather than together) led to a series of 'succession states' in Eastern Europe, each invariably in need of an external guarantee to survive, since their gimcrack structures were too internally divided, lacking in economic viability and rent by territorial jealousies to stand easily of their own accord. Many of these Danubian and Baltic states looked naturally to France as a patron, a connection shortly consolidated for some into what became known as the Little Entente.[10] It was the United Kingdom's relationship to *this* aspect of the new Europe which was the true storm-centre of 'ex-Allied' diplomacy, especially once the United States had availed herself in 1920 of the luxury of detachment, withdrawing her promised guarantee to France and refusing to join the League of Nations. The fundamental problem, as Foch himself admitted, was that the system of Versailles needed twenty-four divisions to keep upright even under normal conditions. For Britain the choice that lingered was whether to arm up to the level prescribed by the internal logic of the Treaty, or whether to stand increasingly aloof whilst the natural currents of European power politics imposed, as in the course of time they must, a balance of their own. It was a choice which became hedged round by rival imprecations of realism, justice, honour and obligation.

The underlying issue for Britain was first manifest in the 'Intervention' against the Bolshevik takeover in Russia, which continued to consume huge resources even after the main fighting in Europe against the Central Powers ended. The campaign's chief advocate was Winston Churchill, whom Lloyd George had eased back into office as Minister of Munitions in 1917, and then made Minister of War in 1919. Churchill's principal political belief, having long since lost touch with Liberalism, reposed in the triple entente of 1914, and it was only by putting the Archdukes back into their dachas that this ideal could now be reconstituted. But there were other, more profound, connotations. 'I want to build up the nation', Churchill responded when his anti-Soviet obsession was criticized in private, 'with the gallant men who have fought together. I want them to combine to make an ever greater England.'[11] On another occasion the Minister for War suggestively defined his ideal of the Intervention as a point of concentration for '. . . the strong and dominant forces in our national life' which only a Coalition, locked in foreign combat with a cruel tyranny, could provide.[12] The Great War had fused such sentiments of martial ardour, nostalgia and implicit social reaction into a powerful force, and although it was to be pushed onto the defensive for much of the 1920s and 1930s the traces were not by any means to be entirely expunged from the body politic. Meanwhile, the emotional and ideological stress it pointed to within the Coalition was illustrated by the diatribe which Churchill levelled at his political chief at a night-club party in London. 'Winston still raving on the subject of the Bolsheviks', Frances Stevenson recorded, 'and ragged D. [Lloyd George] about the New World. "Don't you make any mistake", he said to D. "You're not going to get your New World. The Old World is a good enough place for me, and there's life in the old dog yet. It's going to sit up and wag its tail".'[13] Afterwards, in so far as Churchillianism stood for any distinct principle in English public life, getting the old dog to wag its tail was it.

Even Churchill, however, had shortly to recognize that the United Kingdom had not the troops or the cash to guard against social disorders at home, fight Irish rebels, dish the Bolsheviks and consolidate a new *imperium* in the Middle East, all at once. In fact, whilst the Interventions in the Ukraine and Transcaspia were inexorably running down, a crisis of major proportions was brewing in Mesopotamia. Developments in the latter region epitomized the United Kingdom's Middle Eastern ambitions as they had taken shape in the wake of Allenby's wartime victories. 'During . . . [1919] a tight, centralized, Indian-style government was officially reinforced [in Mesopotamia] and heavily staffed with Indian civil servants under the direction of British senior officials', one historian has written. 'The very titles carried by the bureaucracy in New Delhi – Civil Commissioner, political officer, revenue officer, judicial officer – were precisely reproduced in this miniature Indian administration.'[14] In 1920, however, a dispersed but devastating revolt broke out in the vast hinterlands of what was a tribal and lawless realm. The nascent Mesopotamian Raj called on the British taxpayer for reinforcements; the reply it got was dusty. An 'Anti-Waste' campaign run by *The Times* depicted the territory as a bottomless hole down which British money was being nonchalantly cast, and the public gorge rose against 'Squandermania'. The rebellion was contained, but only at the price of conciliation which included the substitution of local Iraqi officials for Anglo-Indian imports, the latter being dispatched to their homes 'complaining bitterly that the "wogs" would never succeed in managing their own affairs'.[15] Thus it was along the flood-plain of the Euphrates that England's 'war imperialism' at last began to sink beneath the weight of its great, but ultimately unsustainable, expectations.

Events certainly proceeded to bear out Maynard Keynes's prediction that when peace came, British public opinion would insist that wartime inflation be squeezed out of the system, along with whatever accretions (social or strategic) had become attached to it. A policy of active deflation was the chosen method to effect this goal. As Chancellor of the Exchequer, Austen Chamberlain boosted indirect taxes, cutting consumption where it had risen most – amongst the working classes. But thorough-going retrenchment (what became known as 'Geddes' Axe', after the man who at this time presided over an emergency review of public expenditure) was no nice discriminator once it got into its stride. A bonfire of controls and subsidies took place, whilst the Bank rate was hiked up to 6% 'and kept at . . . or above [that figure] for eighteen months when prices were falling and the money-supply . . . fell in 1921 and 1922.'[16] Not surprisingly, unemployment rose to 12.2% of the work force (a higher figure than obtained at any point in the depression of the 1930s). In sum, government finances were restabilized through a deflationary cycle which spat out corn price guarantees[17], housing benefits, Russian interventions and the aspirant raj in Mesopotamia, if not simultaneously, then one after the other.

In cracking open the wartime political economy, however, the social and political basis of the Coalition itself began to unravel. Lloyd George sought to reconstitute it on a new basis, at the heart of which lay the ideal of a reconstruction of Europe in which the United Kingdom might play an innovating role. 'I mean to go wherever the policy of European pacification leads me', he told Lord Beaverbrook, the press magnate. 'There is nothing else worth fighting for at the present moment.'[18] One place it soon led him was up against the French. At a series of Allied conferences – the current fashion for resorts being reflected in such venues as Hythe, Lympne and Spa – Lloyd George pressed not only for the scaling down of war reparations but for a recognition of the need to *encourage* German recovery as a precondition for international stability. When those around him argued that the key to Continental pacification lay in the assuagement of French 'insecurity', his response was that the problem of insecurity ceased once you stopped thinking about it. The successor states of Eastern Europe, with their old minorities posing aggressively as new majorities, interested him little. It was inherent in his formulations at this time, however, that the Soviet Union should be brought within the mainstream of European affairs, since only thereby could a vent be found for Germany's industrial surplus. Propelled by these insights, Lloyd George invented shuttle diplomacy, traversing Europe on *trains de luxe*, surrounded by secretaries, interpreters and golf clubs; he is, perhaps, the first leader ever to have carried out a major international negotiation *whilst* going round a links (at Cannes, with Aristide Briande).[19] Undoubtedly, as his critics at home and abroad alleged, much of this feverish activity smacked of a 'great man' searching for a refurbished image, but in the light of later British diffidence towards European restoration after another great war, it is at least notable that on this previous occasion it was a British premier who was full of visionary ideas, and got laughed at for his pains.

Lloyd George's diplomacy eventually fell apart, in effect, at the Genoa Conference on European Reconstruction during April 1922, when the German and Russian delegations withdrew unilaterally to the more refined ambience of Rapallo, thumbing their noses at Allied pretences to leadership of the 'new Europe'.[20] Even before then his position had become politically tenuous. In particular, many among Lloyd George's Tory partners in the Coalition took grave exception to his quarrelling with France, since that country continued to constitute a repository of British Conservative emotion. More generally, the very novelty and panache of his foreign policy, especially when it began to embrace the Soviet Union, became a conductor for the nagging anxiety among Unionists – never wholly dispelled after December 1916 – that one day the Welshman would return to his demagogic roots and attempt to lead them up a garden path of his own choosing. The road to Genoa was paved with ill-concealed suspicions of this sort; and on his return from that abortive gathering the premier quickly found the ground moving beneath his – and the Coalition's – feet. The long-simmering revolt amongst Unionists came to a head at a famous party meeting at the Carlton Club on 19 October, the highlight of which was a withering interjection by Stanley Baldwin aimed at the 'dynamic' (and disintegrative) force of Lloyd George's political personality.[21] The truly decisive factor was the change of front by Bonar Law, who at the last moment shifted his alignment from the reluctant elders still mesmerized by the appeal of an anti-socialist front with Lloyd George at its head, to the younger and more impatient cadres pressing for the restoration of the party's independence before its identity was irretrievably lost. After some hard words, the majority voted to withdraw support from the Government; and with this – since the Unionists were by far the largest party in the House of Commons – Lloyd George's tempestuous tenure of the premiership came to an abrupt end.

The fall of Lloyd George served as such a litmus-test for the prevailing chemistry in British affairs that the background to it merits further attention. If foreign policy was one index of Conservative reaction against Coalitionism, imperial policy-making provided another – in fact several others. Thus amidst the hubbub at the Carlton Club, Austen Chamberlain – ever a loyal Coalitionist – had opened proceedings by announcing that '. . . there was no divergence of policy between the Conservative and Liberal wings of the Government', only to be met with angry shouts of 'Ireland', 'Egypt' and 'India'.[22] As regards the last of these, it had been the Liberal element in the Coalition which had associated itself, albeit tentatively, with the protests following the tragedy in the Punjabi city of Amritsar in April 1919, when an Indian demonstration was broken up by Army fire, killing three hundred and seventy-nine Indians and wounding many more. In its wake the Secretary of State for India, Edwin Montagu (himself a Liberal), had lectured his Cabinet colleagues on the folly of asserting 'a force which we do not possess in preference to the doctrine of goodwill'.[23] To many Unionists, this was just the kind of pusillanimous talk they had so despised in English Liberalism before 1914; and when the British officer who had ordered the Amritsar shooting, General Dyer, was cashiered, the popular outrage in Britain outstripped whatever voices had been raised in condemnation of the original action. Lloyd George had little option but to straddle these contrary waves of injustice. As outraged Unionists bayed for Montagu's blood, Lloyd George sought to buy time by throwing the latter's scalp to his enemies during an unseemly parliamentary debate, in which anti-Semitism added further spice to proceedings.[24] Assisted by a further touch on the tiller of Indian repression during the following months, the Prime Minister managed to ride out these particular difficulties, but the scars left by the abrasive aftermath of Amritsar were to be revealed when the

Unionists subsequently bared their souls in the privacy of the Carlton Club.

The story with respect to Egypt was not dissimilar. The British had long considered the populace of the Lower Nile valley to be a peculiarly docile breed, so that Imperial forces in the country were generally used as a reservoir for use elsewhere. The violent disturbances which marked the summer of 1919 thus came as a nasty shock. Lord Milner was dispatched to investigate the situation, and it was his conclusion – adumbrated in a historic Report to the Cabinet in the spring of 1921 – that considerable scope existed for defusing Anglo-Egyptian tensions. 'It is possible', he wrote in conciliatory vein, 'that what *we* mean by "Protectorate" is not really incompatible with what *they* mean by "Independence"'[25], by which he meant that so long as Britain continued to be able to guarantee the exclusion of all foreign influences other than its own, there was no reason why the Egyptians should not be allowed to get on and run their own fly-ridden affairs as they wished. It is piquant that the man who had once insisted on laying so heavy a hand on South Africa should have come in the course of time to advocate a more delicate policy in Egypt, though whether this contrast arose from the venues themselves, or an adaptation over time of Milner's guiding philosophy, is a question we must leave aside. What is certain is that for many Unionists the 'Independence' of Egypt, whatever gloss might be put upon it, was no more congenial than the doctrine of 'goodwill' had been in India, on the grounds that both were euphemisms for surrender. In this milieu a counter-argument (by no means lacking in intellectual or moral force) took shape: that the *appearance* of power could not be conceded without its *substance* being lost at the same time. The Egyptian and Indian cases were to interact in this manner within the canon of English Die Hardism for over twenty years thereafter. Meanwhile Lloyd George's hand was forced, ironically, by Lord Allenby who, though something of a Die Hard himself, was responsible for law and order in Cairo. As such, he demanded that the Cabinet either send him more troops, or failing that a piece of paper (in the form of a proffered agreement) which could get the protesters off the streets. Since there were no troops to send, the British Government reluctantly authorized what became known as the Allenby Declaration of February 1922, recognizing Egypt as an independent country whilst reserving 'absolutely' a series of matters – principal among which were imperial communications, defence, finance and the administration of the Sudan – for British discretion. '[T]he white flag is once more up over 10 Downing Street' sneered one disenchanted observer.[26] In these opposed responses, one expedient and practical, the other self-consciously robust and absolutist, could be detected not only the visceral sentiments that were to mark Egyptian debates in British politics for many years, but also a more generalized and ultimately explosive conflict as to the purposes and nature of British power overseas.

It was Ireland, however, which some later held to have been the true graveyard of the Lloyd George Coalition. At the 1918 general election Sinn Fein ('Our Freedom') candidates had swept the board outside Ulster; but instead of taking their seats in Westminster they set up an independent Assembly (or 'Dail') in Dublin. Then, on 23 June 1919, a Royal Irish Constabulary officer was gunned down in Thurles, County Tipperary; witnesses suffered an instant loss of memory as to the assassins' likenesses and mode of departure. This was the start of the gun war, under cover of which the structures of a provisional republic surreptitiously displaced those of the Union.[27] In 1920 the British Government responded with another Government of Ireland Act, which proposed to set up local legislatures in Dublin and Belfast, whilst reserving such matters as defence and the bulk of taxation for Westminster. But it was too little and too late to stop the slide into civil war. The southern Parliament never met, and the shooting got worse. Martial law was introduced in stages, and 'retaliation' began. 'I see no alternative but to fight it out', Lloyd George declared. 'A republic at our doors is unthinkable.'[28]

There followed a brief but bloody interlude in which intimidation was offered as a solution to intimidation. The champion of this new intervention was again Winston Churchill. As Minister of War, he was responsible for the recruiting of an auxiliary force known – owing to its job-lot uniforms – as the 'Black and Tans', the mechanized units of which rolled through villages and small towns doling out retaliatory medicine, sometimes with scant regard for their victims other than their ill-advised proximity. 'Winston [Churchill] saw very little harm in this', noted Henry Wilson, the Chief of the Imperial General Staff, who was not known for being fastidious himself where Ireland was concerned, 'but it horrifies me.'[29] It came to horrify British opinion more widely, not least because pacification along these lines was very expensive. In the end it was the dominant ethic of public economy ('Anti-Waste') which undermined British authority in southern Ireland, as it had in Iraq. Ultimately, the foundation of the Union of 1800 gave way, not because it was no longer possible to chase renegade Irishmen across the bogs of Kilkenny, but because it was no longer a business proposition.

Impelled by these pressures, Lloyd George finally closed with the Sinn Feiners. He was not without bargaining counters. Irish rebelliousness thrived on republican rhetoric, but its essential spirit was practical and bourgeois; its representative hawkers, publicans and horse-breeders were not constitutionally choosy. In Ireland the yearning for normality after all the travails since 1914 was no less (and probably more) intense than it was in England. The British premier was adept at exploiting such tendencies, enticing Michael Collins at the head of an Irish Republican Army delegation to the negotiating table in 10 Downing Street during December 1921, and then confronting them with the choice between accepting a peace Treaty or the alternative of 'war, and war in three days'. Faced with this ultimatum, they concurred in an agreement which partitioned Ireland between North and South, creating in the latter an entity to be known as the Irish Free State. This polity, however, was not to be the unthinkable republic, but a very thinkable Dominion, and as such one which would continue to be in formal allegiance to the British Crown. The compromise was not one likely to recommend itself equally to all Irishmen. 'This is my death-warrant' Collins told Lloyd George as he appended his signature to the document[30], and before long he was indeed to be gunned down in the fratricidal struggle between pro- and anti-Treaty forces before the constitutionalists eventually (but not definitively) emerged as the winners.

In mainland Britain some hailed the Anglo-Irish Treaty of 1921 as a 'great triumph' for Lloyd George[31]; others despised it as an act of treachery; most probably accepted it as making the best of a bad job. Behind the kaleidoscope of reactions, there was little doubt that just as the Easter Rising in Dublin during 1916 had helped to seal Asquith's fate, so the later settlement in Ireland had a similar effect on Lloyd George's position. It is against this background that one may grasp the motives which led the flailing premier into the remarkable antics associated with the Chanak Crisis of September 1922, when, having abjured an unwinnable war in Ireland, he unavailingly tried to orchestrate a fresh offensive against his old foes, the Turks. That a premiership which in its more recent manifestations had often flagged its commitment to the ethic of peace should finally have come to grief through a surge of bellicosity was fully in line with a character trait of modern British politics. For most of the twentieth century British leaders possessed two stock pieces of repertoire: a peace policy and a war policy (or what Harold Macmillan, in outlining this gambit, always typified as the rival advocacy of the Gown and the Sword).[32] Lloyd George was special only in the remarkable versatility with which he was capable of slipping between the two as circumstances prescribed. Furthermore, one of the lessons he had derived from the Great War was that if a cheap and easy triumph overseas was required, the Mediterranean was the place to go in search of it. 'These ambitions', Harold Nicolson remarked of Lloyd George's growing concentration on the Near East as his domestic political position worsened, 'were symbolized by the word "Greece"'.[33]

Greece had become more than ever vital to Lloyd George as a British proxy in the eastern Mediterranean and western Asia because it was thought to provide the key to upholding the Treaty of Sèvres (October 1920) which, if anything, imposed even harsher terms on Turkey than that of Versailles had on Germany.

In its wake Constantinople looked set to become virtually a British possession, and with it, control over the Straits was assured. In this dispensation Greece obtained not only the whole of Thrace, but also Smyrna and a broad enclave driven into the interior of Anatolia. The stability of such a settlement depended not only on Anglo-Greek bayonets, but on the exhaustion of the Turkish people and the preparedness of other European 'victor' powers to make do with only minor territorial compensation. These expectations were belied by events. The humiliation of Sèvres led to the fall of the religious Caliphate in Constantinople, and also sparked a secular, nationalist and militant revivalism headed by Kemal Ataturk from his fastness of Ankara deep in the interior of Turkey. Nor was Ataturk's revolution isolated: it was armed by the Bolsheviks, and diplomatically insured by France, the latter happy to forgo its allotted Cilician spoil for the pleasure of seeing the British get a come-uppance. Thus embarrassed, Lloyd George became increasingly dependent on Greek force to hold together an arrangement which looked like coming apart at the seams. Finally, on 4 August 1922 he delivered a speech in the House of Commons which was widely interpreted as 'a thinly-veiled invitation to Greece' to launch a frontal assault on the Turkish forces in Anatolia.[34] The Hellenic armies advanced under the personal command of King Constantine; however, after fierce fighting they broke ranks, and in retreating were pushed literally into the Aegean Sea; amidst the turmoil Smyrna was razed by the triumphant Kemalists, its Greek inhabitants being indiscriminately slaughtered. This, combined with the great movement of population it made necessary, was one of the worst man-made catastrophes of the twentieth century. One of its victims was Lloyd George's policy in the Near East.

The dénouement which followed this tragedy may be briefly stated. As the Kemalists turned north to approach the British lines at Chanak, just across the Straits from Constantinople, Lloyd George's instinct was to fight. The colourful prospect of a showdown on which an impending election might be made to turn aligned the Prime Minister once more with the perennial enthusiasms of his natural soul-mate; and together

Lloyd George and Churchill dispatched urgent telegrams to the Dominion Governments calling for immediate military support, not forgetting (in the case of Australia and New Zealand) to touch the delicate chord of 'the safety of the graves' at Gallipoli. Answers to these pleas, however, were either churlish, or simply not sent.[35] In the Dominions – as in Britain itself – a reaction set in against ministers who had, as Curzon observed from his place within the Cabinet, 'the smell of gunpowder in their nostrils'.[36] What really spoiled the calculations of the two ministers, however, was the initiative of the British Officer Commanding on the spot, General Tim Harington, in parleying with Ataturk. 'Our country wanted no more war' was the latter's explanation for his pacific conduct.[37] The crisis evaporated almost as quickly as it had arisen, so that Lloyd George and Churchill, having marched themselves up to the top of the Turkish hill, had to march themselves down again – alone.

The abortive war-ramp of Chanak provided the immediate background to the Unionist revolt in the Carlton Club. The deeper motives for the reassertion of independent Conservatism, however, remain a matter for speculation. This phenomenon has been variously attributed to frustrations amongst the younger Tories, such as Stanley Baldwin, for whom the Coalition was a disreputable means by which their seniors continued to cling to positions of authority, and to currents of feeling among more established elements – '. . . an aristocratic reaction, the response of the Salisburys, the Selbornes, and the Devonshires to the passing of ancient patterns of deference, control and stability'.[38] These explanations are not mutually exclusive. Thrusting youth (though this term hardly ever precisely described Stanley Baldwin), or crusty age, both formations were driven by a strongly felt need to recapture the sense of quietude, caution and balance which had been forfeited amid the tumult of recent years. It was a tendency which temporarily found its champion in Bonar Law, who now became Prime Minister in a Conservative Government about whose prospects he had once been so gloomy.[39] 'We cannot act alone', Law summed up the new doctrine in an instantly renowned letter to *The Times*, 'as the Policeman of the World'.[40] 'Tranquillity', indeed, was the watchword of the emergent ministry, and implicit in this slogan was a rejection of adventurism, fiscal licence and (something about which Baldwin felt especially deeply) the brazen corruption which had marked the Lloyd George regime. The tenacity of purpose which was to infuse this new (or rediscovered) version of Toryism derived above all from the depth of feeling and prejudice which surrounded the *bouleversement* of October 1922.

Yet even at the outset of this incipient pattern of politics many of the Unionist elders remained unconvinced by it, and hankered for the more crystalline and versatile politics which had come to be secreted in the Coalition. These elements, with Austen Chamberlain as their titular spokesman, made their peace and accepted office when Baldwin replaced the dying Bonar Law as party leader and premier in May 1923, but the basic rift remained; and when Baldwin's ensuing administration (broken only by the brief but historic interregnum of the first Labour ministry led by Ramsay MacDonald between January and November 1924) itself went down to electoral defeat in May 1929, these endemic party rivalries were to boil up anew. It is with the curiously uncertain years immediately preceding the era inaugurated by the Great Depression that the rest of this chapter will be concerned.

The years from 1922 to 1929 are not among the most dramatic in modern British history. Lloyd George called them a 'yawn'[41] – although this perhaps tells us as much about Lloyd George as it does about the period in question. Nevertheless, it became axiomatic of the critique levelled at 'tranquil' Toryism that its practitioners' common trait was the possession of what was often characterized as 'Second Class Brains'. Baldwin himself became conventionally lampooned as the quintessence of prevailing mediocrity. None was more vitriolic in such lucubrations than the arch-coalitionist, Lord Birkenhead, most notably in his rectoral address to Glasgow University in October 1923 when he declared that 'the world continued to offer glittering prizes to those with stout hearts and sharp words' – equipment which

Baldwin and his circle, by implication, conspicuously lacked.[42] Baldwin's response to hits of this kind was to retort that the British people instinctively preferred to be governed by men of second-class brains than by those with second-class characters. Between Birkenhead's promotion of pushy talent on the one hand, and the new Prime Minister's alternative ethic of sound respectability on the other, existed the real battle to be fought out within modern British political culture. Arguably the most effective rejoinder to the lure of 'glittering prizes' was the comment made by the man Baldwin appointed to be President of the Board of Trade, Philip Lloyd-Graeme, when the latter observed of the prevailing mood of the day that the nation was no longer prepared 'to be buggered about' by politicians with a strong tendency to mix up the glorification of themselves with the glorification of their country.[43] Baldwin's success in making himself so dominant a figure for many years thereafter arose from the way he identified himself precisely with this popular desire to avoid unnecessary and, in his view, frequently specious excitements.

Baldwin's essential political instinct, in fact, may be said to have been summed up in his foreign policy – or rather, in his proclivity, as far as circumstances allowed, to have no such thing. At first the Conservative Government after October 1922 aimed to restore the entente with France which Lloyd George had recently done so much to weaken. This good intention was swiftly belied by the French invasion of the Ruhr in January 1923 – 'the use', as it seemed to much British opinion, 'of bayonets to dig out coal'.[44] Since hopes in the United Kingdom of getting to grips with domestic unemployment – the 'intractable million' on the register, as it was called – hinged above all on recovery in Europe, the blow was a hard one. Baldwin's disillusionment was complete when, as his first major diplomatic initiative after becoming Prime Minister, he paid court to the intransigent President Poincaré in Paris during September 1923, only to find that the agreement he thought he had secured to ease the position in the Ruhr turned out to be a mirage. Some years later Baldwin's first biographer, G.M. Young, asked him whether he recalled his meeting with

Poincaré. "'I do indeed", he answered with a wry mouth';
Young then asked "'Did you ever talk with any other leading
men in Europe?". "No", he [Baldwin] said simply, "I did not
like them"'.[45] The isolation this implied might not be splendid,
any more than it had been in the age of Lord Salisbury, but to
Baldwin's way of thinking it remained a true reflection of British
national interests. Henceforth he inwardly dedicated himself to
what a journalist classically defined as 'the insatiable conquest of
the English heart'.[46]

To one so essentially a late Victorian as Baldwin such a
reversion came naturally. Yet for those of his peers who bore the
marks of recent theories of British prestige – theories inextricably
entwined with a Continental commitment – it was not so easy.
The connection with France provided the main continuing
linkage between the entente idealism of Edwardian vintage
and post-war British foreign policy. Thus Austen Chamberlain,
whom Baldwin made Foreign Secretary in 1924 in order to palliate
the Coalitionist wing in the party, often professed to love France
'as a woman'.[47] The root of this passion was as much moral
as diplomatic, for the cross-Channel neighbour – aristocratic
(for all her republicanism), rural, sacrificial – appealed to a
certain segment of English Conservatives because she ostensibly
offered a welcome contrast to the pullulating industrial bias and
overt social disaffection all too evident in contemporary urban
Britain.[48] 'If we withdraw from Europe', Austen Chamberlain
rationalized part of this impulse, by which he meant that if
Britain withdrew from France, 'I say without hesitation that
the chance of permanent peace is gone and that the whole
world must make up its mind that sooner or later . . . a new
disaster will fall upon us and civilization itself may perish'.[49]
Steering between the Charybdis of this apocalyptic vision, and
the Scylla of a more prosaic diffidence towards Continental
entanglements, absorbed all of Chamberlain's indefatigable, if
pedestrian, skills as a negotiator. His efforts – indeed, his entire
career – climaxed with the signature of the Locarno Treaties in
May 1925, by which the United Kingdom became a co-guarantor
of the Western boundaries of France, Belgium and Germany,

without any similar imprimatur being given to the status quo in the East. But could one be committed to the frontiers in the West *without* being committed, whether one liked it or not, to those in the East as well? The British Dominions, where Francophobia was rife throughout this period, thought not and refused to have anything to do with Locarno – a significant rupture in the fabric of the 'united foreign policy' of the British Empire.[50] More importantly, not only did France herself also hold such distinctions to be untenable, she was determined to prevent any such choice crystallizing for others. Barely was the ink dry on the Locarno parchment when the French Government quickly signed a 'friendship treaty' with Czechoslovakia, so making the latter into a potential trip-wire in the minefield of European power politics. Whilst Locarno, therefore, ushered in a famous 'spring' during which relations generally in Europe warmed to expectations of peace and prosperity at last, the essential structural faults – should anything go wrong – remained to be revealed.

One notable aspect of the aftermath of the Carlton Club revolt in the sphere of foreign policy was that for the first time relations with the United States became a first-rank concern in British policy-formation (as opposed, for example, to panic reactions in moments of crisis such as that of March 1918). Thus Baldwin, whose acute intelligence was masked by his rustic affectations, instinctively grasped that a corollary of giving up being the 'Policeman of the World' was the need to identify a like-minded and well-heeled power on whom to devolve some of the responsibility for managing international security. There was little doubt who that putative partner might be. Yet any wider political understanding with the United States clearly hinged on clearing away the problem of war debts, which since 1919 had threatened to put London and Washington seriously at odds with each other. Soon after becoming Chancellor of the Exchequer in October 1922, therefore, Baldwin travelled to New York and negotiated a debt settlement on the terms demanded by the local bankers.[51] The news of this caused something of a Cabinet storm back in London, and Bonar Law even threatened to resign – proof that Law's own understanding of the implications of 'Tranquillity' was distinctly limited. Despite much huffing and puffing, the Chancellor's colleagues let him have his way, and in so doing swallowed the unpalatable logic that the War had smashed British hegemony of world financial markets beyond repair, its best hope for the future now residing in a joint primacy alongside the American dollar. The scene was therefore set for the interweaving of the Bank of England and the Federal Reserve Bank of New York which was to survive many diplomatic bumps between the two countries thereafter.[52] 'Special Relations', after all, are usually specially about money, and in this the Anglo-American tie was no different from any other.

Financial accommodation between the British and Americans was to prove one thing, and naval accommodation quite another, so that when Stephen Roskill, a leading chronicler of British naval affairs during the twentieth century, composed his survey of the inter-war years, he chose for his sub-title 'The Period of Anglo-American Antagonism'.[53] It is not an inaccurate portrayal. This may seem surprising, given that in 1921 the British Government had participated fully in the Washington Naval Conference convened by President Harding, and agreed both to a fixed ratio in battleships of 5:5:3 between (respectively) the United States, Britain and Japan, whilst simultaneously agreeing to a 'holiday' covering new construction in that category. The Washington Naval Treaty, nevertheless, by concentrating exclusively on 'capital' ships, merely served to transfer rivalries between national marines to other types of naval craft. In the backwash of the 1921 settlement, furthermore, a fierce campaign got under way among British navalists to draw the line against any further concessions of 'parity' to foreign powers. It was a campaign, reinforced by the turning away of British defence policy generally from the Continental Commitment and the yearning for the old familiar benchmarks of national prestige, which gathered pace throughout the decade and was, indeed, to continue in one form or another for much of the 1930s.

The First Sea Lord during this era, Lord Beatty, epitomized, not least in his conscious evocation of the Nelsonian spirit, the tendency we have described. His essential goal became wrapped up with the ideal of the 'Seventy Cruiser Navy'[54] – in effect, reversing the direction of Fisher's reforms earlier in the century, with their emphasis on fire-power and concentration, and putting in their place the more traditional ideals of speed, dispersion and cost-effective flexibility. The renovation of a modified *Pax Britannica* along these lines remained an expensive proposition, which the domestic taxpayer in his current stingy mood was not likely to agree to shoulder unless convinced of some concrete threat to justify the extra levy. Here there was a problem, since the German Fleet was still under water off the Scottish coast; the Soviets not only had no ocean-going navy, but were immersed in a bloody civil war; whilst it was scarcely politic to frame the United States as a hypothetical foe (though the more risqué, or more stupid, admirals sometimes fell victim to this natural temptation). In scanning the seas for a suitably inimical object, however, Beatty soon discovered Japan, and it was on the promotion of a Japanese threat to the trade and possessions of the British Empire in the Far East that much British naval lobbying came to turn. The building of a great new war-base at Singapore thus emerged as the leitmotif of the Admiralty's strategic planning after 1921[55], a development assisted by the non-renewal of the Anglo-Japanese alliance two years later. Whether Beatty's prognostications may be hailed as far-sighted, in the light of later events, or, as Labour Party critics (who during their own brief first taste of responsibility 'mothballed' the work under way at Singapore) alleged at the time, to have created the very Japanese threat it claimed to prevent, is not something that may be resolved in these pages. For the moment it is sufficient to note that in seeking to restore a high-profile role for the Royal Navy, at a time when the latter was involved in some of the fiercest inter-service disputes of the century, the British half-accidentally traded in an understanding with Japan on which her regional security in East Asia, and that of a good many others, had depended since 1902.

The Americans could not fail to notice that in seeking to build against Japan, the United Kingdom was conveniently building against everybody else – including themselves. Thus whilst in Admiralty circles in London naval disarmament was described as a canny American ploy to 'catch the Lion by the tail', in Washington, where Anglophobes were not thin on the ground during the age of American 'Isolation', the English were stereotyped as a barrier – even *the* barrier – to authentic pacification in world affairs. The stereotype was one which obstructive British behaviour at the 1927 Geneva Disarmament Conference did nothing to rebut.[56] The fact that it was generally held that the really difficult issue of disarmament on *land* could not even be approached until progress had been made on the *sea* made the deadlock appear all the more culpable to some. One of the early actions of the new Hoover Administration after November 1928 was to authorize a big cruiser programme of its own 'just to give the Britishers what's coming to them'.[57] The disillusionment was wholly mutual. 'S.B. [Stanley Baldwin] says he loathes Americans so much', Neville Chamberlain noted in his diary, 'he hates meeting them.'[58] These resentments were to spill over into the 1930s, one of their significant effects being to influence the thinking of Neville Chamberlain himself. Behind all the name-calling, however, the simple fact remained that whilst the interests of the two countries might now overlap in certain important spheres, such as finance, their positions with respect to more fundamental questions regarding the shape and balance of the international system remained as yet a long way apart.

The Seventy Cruiser Navy aroused acute controversy inside as well as outside the United Kingdom. One of its principal opponents was the Treasury, whose attenuated voice had become more audible in recent years by virtue of having at its back 'the heavy breathing of a pacific and parsimonious electorate'.[59] At the helm of the Exchequer after November 1924, furthermore, was the determined figure of Winston Churchill. Quite why Baldwin should have extended such amazing largesse to one whose claims to his affections were so slight has puzzled many commentators. Churchill certainly evinced surprise at the time. 'Of the Duchy?' he enquired when Baldwin offered him the Chancellorship, responding with an effusion of gratitude when the correction came 'Of the Exchequer'.[60] This self-deprecating recollection on Churchill's part is to some extent misleading. Ever since ceasing to be Minister for War in late 1920, and in his subsequent role as Colonial Secretary, he had been careful to adopt a more pacific, cooled-down style of politics. It was Churchill's management of the Cairo Conference in March 1921, for example, which put the British presence in the Middle East on a lighter, but still effective, rein. After the aberration of Chanak, and its aftermath in the Carlton Club, he was quick to send out the requisite signals to the new Tory dispensation that, as a mobile quantity in British politics, he was prepared to gravitate back towards the party of his birth. Whether Churchill *really* mistook the Duchy for the Exchequer in the manner implied above, therefore, must be problematical; and although he boasted to his old Coalitionist friends still out in the cold that he would capture Baldwin and keep him incarcerated in a 'padded cell'[61], the reality was all in the other direction. The new Chancellor proceeded to beat his sword, and that of the nation, into ploughshares, and reverted to the economical concerns he had harboured prior to his conversion in 1911 to a more martial set of principles. This was arguably the most striking testament of all to the sea-change in the nature of British public priorities and feelings from late 1922 onwards. The ark of this fiscal Covenant was the return to the Gold Standard in April 1925.

The pegging of the pound to the dollar (and therefore to gold) at the old ratio of $4.86 has invariably been characterized as the Dardanelles of British economic policy in the twentieth century. According to its subsequent critics, the policy overvalued the British currency by approximately ten per cent at a time when industrial competitiveness was growing in other countries, thereby laying the foundations for an export slump and intensified unemployment. Consequently the United Kingdom *entered* the world depression in a debilitated and vulnerable condition.[62] Whether this analysis is correct or not we cannot say, except to note that economists (including economic historians) are congenitally prone to great wisdom after the event. More interesting for our analysis is the reasoning which lay behind the departure. Martin Gilbert, Churchill's official biographer, finds the key to the Chancellor's decision in his 'romantic attachment to British greatness'[63] expressed in the determination to elevate the pound sterling once more on to the gold-pedestal. There is surely something in this: the policy appealed to Churchill partly because of its quasi-military overtones, providing a 'Standard' to defend in the open combat of the market-place; whilst it will be essential to our argument that within a few years, when this 'Standard' perforce began to droop, he returned to other preoccupations which were naturally more congenial. The fact is that Churchill never did feel comfortable handling abstruse matters of economics and finance, an unease reflected in the findings of recent research that as Chancellor his practice was merely to put an appropriate flourish on decisions which stemmed from the advice of his senior officials.[64]

What increasingly concerned senior Treasury servants at this juncture, then, was the *relative* performance of the British economy compared to its traditional competitors. Taking 1913 as a base year (100), in 1924 British exports stood at 80.1, compared to 107.4 for world exports, and 82.2 for *average* European exports. 'Thus even in a period when most of Europe was recovering from the ravages of wartime damage and postwar disorganization', one commentator has concluded, 'British exports had done relatively badly'.[65] The deduction drawn from such gloomy statistics was that, earlier retrenchments notwithstanding, British costs (including wages and taxation) remained too high. Within the Treasury, the Gold Standard was seen as the only mechanism which could be relied on to bring those costs down, and, once equilibrium had been attained, to police them on a strict and permanent basis. Meshed in with this orthodox economic analysis, however, was a political critique which one of the Chancellor's closest departmental advisors gave voice to when he pointed out that the real beauty of the Gold Standard lay in its being 'knave-proof'[66] – in sum, that it provided a check to the modern politician's itch to raid the public till on behalf of the special interests invariably standing at his elbow. In developing such a thesis Exchequer officials had in mind the novel bogey of Socialism; but they were equally conscious – not surprisingly in the shadow of the Great War – of that older bogey, the insatiable appetite of the military services. It was, then, with both of these dangers in mind that one senior Treasury hand remarked that in returning to the immutable laws of the Gold Standard, the country would 'be doing no more than shackling ourselves to reality'.[67]

Considering how later on Churchill came to revel in the aspersions of others that he *lacked* any sense of realism where British power was concerned, the struggle he conducted over the second half of the 1920s to shackle his compatriots to the realities established by Gold Standard finance is full of ironies. Thus he pitted himself against the Seventy Cruiser Navy. 'There will be nothing for the taxpayer', he railed at Baldwin. 'We shall be a Naval Parliament'.[68] He was just as combative towards the Trade Unions, and emerged as the most violent of Baldwin's ministers during the General Strike of 1926, calling for machine-gun convoys not only to ensure the passage of food from the East End docks to London Town but as an 'encouragement to the great mass of loyal people'.[69] There were those close to Churchill at this time who found his bellicosity towards fellow-countrymen deeply unsettling. Yet it was, in its way, wholly consistent. For Churchill, politics was by its adversarial nature a form of war; it was something to be waged; the only question was whether one did so at home in the quest of running a great commercial state (in which case the primal conflict lay between the classes), or abroad in pursuit of the Balance of Power (in which case it lay between the dominant nations). Hence in accepting the Chancellorship from Baldwin's hand, he had reluctantly accommodated himself to the shift of focus in British affairs from overseas to the domestic sphere. What he did not accept was that the one set of goals could be attained with any more tranquillity than the other. In trying to beat down the Admirals with their spendthrift plans with one hand, and the northern coal operatives with their impossible wage demands with the other, he was only seeking to implement the logic of independent Conservatism according to his own instinctively glaring lights.

Herein lay the taproot of a profound difference between the increasingly disaffected Chancellor and his political chief. For Baldwin, in contrast, the art of politics lay in endlessly splitting the differences between the estates and institutions of the realm – not a form of war, but a form of brokerage replete with necessary subterfuges. Affected also by the fact that the First Lord of the Admiralty, Willie Bridgeman, was his closest friend, the Prime Minister came down largely on the side of the Admiralty in the matter of cruisers. In the same vein, he essayed a studied, if firm, moderation throughout the General Strike of 1926, and once it was broken adamantly held out against those of his colleagues who contended that the opportunity should be taken to 'go for broke' and smash the Trade Unions once and for all.[70] The Trade Disputes Act which followed, whilst deeply unpopular on the Left, nevertheless fell far short of the ideals of Baldwin's more *enragé* colleagues. The incipient fissure in British Conservatism was summed up both by the 'Safety First' slogan which Baldwin subsequently chose as his rallying cry at the 1929 General Election, and by the strong reaction it evoked in some circles of the party – a 'blank negation' was how Churchill referred in private to the Baldwinite platform.[71] The antagonism this pointed to looked back to the tensions attendant on the fall of the Coalition in 1922, in which 'Second-Class Brains' had been set off against 'Second-Class Characters'; it also looked forward to the more clear-cut, and ultimately more historic, parting of the ways which was to lie at the heart of the controversy over Appeasement after 1935.

In this context mention should be made of the interpretation of British politics during the twenties as being overwhelmingly shaped (in the words of Maurice Cowling) by the 'Impact of Labour'.[72] To the extent that it was during these years that the Labour Party successfully displaced the Liberals as the second great party in the state, the thesis is not to be wholly refuted. Indeed, the increasing emphasis ever since the death of Queen Victoria on national unity stemmed not least from the paranoia amongst the governing elite at the evident signs of class disunity. Yet Cowling's argument has a central flaw, for if the proletarian challenge had been the *critical* factor in British developments the quintessentially anti-socialist Coalition would surely not have been disbanded in the first place. It was Lloyd George whom the Baldwinites hated and held to be a threat to the national good, not Ramsay MacDonald, or come to that A.J. Cook, the fiery leader of the Miners' Federation. The few waves made by the first Labour Government after coming to office with the help of Liberal parliamentary votes in January 1924, and the very ease with which it was swept out of office ten months later by a 'Red Scare' arising from a convenient forgery (the so-called Zinoviev Letter), showed how fragile a growth socialism remained in British politics. The true storm-centre in the United Kingdom remained that between various fragments of the great anti-socialist majority, and not least between contrasting brands of Conservatism. For this reason, if for no other, imperialism, rather than socialism, still functioned as a more significant lightning-rod within the governance of the nation. The final section of this chapter will therefore return to the subject of empire.

It was logical that the lifting of the war emergency led to the gradual revival of the controversy over a hypothetical Imperial Tariff which had divided Conservatives before 1914. The protectionist case, whilst it continued to draw on traditional inspirations, also assumed an intellectual shape reflecting contemporary conditions. The untiring advocate of this prognosis was Leopold Amery. 'We are in fact', was how the latter defined the new situation, 'no longer the sort of country that can compete industrially in the open market in certain industries . . . It really comes down to this, that we can both carry out our social reform and develop an immense trade, but mainly if not entirely within the empire.'[73] There was present in this rationale a strain of economic defeatism not known to Joseph Chamberlain. But what was most distinctive about Amery's imperial economic thought was the yearning for a *via media* between the roller-coaster uncertainties of the open market and a thorough-going collectivism – in short, a kind of Anglican capitalism. The search for an English political economy along such modulated and imperial lines was to be characteristic of much Conservative doctrine in the years ahead, and helps to explain why 'modern' Toryism was to find the emergency conditions which eventually came to prevail – be they of depression, war or reconstruction – eminently reconcilable with its own innermost impulses.

In retrospect Leopold Amery's persistent imperial canvassing is apt to appear unpersuasive to the point of crassness.[74] The Canadian historian, Ian Drummond, has described his economic conceptions as 'visionary'[75], their chief defect being that even in the twenties it was transparent that the rapidly developing Dominions overseas were bent on building up their own manufacturing industries, and determined to break out of the strait-jacket of Amery's beloved 'complementarity' in which their own place and station was to play farmyard to industrial Britain. Amery certainly grated on the nerves of many of his fellow Cabinet ministers who, having heard the record once, did not relish having it repeated *ad nauseam* in private as well as public. Amongst informed officials in Whitehall, too, the scenario of an integrated economic empire came to arouse sarcastic disdain. 'Of land flowing with milk and honey', one British civil servant reported on his tour through the Antipodes at the end of the decade, 'I saw not a sign'.[76] The flaw in Amery's model of imperial protectionism was that the details could never be made to fit the system, or the facts made consonant with what was at bottom a political theory whereby the United Kingdom might continue to be an economic 'planet' around which minor constellations still revolved, even though the orbits so described were more constrained than had been the case in the nineteenth century. Yet for all these faults and failings the innate attraction of the idea is not hard to comprehend, especially when it is recalled that as late as 1966 a British minister (in a socialist government) could go to Australia and come back saying he had seen Britain's future, and that it worked.[77]

Baldwin as Prime Minister had to skirt the same minefield in this area as Balfour had done twenty years before. Much speculation has surrounded the former's adoption of the platform of Imperial Preference (that is, a systematic preference in favour of fellow 'British' countries at the expense of foreign nations) at the 'snap' General Election of December 1923. It has been suggested that he was panicked into this by fear that Lloyd George was about to appropriate the tariff weapon for himself.[78] Whether this be true or not, the ploy also had the merit of calling the bluff of the protectionists in his own party by testing the genuine popularity of their proposal; and when it failed – leaving the Conservatives briefly in Opposition for the first time since 1915 – Baldwin was able to quietly set about pulling the threads of control firmly into his own hands. This sequence illustrated a critical dilemma: the Tory party could not easily be led *without* protection, whilst the country – for whom 'Dear Bread' remained a bogey – could not be governed *with* it. The Gold Standard drive (coupled with the protectionist sop of 'safeguarding duties') which marked the second Baldwin administration following its come-back at the October 1924 hustings was an attempt to get over this hurdle, but by the end of the decade it was clearly failing. The renewed chorus of imperial-protectionist dissent from 1928 onwards was to be the harbinger of a decade of renewed intra-Conservative feuding.

In the field of imperial policy proper, the most outstanding innovation of the twenties was the recognition at the 1926 Imperial Conference of the Dominions' fully self-governing status (or 'Dominion Status', as it was now officially designated). A formal declaration (under the imprint of Balfour, whose liking for dramatic statements belied his otherwise elliptical personality) was issued defining the *inter-se* relations of the British nations as 'autonomous communities, equal in status, in no way subordinate to one another . . . though united by a common allegiance to the Crown'. The checks and balances implanted in this formulation were nicely judged to finally explode the old bogey of 'Downing Street control' over the affairs of the colonies of settlement, whilst not prejudicing the practical unity of the Empire in a crisis comparable to that, say, of 1914. To the extent that the Dominions continued to be as dependent as ever on the United

Kingdom for much of their economic and political security, and that as a consequence they could be relied upon to 'turn up on the night' should any major war supervene, the British gave little or nothing away by such concessions. Nevertheless, the reforms of 1926 had significant implications for the way that most Britons, at least, looked out upon the world. Thus the dream of an Empire super-state which the Edwardians had largely invented, and which the War of 1914–18 had appeared to legitimate, went beyond the conception of a cultural mass liable to be bonded together if exposed to some common external emergency; it embraced the ideal of a pan-British entity as a conventional element in the world's economic, military and diplomatic system. After the War, for example, the British Admiralty still harboured plans for a grand Imperial fleet which Australian, Canadian and South African taxpayers would help to finance alongside their brothers in the United Kingdom. The outcome of the Chanak crisis in 1922 knocked a good deal of the stuffing out of such extravagant notions, but it was the Imperial Conference four years later which may be taken as the point when these aspirations were finally consigned to the dustbin of history. This was yet another 'reality' of the age which some found distasteful – so that Churchill described the Statute of Westminster of 1931 which eventually regularized these constitutional shifts as a 'repellent legalism' – but there could be no going back. The Dominions may thus have later gone to war alongside Britain in 1939, just as they had in 1914, but they were very careful at the same time to make clear that they did so under their own steam and for their own distinct purposes.

The continuing resilience and suppleness of the imperial principle, however, was evident in the way in which it was simultaneously rejigged to take account of the separatist effects flowing from the demise of Westminster's sovereignty over her 'daughter' parliaments overseas. More precisely, the focus of Empire unity now shifted from the Palace on the banks of the Thames to the other Palace just up the Mall. 'It is one of the odd things of history', the Lord Chancellor remarked in 1928, 'that after the power [of the Crown] has been diminishing through the generations from being an absolute to a constitutional monarchy, he [*sic*] should become the most important thing in holding things together [in the Empire]'.[79] It was indeed a development of the highest importance to the institutional fountain of the British state that after a period in which its confidence had been progressively sapped (not least by the pre-War crisis over Ireland and the constitution), from the mid-twenties onwards a new *raison d'être* was fortuitously developed which nicely blended both real functions and a compelling mystique. For the residue of his reign George V came to personify this concentration on the Imperial and Commonwealth role of his dynasty. Technology helped this process along, King George's Christmas message to the Empire delivered by radio becoming a legend almost from its first transmission on 19 December 1932. Indeed, so powerful was the appeal of this mixture of mediums that it was able to extract a kind of homage in even the most unlikely places: when Edward VIII broadcast his Abdication in 1936, the bars of New York were said to be empty because their habitual denizens were all at home listening to the show.[80]

The critical attribute of this burgeoning imperial kingship lay in its representation of a quintessentially English consensus. In this it was assisted by the fact that after 1922 internecine quarrels over imperial issues remained relatively damped down. Economic recovery, halting and patchy though it was, made the tariff arguments to which we have alluded a pale version of the angry confabulations earlier in the century. India, too, remained quiet. The passive, not to say exhausted, texture of that great dependency's politics in the wake of the Amritsar controversy and the Gandhian non-cooperation movement underlay this quiescence. Yet there was something else, intangible but none the less of considerable moment: the start of a process by which the Sub-Continent began to slip gently off the 'mental map' of the British upper classes. Thus the ill-starred visit to India by the Prince of Wales in 1921 was testimony to the erosion of the cult of the King-Emperor[81]; the once-so-splendid jewel did not add its lustre to the fresh sheen on the imperial monarchy, just as it did not feature in Amery's otherwise encyclopaedic schemes promoting imperial economics. Furthermore, as it became clear that an administrative career in the Indian provinces no longer meant dispensing justice from horseback, or from the District Commissioner's veranda, but under modern conditions involved endlessly buttering-up brown men, the gloss was knocked off the Indian Civil Service as a choice career for the scions of Hampshire gentry. Draining the meaning of India out of British life was necessarily a slow business, and the arguments surrounding the appointment of a Royal Commission in 1927 (to which, pointedly, no Indians were nominated) to review the working of the 1919 reforms was to be the precursor of much controversy ahead. Meanwhile, however, the trouble which India was to cause Baldwin after 1930 was not anticipated during his early years as party leader.

It was Egypt, not India, which during the second half of the twenties served as the principal touchstone for the opposed principles within the diverse corpus of British imperialism. The central figure during this phase of the Anglo-Egyptian saga was Lord Lloyd who – in the troubled aftermath of the assassination of Sir Lee Stack, the British Commander-in-Chief of the Egyptian Army – was appointed in May 1925 to be the new High Commissioner in Cairo.[82] Lloyd had previously displayed considerable conciliatory skills as Governor of Bombay, dousing popular discontent in his province; it was this track-record which recommended him to Baldwin as a man likely to get Egypt back on the rails. As it turned out, Baldwin – and the Egyptians – got more than they bargained for. Lloyd sought to make plain what it had hitherto been thought discreet to keep under wraps: that Egypt was ruled, not by its corrupt monarchy, not by its shaky Parliament, but by the British Resident. This attempt showed up in small things as in large: it was noted, for example, how Lloyd was driven about Cairo in the ceremonial style of an Indian Viceroy, thick with police escorts and klaxons blowing to shoo locals out of the proconsular path. The High Commissioner's extravagances were not merely petty. Lloyd later wrote a two-volume work (*Egypt Since Cromer*), the nub of which was that the outward show of British power had to reflect its substance if the latter were not to be fatally compromised. But if Lloyd genuinely felt himself to be merely upholding the status quo, his political masters at home (and above all the Foreign Office, under whose aegis Egypt came as a formally 'independent' country) suspected that the High Commissioner was bent on turning back the clock – or at least freezing the movement of its hands. At bottom, the vital difference that lay between these rival British doctrines was perfectly straightforward: where the one was concerned to see that Egypt was *ruled*, the other held that it was only necessary for metropolitan interests that she be *influenced*. What made the underlying controversy so resonant in this case was that it touched upon two profoundly contrary evaluations as to the capacity of British power in the wider world, and with it the proper ideals of the British state itself. This acute division was eventually to be transposed onto issues which went far beyond Egypt, and to be refracted through the prism of British Appeasement. Before then, however, there was a Great Depression to surmount. The Labour Government emerged triumphant from the British election in May 1929 only to find that, within a month, the collapse of stock prices on Wall Street transformed the international scene uniformly for the worse.

Reality and Honour in the Age of Appeasement

The new Labour Government, its leader, Ramsay MacDonald, declared in the House of Commons during the debate on the sovereign's address, existed above all to deal with two main contemporary problems – Peace and Unemployment. Of these the former appeared, financial difficulties notwithstanding, indubitably the more important. Distinctive values with respect to diplomacy, not to economics, principally identified the Left in British politics at this time, just as they did on the Right. It was in the sphere of foreign policy, too, that the in-coming (but still minority) ministry looked to make its mark and win the sort of public success capable of affording it a more prolonged stay in power than its predecessor had been able to enjoy in 1924. In his first premiership, in fact, MacDonald had served as his own Foreign Secretary. In 1929 that crucial position had to be given to Arthur Henderson, who made it a condition of his own continued support. In yielding to this pressure (which bore the traces of future disruption), however, MacDonald made it plain that some issues of foreign policy would remain very much under his personal sway. With a more relaxed atmosphere in world politics, and with Baldwin privately assuring the Labour leader of 'fair play' by his principal opponents, neither of which had been altogether the case five years before, the outlook for a renewed experiment in socialist administration seemed, at the outset at least, by no means dark.

The aspect of diplomacy which most preoccupied MacDonald, and for which (as a mark of its significance) he took personal responsibility, was relations with the United States. In particular, where the price of putting Anglo-American naval cooperation on a stable footing had ultimately proved too high for the outgoing ministry, the new Prime Minister was ready to pay up, and in June 1929 the British Government finally conceded parity in cruisers with the Americans. Complex technical difficulties regarding tonnages and gun-calibre limits remained, but the way was none the less cleared for MacDonald to cross the Atlantic. He did so in early October – the first serving British Prime Minister to touch United States' soil. The trip was a magnificent success. MacDonald's speeches and official exchanges attracted innumerable encomiums in the local press; the one which lauded the performance of his mission as 'unparalleled in the history of Christian civilization' was not entirely untypical.[1] The picture of this dour Scottish Victorian Radical receiving a ticker-tape welcome in New York is a fond scene; and it may be said to have laid the foundations of an Atlanticist tradition in the British Labour Party which continued until it came unstuck in the era of Polaris.

In practice, however, Anglo-American naval agreement could only be fully worked out in relation to the strengths of other Powers. To put together such a package MacDonald convened an International Naval Conference in London during January 1930. Two main snags presented themselves. The first was Japan, who showed signs of jibbing at the 'Rolls Royce: Rolls Royce: Ford' formula dating from the Washington settlement of 1921. After some cajoling, and assisted by the fact that the Labour Cabinet again put the construction of the Singapore Base 'on ice', the Japanese eventually fell in with the general plan. The second, and larger, complication derived from France, whose ostensible sticking point was a demand for clear superiority over Italy, but who also saw the Conference as an opportunity to extract a broader political guarantee unlimited by the geographical and discretionary limits of Locarno. Here, indeed, was the traditional gambit by which the French sought to pin their British partner down: if the United Kingdom did not link hands with France on land, France would not assist the United Kingdom to achieve the stability on the seas she craved. Whereas MacDonald had been generally sympathetic to Paris during his first premiership, under these new circumstances his sentiments quickly did a somersault. 'France becomes the peace problem of Europe', he observed in his diary. 'Mentality is purely militarist'[2]. A few days later, still seething, the Prime Minister added that he was above all things determined 'not to drift into the position in which Grey found himself', whereby the United Kingdom had become little more than a 'bound follower' of the French war chariot.[3] Loaded though this might be as history, no appreciation of the tendencies which later merged into Chamberlainite Appeasement is complete without underlining the degree to which many British statesmen in the era felt themselves to be confronted by a 'replay' in Europe of the events of 1911–14 – and were adamant that this time round Britain at least should avoid the trap.

The London Naval Treaty concluded in April 1930 was a considerable achievement for the Labour Government, and for the control of world armaments generally. It highlighted the potential of Anglo-American co-operation in providing an anchor for international affairs, especially when Japan was prepared to 'work in' with the arrangements. Yet in establishing a framework for the future it had several weaknesses. As a Three Power agreement only, it failed to grapple with the central problem of Europe. Above all, its beneficent potential was simultaneously drained off by the commercial tensions emanating from the recent stockmarket crash in New York. Hence even whilst the British and American navalists (some of them reluctantly) were settling their differences, protectionist pressures were building up in the United States Congress, resulting in the Hawley-Smoot Tariff of June 1930. The fresh wedge this helped to drive between the two Anglo-Saxon powers was to critically weaken the forces making for stability in the world at large over the next few years. For MacDonald himself the transition from coping with problems of diplomacy, about which he felt instinctive confidence in his own abilities, to problems of economics, about which he always felt innately uneasy, was painful. The subsequent travails of the Labour ministry in Britain as it battled with inexorably rising unemployment at home, and a matching deficit in government spending as the 'dole' absorbed more and more resources, is a facet of domestic history outside our story. Nevertheless, a brief survey of the background to the crisis of the summer of 1931 must be sketched, since the latter was to determine the shape of British policy in external (and internal) matters for virtually the rest of the decade.

It has often been remarked, invariably in critical undertones, that the impact of the slump put in high relief the classical orthodoxy of the Labour Party's economic beliefs.[4] Yet the unreceptiveness of many socialists, especially of an older generation, to what they regarded as new-fangled nostrums is not surprising, nor was it necessarily misplaced. In their lifetimes classical economics had delivered massive improvements in the purchasing power of the workers. This, of course, had not satisfied them, or their constituency, as to the way in which the national cake continued to be carved up on class principles; but neither did it dispose them to defer to those who advocated a different brand of economics altogether. More often than not, these alternative political economies were based on raking-in enhanced state revenue, not by taxing luxuries, but by putting imposts on articles of mass consumption – penalizing not silk, but bread. Much of this money, furthermore, was usually earmarked for spending on defence, even if this was appropriately rationalized in terms of propping up employment in the arsenals and shipyards of the nation. It was such tell-tale signs, implying that a more 'active' state would as ever be active on behalf of the stronger rather than the weaker orders in society, which on the left of British politics kept alive the old faith in Peace, Retrenchment and Reform. There was no more stubborn defender of this ancient doctrine than the Chancellor of the Exchequer in the Labour Government, Philip Snowden.

Snowden's chief contribution to the second Labour Government was to keep Ramsay MacDonald steady on a Free Trade course even when the premier was tempted by the compromise of a 'revenue tariff'.[5] In this he was assisted by a peculiarly tenacious personality, and by the considerable autonomy which the Chancellor still retained over his portfolio. A crucial moment in this saga came with the Imperial Conference in October

1930, which provided a focus for the medley of protectionist forces in British politics. Many hopes centred on the Canadian Conservative Prime Minister, R.B. Bennett, who barnstormed the conference with his sweeping demands for Empire trade preferences. It was, however, a case of the irresistible force meeting the wholly unmoveable object, the latter coming out on top. Snowden contemptuously dismissed the prognosis that British consumers owed Canadian farm producers a tax to shield them from market forces; advised Bennett in full plenary session to go and talk to the Americans, since Canada evidently could not cope economically on its own; and boasted openly as the meeting dispersed in less than fraternal hysteria that he had 'wiped the floor' with his chief adversary.[6] Such behaviour was a trifle *gauche*, but it was not without a rationale: by so brazenly seeing off the Canadians, Snowden made it plain that no government of which he was a member would embrace the protectionist heresy.

Thus abjuring public works and tariffs (leaving the former to be taken up by the ever-fertile Lloyd George), the Labour Government had no alternative but to batten down the hatches, get a grip on public expenditure and imitate Mr Micawber. Alas, what turned up in May 1931 was a great European banking crisis sparked by the collapse of a Viennese institution, the *Kreditanstalt*, swiftly bringing sterling within the speculators' sights. The Hoover Administration in the United States – whose financial policies were generally more internationalist than those it followed in the trade sphere – responded with the offer of a debt moratorium. This was made conditional on an equivalent contribution being made by the other main gold-surplus country, France. Such agreement was not forthcoming. The authorities in Paris, having themselves pursued a severe deflationary regime for much of the preceding decade, saw no reason why others should be spared the rigours of an adjustment they had already undergone; whilst anything – including banking troubles – which kept the Germans off-balance appeared as grist to the mill of the Versailles order. The trouble for the British was that their own currency stood at the junction of these market and political conflicts. MacDonald regarded French financial policy during these upsets to be 'inconceivably atrocious'[7]; and it was significant that the international circumstances attending the British crisis of 1931 were ones which cast France once more in a lurid light.

The bankruptcy of international financial co-operation, which before long catapulted Germany into the hands of Adolf Hitler and the Nazi Party, also had the more immediate effect of putting the British Labour Government into the hands of the bankers.[8] The money-men, both in London and New York, refused to contemplate an emergency loan unless government spending was curbed along the lines already laid down in the report of a committee chaired by Sir George May, appointed by Snowden to enquire into the state of the public finances. The resulting explosions within the Cabinet are not our concern. As David Marquand has remarked, the controversy did not revolve around *whether* or not spending should be cut.[9] All the principal ministers were agreed it had to be, and during the bargaining the figures touted by the two sides to the argument were never very far apart. Yet the political gulf which had opened up ultimately could not be bridged. For MacDonald, Snowden and the minority in the Cabinet who supported them, not to go the whole hog in making economies was to fail the test of that 'fitness to govern' which it was the whole point of their careers and convictions as socialists to vindicate; for the majority, however, cuts on the scale proposed was tantamount to betraying the class whose interests they claimed to represent. Amidst the din emitted by this scrap between two different versions of British socialism, the Government broke up on 25 August 1931. The MacDonaldites migrated into a National Government with the Conservatives and Samuelite Liberals (MacDonald himself retaining the premiership), whilst the bulk of the Labour Party retired, smouldering, to the Opposition benches. In this way the British Left – for whom Ramsay MacDonald has ever since remained a renegade figure – claimed its most stunning, and over the years curiously heart-warming, example of class betrayal.

Yet probably more important for the future than this dis-integration of governing socialism was the parallel rift in the

Conservative ranks during the period prior to August 1931. How, for instance, did Stanley Baldwin, that inveterate hater of Coalitions, come to embrace a 'National' combination which amounted to something very similar, without even the assuagement of the premiership to sweeten the pill? The reason lay, in part, with the urgency of the crisis itself when it arrived, and the risks it posed to the fabric of the country. But it also had a lot to do with the factional and ideological divisions within his own party. These intra-Tory tensions hinged on two main issues: Imperial Protection and India.

At first the inevitable challenge to Baldwin's leadership after the election of 1929 had focused on Lord Beaverbrook's 'Crusade' for so-called Empire Free Trade (that is, Protection against everybody else) disseminated through the medium of the *Daily Express*, of which he was the proprietor. In fact, Beaverbrook's Empire loyalism, as A.J.P. Taylor has observed, never really stretched beyond a preoccupation with his native Canada.[10] This merely reflected the weakness of imperial movements generally in British politics; they consisted of not one but many essentially disaggregated lobbies; and by and large these elements rarely rallied to each other. The most interesting clue as to the character of the self-styled Crusade may be found in the geography of Beaverbrook's speaking tours in 1930. 'He [Beaverbrook] only once ventured into an industrial constituency, at Preston, and even that was to address the local branch of the National Farmers' Union', Taylor tells us. 'All his other meetings were either in agricultural constituencies or in London suburbs.'[11] In this was detectable the overlap between English rural reaction and imperial consciousness which flowed powerfully into *ultra* Toryism after 1930. In its most extreme form, the solution offered to the problem of industrial competitiveness and employment was simply to force it off the agenda. Baldwin, despite his pose of rustic authenticity, was never drawn to the escapism of the shires. He stoically held the centre ground – laying himself open to the allegation by critics, then and since, that he lacked 'imagination' – whilst mainstream Conservatism struggled to evolve a more credible approach. Gradually a centrist programme geared to 'economy' and industrial reform took shape, the purely sectional claims of the agricultural-cum-imperial interests being successfully 'relegated to the backwaters of politics'.[12] During this process, however, not only had the party fortunes of Baldwin and Neville Chamberlain, hitherto only loosely related, become closely entwined, but the values for which they stood were more than ever defined in ways that were cautious, insular and, above all, national.

The second challenge to 'Baldwinism' from within the Tory machine revolved around the political, rather than economic, dimension of empire. Almost the very first act of Arthur Henderson when he became Labour Foreign Secretary in 1929 had been to dismiss Lord Lloyd from his post in Egypt, a peremptory move inspired (not, as we have seen, without reason) by fear that that eager proconsul would sooner or later embarrass his new masters. What dismayed Lloyd's many Conservative supporters was not only the dismissal itself, but the fact that when the matter was brought to the floor of the Commons their own Front Bench leaders refused to take the bait; indeed, Austen Chamberlain's (and Baldwin's) silence was interpreted as tacit agreement in what had been done.[13] Even this grievance, however, was shortly overshadowed by the historic declaration of the Viceroy of India, Lord Irwin, himself an impeccable Conservative, in October 1929 that the 'natural issue' of India's constitutional progress was Dominion Status. Again, far from Baldwin exploiting the parliamentary debate this occasioned to attack the policy, he showed every sign of wishing to develop it into a bi-partisan approach. The contrary response on some of his own benches – Churchill's intervention bespeaking a man 'demented with fury'[14] – may be taken as the quasi-official inauguration of a doctrinal feud between different schools of Toryism which lasted not only up to the Second World War, but well beyond it.

What considerations, then, governed the increasingly contrasting postures which Baldwin and Churchill took up in these obviously volatile spheres? The former's private conversations at the time were marked by recurrent emphasis on the need to prevent India becoming 'another Ireland' – to stop it, in other words, hardening and festering into a 'Question' which would distort and divide the metropole just as much as it did the dependency concerned. The analogy was not merely analytical; it was no accident that the aged Orange hero, Edward Carson, was prominent amongst those seeking to mobilize Tory sentiment against Irwinite (and Baldwinite) moderation towards India. Cool reflection, not fabricated and rhetorical emotion, was, in contrast, the touchstone of the Conservatism for which Baldwin stood. 'If ever the day comes', he said in the Commons, pointedly addressing his own benches rather than those opposite, 'when the party which I lead ceases to attract men of the calibre of Edward Wood [Lord Irwin], then I have finished with my party.' The implication as to the 'calibre' of Winston Churchill did not go unnoticed, nor was it ever forgiven.[15]

Churchill's motives were in many respects simply the obverse of those of his leader. His hopes of becoming Baldwin's successor had become increasingly frail; by 1930 they had effectively disappeared. As a life-long Free Trader, however, he was in no position to leap aboard the protectionist bandwagon. India was, in Stuart Ball's words, 'the only issue he could take up with credibility'[16], and he proceeded to do so for all it was worth. The issue was tailor-made to evoke the political feelings with which Churchill now sought to identify himself. 'The truth is', he addressed a meeting at the Canon House Hotel on 12 December 1930, 'that Gandhi-ism and all it stands for will, sooner or later, have to be grappled with and finally crushed. It is no use trying to satisfy a tiger by feeding him cat's meat . . .'. On the one side grappling and crushing, on the other side the feeding of cat's meat – these metaphors were ultimately to translate more successfully into European than into Indian terms. Meanwhile, given language such as this, when Ramsay MacDonald convened a Round Table Conference on India in early 1931, it was inevitable that Baldwin and his party managers should make sure that neither Churchill nor anybody associated with him were accorded places on the Conservative delegation. The result was to make an incipient breach virtually complete.

Given the diverse and highly fissiparous pressures within their two parties, therefore, it was understandable that MacDonald and Baldwin came to suspect that they had more in common with each other than they did with some of their respective colleagues. Such sentiment undoubtedly would have remained inchoate if it had not been worked upon by the force of the financial crisis itself; and it was only at the last moment – under the promptings of King George V (always a coalitionist at heart) and impelled by the logic of spreading 'the load of unpopularity [of further economies] across as many shoulders as possible'[17] – that a National Government finally emerged as the solution. Like many temporary expedients, however, this one was to prove more long-lived than anyone anticipated at the outset.

'Its origins', wrote Sam Hoare in his memoirs of the National Government in which he was to be such a controversial figure, 'determined its whole existence.'[18] This was profoundly true: August 1931 defined the mainstream of British politics in terms of balanced budgets and instincts which were fundamentally introverted and risk-averse. Apart from MacDonald's retention of the premiership and Baldwin's assumption of the Lord Presidency of the Council, the crucial appointment was that of Neville Chamberlain to be Chancellor of the Exchequer, and it was in his personality and intellect that the impulses stemming from the recent crisis were finally to cohere into a rigid philosophy of government.

In fact the immediate goal which the new ministry, superficially at least, had been formed to secure – that of 'saving' the pound – soon evaporated.[19] On 21 September continued speculation resulted in the British currency being unpegged from gold, after which it drifted lower against the dollar and the franc. Had Britain's overseas suppliers proceeded to do what many in Whitehall feared they might, and raised their sterling prices in order to compensate for the depreciation, the National Government might have been confronted – and possibly before long swept away – by a tide of rising commodity and raw material prices. Yet they did not do so, and the United Kingdom pulled off a most rare triumph: that is, a successful devaluation, in which depreciated currency is foisted on the outside world without incurring retribution. 'I did not know we could get away with this', muttered one Government minister in happy surprise. None the less, the entire conduct of Government policy in the years ahead was marked by that *grand peur* of inflation which had attended its birth.

The devaluation gamble in 1931 worked for the simple reason that, as world trade shrank rapidly through the early phases of Depression, the relatively open market of the United Kingdom remained far too valuable for millions of overseas producers to put their share of it at risk, even if it meant accepting devalued sterling in return for their goods. This is the chief reason why Britain had the 'best' Depression of all the major industrial countries in the 1930s: being the most uniformly industrialized, she creamed off huge profits from the advantageous terms of trade accruing to manufacturers during this period, an advantage which sterling devaluation only served to intensify (the Canadians, on the receiving end as an agricultural exporter, invented a phrase to describe this dual process – 'skinning the ox twice').[20] Hence it was the stimulus resulting from these lowered costs which allowed *average* living standards in Britain to improve very markedly in what afterwards came to be too simplistically pictured as a time of unrelieved woe. Whilst subsequent orthodoxies in British politics made it virtually *de rigueur* to regard anything that happened under the aegis of the National Government as 'a bad thing', recent scholarship has begun to focus more dispassionately on the long-delayed structural transformation of British industry, which, prompted by the necessities of recession, was set in motion after 1931.

As part of its recovery programme the National Government adopted a measure of Protection combined with Imperial Preference, but the former was distinctly mild and the latter very diluted. Thus the British Tariff introduced by the Abnormal Duties Act of November 1931 was never really more than an exercise in international trade bargaining: its theme was that of

'Retaliation', not full-blooded tariff-mongering. The orthodox account that Britain 'went off' Free Trade in this period, as she went off the Gold Standard, therefore needs to be carefully qualified; she remained – certainly by the standards set by other nations during the decade – a remarkably open market. Equally restrained was the National Government's commitment to imperial economic co-operation. The devaluation of sterling (leading to an informal monetary entity known as the 'sterling bloc') added, admittedly, to the putative attractions of an imperial refuge from the storms afflicting the world economy. Domestic political factors increased the pressures tending in this direction, since empire trade agreements, quickly cobbled together, were one of the few cures which the National Government, having won a smashing election victory in November 1931 on a Doctor's Mandate, could be seen diligently applying to the patient. Hence when an Imperial Economic Conference convened in Ottawa in September 1932 more than half the British Cabinet was in dutiful attendance; and when negotiations resulted in a series of commercial agreements including new preferences, quotas and duties between various Dominions and the United Kingdom, a small number of Free Trade ministers who had remained rather sulkily at home (including Philip Snowden) promptly resigned.

The outstanding feature of the Ottawa Conference, however, was not so much what various Governments had agreed upon, but what they failed to agree.[21] So desperate were conditions in parts of the overseas (primarily agricultural) Dominions that their representatives understandably lobbied hard for 'quick fix' inflationary solutions to their problems, only to find that for the British inflation was forbidden fruit. Reduced to bartering about merchandise trade, the Australians, Canadians and South Africans refused to dismantle their own 'infant' secondary industries, whilst the United Kingdom refused to grant the other Commonwealth countries the effective monopolies of the metropolitan market they so desired. Personal relations took a dive, as they had in 1930. Thus one British participant described the host Prime Minister, Richard Bennett, as having 'the manners of a Chicago policeman and the temperament of a Hollywood film star'[22], whilst what Bennett thought of the British by this time was not always printable. It was the measure of their mutual disenchantment that some of the Englishmen present found that their most enjoyable exchanges at the conference were with the Irish, against whom they were (for wholly non-commercial reasons) conducting tariff hostilities at the time.[23] The agreements which emerged out of the mêlée were necessarily rather limited, and one historian has calculated that they added a mere one per cent to British industrial production thereafter – not enough to have any discernible employment effects whatsoever.[24] In their favour it may be said that they bucked up business and consumer confidence when spirits were otherwise at a very low ebb. The fact that Snowden chose to regard Ottawa as a resigning matter said more about his desire to leave politics than it did about any fundamental sea-change in British political economy.

After the summer of 1932 imperial commercial relations often got worse rather than better. The Dominions desperately sought to shore up their domestic employment by *accelerating* industrialization; meanwhile the United Kingdom diluted what had been agreed at Ottawa by negotiating agreements with non-Empire trading partners in Europe and Scandinavia (the 'Black Pacts', as these commercial agreements were known in Canada). Each side thus felt let down. Of course, mutual recrimination was restrained by awareness that deflation remained even more rampant outside the sterling system than within it; and overall the Dominions were probably no less dependent on Britain economically at the end of the 1930s than they had been at the beginning. This continuing reliance on the imperial connection, however, was itself merely a reflection of the present curtailment in world-wide exchanges; and as countries such as Canada and Australia emerged after 1935 from their local depressions, they showed more interest in developing commercial relations with 'foreign' nations (above all, the United States) than they did with the Mother Country.[25] In sum, the chief lesson derived from the often dismal experience of the decade was that an imperial economic *zollverein*, beguiling an idea though it might be in hard times, was really an answer to nobody's problems, because none of the countries concerned were prepared to shoulder the burdens which it indubitably involved.

Whatever irritations the National Government came to entertain on economic matters *vis-à-vis* the Dominions, however, paled beside the disillusionment experienced with respect to the United States. The legacy of the Hawley-Smoot tariff in 1930 was important here. None the less, early in its term of office the National Government invested considerable hopes in maintaining a commercial dialogue across the Atlantic, and with this in mind British officials minutely scanned the runes of the American presidential election in the autumn of 1932. The victory of Franklin D. Roosevelt, at first assumed in London to be a traditional low-tariff Democrat, fuelled these expectations. The recovery programme which Neville Chamberlain provisionally hammered out as Chancellor of the Exchequer, and intended to unveil at the World Economic Conference in London during June 1933, therefore hinged on the Anglo-Americans jointly giving a lead to the renovation of world trade. Yet driven by the depths of the domestic crisis prevailing when he took office, including banking closures threatening the financial fabric of the Union, President Roosevelt immediately presided instead over an emergency 'New Deal' in which international co-operation – with the British or anybody else – was subordinated to purely internal reflationary goals.[26] This got American farmers temporarily off the hook, but it greatly intensified deflation elsewhere in the world. Most dramatically of all, Roosevelt's famous 'bombshell' message to the World Economic Conference when it finally met in the British capital, declaring his intention to devalue the dollar as far and as fast as the needs of America's domestic circumstances required, finally put paid to any prospect of a multilateral recovery package for the rest of the decade.[27] It is not an exaggeration to say that Neville Chamberlain never forgave Roosevelt, or America, the transgression; and when he moved from No. 11 Downing Street to the premises next door he took with him the conviction that an understanding with her transatlantic cousin was the *least* reliable basis on which to plan the United Kingdom's long-term interests.

Disappointment with the Americans apart, the key to much of Chamberlain's economic thinking in this period came to lie in his appreciation of the *fragility* of British recovery. The orthodox version of events is somewhat misleading on this front. Hence the conventional view is that the United Kingdom endured the worst of the slump in 1930–2; bumped along the bottom for a while; and from 1934 onwards enjoyed a sharp recovery, broken only by a 'blip' (imported via a recession in the United States) during 1937 which rearmament expenditure, in good contra-cyclical style, happily ironed out. The only puzzle this leaves is why the National Government spent so little on armaments during the mature phase of the recovery, considering what an excellent tonic it would have been for the economy; and the answer is unerringly found in the obtuseness of Stanley Baldwin (who became Prime Minister once again when MacDonald finally retired in June 1935) and the flint-like disposition of his Chancellor of the Exchequer. To those who actually had responsibility at the time, however, things did not appear in anything like this light. By 1935 the stimulatory formula of 'easy money', a residential housing boom and access to cheap (often dirt-cheap) imports was running out of steam in the United Kingdom. The fundamental problem of British manufacturing competitiveness remained, and it was starkly revealed by the scale of the balance of payments deficit in 1936. In the annals of British economic history, indeed, 1936/37 may be taken as the first discernible era of what later commentators came to call 'stop-go', whereby a pronounced spurt of British economic growth invariably had the effect of sucking in excess imports, weakening the country's balance of payments position and so bringing itself to a dead stop. Foreknowledge of this sort was clearly not available in Treasury Chambers during the 1930s; yet the official experts could see the figures and deduce from them that it was not the moment to throw away what had been gained at very considerable cost (not least in employment terms) during recent years by a bout of fiscal largesse. In short, keeping taxes low, inflation smothered, public expenditure under restraint and demand in line with ability to supply appeared on the eve of Chamberlain's own premiership to be just as compelling as in August 1931, when the priorities of the National Government had first been set in stone.

Against this background, the campaign which shortly got under way to transfer massive resources to rearmament on the grounds of preserving a slippery phenomenon called the 'Balance of Power' seemed, as one leading industrialist bluntly put it to Churchill, to lose all touch with 'the true proportion of affairs'[28]; and when the latter led a vocal deputation to Baldwin in order to demand that one-third of British industry be put at the disposal of the military, the Prime Minister could not resist remarking on the telling fact that not one of his visitors haled from an industrial constituency – clearly the shires expected other people to do all the mobilizing.[29] Yet it was precisely such diametric notions as to what was the 'true proportion of affairs' which made Appeasement the most seminal divide in twentieth-century British politics. Before turning to the central tenets of British foreign policy, however, we must say something more about Indian developments, since the continuing metropolitan arguments on this front in many ways prefigured the larger and ultimately more important antagonisms over Europe.

Import quotas, currency devaluations, debt conversions – these provided the stuff of British politics during the early thirties. They were arcane matters, about which it was difficult (if not quite impossible) for politicians, or people sitting in pubs, to claim to have all the answers. India was different. It was a good, old-fashioned question of power, and it may be suggested that at this time Britons welcomed a polemical diversion from the baffling and often very technical dilemmas of the slump. It is a nice conundrum that whereas the final granting of Independence to India in 1947 caused scarcely a stir in British politics, the much more modest reform legislation first considered by a Joint Committee of the two Houses of Parliament after April 1933, and which finally received the Royal Assent as the Government of India Act on 2 August 1935, was the occasion for tremendous eruptions.[30] The reason for the contrast lies not so much in Indian conditions, as in those obtaining in the United Kingdom itself.

The proposed legislation presided over by the relevant Secretary of State, Sam Hoare, fell into two main parts. It extended a full measure of responsible government to the provinces of British India, subject only to emergency safeguards on the part of Governors. In addition, it sought to bring into being a new Central Government on a federal basis which joined the Princely States (with their feudal ruling families) to the rest of the Sub-Continent. Combined with the Viceroy's continuing power of veto where British, or 'imperial', interests were concerned, it was the novel ingredient of conservative federalism which has been taken to give the lie to the underlying purposes of the authorities in London. Undoubtedly the basic conception of the Bill was to 'find nationalism out'; to confront it, in other words, with a real Indian electorate (which under the rubric of the franchise would amount to approximately forty million voters) and so finally prove that the claims of the Congress Party to represent something called 'the Indian nation' were wholly fraudulent. Once this wedge could be inserted, the British presence in India might be guaranteed for many years ahead. 'It is no part of our policy', Lord Linlithgow, the incumbent Viceroy, summed up the essential spirit of the Bill, '. . . gratuitously to hurry the handing over of controls at a rate faster than that which we regard as best calculated . . . to hold India to the Empire.'[31]

Seen purely in this light, recent scholarship has tended to emphasize the machiavellian aims of Hoare, in which *plus ça change, plus c'est la même chose* was the guiding theme. John Darwin, in particular, has posed the question as to whether British Imperialism was in decline during the *inter-bellum* years, and, not least with respect to the conduct of Indian policy, has concluded that far from being terminally ill it was alive and well and busy thinking up new methods of pursuing its age-old goals.[32] This interpretation clearly has a good deal of validity, but arguably it fails to capture the essence of the National Government's tendencies in the imperial field in general, and India in particular. After all, Hoare and his colleagues, machiavellian as they were, could hardly have been so naïve as to think that by thus Indianizing the administration and basing it on an electorate of forty millions, the appearance of power might be altered without simultaneously affecting its content and operation as well. '[The Bill] was based upon what could be called India's financial and international morality', Carl Bridge has crisply remarked. 'Britain had to have the means to ensure that India met her obligations to pay sterling bond-holders and Indian Civil Service and army pensions and salaries, and maintain an army adequate for Indian and Imperial defence.'[33] Yet there could be little doubt that an Indian Government constructed along these lines would interpret what was 'adequate' with respect to Imperial Defence rather differently than the War Office in Whitehall. Indeed, as Jack Gallagher has stressed, one of the most telling facts relating to imperial affairs by the *end* of the 1930s was that the Indian Army could only be modernized, and thereby equipped for imperial purposes, when the authorities in London agreed to find the money themselves; clearly the days had passed when the metropole could depend on Indian taxpayers to subsidize its own strategic visions.[34] In brief, for all their subtle draftmanship designed to guard 'Imperial interests', Hoare's proposals marked a critical move away from rule and towards the influence of Indian politics; and, as its critics were not slow to point out, influence, like love, may be here today and gone tomorrow.

Throughout the long parliamentary battle which was waged in Britain over the Government of India Bill, its most intransigent opponent was Winston Churchill. Some suspected that he continued to be attracted to the India issue in these years because it was capable of being manipulated in line with the widely-held thesis of 'England going Fascist'[35], and certainly the bankruptcy of liberal democracy formed a recurrent part of Churchill's oratory in these years (as it did of many others). 'Is this the time', he asked somewhat shrilly in one of the great India debates, 'fatally to dishearten . . . all those strong, clean forces at home upon which the strength and future of the country depends?'[36]

His auditors did not need to be reminded from which branch of contemporary European philosophy this mode of discourse was drawn. Such posturing, however, was largely cosmetic. Churchill's real purpose comes out more clearly in an earlier letter he wrote to Lord Irwin on the latter's retirement from the Viceroyalty, warning him that India was destined to become 'the dividing line in England'.[37] What he meant was that he intended to make it so, just as Ireland had been the great demarcator in British affairs after 1910, and South Africa before that. Most profoundly at issue during the India controversy between 1933 and 1935, then, was not only how the Sub-Continent should be governed, but how (and against whom) England should be divided.

In his main purpose Churchill failed completely. He was never able to mobilize against Hoare anything more than a small caucus of disaffected back-bench Tories; and although this slowed the legislation down in its constitutional evolutions, it never came anywhere near killing it outright. In the country at large, talk of the 'strong clean forces' fell largely flat, and most people felt as Linlithgow did when he pointed out to Churchill that it served no purpose to talk of India as if it was the 1890s, not the 1930s.[38] The Bill finally secured an overwhelming majority on third reading, and, although the federal clauses eventually foundered owing to a change of mind by the princes, the eventual independence of that country (within, that is, some recognizably human time-scale) may be said to have become a foregone conclusion. Nevertheless, from the perspective of Churchill's career, the Die Hard onslaught which he led against Hoare had its uses. It identified him, subliminally at least, with conceptions of British strength and prestige, and gave him a platform when none other was available; and by the time the India campaign was running into the sands, the question of German revival (especially, or so it was alleged, in air-power) afforded a fresh peg on which to hang a certain rationale of British action. The rest of this chapter will concentrate, therefore, on the paths which led to the United Kingdom's participation in a 'second round' in the struggle for mastery in Europe.

*

Although in considering the course of British diplomacy we shall, for reasons of brevity, largely confine ourselves in this chapter to the European dimension, we should start by making some remarks on the situation in the Far East. Thus it is sometimes said that it was the Japanese incursion along the Chinese Eastern Railway into Manchuria during September 1931 which began a long crisis finally issuing in the world war of December 1941; and undoubtedly the British role in helping to whitewash this initial act of aggression by Japan (through the helpful medium of a League of Nations Enquiry) was a foretaste of other appeasements to come. Yet from the United Kingdom's point of view one of the prime effects of the Manchurian episode, ironically, was to highlight Anglo-American, rather than Anglo-Japanese, differences. London's refusal to participate in the plan of the American Secretary of State, Henry Stimson, for collective non-recognition of the resulting puppet-regime of Manchukuo led to bitter recriminations on both sides of the Atlantic. A Whitehall lobby – in which Neville Chamberlain was prominent – soon began to promote the merits of a *new* Anglo-Japanese alliance; it was argued in this respect that Britain had given one concession after another in recent years (by refraining from the coercion of Ireland in 1921, pulling out of Treaty friendship with Japan in 1923, and settling her war debts on unfavourable terms) in order to win the United States' favour, only to find that the latter took and never gave in return.[39] There was much rewriting of history in all this, but it reflected accurately enough a tough-minded anti-Americanism which became a distinctive feature of official British attitudes during much of the decade.

British and American perspectives in the Far East were, in fact, substantially different. The United Kingdom's stake in the Asian mainland was pre-eminently colonial (embracing Hong Kong, Singapore, and Malaya) and, of course, commercial (the latter centred on the riverine and coastal trades of central China). Her ambitions did not go beyond the preservation of these relatively circumscribed assets; and providing the Japanese were deferred to in what was, at bottom, their own region of mastery, there was every reason to hope that the latter might advance around, rather than through, Britain's spheres of interest. In London it was thus feared that American calls for co-operation against Japan concealed a propensity to entertain a war in which the British – as the most exposed – would endure the losses, and do most of any fighting which might eventuate. This is paradoxical given what happened after December 1941, when it was the Americans who overwhelmingly shouldered the burdens of defeating Japan. Nevertheless, in the context of the thirties it was logical that British policy should be governed by the suspicion that, should things go off the rails, they had everything to lose and the United States – as an *expanding* naval and commercial power in Asia and the Pacific – everything to gain. Here, then, were the roots of transatlantic suspicions that were to contribute towards the stunting of co-operation between the two Anglo-Saxon powers on matters that went beyond the configuration of East Asia.

Anglo-American difficulties apart, most British diplomatic narratives of the thirties analyse the East Asian crisis in terms of Whitehall's fear of a hypothetical 'two-front' war – that is, one occurring in Europe and the Far East simultaneously, thereby stretching the United Kingdom's resources beyond breaking point. By linking the two main fronts in this way, the appeasing instinct can be seen to have fed off itself, and in the end to have underpinned an overwhelming preoccupation with the requirement for political solutions in the European theatre. These tendencies were undoubtedly important, and the breathtaking risks inherent in the scale of Britain's world-wide responsibilities certainly reinforced a prudential bias which drew the armed services as well as the diplomats into a temporary, if always brittle, consensus over appeasement. Yet there is no need to strain too much to view the European and Asian crises in their precise relation to each other. Almost certainly the British Government's policies towards Europe would have been what they were even if the Japanese had got on with their silk-worming, instead of building aircraft-carriers. Nothing exemplifies this more strikingly than the fact that Alexander Cadogan, as Permanent Head of the Foreign Office, was only dimly *aware* of the Tsientsin crisis of June 1939 – certainly the relevant papers were not put on his desk for attention.[40] As we shall see, this marginalization of Far Eastern developments was to be even more stark during the Second World War. Meanwhile, following Cadogan's practice, we shall turn our attention to the eye of the storm on the adjoining Continent.

If the Manchurian incident inaugurated a crisis in Asia that was to run and run, the breakdown of the Geneva Disarmament Conference in early 1933 may be said to have had a similar aggravating effect in Europe (especially as amidst the unpleasantries Adolf Hitler became Chancellor of Germany on 30 January). The blame for the impasse over land disarmament in Europe, however, was in many quarters ascribed to the government in Paris for setting too high a price on their co-operation. 'The French had fired the starting pistol for the arms race', A.J.P. Taylor remarked in his impish work, *The Origins of the Second World War*, 'characteristically they failed to run it.'[41] Instead, in the tradition of the ententes, the incumbent premier, Louis Barthou, sought reinsurance through Russia, issuing in the Franco-Soviet Pact of 1935. Nothing was more likely to set alarm bells ringing in London, and to stimulate afresh harrowing memories of the road to 1914. 'It is the Louis Barthous of this world', Anthony Eden, an up and coming young Conservative, summarized the widespread sentiment in Britain, 'who have made Hitler inevitable.'[42]

The débâcle of the disarmament process in Geneva naturally led the National Government to review the United Kingdom's own position. The Defence Requirements Sub-Committee of the Committee of Imperial Defence was therefore set up, and its report in mid-1934, in addition to recommending the abandonment of the highly contentious 'Ten Year Rule' whereby it was a rolling assumption in Whitehall that Britain would not be confronted with a major war for a decade ahead, led to the funding of deficiency programmes to make good the gaps which earlier economies had created.[43] Two distinguishing features of British rearmament in this early phase stand out. The first is that the politicians who presided over it were constantly on the look-out for signs that the policy itself was getting out of control.

'We are back to 1912', Ramsay MacDonald warned, dismally pondering a new set of Naval estimates.[44] The second (and related) aspect of the 'deficiency' approach to British rearmament was its emphasis on purely defensive priorities, and hence the strict restraint that was kept on any expansion of the Continental Commitment. As we shall see later on, this had implications, not only for the aggregate amount of defence spending, but also for the distribution of monies between the various services – never to the advantage of the British Army. Overarching these responses was a continuing, and if anything stiffening, resolve that the forces which had taken control of British policy-making on the eve of the Great War should this time be kept firmly in their place.

A continuing restraint on British rearmament was the public's belief in 'Collective Security' organized through the League of Nations. The most striking evocation of this was the Peace Ballot of June 1935, in which some twelve million people responded to a questionnaire circulated by the League of Nations Union, with an overwhelming plurality professing themselves in favour of collective action against aggressors. The significance of this outcome has been contested ever since. Some have claimed that it evinced an incorrigible pacifism; others that it indicated a preparedness to fight for what was still quaintly called 'the Public Law of Europe'. The truth was that the Peace Ballot (or the Blood Ballot, as Beaverbrook called it, in recognition of its slippery qualities) meant neither – or rather, both at once. For the man on the Clapham omnibus, or now beetling along in his Morris motor, 'Collective Security' had a solid, reassuring sound because it legitimated and upheld what was, for the United Kingdom, the best of all possible worlds. In private, none the less, the politicians had to begin guessing for themselves how – if push came to shove – the tide of national opinion might break; whether, in particular, it would surge towards a peace of realism and readjustment, or towards a war ostensibly 'on behalf of the League'. The ambitions and rivalries of individuals and factions (Birkenhead's ideal ethic of 'glittering prizes') continued to cut across these issues as, in Maurice Cowling's rendering, 'foreign policy [became] the form that party politics took' in the second half of the decade.[45] Embedded in these politics, inevitably, were alternative visions not only of the 'true proportion of affairs', but of the character and values infusing British society as a whole.

Despite the progressive renewal of tension in Europe after 1933, for some while it still seemed feasible that compromises could be found within the framework of Locarno. This hope effectively disappeared during the course of 1935. Three events contributed to this sea-change. In January the long-awaited plebiscite in the Saar region took place, and ninety per cent of the inhabitants voted to rejoin Germany. After this result the racial reintegration of the German diaspora was on the agenda – not without democratic credentials to its name. Secondly, in March Hitler unilaterally renounced the armaments limitations imposed on Germany in 1919. After this it was only a matter of time before Germany emerged as the strongest military power in Europe, or, as some believed, the world. The third crucial departure was the Franco-Soviet Pact referred to earlier. British opinions might differ as to which of these was most to be regretted or deplored. Their most important effects in Britain, however, were psychological. 'Everyone seemed to be overexcited', Sam Hoare recalled of his first visit to the Foreign Office on being appointed to head that department in May 1935.[46] The excitement was already being compounded by the impact of the crisis surrounding the claims to Abyssinia of the Italian dictator, Benito Mussolini, for whom an enlarged empire in Africa was the index of his country's Great Power status. It was this crisis – and specifically the 'Hoare-Laval' scandal to which it eventually led – which defined the shape of British controversy over foreign policy in the years which followed.

The first British response to Mussolini's demand for Abyssinia had been to ignore it, as they did at the Stresa Conference between Britain, France and Italy in April 1935; then they tried to buy it off at bargain-basement prices – the Zeila 'corridor' offer of the following June; eventually they cracked the whip of Collective Security.[47] In a speech to the League of Nations Assembly in Geneva on 11 September which raised Britain's prestige – that is, other nations' relief at an action they considered too ill-advised to take themselves – to new heights, Hoare famously declared that '. . . the League stands, and my country stands with it, for collective maintenance of the [League] Covenant in its entirety and collective resistance to all acts of unprovoked aggression.'[48] Afterwards it was alleged by the Government's critics that this brief spurt of militant internationalism was designed merely to buy the League of Nations vote at the general election of November 1935, after which it was quickly ditched for an altogether different policy. This is not entirely persuasive, if only because the cynicism would have been so overt as to be ultimately self-defeating. More persuasive is the theory that the National Government saw in the current situation an opportunity to annex the popular theme of Collective Security, but in so doing to give it a twist better fitted to the United Kingdom's special position and interests. Thus the 'collective maintenance' of the Covenant in the Mediterranean had an appeal for Britain that any putative counterpart in the marches of Danubia did not.

Events quickly showed, however, that League Collectivism did not work very well even in the 'second eleven' Mediterranean. No sooner had Hoare unsheathed the weapon of sanctions following Italy's invasion of Abyssinia in early October, than all the other member-nations fled from beneath his banner. Prominent among these was France, whose motive was the complete reverse of that prevailing across the Channel, in so far as the Gallic conception of Collective Security was of an instrument which should either be used against Germany or not at all. The British Dominions (shades of the Chanak crisis in 1922) did not do much better. Canada gallantly proposed an oil embargo, especially as she had very little of her own to export, but quickly retracted once this was defined in Rome as a *casus belli*.[49] Amidst these disappointments a sharp reaction developed in London against being framed in the role of 'unpaid policeman of the world'[50] – the recurrence in this context of Bonar Law's phrase was very telling. Having thus pushed out the boat, and found the conditions inclement, Hoare now strove to regain the safety of shore. He fixed a deal in Paris with his French opposite number, Pierre Laval, effectively giving Mussolini all he wanted. News of this leaked out, and there followed one of the great foreign policy 'storms' in modern British history. Baldwin bought time by dropping the beleaguered Hoare and appointing in his place the brilliant prodigy Anthony Eden, who had struck lucky with his rich blend of English nationalism and progressive League ideals. Like most such indignations, the public fury over 'Hoare-Laval' evaporated as quickly as it had arisen, leaving the National Government chastened but intact, and the Duke of Aosta and his legions undisturbed in their advance on the slave-owning paradise of Haile Selassie, Emperor of Abyssinia.

Within the realm of high politics in Britain, however, the ramifications of 'Hoare-Laval' were deep and lasting, and out of its toils Appeasement was to emerge in its mature form. The psychological essence of that policy was not to get excited about other people's excitements, just as its strategic essence was a fine appreciation of where British interests began and, just as importantly, where they ended. In this connection the residual sanctions in operation against Italy were a loose, undesirable end, made more complicated by the fact that the new Foreign Secretary was all too conscious that he owed his own remarkable elevation at the tender age of thirty-eight to his association with the League lobby. It fell to Neville Chamberlain, whose Treasury responsibilities embraced commercial restrictions, to pull the necessary trapdoor when in a speech on 10 June 1936 he described sanctions as 'the very midsummer of madness'. They were dropped, the Foreign Secretary omitted to resign, and – as a colleague percipiently noted – from that moment Chamberlain knew he had the measure of the glamorous but feminine Eden.[51]

Yet if the Hoare-Laval pact thus served as a lightning-rod for Appeasement, so it did for anti-Appeasement. The episode illustrated what a heady cocktail could be produced by the mingling of Collective Security emotion and hurt national pride. It had shown a capacity to bring together such opposites as Die Hard Tories, 'progressive' Conservatives, Liberal internationalists, and socialists for whom League idealism was a bridge they began, tentatively at first, to cross from a passive (if not always pacifist) foreign policy to one that was almost belligerent in its desire to get to grips with dictators (except, of course, in the Soviet Union). Hence for the first time there existed a disparate and potential mass of discontent which Winston Churchill could hope – or threaten – to bring to bear against the incumbent ministers. It was the opening of these hairline fractures which in the end translated into such a splitting of loyalties throughout the Party and the establishment that, as one senior Whitehall official was to remark, the final coming of war was to be a distinct relief from the anxieties and bitterness which had preceded it.[52]

This is to look ahead of events, for from early 1936 onwards one crisis after another appeared to have the effect of strengthening the National Government's position. Thus it was only much later that the reoccupation of the Rhineland by German troops in March 1936 had superimposed upon it the myth (later much used by historians) that it represented the last, lost opportunity to stop Hitlerism in its tracks. At the time it was very generally regarded in Britain as having cleared away an inconvenient and unsustainable anomaly; there was not, for example, any sign of the sort of reverberations which had been generated by the Abyssinian episode. Subsequently another Mediterranean matter – the Civil War in Spain, which broke out between Republicans and insurgent Monarchists in July 1936 – occasioned much political and ideological anguish among many Britons. Although it gave rise to many delicate problems of policy for the British Government, its main domestic effect was to keep the ministry's critics at odds with each other, for whilst the discontented Left bayed for the blood of General Franco, the frustrated Right considered him the very model of modern statesmanship – as Churchill admiringly phrased it, the only contestant who grasped the 'power of attack'.[53] Above all, it was the course of the Abdication affair which brought Baldwin's prestige to its apogee, and Churchill to one of his periodic nadirs in public esteem. The reason why the latter blundered so badly in dabbling with a forlorn and dangerous King's Party of Divine Right royalists,

Ulster mavericks, and press barons remains obscure.[54] Regal romance brought out the sentimentalist in him, and cut across the 'old world' reaction which he had for so long wished to weld into a real political force. Fundamentally, however, his actions at this time constituted a last gamble to upset the ageing Baldwin's apple-cart before Neville Chamberlain, the official heir, took over the cargo. Churchill's role in the private tragedy of Edward VIII was doubtless chivalrous and, in so far as it was possible for such an engaged spirit, disinterested; his contributions in the public domain on this matter, nevertheless, raised anew the doubts which many entertained as to the stability and ultimate direction of his career. When Neville Chamberlain finally assumed the premiership in April 1937, his hold on the job was unusually secure; and the sense of both confidence and rectitude this inculcated was to lend a distinctive texture to his leadership thereafter.

No premiership of as short a duration as Neville Chamberlain's (it lasted, after all, for only thirty-eight months) may be said to possess a comparable significance in British history. Indeed, no single 'snapshot' of a British leader in modern times has such instinctive resonances as that of Chamberlain, having returned from a conference with Hitler in Munich, declaring on the rainswept tarmac of Heston Aerodrome on 30 September 1938 that the piece of paper he waved aloft guaranteed 'Peace in our Time'. Quite why and how the son of *père* Joseph, who made such a fetish of British 'strength', should have ended up becoming a metaphor for British 'weakness' – a metaphor still in use fifty years later when it is desired to ascribe pusillanimous qualities to one's domestic opponents – is to touch on an unexplained and profound paradox in United Kingdom developments during the century.

This intriguing linkage between father and son might be drawn in several ways. Hence, just as Neville Chamberlain felt that with the conclusion of the Empire trade agreements at Ottawa in September 1932 he had brought to a climax his father's dreams of an Imperial commercial *zollverein*[55], so in later reaching out towards Hitler he almost certainly conceived of himself as effecting an Anglo-German understanding which Joseph had promoted at the start of the century, only for it to slip through his fingers.[56] More fundamental, however, was the plebeian impulse which always underlay the politics of the Chamberlain dynasty. The founder of the line had been drawn to Great Power prestige not least as a weapon to use against that patrician and lackadaisical Toryism – the 'House of Cecil' – with which he found himself in such uneasy harness. Subsequently the vocabulary of prestige and greatness had been largely appropriated by a new cadre of young magnates (flying under Liberal as well as Unionist colours) striking dramatic postures as men of vigour and glittering national ambition. In the wake of Joseph's death (ironically in 1914), not only did the gilt go off the gingerbread of British 'prestige' for Neville, but his intensely disillusioning wartime experience as Director of National Recruiting deeply affected his mental outlook. He escaped to be a planter in Bermuda; and after returning to political life he spurned Baldwin's offer of the Chancellorship and claimed instead the Ministry of Health[57] – just as his father had once chosen the portfolio of Colonies rather than more glamorous posts open to him. Subsequently Neville's concentration on health matters confirmed and publicized a radical focus on the intrinsically *internal* needs and interests of the United Kingdom. When he was later translated to the Exchequer he evolved an economic brand of the same philosophy, in which the reform of domestic industry became the essence of his policy, to which end he was prepared, for example, to go off the Gold Standard which others revered as the symbol of financial greatness. In so far as the evolving situation of the thirties necessarily led to a concern with foreign policy proper, Chamberlain thrashed out a set of attitudes which were wholly consonant with these main priorities. Central to his overall approach was the belief that the welfare of British society should under no circumstances be subjugated to the temptations of power politics; that the case for Great Britain as a disposing power in great Continental questions was marked not only by stupidity, but by bad faith; and that, in sum, true British interests lay in working with, not against, the grain of reality. As a later generation nears the end of the millennium, with Europe once more on the Mark Standard, the basic validity of these insights may be better appreciated than the artificial dogmas prevailing after 1939 usually allowed.

The nature of the agenda which Chamberlain was determined to set on first becoming Prime Minister was reflected in the 'cap' of £1,500 millions which he promptly put on overall defence expenditure. This was done without any precise attention to military or strategic logic; but as later experience might be said to show, if public expenditure is to be truly controlled, no real alternative exists to the imposition of somewhat arbitrary limits. A concern for economy did not prevent Chamberlain (contrary to the picture often painted of him) from being a genuine enthusiast for rearmament, providing it fitted with his increasingly supple conception of the real nature of British concerns. This led to a bias – in the public mind, as well as the Prime Minister's – towards naval rearmament. A crowd of twenty thousand people attended the launch of HMS *Ark Royal* at Birkenhead amidst scenes of Nelsonian bravura. In this connection it was symbolic that Admiralty House was refurbished by the Chamberlain Government, and the Admiralty's official yacht, *Enchantress*, taken out of the 'mothballs' she had been in ever since 1914. The latter was sent off on a string of Mediterranean inspections. 'Our visits', wrote Sam Hoare, back in harness as First Lord and evidently enjoying the jaunts, 'were the outward and visible signs of a new chapter of reviving national prestige.'[58] The revivalism of which Hoare spoke was focused in particular on the Mediterranean, and it was to this area that Chamberlain's own mind increasingly turned. Whereas, for example, the Chiefs of Staff still assumed that in a crisis that throughway would be largely vacated in order to release a 'serious' fleet for despatch to the Far East, inside the Cabinet the 'maintenance of the existing position in the Mediterranean and the Middle East' was already hardening into a dominant national principle.[59] There are intriguing anticipations here of the strategies which, in the end, Churchill and his military advisers were constrained after 1940 into making their own; but for our present purposes it is enough to note that Chamberlain's policies carried within them the insight that in the real, as opposed to merely rhetorical, world the practical limits of British belligerency as an independent great power, over and above the defence of its own shores, lay in and around the southern European sea.

If the Royal Navy was thus the favoured child of Appeasement, it followed that there were lesser roles for the Army and Royal Air Force. Financial rationing was used to strip the latter of the long-range bombing role for which it yearned, and to concentrate the mind of the higher command on short-range 'fighter' tasks. The job of the air arm, under this dispensation, was not to 'beat' anybody, but to ensure that the United Kingdom herself could not be beaten – in this respect, too, experience was to prove the wisdom of the policy. By the same token, the Army's job remained that of the imperial garrison which it had fulfilled ever since 1919, so that almost one-third of its available cadres in 1937–8 were engaged in quelling an Arab revolt in Palestine; and although the 'Continental Commitment' to France was never completely expunged from the planners' notebooks, its credibility became increasingly exiguous.[60] Yet if this defence policy was eminently coherent and even innovative, the manner of its execution often alienated Service opinion and depressed morale. In this context the promotional log-jam which had built up since the end of the Great War was a major source of disaffection; and although the Prime Minister was too canny a politician to forget the necessary tricks of his trade – the announcement of 2,500 Army promotions in August 1938 being the longest list of its kind[61] – the pressure could never be fully syphoned off. Here was one rivulet of emotion and general unhappiness which fed directly into the essentially moral crisis of Appeasement.

As far as potential obstructionism in the labyrinthine world of British administration was concerned, it was the preparedness of the Foreign Office to 'play up' which more than anything else worried Chamberlain.[62] There were many 'Foreign Office Conservatives' on the party benches in Parliament ready to be prodded into action against anything which smacked of heresy, whilst the remit of that department cut across the daily grind of politics in a way that was not true of the Services. In fact the Foreign Office was split by the fissures which Chamberlainism triggered amongst the chattering classes as a whole. 'We do not possess the means to prevent Germany from treating Austria and Czechoslovakia as satellite states', minuted one official in mid-1937, only for a colleague to annotate pointedly in the margin 'Don't we?'[63] Thus arrayed at an early stage were two views encompassing not only opposed estimations of British power, but (by implication) of the price that the United Kingdom should be willing to pay in certain circumstances to achieve the desired ends; on the one hand the doctrine, as one protagonist put it, that 'the sooner we cut our coat according to our cloth, the better it will be for the British Empire'[64], and on the other hand the conviction that the 'hard fibre' of the British nation would respond if only the politicians gave it the necessary lead. The reverberations of this debate were all the greater because the various participants could draw upon stereotypes, prejudices and genuine (but opposed) ideals which, as we have stressed, had long been current in the nation's political life.

For at least the first eighteen months of Chamberlain's premiership, however, the anti-appeasers were divided amongst themselves as to *which* European dictator should figure in their scenarios as the chief enemy. Anthony Eden, as Foreign Secretary, sought to finesse his difficult relationship with his leader by adopting a 'soft' line on Hitler, but a 'hard' line towards Mussolini – posing, as it seemed from Rome, 'as a sort of new Pitt facing the Napoleon of Italy'.[65] This was to misunderstand the premium Chamberlain now put on avoiding trouble with the latter country, situated as it was athwart the crucial axis of British power, and in February 1938 the Prime Minister more or less forced Eden out of his Cabinet by taking Anglo-Italian relations in hand himself. Eden was to be disappointed if he hoped that his anti-Italian *machismo* would win him the plaudits of the Churchill group. Members of the latter were always contemptuous of what they regarded as a diversionary ruse, and the echoes of this particular divide, as we shall see, were still to be heard in the 1950s, when the Churchillians watched with some glee as Eden's own premiership began to come apart at its Mediterranean seams. Churchill himself was adamant after 1937 that only a confrontation with Germany could provide 'the unattached flowing mass' of British opinion with 'a real awakening and a clear goal'[66], which was what, in his mind, foreign policy was all about. Against this background, one of the central features of the Czechoslovakian issue, as it concerned Britain, was that it wrenched the focus away from the erring (but increasingly tentative) Mussolini and set anti-appeasement definitively in the mould of 'facing up to Hitler'.

The larger, moral significance of Czechoslovakia for the anti-appeasers, however, derived from two further aspects. First of all, in taking up the rights of the *Sudetendeutsch* in that country, Hitler encroached up to – and beyond – the limits of the German diaspora in a way the *Anschluss* with Austria in March 1938 had not. The second, more practical, reason was that France had a treaty with Czechoslovakia dating back to 1925, and it was to arguments about the honouring of treaties that Chamberlain's opponents looked as the most likely method of pinning him down, just as the Liberal Government had been pinned down with the help of an even fustier treaty with Belgium in 1914. This was the subtle trap which the Prime Minister identified when he pointed out that if general hostilities broke out over Czechoslovakia, it would be not a war *for* the latter's freedom (since there was no way for the Western powers to ultimately affect the outcome in the matter), but the *pretext* for a war. Pre-empting the pretext was therefore the aim of the ultimately abortive Runciman Mission which Chamberlain dispatched to Prague in early August 1938 to explore an 'autonomist' solution to the problem of the Sudetenland, and, after its failure, the flurry of personal conferences in Germany the following September between the British Prime Minister and the Chancellor which are generally lumped together as the 'Munich Crisis'.

The story of Chamberlain's triple encounter with Hitler cannot detain us long.[67] At Berchtesgaden (15–16 September) the British premier thought he had extracted an agreement on a plebiscite in the Sudetenland to determine new frontiers. But when – having secured the concurrence of his own Cabinet and that of the French Government – he flew again to Germany, this time to Bad Godesberg (22–24 September), he found that the terms had hardened to include the immediate occupation of territory by Reich forces. It was, as Maurice Cowling has explained, the 'character of violence'[68] in these fresh German desiderata which created a 'moral disturbance'[69] around and within the British Government. 'Pray God may there be a revolt', wrote Alec Cadogan, who had for some time been wobbling on the central issue. 'I know they [the French] are in no condition to fight: but I'd rather be beat than dishonoured. How can we look any foreigner in the face after this? How can we hold Egypt, India and the rest.'[70] The blurring of British interests as the crisis mounted, so that the security of the British Empire was held to depend on the precise contours of Czechoslovakia's borders, was not only to undermine the edifice of Chamberlain's strategy, built as it was on finer discriminations, but to turn the logic entirely inside out.[71]

One of the intriguing aspects of the Munich crisis was the prefiguring of individuals and groups who were later to coalesce into a new regime in Britain. 'If Chamberlain rats again', Harold Nicolson summed up affairs after one council of war at the Savoy Grill, 'we shall form a united block against him. We do not think he will rat, and therefore we shall "rally behind him" (poor man). We shall press for a Coalition Government and the immediate application of war measures.'[72] Evidently not all the martial ardour of the times was abroad. But the Prime Minister did rat, or more to the point, when the French representatives came to London on 18 September he asked them what they would do if war broke out against Germany. This was precisely the question which his critics considered unnecessary and distasteful – 'Fire your cannon', was Churchill's vague prescription, 'and all will be well.'[73] Chamberlain was no more swayed by this prognosis for a 'second round' against Germany than he was by the answer to his enquiry he actually received from the French

Prime Minister – ' Each of us will do our duty.'[74] Under penetrating cross-examination in Downing Street, it appeared that the French conception of their 'duty' was to launch a few 'probing offensives' in front of the Maginot Line, whilst awaiting the arrival of Britain's Kitchener-type armies.[75] This was Chamberlain's secret weapon against the waverers within his own government: that the *only* alternative to his own policy – and the natural consequence of the exhortations of those who opposed him – was a straight-forward repeat of 1914–18. The threatened revolt collapsed, the French (whose willingness to go to war had anyway been problematic throughout) were isolated, and on 29 September Chamberlain flew to Munich where, after some stormy exchanges including the Italians as well as the Germans and British, but in which the Czechs themselves were represented only vicariously by the last of these, a treaty was signed which amputated the Sudetenland and supposedly guaranteed the rump of Czechoslovakia.

Chamberlain's key source of strength in the immediate post-Munich period was the great personal popularity which the preservation of peace had earned him. Probably his greatest mistake was to have decided against holding an immediate election (thus advised by his Foreign Secretary, Lord Halifax); had he done so, and secured the virtually certain triumph that could have been his, the covert defections from his side which soon got under way would probably have been stemmed. 'Rab' Butler, whose own loyalty to the Prime Minister never wavered, recalled in his memoirs how in the winter of 1938–9 Halifax himself began to trim, soliciting private contacts with Churchill, Eden and the Labour leaders.[76] These tendencies received an enormous boost from the German 'liquidation' of Prague on 15 March 1939. 'An explosion of public opinion', A.J.P. Taylor has referred to the impact of this event in Britain, 'such as the historian cannot trace in precise terms'.[77] It cannot be traced precisely because it did not really happen. The only explosion of British public opinion over foreign policy during the 1930s occurred over 'Hoare-Laval'; afterwards the recognition of what a war with Germany – as opposed to one with Italy over Abyssinia, for example – might bring in its wake had an understandably sobering effect on the population at large (the fact that the war of 1939–45 proved to be *less* sanguinary than that of 1914–18 being, of course, irrelevant to these fearful premonitions). The 'explosion' of feeling which Prague ignited was, in brief, parliamentary rather than popular in character, and was all the more important for being so, since governments are usually able to survive detonations (such as that in 1935) which go off *around* them, but are invariably fatally weakened by those which do so within. The measure of Chamberlain's growing weakness after March 1939 was that for the first time in his premiership he had, in effect, to share control over the administration of foreign policy, as the subsequent dispatch of guarantees to Poland, Romania and Greece may in part be said to show.[78]

A British guarantee to Poland against German aggression, quite obviously, could only be made credible by an understanding with the Soviet Union; and relations with that country emerged as a major flashpoint between the Chamberlainites and their varied opponents during the final stage of the Appeasement saga. A.J.P. Taylor, indeed, remarks that the real historic significance of the diplomatic events of this time lay principally in the emergence of the Soviet Union as a Great Power capable of arbitrating the fate of much of Europe.[79] True as this may be, there was nothing preordained about the outcome, and it was always inherent in the thesis of Appeasement that Britain had nothing to gain from 'saving' Eastern Europe with Russian bayonets. Desultory Anglo-Soviet military talks tailed off in the summer of 1939, finally cut rudely short by the 'Hitler-Stalin Pact' of 23 August. Meanwhile, a surge of pro-Sovietism in Britain acted as a screen behind which the discontented Right and the discontented Left could begin at last to draw together. This accommodation was helped considerably by the rhetorical likeness of the twin conceptions of the Balance of Power and Collective Security, so that a diverse group of politicians could link up without departing from their respective ideological attachments. The Labour Party, anyway, was in no position to be fussy about labels – or, indeed, about the identity of its friends. After

1931 that party had been converted into what has been aptly called an 'office-seeking intelligentsia'[80]; by the summer of 1939 not only had its leaders become soured, as all factions are in such circumstances, by a long and lean period of opposition, but they were deeply afraid that Chamberlain was about to spring upon them an election which, since they had no chance of winning it, was likely to kill off altogether the prospect of 'office in their time'. 'In truth, Labour by the end of the 1930s', Paul Addison has written in one of the few accounts to penetrate this murky period, 'was looking to one wing of the Conservatives to save them from the other.'[81] Chamberlain was well aware that the chief danger to his own position lay in a parliamentary censure which would forge together (however temporarily) an excitable mass of Socialists, Tory *ultras* and the inevitable waverers and opportunists. This was the unusual British chemistry set off, first by Hitler's pressure on the Free City of Danzig, and finally by his invasion of Poland on 1 September 1939.

The details of this final crisis we may pass over, except to note that throughout Chamberlain was on the look-out – as during the Czech difficulties of the previous summer – for some peg on which to hang a negotiation.[82] It was only two days *after* the German troops had crossed the Polish frontier that the Prime Minister finally went down to the House of Commons, and when he did so it was not to announce the expected ultimatum to Germany, but to float the possibility of the United Kingdom being 'associated' with talks to bring the present hostilities to an end. What followed was the fusing of parliamentary elements he had long dreaded. Thus amidst the hubbub one of the Labour leaders, Arthur Greenwood, rose from his seat, to be greeted by Leopold Amery, arguably the most arch anti-Socialist of his generation, with the words 'Speak for England'. Greenwood did as he was bade by his unlikely comrade-in-arms, and in the remarkable euphoria which ensued Appeasement effectively evaporated as a political force. 'There was no doubt', Churchill later wrote of this debate, 'that the temper of the House was for war. I deemed it even more resolute and united than in the similar scene of August 3rd, 1914.'[83]

There was one aspect, however, in which August 1914 and September 1939 were marked by a significant difference elided by Churchill's description. On the former occasion the British had debated whether or not to *follow* France into a war which the latter was clearly determined to wage vigorously anyway. In September 1939 it was France who held back, and was, in essence, pulled in the British wake. This was a rather different basis on which to go to war with Germany over the fate of a third party situated (not, as in 1914, in the Low Countries) on the thither side of Europe. Time was to show what the implications of such a distinction might be.

The Elusive Triumph

The Second World War, John Vincent has written, was, for Britain, 'the right people's war . . . The last great achievement of an imperial ruling class'[1], and the insight throws light on why it was that the experience became such a potent reference point in British political life thereafter. Thus Lord Lloyd, whose latest task had been the mock-proconsular one of establishing the British Council, wrote excitedly to his son shortly after the outbreak of hostilities that he harboured '. . . a most confident assurance that the war is going to mean not only life but a great avenue to success – I think all is coming your way'[2]; and so for many like the younger Lloyd, or like Widmerpool in Anthony Powell's *roman-fleuve*, *A Dance to the Music of Time*, it undoubtedly proved. But if the Second World War represented a social as well as national apotheosis ('the Finest Hour'), it also resulted in the United Kingdom's effective insolvency, and grossly attenuated her claims to be a truly independent Great Power. This darker side of the picture has received a remarkably gloomy portrayal in Correlli Barnett's study *The Audit of War*[3], in which all the tell-tale signs of Britain's later sclerosis as a modern capitalist society are held to be identifiable during, and indeed to have been accentuated by, the war. The fact that what was the central, defining experience of the British people during the twentieth century should be simultaneously its greatest achievement and the cause of subsequent failure indicates a complexity which, being sociological as well as merely diplomatic in its meanings, historians have only recently begun to unravel.

In fact the anticipatory excitements attending the outbreak of war in September 1939 were soon curbed, for it became apparent that there was to be a striking departure from the pattern of 1914: to wit, that the continentals themselves did not feel very much like fighting – except, that is, the Russians, who swiftly gobbled up eastern Poland (combining with Germany in what was effectively a programme of joint-genocide), and then fell upon the Finns. Hitler evidently had no immediate thought of invading the West, whilst the French satisfied themselves by promenading in front of their fortifications. In Britain, welcome though the breathing-space might be in some respects, it also meant that second thoughts were apt to intervene, with all the uneasiness this induced. A sure signal of such an awkward proclivity was that Halifax began to trim once more, asking the Permanent Secretary of the Foreign Office, for example, what Britain's war aims now actually amounted to. Alec Cadogan noted in his diary:

> I told him I saw awful difficulties. We can no longer say "evacuate Poland" without going to war with Russia, which we don't want to do! I suppose the cry is "abolish Hitlerism". What if Hitler hands over to Goering? Meanwhile what of the course of operations? What if Germany now sits tight? What do we do? Build up our armaments feverishly? What for? . . . Must try to think this out . . .[4]

Clearly the 'phoney war' (as this interim is pejoratively known to history) was a puzzling experience for Britain's nascent war establishment. Meanwhile, it followed that amidst these confusions Neville Chamberlain's stock as Prime Minister began to recover. He had, perforce, to let Churchill into the war ministry as First Lord of the Admiralty, and Eden too, though the latter only in a half-job as Secretary of State for Dominions. Chamberlain, none the less, was able to give an 'irritated snort' when Churchill tried to advance the claims of his clients such as Leopold Amery[5], and the long 'tail' of the latter's supporters continued to be kept frustrated and jobless. The gulf between the two schools of English Toryism remained as wide as ever:

'vulgar beyond words' was all that could be said by one Downing Street aide of a tub-thumping, raucous broadcast by Churchill.[6]

How, then, might we sum up Chamberlain's intentions at this point? That wizened observer of Downing Street affairs, Thomas Jones, found him 'costive and dull and talks of endurance and victory in the most defeatist terms'.[7] This passivity sprang naturally from Chamberlain's belief that since the war could not be won, there was no sense in striving excessively to fight it; the best to be hoped for was the avoidance of defeat – a point about which the Prime Minister was always confident – and thus a return to the negotiating table. Nor were such assumptions necessarily misplaced. Field Marshal Lord Alanbrooke, later Chief of the Imperial General Staff, for example, was quite clear in his own mind that, up to December 1941, a strategy to *win* the war simply had not existed, after which the Americans invented one.[8] By then Chamberlain was dead, which perhaps was just as well, since a conflict in which the United Kingdom became progressively squeezed between the United States and the Soviet Union on the one hand, and Germany on the other, was one which he could not easily have reconciled with his preconceptions as to the nature of British national interests. In short, after September 1939 Chamberlain calculated (and hoped) that the war might fizzle out as suddenly as it had ignited. To this extent his war policy always retained the impress of Munich.

Against this background it follows that the Prime Minister (like Herbert Asquith in comparable circumstances) sought to preserve as much 'normalcy' and flexibility as possible. This involved turning Trade Union leaders – who were quick to spot the advantages which 'consultation' might give them – away from the door of 10 Downing Street. It also meant being unmoved by letters to *The Times* from such assorted luminaries as Arthur Salter, Walter Layton and Maynard Keynes calling – in the idiom of planning – for an 'economic general staff', a War Cabinet 'on the Lloyd George model' and a 'Ministry for Economic Co-ordination'.[9] Chamberlain's immobility barred the way to these interventionist ideals, just as Asquith had earlier obstructed the rich panoply of the 'machinery of war'. His critics, inside and outside the Government, sought for ways around the impasse, criticism focusing on such items as the omission to retaliate against 'so-called Eire' (as Churchill referred to that country) for her neutrality[10], and the modest build-up of the British Expeditionary Force (BEF) in France. In particular, those who favoured a more active stance looked about for an opportunity to tilt the balance of events; and their glance fell upon Norway. The ostensible rationale for a strike at the northern Norwegian port of Narvik – in which Chamberlain only reluctantly concurred – was to stem the flow of iron ore to Germany, although the desire to gain some leverage over Scandinavian neutrality was also part of the inspiration. Whatever the motive, the plan was speedily nullified by the pre-emptive action of Hitler in invading both Denmark and Norway on 9 April. Anglo-French forces were rushed to Trondheim, but they lacked any air cover (a complication Chamberlain had earlier pointed out), and were humiliatingly evicted on 3 May. Sporadic fighting continued around Narvik, where troops had also been dispatched in fulfilment of the original scenario, but there, too, the Anglo-French command had to be withdrawn on 9 June, defeated more by the cold than anything else. By then, however, British politics had been transformed.

A striking facet of the British parliamentary *coup* of 9 May 1940 which finally brought Chamberlain's premiership to a close was its resemblance to the similar occurrence of 15 May 1915, when the Liberal Government had fallen. The likeness did not go unnoticed. 'It's 1915 over again', 'Chips' Channon remarked in his diary[11] as the air became thick with calls for a leadership imbued with the necessary 'war spirit'. In this regard it was ironic, as many were to comment both at the time and after, that the bungled campaign which, in effect, elevated Churchill to the highest office in the land was one he himself was responsible for (his 'rampages' at the Admiralty as the crisis unfolded reminding some long-serving officials forcibly of similar tantrums during the Dardanelles disaster).[12] None the less, it was the House of Commons which dispensed power, and in that arena the finer points of administrative competence or military strategy were not relevant. It was Chamberlain who found himself under fire for the course recent events had taken, and although Churchill vouchsafed 'complete loyalty' to his chief (again, just as Lloyd George had once done to Asquith) the appropriate leaks of the First Lord's general unhappiness with the status quo were enough to keep the backbenches on the boil. During the crucial debate in the Commons Churchill stood by Chamberlain throughout, but since one of his own private secretariat did not take this at its face value, it can be presumed that nobody else did either.[13]

The parallelism between the parliamentary events of May 1940 and May 1915 was so uncanny in one particular respect that it merits remark, not because it indicates any greater degree of manipulation than naturally attends any struggle for political leadership, but because it throws light on the nature of the emotions at work. In 1915 the *coup de grâce* to the Liberal Government had been delivered by a combination of Tory war-patriotism and navalist sentiment exploiting Jacky Fisher's act of protest in deserting his post as First Sea Lord. In 1940 something very akin to Fisher's starring role was taken by another – even more consciously antediluvian – Admiral, Sir Roger Keyes, whose professed philosophy was 'the Restoration of Sea-Power'.[14] Keyes, a retired sexagenarian, had previously gone personally to 10 Downing Street and demanded the naval command for the Trondheim operation. He had been refused by Chamberlain, and retired to his rural constituency in Devon to nurse his grievance. When during the fateful debate over Norway, the Liberal leader, Sir Archibald Sinclair, was winding up his acrid remarks on the Government, Keyes strode into the Chamber in the full dress uniform of a Fleet Admiral, sporting six rows of medals, and proceeded to deliver a vitriolic attack on the Prime Minister which purported to come from the 'fighting men' of the Royal Navy.[15] Only younger tribunes in the House could have misconstrued the scene that was being re-enacted; and if in retrospect this particular episode in the proceedings seems to verge on farce, and even at the time had a symbolic rather than substantive importance, the undercurrents were none the less powerful. When the vote was called after Keyes' intervention, the Government won only a thin majority, which in the circumstances was universally regarded as a moral defeat. 'As soon as the figures were announced', Martin Gilbert relates, 'the Labour M.P., Josiah Wedgewood, led the Government's opponents in the singing of "Rule Britannia". But even this unprecedented demonstration was drowned in cries of "Go! Go! Go!" directed at Chamberlain as he left the Chamber.'[16]

Nelsonian reaction, Socialist ultra-patriotism, a great gust of Tory *schadenfreude* – this was the curious but not wholly unprecedented combination which now set the scene for a new Coalition in a nation which was reputed not to love them as a constitutional form. Admitting the force of circumstances, Chamberlain approached the Labour leaders, and when they predictably refused to serve under him, but welcomed the opportunity to do so under an alternative Conservative figure, the choice lay between Halifax and Churchill. The story has often been retold of how, in the fateful interview, the outgoing premier asked Churchill whom he might advise the King to send for; a long silence ensued, after which Halifax drew his own conclusions and retired from the contest. Only Churchill, in truth, could deliver the balance of parliamentary support on which the new patchwork ministry would rest, and his silence betokened that he would deliver it to nobody other than himself. The First Lord of the Admiralty went to the Palace and came back still a First Lord, but this time of the Treasury. His trip up the Mall inaugurated a more profound transition than is usually the case when one Prime Minister gives way to another, despite the fact that this handover was ostensibly one between members of the same political party. 'I spent the day in a bright blue suit from the fifty shilling tailor', John Colville, a Downing Street habitué, recalled the feeling of not a few 'insiders' at the time, 'cheap and sensational looking, which I felt appropriate to the new Government.'[17]

Paul Addison has discussed in an absorbing study the broader significance of the political *bouleversement* of May 1940 in

British affairs.[18] The critical divide amongst the political cadres had for some while come to lie between different branches of Conservatism; Liberals and Socialists simply waited on the sidelines to see what scraps might come their way. On one side of the chasm was a prudential, economistic and 'respectable' Toryism which for many years had recrudesced around Baldwin, but which rapidly changing circumstances had forced his successor to hammer into a more coherent and ruthless programme – a programme infused by an ideology which Maurice Cowling has nicely summarized in the caption 'Civic Radicalism'.[19] The moving spirit of this philosophy was that the British state and society would never regain the equipoise of their Victorian forebears until a sustainable and realistic balance between domestic priorities and external responsibilities had been restored to the heart of the governing process. On the other side was, in Addison's portrayal of this situation, the 'rugged, leonine patriotism of the 1914 school'[20], whose core belief was that the nation should be scaled up to meet the responsibilities, not that the responsibilities should be curtailed to fit the nation. This was a doctrine of adventure, or 'pluck', which came to rest pre-eminently in the personality of Churchill himself; and it was arguably of some practical, as well as merely symbolic, importance that during the controversy over Appeasement Churchill had written an apologia for the exploits of his ancestor, the Duke of Marlborough, whose contribution to British greatness had been to plant his standard so forthrightly on the banks of the Danube. What made the clash between these forces so promethean was not only, then, the precise stakes implicit in contemporary developments in *Mitteleuropa*, but the fact that the latter issue had become inextricably interwoven with other, more deep-seated, differences within the British polity itself. The historic domestic transition of May 1940 thus involved not only a change of personnel at the top; it automatically implied a shift in the basic values and instincts behind British statecraft as a whole. The approach was soon put to the first of its tests, for on 10 May Hitler's *blitzkrieg* on western Europe had begun.

The events surrounding the Fall of France in the early summer of 1940 are self-evidently the main pivot of French history in the twentieth century; less recognized is the degree to which they constituted a principal rupture in British developments as well. Since the opening years of the century, the United Kingdom's conception of her own power and influence in Continental affairs had hinged on being able to work through the instrumentality of France; and although, as a *quid pro quo*, this had meant giving France a matching access to British diplomacy and force, the subscription had been paid, albeit often in a grudging spirit. No English politician was more intensely loyal to this connection than Winston Churchill. During the 1930s, for example, the latter went to America when he needed to earn money on the lecture circuit; when he wanted to be truly happy he joined the French Army on its annual manoeuvres.[21] Thus it was not merely an ally which 'went under' in 1940; it was also a method, one might say an emotion, of British foreign policy. By the time the mass evacuations of Dunkirk and Cherbourg were complete, the United Kingdom had effectively been evicted bag and baggage from the neighbouring land mass. German military dominance was not the only factor which ensured that (psychologically at least) she long remained so.

No version of what happened at this historic juncture, of course, can possess a monopoly of truth.[22] The orthodox British rendering came to be characterized by a bluff straightforwardness – in fact, the archetypal British Second World War style. Thus it was pointed out that the British Expeditionary Force (BEF) under General Gort had taken its place 'in the line' during September 1939. Preparations were made to expand it, conscription (in contrast to the First World War) having been introduced in Britain even before the conflict began. When the German *blitzkrieg* erupted, it was the United Kingdom's allies who buckled. The enemy's panzer divisions swept through the Ardennes and into Belgium, Holland and Luxembourg, pulling French forces into the northern 'gap' in their defences. At this point much depended on the Belgians, but King Leopold prematurely sued for an armistice, leaving the British formations

– who had moved up in support – dreadfully exposed. Even then all need not have been lost if only another 'Miracle on the Marne' had intervened. On this occasion, however, the French Army became enveloped, despite exhortations from London, in a paralysing defeatism as the fighting spread. Finally, the imminent closing of the jaws of the German advance made it absolutely necessary for the BEF to retreat to the coast, from whence its disembarkation was completed on 4 June. Unfortunately, amidst the confusion much of the French Army congregated on the beaches got left behind in the British exodus.

Whilst this drama was unfolding in northern France, Churchill and his military advisers flew several times to meet their French counterparts behind the main fronts, begging them to continue to resist, and promising British help funnelled through the southern ports. But as the defeatist shadow of General Pétain spread, grim realities had had to be faced. Principally this meant refusing to commit the Royal Air Force to the Battle of France, in order to conserve it for the Battle of Britain. Hence the United Kingdom retreated into her island fortress, the residual trustee for the freedom of Europe. Most sadly of all, however, the new regime crystallizing in Vichy appeared intent on suing for a separate peace with Germany, an exercise in which – since they had few other bargaining chips at their disposal – they were bound to dangle the bait of their marine. It was from this imminent likelihood that there sprang the necessity for the Royal Navy's lightning attack on the French fleet in Oran on 3 July (killing 1,250 French sailors in nine minutes of firing). This was the only occasion in British history when her guns had been turned on a defeated ally. That ordinary Frenchmen appreciated the *raison d'état*, however, was said to be illustrated by the fact (of which no photographs are extant) that the mariners' coffins were disembarked at Toulon draped in the Union Jack.[23]

Viewed from Vichy (or even from Toulon) things tended to be seen in a different light. Despite their own hesitations, the French had followed in the wake of the British ultimatum in September 1939, assuming that their entente partner was prepared to make the same sacrifices on land as she had after

1914. Yet from the start the BEF had exhibited disturbing traits. General Gort set up his Headquarters suspiciously close to the sea. As the fighting spread, British reinforcements were unaccountably slow in appearing. Thus when, at the peak of the crisis, Churchill called for a last-ditch resistance like that of March 1918, Marshal Pétain scathingly pointed out that on the earlier occasion there had been *twenty-four* British divisions to be sent into the fray – a comparison not becoming to the relatively puny BEF of 1940.[24] The more dire the situation became, the closer Gort's commanders loitered anxiously by the exit; and when the decision was finally made to bolt, not only was it taken without consultation with the French and Belgians, it was at first not even communicated to them. Under these distressing circumstances, King Leopold sued for peace in order to stop the needless devastation of his people, and whilst that monarch subsequently became the butt of official British scorn, his own valour and that of his troops during the hostilities of 1940 have since received their due. Wherever the balance of truth lies in these tragic convolutions, one thing was plain: when the small boats had ceased their plying, the reputation that Gort's army left behind them was more equivocal than that which lay ahead.

At the heart of this saga lay the critical fact that the British Army had no intention of allowing itself to be sacrificed like their 'old contemptible' predecessors of 1914–15. The high command in London, therefore, may initially have clung to the traditional belief that the 'first line' could never be anywhere other than across the Channel, but in the BEF, where the dying had to be done, priorities were apt to take on a different complexion. One index of this was its characteristically pejorative assessment of the French. 'I can still see those [French] troops now', the then General Brooke recalled of his experiences as commanding officer of II Corps during 1940. 'Seldom have I seen anything more slovenly and badly turned out. Men unshaven, horses ungroomed, clothes and sadlery that did not fit, vehicles dirty, and complete lack of pride in themselves or their units.'[25] Yet it was precisely such scenes of *déshabillé* which had been lauded during the Great War as the honourable badge of 'patriotic

France'.[26] In short, by 1940 it was not the French Army which had changed – dirty harness and all – but the preparedness of the British soldiers to participate to the hilt in its travails.

It was air power, however, which cut most painfully across the tottering entente. As one British observer noted of Air Marshal Dowding, for example, the latter consistently appeared 'very much inclined to regard himself as outside operations in France'.[27] At the Anglo-French conferences already referred to – arguably the most dramatic of all the 'top tables' that any British leadership sat at during the twentieth century – it was the commitment of the RAF's reserves to the struggle that the French representatives most warmly demanded. The final break came at Briare on 10 June. 'Here', General Weygand implored Churchill, 'is the decisive point. Now is the decisive moment. The British ought not to keep a single fighter [aircraft] in England.'[28] The British Prime Minister's entourage held bated breath lest Churchill's innate loyalty to France outweigh all other considerations. 'Thank God', his Chief of Staff, General Ismay, remembered the episode, 'my fears were groundless. After a pause, and speaking very slowly, he [Churchill] said "This is not the decisive point. This is not the decisive moment. The decisive moment will come when Hitler hurls his *Luftwaffe* against Britain. If we keep command over our own island . . . we will win it all back for you".'[29] Yet for most Frenchmen the decisive point was France, and the decisive moment the imminence of her defeat. Nor, once the English drawbridge was pulled up, was it easy to believe that the island race would willingly come back into the continental fray, an apprehension which to a not inconsiderable extent was to be borne out by events. Later developments and attitudes were, of course, to play their part in ensuring that relations between Britain and France remained cool for virtually the rest of the century, but the 'iron in the soul' which attended the separation of 1940 may be said to have set the lawyer's seal on a document of divorce. It was, as one study has called it, the 'End of an Affair', and as in many such partings the anger and the scorn never entirely evaporated.

Meanwhile it was inevitable that this turbulent passage should have powerful effects in British politics as well. At first the aftermath of Dunkirk witnessed the revival of 'peace talk'. 'I can't work with Winston any more' the mercurial Halifax moaned anew[30], and although Churchill's martial addresses in the House of Commons continued to be met by the effusions of the Labour Party, for whom office in the existing Coalition constituted the best of all possible worlds, elsewhere there were signs of renewed reserve. These were to be finally excised, however, by the brief cannonade which sank the French fleet. When the news of that episode reached the lower chamber, there was an unparalleled explosion of approbation. This mystified some observers. 'I still don't know what it was all about'[31] noted a bemused on-looker, for whom the occasion rather appeared one of profound melancholy, if not actually of shame. Yet this was to miss the essential point. The attack at Oran meant that for the United Kingdom there could be no going back, no negotiated peace with Germany, no Vichy English-style. As such, it fused the Coalition once and for all into a real war administration, the various constituencies within which accepted that they would have to sink or swim together. Although subsequently Churchill's own position was not to be entirely without threat at moments of crisis from those who saw themselves as alternative war leaders[32], after July 1940 the road to a compromise peace was, for Britain, roped off.

Parallel to the British repulsion from Europe there went, logically enough, a turn to the United States; indeed, political Anglo-Saxonism in many ways may be said to have been finally consummated by the Fall of France (which was why Charles de Gaulle, enemy of Vichy though he was, hated the phenomenon with such passion). 'I think I can see my way through', Churchill summed up the dilemma in the dark days of June to his son, Randolph, '. . . I shall drag in the United States.'[33] This was to prove easier said than done. The first requirement was to establish British belligerency in American eyes as a paying proposition. The outcome of the Battle of Britain – by proving the United Kingdom's invulnerability to defeat – in the late summer of 1940 helped this process along. The critical departure in Anglo-American relations, however, came the following January with the visit to London of Roosevelt's personal emissary, Harry Hopkins. Not only did Hopkins see 'all the books', which Churchill ordered his aides should be made available without any reserve, he went up to the roof of Chequers during a supper party and watched the capital burning from afar during an air-raid.[34] The books, and the burning, convinced him of something that hitherto American opinion had found hard to credit: that the British were resolutely bent on continuing the war against Germany. Hopkins advised Roosevelt accordingly, and in March 1941 the Lend-Lease Bill was passed by Congress, providing – in tandem with the Mutual Aid Agreement between the two governments – the financial framework for Anglo-American co-operation during the following years.

A.J.P. Taylor has described the Mutual Aid Agreement as the most decisive departure in modern British history, since it legislated the United Kingdom's status as a permanent pensioner of another power.[35] Debits and credits have changed since Taylor made this observation, but the analysis still retains some force. Under Article VII of the Agreement Britain was precluded from using materials acquired (even indirectly) under Lend-Lease for the purpose of manufacturing for export and hence for the support of civilian industries in general. The United Kingdom was thus to be fully mobilized as a war economy, the bottlenecks being kept open by American gifts. During the 1914–18 War, for all its inevitable distortions of commerce, the British economy had never been completely taken off an 'export basis', if only because the United Kingdom had needed to earn the wherewithal to subsidize her own junior allies. In 1941 Churchill, once the Gold Standard Chancellor, cut this Gordian knot, so that by 1944 British exports had fallen to 34% of the figure for 1938, the year of Munich.[36] Ironically, therefore, in forging a putative 'special relationship' with the greatest free-enterprise nation in the world, Britain adopted for herself the principles of the command economy; the first Keynesian Budget in a long line of such Budgets was, indeed, that introduced in March 1941 by the Chancellor of the Exchequer, Kingley Wood.[37] The logic of political economy this shortly entrenched in the United Kingdom was, as Correlli Barnett has lamented, to be far too powerful to reverse when the shooting stopped, even by those governments which might theoretically have wished to do so.

Apart from the progress made towards a preliminary understanding with the United States, the period following the Fall of France was significant for the gradual evolution of the operational strategy to which the United Kingdom subsequently cleaved with great singlemindedness for the rest of the war. This was pre-eminently a strategy in the Mediterranean, triggered initially by the accession of Italy to the fray in the aftermath of the French capitulation, and then by the excursion of her troops across the Libya-Egypt border the following September. The strongest early pointer in this regard was the fact that even at the height of the Battle of Britain, when the possibility of a German invasion of England had yet to be fully discounted, precious cargoes of American tanks were being diverted to Alexandria. The remarkable plasticity of British strategic conceptions at this juncture, indeed, was evident in the way that the 'decisive place' could thus shift almost in the twinkling of an eye from northern France to the skies over Britain and finally to the Levant. As Michael Howard has observed, from mid-1940 onwards Egypt became a British imperial war-base second only in importance to the United Kingdom itself.[38]

From whence arose this Mediterranean bias, which subsequently came to generate, as we shall see, a good deal of suspicion as to the true nature of British war aims? Here again there are suggestive parallels between the British experience in the First and Second World Wars. Thus Lloyd George's search for 'compensation' in 1917–18 had drawn him inexorably towards the eastern Mediterranean. The defeat of France in 1940 meant that Churchill did not labour long under the delusion that Britain would prove any more successful on the Continent of Europe this time round. Simultaneously, Italy had pushed herself into the martial reckoning; and Italy after June 1940 – like Turkey after November 1914 – was a Power whom the United Kingdom, it was assumed, could indubitably defeat. In brief, the ensuing struggle in the Mediterranean was one which it was within Britain's capacity to wage without excessive strain militarily, and which also held out hopes of that flow of successes and spoils which are, perforce, the blood and bone of any war regime. As a consequence, this was the struggle which the Churchill Coalition and its military staffs were to insist on conducting even when its allies, once they made their appearance, began to question the actual *strategic* purpose of the exercise.

The ideal British strategy in the Mediterranean, furthermore, was always one which included Greece within its sway; a formal guarantee to that country had been one of the markers denoting Britain's shift away from Appeasement after March 1939. The growing Axis pressure on the southern Balkans from October 1940 onwards (with Greece at first fending off an Italian invasion, but only at considerable cost) was thus bound to evoke strong reactions in London. To this extent David Carlton's ascription of the British decision to intervene in Greece during March 1941 to the need of Anthony Eden, back in harness as Foreign Secretary, to live up to his reputation for 'vigour and valour' is unduly confined in its judgement.[39] The effect of this ill-fated initiative was merely to invite – *pace* the earlier Norwegian venture – an even more powerful counter by Germany, whose armies in a fast-moving campaign drove first into Yugoslavia, and then into northern Greece itself. On 16 April 1941 General Wavell, the British Commander-in-Chief in the Middle East, was constrained to order British troops out of the Peloponnese; the following day Yugoslavia sued for an armistice; and on 20 May German airborne troops descended upon Crete, inflicting a devastating defeat on its British Commonwealth defenders, themselves bereft of air support. In fact the recovery of Greece was never to be far from Churchill's mind thereafter, just as that country had so preoccupied Lloyd George after 1916 (and for essentially the same reasons). Meanwhile, the complete excision of a British presence, military and diplomatic, from the Balkans, coming on top of her eviction from western Europe, meant that the United Kingdom's only significant purchase in land warfare was limited to the southern littoral of the Mediterranean. It was by this process of strategic reduction that Cairo was confirmed as the 'overseas capital' for Britain's war leadership, so that afterwards its official entourages – as one recent social study has evocatively illustrated – were in almost constant perambulation through the crowded thoroughfares of that city, with consequences for Anglo-Egyptian relations at a variety of levels that were to prove far from happy.[40]

Even this crucial refuge was soon put at risk, with the arrival in Tripoli of a newly-formed Afrika Korps under General Erwin Rommel in February 1941, and the considerable tactical skill he proceeded to display in exploiting the diversion of British Commonwealth troops from North Africa to the Greek theatre. Thus although British forces had initially swept their Italian adversaries back across Cyrenaica, taking the important prize of Tobruk in so doing, Rommel soon succeeded in reversing this direction of movement; and while Tobruk itself remained at this stage in the hands of a tenacious British Commonwealth garrison, the Afrika Korp's drive eventually carried it up to, and then across, the Egyptian frontier. Amidst these roller-coaster events, in which initial heady success was followed by renewed threats of disaster, the situation in North Africa in general, and the security of Egypt in particular, emerged as a major test by which British public opinion came to judge the course and conduct of the war.[41] For this reason the urgency of Churchill's requirement for a counter-offensive by his commanders in the zone, and the propensity of the soldiers for cautious consolidation rather than a premature surge across the treacherous desert, proved a source of explosive criticism and resentment on all sides. In such circumstances Churchill's instinct was always, as he liked to put it, to 'show his power', and in June 1941 – following the disappointment of 'Operation Battleaxe' – he abruptly dismissed General Wavell from his position in the Middle East, sending him to 'sit under a pagoda tree' as Commander-in-Chief in India (where he eventually succeeded as Viceroy).[42] As we shall see, the Prime Minister's anxieties regarding North Africa were not to be solved by a single change of personnel, but the action underlined just how critical success in this sphere had become for the prestige and possibly even the political survival of the government in London.

If the British venture into Greece was the source of much temporary mischief, however, it was afterwards accorded an *ex post facto* justification: by delaying Germany's invasion of Russia to June 1941 it condemned 'Operation Barbarossa' to the winter snows, and so contributed signally to the ultimate outcome of the war. More recently, historians have been sceptical as to the efficacy of the links between the relative skirmishes fought in the Mediterranean and the gigantism of modern war as it was expressed on the flatlands of the Ukraine. What is not in doubt is that June 1941 represented a critical turning point in the Second World War which tilted the odds against Germany. Yet at the time the Soviet Union's entry into the war gave Churchill a very bad moment. Neville Chamberlain's past injunctions against entering into an alliance with Stalin had struck a genuinely popular chord; above all, the departure was one which went so entirely against the grain of much Conservative sentiment that it had the potential to smash the delicate compromises on which the incumbent ministry was based. That it was the political, rather than military, implications of 'Barbarossa' which first preoccupied the Prime Minister is indicated by the fact that when woken to be told the news, his first instinct was not to call together his Service advisers, but to set afoot the preparation of his script for the BBC.[43] Listeners who recalled the 'raving' anti-Bolshevik of 1919 must have been bemused (or at least amused) that night to hear Churchill's eulogy of 'the thousand villages of Russia . . . where maidens laugh and children play'[44], but the tone of discourse was thus established and before long the Anglo-Soviet alliance became knit into the wartime fabric. None the less, not even the ritual circuit of the 'Sword of Stalingrad' through the thousand villages of England could subsequently dispel entirely the fact that for some people (many Tories especially) the link-up with the Bolshevik dictator – whose own misdeeds were certainly not less, and arguably more, striking than those of Hitler – was a moment of bitter gall indeed.

In fact it may be doubted whether British opinion could for long have been reconciled to a war in which the United Kingdom was teamed up alone with the Soviet Union against the great mass of hostile or neutral Europe in between. For this reason the United Kingdom's need for the outright participation of the United States to even up the political and moral logic became much greater *after* June 1941 than it had been before. The problem was that at the same time opinion in America became progressively less willing to go beyond its financial and logistical assistance conveyed under the Lend-Lease agreement. During 1941, the British mercenary, as it were, having signed up to do the actual fighting against Germany, Congress legislated a *reduction* in overall defence expenditures. Increasingly the only likelihood of this drift being reversed lay not in Europe at all, but in the Far East, where American interests and prestige were more explicitly at stake. At this point our narrative touches on imponderables which have always been shrouded in a good deal of mystery, and will remain so. In a recent manifestation of the perennial controversy over the outbreak of hostilities in the Pacific, it has been alleged that the British possessed foreknowledge of the impending Japanese attack on the American Fleet in Hawaii's Pearl Harbor, which took place on 7 December 1941, but kept it discreetly to themselves and waited confidently for the moment when the Americans would thus be 'bounced' into war alongside them.[45] Against this, it may be said to have been highly unlikely that Churchill, who fully appreciated that Roosevelt had it in his power to make or break the British war effort, would have taken such a risk with American goodwill. Yet there is undoubtedly an underlying sense in which the British came to look upon the rapid deterioration in Far Eastern security from the middle of 1940 onwards as at worst something of a mixed blessing, since it did not escape their comprehension that the only way of getting off the hook of an unwinnable war in Europe was to see it swallowed up in a *world* war, in which the United States' involvement reworked the odds. Paradoxically, therefore, although during the 1930s British strategic planners had agonized over the awful prospect of a simultaneous 'two-front' war in Europe and East

Asia, once this 'nightmare' eventually dawned it was greeted in Whitehall, and certainly by Churchill himself, as nothing less than the harbinger of salvation. After all, what mattered almost as much as beating Hitler, was the company one kept in doing so.

Before turning to the era of the Grand Alliance between Britain and the United States after December 1941, however, a brief comment should be made on that apogee of the English social commonwealth when the United Kingdom 'stood alone' against Nazism. 'It is difficult to think politically or socially – in classes – any more', Churchill remarked on this phenomenon. 'There is a warmth pervading England.'[46] Nothing could better exemplify how the fight against Hitlerism jelled with the essentially Edwardian idyll of an integrated and disciplined nation, from which all class feeling had been expunged. The most striking test of the legitimacy which sprang from this climactic achievement came when the premier toured the smashed terraces of the East End working-class and was cheered to the echo. 'It was good of you to come, Winnie', a local denizen called out on one recorded occasion. 'We thought you'd come. We can take it. Give it 'em back.'[47] It is true that a 1940s Cockney who greets a visitor with 'It was good of you to come' is not entirely persuasive in the role, and stories leaked out where sympathetic dignitaries were abused by East Enders who felt that, whatever might be true in other quarters, this was not their finest hour. Yet the fact remains that such idealizations were authentic in so far as they effectively blended with the national culture, even if the blending was largely done by the modern cadre of news-managers to which the Second World War gave rise. This is remarkable testimony, as Paul Addison has written, to how little class-consciousness has counted in the final analysis of twentieth-century British politics.[48]

Whilst Churchill was certainly justified in his related prediction that the present hostilities were 'the sort of war which would suit the English people once they got used to it'[49], the equilibrium was only likely to last so long as the cost did not prove excessively sanguinary; in short, so long as nothing very much happened.

After December 1941 a great deal was to happen, and if the escalation of a European War into a showdown of incipient world superpowers got Churchillian England off one hook, it was, before long, only to pinion it on another.

London's relief at America's enforced entry into hostilities was quickly tempered by the military disasters which overcame British arms in south-east Asia. On 10 December the Royal Navy battleships *Repulse* and *Prince of Wales*, which had been rushed to the area as the tension rose prior to Pearl Harbor, were caught in the open sea and sunk by Japanese dive-bombers. Meanwhile the Japanese Army had effected a surprise landing at Kotu Bahru on the northern 'neck' of the Malayan peninsula, pushed its way south against rapidly disintegrating resistance and received the capitulation of Singapore on 15 January 1942. This was generally reckoned to be the most shattering imperial military defeat since General Cornwallis's surrender at Yorktown in 1781, and the very ease with which it had been inflicted – the seeming lack of 'heroics' on the part of the defenders, despite a personal injunction from the Prime Minister himself to 'fight to the last man' – caused a great deal of heart-searching. Afterwards a biting critique of old-fashioned, amateurish and allegedly indulgent colonial administration was poured out in books bearing such titles as *Post-Mortem on Malaya*.[50] It was the naval losses, however, which mattered as much (and really more) than those on land. 'It means', the Chief of the Imperial General Staff declared, 'that from Africa eastwards to America through the Indian Ocean and Pacific, we have lost command of the sea.'[51] If a symbolic date is needed for the final liquidation of British aspirations to naval mastery on a global scale – exceedingly tenuous though such aspirations had been for some years – the sinking of *Repulse* and the *Prince of Wales* may be said to supply it.

For Australia and New Zealand, dependent as they were on the efficacy of the Royal Navy's protective screen, these developments were dour indeed. The Australian Prime Minister, Philip Curtin, was driven to announce that his country would turn 'free of any pangs' from Britain to the United States, in the hope that the latter would provide the guarantees now clearly beyond the capacity of the former.[52] There was an implicit gripe here at having been let down which in the hands of one recent Australian historian has festered into a study which bears the headline 'The Great Betrayal'.[53] In its connotations of consistent and calculated duplicity on the part of the United Kingdom authorities, this is certainly misleading. Nearer the truth (though not itself free of self-pleading) was the exculpation given by one senior British military official at the time with respect to the Japanese onslaught: 'We just hoped it wouldn't happen. And it did.'[54] In fact, any veering away from the Commonwealth connection by Australia was subsequently checked not only by the gossamer ties of a common Britishness, but by the experience that America did not necessarily provide a more pliable or easy patron than the United Kingdom – in many ways, in fact, less so, if only because the relationship was even more unbalanced in power-political terms than the old imperial equipoise.[55] Before long the British Commonwealth was to assume a new lease of life precisely because it provided an off-set to that dependency on the United States which almost all the 'small democracies' came to exhibit after 1941. Such countervailing tendencies apart, the effect of British defeats in Asia was profoundly to undermine her claims to be a protecting power on the old lines, thus intensifying the long-standing bias of the Dominions to concentrate on their own regional security arrangements; certainly Australia's contribution in the Middle East, for example, was much less during the Second World War than it had been during the First. All in all, Imperial Defence, so long part of the 'glue' in British official thought, could never be quite the same again after early 1942. According to the metaphor which came naturally to the subject, the metropolitan parent might continue to be looked upon with a certain fondness, and was resorted to in a wide variety of circumstances where a helping hand was needed, but Australians, Canadians, South Africans and even gentle New Zealanders acknowledged among themselves that the *materfamilias* was on the skids at last.

The early phases of the Pacific War also suggested that potentially serious tensions within the Grand Alliance might stem from the pressure inside the United States exerted by those who wanted their country to concentrate its resources exclusively against Japan, thus deviating from the 'Beat Hitler First' principle previously inscribed in Anglo-American joint planning.[56] The naval lobby, traditionally averse to close ties with Britain, particularly evinced views along these lines. Such frictions subsequently remained largely dormant, if only because the logistical demands posed by the two main theatres in Asia and Europe never clashed too drastically with each other. This was a tribute to America's war economy, which proved able to supply both fronts at once, whilst simultaneously putting millions of uniformed men into the field. The relatively rapid peaking of Japanese expansion in the Pacific naturally eased the overall position considerably. Thus the United States Navy stopped that country's further maritime advances in its tracks at the Battle of the Coral Sea – the first major naval engagement in history during which neither of the combatant fleets saw the other – on 8 May 1942, and then threw their opponent on to the defensive after the Battle of Midway during early June. Afterwards there was much bloody fighting on atolls and in jungles, but the ultimate outcome in the Pacific was never really in doubt. Under such circumstances the American commanders in the region had no desire to welcome Britishers into their wartime circuits. For such heroes of America's Pacific struggle as Admiral Nimitz and (especially) General Douglas MacArthur, the Grand Alliance was, in the main, a ritual rather than a practical bond.

The most profound differences between the British and the Americans over the conduct of strategy came instead to be concentrated in the Western theatre. Thus from their entry into the war the Americans – taking 'Beat Hitler First' literally, as befitted their instincts as a people – looked towards the opening up of a 'Second Front' in north-west Europe, not least to provide some respite to the Soviet Union against Germany's continuing assault. Conversely, however, the United Kingdom's southward bias towards the Mediterranean became *more* marked once the machinery of the Grand Alliance had been slotted into place. Under the new circumstances the British had to ask themselves if they genuinely looked forward to being swept back into northern Europe on the Americans' coat-tails, and they soon discovered that their feelings on the matter were distinctly equivocal. They peered into the future and saw looming a hypothetical peace in which the Americans, having blasted an allied path back into Europe, would retire once more into their shell – as they had in 1920 – leaving the United Kingdom to pick up the pieces. This was not an inviting prospect, and the natural British response was to recoil from it. Churchill, of course, was never so indiscreet as to oppose a cross-Channel invasion *on principle*, though some of his senior military advisers were not so veiled in their observations.[57] To American sceptics it increasingly seemed that British thinking had an innate tendency to become decoupled from any larger vision of beating Germany where it mattered – in the heart of Europe. All in all, attitudes in London towards the liberation of the adjoining continent came to bear a certain resemblance to St Augustine's famous ambivalence on another subject: make me chaste, Lord, but not yet.

In fact Churchill initially enjoyed a considerable measure of success in determining the 'lay-out' of the war in the West, first by scuppering the American plan for a cross-Channel invasion in 1942 ('Operation Sledgehammer') and then by putting off a similar scheme for 1943 ('Operation Round-Up'). In the immediate aftermath of Pearl Harbor he enjoyed acting as if the Americans had been delivered into his hands. 'Oh!', he protested archly when one of the Chiefs of Staff stressed the need for tact in dealing with the United States, 'that is the way we talked to her when we were wooing her; now she is in the harem, we talk to her quite differently.'[58] Despite such characteristic bravura, however, the Prime Minister knew very well that the faster America's domestic mobilization proceeded, the more men she put into the field, the more transparent would be the United Kingdom's subordination to her great ally. It was to ameliorate and to some extent confound this process that

Churchill began to talk in terms of 'mixing up' the American and British decision-making systems, in the hope that by so doing the allocation of power would become diffuse and, at the least, less embarrassingly overt; before long the build-up of British personnel in Washington was to become so vast as to constitute what has been called 'a second Whitehall overseas'.[59] Yet in truth the fig-leaf of equality between Roosevelt and Churchill was not long in place. Its dislodgement can be traced quite precisely. Thus in June 1942 the Prime Minister visited Washington, and was breakfasting with the President one morning when a messenger entered with a pink piece of paper which Roosevelt took and read, before passing to his guest. It bore the news of the fall of Tobruk. After a silence Roosevelt said simply, 'What can we do to help?', and in a flash any pretence to equality between the two men disappeared.[60] What the Americans subsequently did to help was to concur in a joint Anglo-American invasion of north-west Africa ('Operation Torch') planned for November of that year. Self-evidently, even in what the British leadership took to be its distinctive theatre of operations, the United Kingdom was now dependent on the United States for pulling its chestnuts out of the fire.

The fall of Tobruk represented the nadir of Churchill's war, the moment when his premiership was most tangibly at risk. The domestic details of how this thread was fended off are not our concern.[61] The fall-out, however, was soon felt in Britain's Middle Eastern Command. Hence although General Auchinleck had by July 1942 successfully stemmed the Axis advance along the El Alamein line and foiled any credible threat to Cairo, he nevertheless found himself seriously at odds with his political master. The trouble was that what seemed to the commander on the spot as a continuing practical necessity for 'consolidation' struck others, especially the Prime Minister himself, as stubborn 'defeatism'. Above all, the British, according to Churchill's broader calculations, had now quickly to be *seen* saving their own bacon in North Africa before the Americans could turn up and claim to have done it all themselves. Such were the ingredients in the dramatic intrigues in Cairo and London climaxing when

Churchill (en route to Moscow in August 1942) made a special detour to preside personally over the dismissal of Auchinleck from his post, dispatching him, in Wavell's footsteps, to the backwater of India.[62]

The new British *generalissimo* in the Middle East was General Harold Alexander, but almost as significant an element in the new dispensation was Bernard Montgomery's appointment to head the Eighth Army. The latter swiftly emerged as the quintessential Churchillian solder. His dominant ability was that of 'putting himself over', rather than the display of any sophisticated tactical thought. In the field, as most military historians have agreed, his forte was the set-piece battle in which superiority of manpower and metalpower afforded the absolute assurance of triumph. Newly-reinforced by consignments of American Sherman tanks, such a guaranteed victory was secured in the Battle of El Alamein when on 23 October the Eighth Army launched itself at Rommel's formations (by now under a huge numerical and logistical disadvantage), and finally managed to evict them from Egypt. Here was the supreme example of Montgomery's gifts; and the painfully laboured aftermath in which, as Auchinleck had predicted, the British advance got bogged down in the wastes of Cyrenaica, did not forcibly detract from the instant fame of the victory which had been gained. In brief, it was the cannonade, not the campaign, which mattered, since barely had the echo died away than the bells of Westminster Abbey were rung out in a peal of triumph for the first time since the start of the war. El Alamein, indeed, gave a genuine patina of success to the Mediterranean strategy and thereby to the political and military leadership with which it was associated; it was a formula, having thus been proved, to which Churchill afterwards clung with all his innate tenacity. As a result, the Eighth Army ('the Desert Rats') came to represent the principal British military 'legend' of 1939–45, just as Lawrence of Arabia more single-handedly had epitomized that of 1914–18. It was a suggestive act of pique in this regard that when the veterans of the Army were awarded a special clasp as a mark of honour, it was reserved for those who had served under Montgomery after August 1942, and denied to those whose exertions (without benefit of Shermans) had gone before.

Whilst the Anglo-American landings in north-west Africa were a source of gratification for Britain, in so far as the Americans were now successfully embroiled in Mediterranean campaigning, they unhappily cut across relations with the Soviet Union. Roosevelt, in agreeing to 'Torch', had insisted that Churchill assume the unedifying task of telling Stalin in person that the 'Second Front' the western allies were about to open up was not in Europe at all, but in Africa. The experience awaiting the British leader in the Russian capital was not pleasant. Stalin bluntly expressed the view that the fracas in the Mediterranean bore no credible relationship to the war *he* was fighting against Hitler; and since at that moment only five (somewhat makeshift) German divisions under Rommel were keeping the British war machine in a permanent spin, whilst two hundred divisions were smashing their way across the Russian countryside, his frankness was understandable. 'You British are afraid of fighting', Stalin lashed out; 'You will have to fight sooner or later', and he was not appeased when Churchill fell back rather lamely on a purple passage about the 'Finest Hour.'[63] When, at the last formal banquet of the conference, and with the Russian dictator in one of his most rollicking, black-booted, sardonic moods, a British delegate rose and proposed a toast of 'death and damnation to the Germans', the wry spirit in which it was received by the hosts may well be imagined.

Before this social climax was reached, however, Churchill succeeded in discovering a technique to ease his stormy relationship with the Russian leader. In an interlude between the latter's aspersions on British virility in general, and the Mediterranean diversion in particular, he wrenched the discussion towards the bombing campaign against Germany. 'The Prime Minister said we hoped to shatter twenty German cities as we had shattered Cologne, Lübeck, Dusseldorf and so on . . .', the transcript recorded. 'If need be . . . we hoped to shatter every dwelling in every German city. These words had a very stimulating effect upon the meeting, and thenceforward the atmosphere became progressively more cordial.'[64] This lightened mood was comprehensible, since in effect the British were promising to mitigate the Mediterranean strategy on land by committing themselves to flattening the heart of Europe from the air, thus making it tractable for Soviet tanks when the planned counter-offensive got into its stride. Afterwards regular telegrams were dispatched from London to Moscow tabulating the tonnage of bombs recently dropped on German cities – culminating in the fire-bombing of Dresden on 13–14 February 1945 (killing 135,000 people). Both the ethics and the strategic logic of the RAF's subsequent 'heavy bombing' of civilian as well as military targets in Germany have been the subject of debate, some of it heated. Yet from the perspective of our present analysis the interest in this emerging pattern lies not in the technical merits of the campaign from the air, but in the essentially political relationship which existed between the fighting in the Mediterranean and the blanket-bombing of *Mitteleuropa*. Stalin, in effect, afterwards turned a blind eye to the peripheral bias of his British ally, in return for a residual, but still significant, form of assistance to the Red Army in breaking into East Central Europe.

Having thus braved Stalin's displeasure, the British premier was soon to gain his modest North African reward. In the aftermath of the 'Torch' landings, Rommel's main force was tied up in the west, leaving the Eighth Army to continue a somewhat laggard advance from the east, finally arriving in Tripoli on 23 January 1943. At the march past to celebrate the occupation of this city, the British troops were amazed (though perhaps they should not have been) to witness Churchill among their number. Many present testified to the high emotion of the occasion. 'The bitter moment in the White House when Tobruk fell', one senior British officer noted, 'was swallowed up in the joy of the morning in Tripoli.'[65] This was precisely the point. That the supreme moment of fulfilment for the British leadership during the war came in a Tripolitanian amphitheatre, far from the hell of Stalingrad (where what was left of General von Paulus' Sixth Army had surrendered only days before), and when the conflict was only at the half-way stage, conjures up the curiously ambiguous, almost evasive, role which – by the inevitable mixture of choice and accident – came to be the United Kingdom's lot after 1941. That Churchill himself recognized the apogee when it happened is suggested by the fact that, about to be air-borne again for the gloom of London, and contemplating the risk of a crash en route, he turned to an aide and remarked that 'it would not be a bad time to go'.[66]

One disturbing trend for the future was the bouts of feuding between British and American soldiers 'in the field' which quickly surfaced, and which only got worse with the final liquidation of the enemy's presence in North Africa during May 1943. These vibrations were most evident during high-level discussion of strategic plans. One senior American planner now called, for example, with a touch of sarcasm for 'a land offensive against Germany in the strategic sense'[67], and it was with this in mind that Washington began to canvass the possibilities of a thrust into southern France (which in a later phase of the war was coded ANVIL). ANVIL and its precursors were anathema to the British, who spent much of the rest of the war trying to put the idea off (it was later only eclipsed by the invasion of Normandy). Nevertheless, with the American military machine yet to attain peak mobilization, the British leverage over western policy-making remained considerable, so that the compromise decision to attack Sicily as the next step was a fresh political triumph for Churchill. Above all, the invasion of Sicily ensured that the Mediterranean would remain a principal theatre of warfare for the foreseeable future, if only because the logic of a further lateral move into Italy became inescapable.

It was on the adjoining peninsula, in fact, that the tenuous understanding between the British and American high commands finally began to come seriously unstuck.[68] In the wake of the invasions at Salerno (September 1943) and Anzio (January 1944), Hitler – far from deciding to withdraw his legions – actually reinforced the German presence, first along a line from Pisa to Rimini, and later along a defensive axis cutting transversely across the River Po. Once it became clear that Italy was not to prove a rapid highway to the north, American interest rapidly evaporated, with the result that Washington began to ration a campaign which it regarded as tangential at best to the outcome of the main war. By the very same token, however, the British strategic mind began to drift off in alternative directions, lured by the compensatory prospect of a series of insular acquisitions in the eastern Mediterranean proper. Hence as the gilt came off the Italian ginger-bread, Churchill's concentrated gaze shifted to such prizes as Corfu, Kos and Rhodes, exhorting his commanders in the region to emulate the eighteenth-century example of 'Clive and Peterborough and Rooke's men taking Gibraltar'.[69] In this context the solidarity of the 'Grand Alliance' became distinctly strained.

If the 'Kos syndrome' came to exasperate the Americans, it sometimes reached a pitch which reduced even Churchill's own advisers to despair. His Chief of Defence Staff, 'Pug' Ismay, when recalling the trait years later, was driven to reflect that, whilst Churchill had possessed a 'political genius' for war, he had also been distinguished by 'the mind of a child' in strategic matters.[70] The distinction is apposite with respect to many episodes in Churchill's career. In essence, however, by 1943 Churchill appreciated that whoever might end up winning the war in Europe, it could not possibly be the United Kingdom. In the Continental heartland the British could never be more than subordinate to people more powerful than they were. Along the southern littoral it was different; there Britain *could* assert herself as a genuine principal. 'We command the Mediterranean Sea itself', George VI himself put the case, 'Sicily, Sardinia, Corsica, half the mainland of Italy is ours.'[71] This was the venue, in brief, where Britain might aspire to go on fighting a war on its own terms and *in its own national interests*, rather than in those of others; and Churchill's genius for belligerency seized on this crucial point, even if the enthusiasm with which it was expressed sometimes appeared to verge on the ridiculous. It was a conception, furthermore, that caught on at all levels, to the extent that in British official circles it became a stock joke that the best thing to happen to OVERLORD (the plan for a cross-Channel invasion) was to be thrown OVERBOARD.

Yet try as one might to kick against the pricks, the plain fact was that as the outlines of a new bi-polar world became discernible the United Kingdom forfeited the trappings of a truly Great Power (as Neville Chamberlain had prophesied would be the outcome of her participation in another land war). The Tehran Conference in November 1943 between the three senior allies – called, suggestively, to decide finally on the timing of an invasion of north-west Europe – marked the on-set of this demotion. Churchill lobbied strongly to have the 'circus' held in Cairo or Khartoum, where imperial ambience and protocol could help to mask the weakness of his position. Stalin, however, insisted on the 'neutral' ground of the Persian capital. Not only did the Americans concur in this, but they refused to have any preliminary exchanges with their British cousins lest the Soviets feel 'ganged-up' upon. When the Conference met, it was the British who found themselves subject to exclusion: Roosevelt refused to meet alone with Churchill, whilst having extensive conversations *à deux* with Stalin. In the plenary sessions the Americans kept a cool detachment whilst the Soviet leader tweaked the British tail, scoffing that the Alps still lay between the war the British were conducting in the Mediterranean and Hitler's main force. When Churchill was at last confronted with the blunt question – was he for or against OVERLORD? – there could, in truth, only be one answer. Alone with his delegation after a fearful hammering, he suddenly looked, according to one observer, deeply wan and said 'in a tired, slow voice, with his eyes closed . . ."I want to sleep for billions of years".'[72]

As an elderly man of sixty-nine years, having shouldered such crushing responsibilities, Churchill's mental and physical fatigue at this juncture is not to be wondered at; the scene we have described is, in its way, deeply moving. Yet the depression which came over him after Tehran, and which stayed till the end of the conflict, did not only arise from accumulated stress. He began, for example, to opine among his intimates that his premiership was in danger of ending up a complete failure. It was undubitably the case that the aims for which Britain had gone to war in 1939 had not so much been defeated outright, as completely overtaken by events. She had entered the fray to preserve the balance of power; by 1943/4 that balance had disappeared without trace, and its incipient successor was one on which Britain could only lay a palsied and ineffective grasp. For the rest of the war the Prime Minister was in the words of one on-looker, 'little more than a spectator'[73], and in a curious way this may be said to have been the fate of the Home island itself, as its southern coasts were converted into a floating platform from which the quintessentially American achievement of invading and liberating German-occupied western Europe was finally launched on 6 June 1944. During the final stages of the war, therefore, Churchill's focus was on deflecting these inimical tendencies, cultivating the appearance of victory for the British nation, and trying to discover a method by which British power and prestige could be put on a viable basis for the future. Thus it was that whilst the attention of the world might be fixed on the Normandy landings and their aftermath, Churchill concerned himself – in their ascending order of importance – with the Bay of Bengal, the Balkans and, as he evocatively put it, 'the Air'. The first of these takes us back briefly to the war in the Orient.

The course of the Second World War in Asia after January 1942 may properly be considered outside the mainstream of British history, particularly once the Japanese threat to India lifted after its repulse at the Battle of Imphal. Thus at the time the researchers of the Ministry of Information revealed that Home opinion took no interest whatsoever in anything 'east of Rommel'.[74] This obliviousness did not apply only to the man in the street, or cooped up in the NAAFI canteen. The Chief of the Imperial General Staff himself hardly ever referred to the Far East in a personal diary otherwise full of agonizing detail[75]; the soubriquet of General Slim's Fourteenth Army in Burma – 'Forgotten' – was therefore entirely merited. In the later stages of the war, it is true, the British were instrumental in setting up a Supreme South-East Asia Command (SEAC). It was, however, put under the aegis of Lord Louis Mountbatten, whose propensity for empire-building was legend, and before long its Headquarters at Kandy in Ceylon was renowned as the 'Rest and Relaxation' capital of the entire Eastern war zone.[76] In American parlance SEAC instantly translated as 'Save England's Asian Colonies', but even this signified a certain level of military activity belied by Kandy's life-style, so that some United States personnel – such as the brash and brazen 'Vinegar Joe' Stillwell – adopted renderings of an even less decorous sort.

British ambiguity towards the war in Asia did not derive so much from *ad hominem* factors, as from central assumptions in British war policy. At the heart of the relationship between the political and military authorities in Whitehall after 1939 was the understanding (profoundly influenced, as we have previously underlined, by memories of 1914–18) that the politicians would not seek to impose on the Services tasks which were beyond their collective capacity to carry out. But whereas the Mediterranean strategy met this criteria very neatly, a putative offensive against Japan in south-east Asia did not. SEAC, in short, had a watching and (to some extent) preparing brief, not a fighting one. For a short but stormy period, as Churchill thrashed about for some means of diluting the commitment to the re-invasion of Europe, the latter challenged this compromise by relentlessly advocating what he called the 'Bay of Bengal' strategy. What this amounted to was not entirely clear, except that it involved lopping off a slice of Sumatra. 'I began to wonder', the Chief of the Imperial General Staff wrote in his diary at the time, 'whether I was in Alice in Wonderland or qualifying for a lunatic asylum.'[77] This indeed was the only occasion during the war when the British Chiefs of Staff were forced into threats of collective resignation to bring their often hectoring master to heel. The fact was that the British military had no intention of risking exposure on any extended scale (with the exception of General Slim's advance on Rangoon) to the sort of bloody fighting in the East which ensued between the Americans and Japanese at Iwo Jima and Guadalcanal; their forces eventually went back into Malaya on tip-toe only *after* the Japanese surrender in September 1945. Nevertheless, even in this case Churchill's Indian Ocean dreams can be credited with a certain prophetic dimension: the Bay of Bengal strategy, phantasm though it remained during the Second World War, resembles nothing so much as the East of Suez defence policy which came to be the lynchpin of the United Kingdom's 'overseas' role for much of the 1950s and 1960s.

After June 1944, however, it was to the Balkans that Churchill looked most eagerly as a conventional bastion of British post-war interests. He went again to Moscow in October of that year and drew up what he called a 'naughty document' amounting to an Anglo-Soviet partition of south-eastern Europe: Romania was to be 90% Soviet and 10% British (the implication for Poland scarcely requiring emphasis), Greece 90% British and 10% Soviet, and Yugoslavia split 50/50. Churchill later described in his history of the war how Stalin perused this piece of paper when it was presented to him, took out a blue pencil, gave a tick and pushed it back across the table. 'After this there was a long silence', Churchill wrote. 'The pencilled paper lay in the centre of the table. At length I said, "Might it not be thought rather cynical if it seemed we had disposed of the issues so fateful to millions of people, in such an off-hand manner? Let us burn the paper." "No, you keep it," said Stalin".[78] It is a riveting picture – one which, in its breathtaking audacity, puts in the shade Chamberlain's modest version of *realpolitik* at Munich, when a mere Bohemian province was converted into territorial cash. Unlike Munich, however, Churchill's (and Stalin's) 'naughty document' had an insecure purchase on reality. Whilst British 'advisers' began parachuting in large numbers into Yugoslavia to secure their stake, Josip Tito's Communist partisans saw to it that they soon had to take their advice elsewhere, as eventually did their equally luckless Soviet counterparts. The Balkan spoil which remained within British reach – and which gave credence to the United Kingdom's Mediterranean strategy as a genuinely European phenomenon – was Greece, and it was to renewed intervention in that country that much of Churchill's efforts were bent during the latter stages of the war against Germany.

One complication with this exercise was that the Americans did not approve of it. After all, it was not an intervention against the Germans, who had already evacuated Greece as their southern flank collapsed under Russian pressure, but against the local Communist-cum-republican insurgents whom the British themselves had previously armed and encouraged. When London therefore requested extra landing-craft to shift their troops from Taranto to Piraeus, the United States Chief of Naval Staff, Admiral King, bluntly refused, sourly remarking that the expedition the British were embarking upon 'does not appear to be a war in which the United States is participating'.[79] By scrimping and scraping, and steeling their nerves, the British nevertheless succeeded in breaking anew into the Peloponnese. The moving spirit in this venture was Churchill himself, who in the most remarkable personal episode of his wartime career made an emergency visit to Athens over Christmas 1944, where he was driven steel-helmeted in a tank through the strife-ridden city, and went into a conference with a motley group of Greek clerics and politicians, with troops guarding the windows as the tenement was engulfed in sniping-fire. It was, as the Prime Minister later recalled, 'intensely dramatic', and the meaning of it lay as much in the drama itself as in the content of the negotiation.

The spectacle in Athens implicitly summed up the singularity of the United Kingdom's aims and experience as the great world-wide conflict entered its closing phases. Where the American and Soviet principals stared at large-scale maps, moving vast armies this way and that, engaged on a struggle for mastery in the broad geo-political sense, the British leader was ducking and weaving in the fragmented world of Greek politics, dealing in scarce landing-craft rather than whole divisions, *but determined for all that* to ensure that Britain got her dues as she conceived them to be. Not only American opinion looked askance at these initiatives; they were almost universally criticized in the British press at home, whilst at the Labour Party Conference only Ernest Bevin was prepared to defend them. Yet it was the exception which proved the rule. The successful British intervention in Greece presaged the Mediterranean's pre-eminence as the forum of distinctively

British interests and world influence for over a decade after 1945, even when other long-standing political investments, as in South Asia, were to be abandoned. The precedent was significant, too, for its confirmation that here was one region where the United Kingdom could still act unilaterally, confident in the expectation that the Americans would have no option but to accept any *fait accompli* with which she was confronted. It was not accidental, for example, that when those close to Anthony Eden urged him to take military action against Egypt in 1956, it was the precedent of Churchill's wartime coup in Athens that they used to highlight the practicality of their case.[80]

Whilst Churchill indulged in his Grecian odyssey, it was scarcely surprising that the fate of Poland, the ostensible *casus belli* of 1939, should have been sharply relegated in the pecking order. In this respect the rot had set in very early. 'We are selling the Poles down the river', Alec Cadogan already exclaimed in 1942[81], and by the beginning of 1945 – with the Red Army closing in on Berlin – the process was much too advanced to consider reversing, even if one had wished to. Thus the sporadic latter-day criticism of the Anglo-American leadership that at the Yalta Conference in February 1945 it 'sold' the pass in East Central Europe is not very persuasive; the pass to all intents and purposes, had been auctioned off some while before. The reference to 'free elections' for Poland in the Yalta document was designed in part to get Churchill out of a potentially awkward corner in the House of Commons, where the resonances of 1939 with regard to that forlorn country had not entirely disappeared. As it turned out, the debate in the British lower chamber proved something of a damp squib, a resolution approving of Yalta being passed with 365 'ayes' against 25 'noes' – the latter rump being mostly composed of old Chamberlainites. Some cynics noted of this outcome that the hawks had miraculously turned into doves, and the doves into hawks.[82] This itself, of course, was a criticism which was potentially very damaging, and here lies a key to explaining the curious zeal among senior British Army figures at the time – especially Montgomery – in blaming the cautious, broad-front advance towards Berlin from the West insisted upon by Supreme Commander Eisenhower for the fact that so much territory fell under Soviet control in the final days of the war. In truth, as Eisenhower never tired of pointing out, since Yalta had already defined precisely where the post-war spheres should lie, the only result of Montgomery's much-vaunted 'pencil-line thrust' to the German capital would have been to expend yet more American lives for no concrete purpose. This dispute, egged on by the publication of barbed memoirs on both sides of the Atlantic, was to run on into the 1950s. The essential point from the perspective of this study, is that just as the British Army sat on the sidelines when Germany surrendered in 1918 to Marshal Foch, so none of its units were in attendance when the American and Soviet forces duly joined up by appointment at Trochau on the Elbe on 23 April 1945. After the Second World War, therefore, even more than after the Great War of 1914–18, the instinct to keep Europe at arm's length was deeply etched into the British psychology.

In London the celebrations began as soon as the rumours of the German surrender on 7 May 1945 were bruited. Crowds gathered in Parliament Square and called for Churchill. 'My dear friends,' he declared when he appeared before them, 'this is your hour. This is not a victory of a party or of any class. It's a victory of the great British nation.'[83] It is unlikely that any of his auditors recalled at that moment his comparable 'victory' speech in November 1918. 'The victory which has been won amidst these hazards', Churchill had announced on the earlier occasion, 'does not belong to any party or any class. It belongs to all.'[84] The striking similarity of the two declensions does not belie any element of banality. Rather, it conveys, in necessarily rhetorical form, the most authentic and insistent war aim of all, which had sustained the United Kingdom through two world wars in less than half a century and which fused so completely in the persona of Churchill himself: the ideal of an armed and disciplined nation, purged of all traces of class and section, its inner tensions – which once had seemed likely to pull asunder the fabric of the nation – sublimated in the common struggle for the balance of power in Europe, and, more latterly, in the grim fight against Hitlerism. Whatever the inevitable mix here between myth and reality, appearance and substance, the idea was one which deeply moved the diverse array of clerks, office supervisors and Lyons' tea-maids as they stood and cheered to their utmosts in Parliament Square; and if, for their part, the miners of Durham kept their own, more enigmatic counsel, the conception of 'greatness' thus underwritten was certainly one which went on to infuse British national culture for a long time ahead.

But how was this 'victory of the great British nation' going to be sustained into the post-war world? It was already obvious that the United Kingdom was well-nigh bankrupt, and, Keynes now warned, would be facing an 'economic Dunkirk' when normality returned. The fact that the British were subsequently to prove rather less enthusiastic about 'normalcy' than many other nations had something to do with the bind to which Keynes pointed. Nevertheless, it is doubtful whether such jeremiads issuing from tame intellectuals caused Churchill to lose any sleep. When the General Election of July 1945 took place, for example – inconveniently arising from the Labour Party's insistence on breaking up the Coalition as soon as the war in Europe had ended – the Prime Minister's lacklustre speeches dwelt upon economic matters only very obliquely, if at all. Considering how crucial economic constraints were to soon become, this omission may appear remarkable. Yet since 1939 Britain had fought a great war which economically-inclined critics had once said was beyond her capacity; likewise, after the war the British people, it was possible to feel, would 'pull its socks up' and transcend again whatever passing difficulties arose. Churchill's *sang-froid* in this regard also sprang, however, from the simple fact that his mind was preoccupied elsewhere. Above all, there was one very secret development which, in terms of future planning, put all else in the shade, including the petty and rather disreputable question of money: this was the project known by the code 'Tube Alloys', or, as it became better known, the Atom Bomb. In the curious British interregnum of half-peace and half-war (or three-quarters peace and one-quarter war) between the defeat of Germany and the final surrender of Japan, it was preponderantly towards this most glittering of strategic inventions that Churchill's mental exertions were directed.

What 'Tube Alloys' meant to Churchill may be gleaned from a remark he made to General de Gaulle on the day Paris was liberated. 'Colonies today are no longer a pledge of happiness, or a sign of power', the premier had roundly declared. 'India is a very heavy burden to us. Modern [air] squadrons are worth more than overseas territories.'[85] De Gaulle, whose troops had just been evicted from Syria by their supposed United Kingdom ally, retorted that he had not noticed the British in any hurry to give away their own empire; whilst it was only gradually that the scale and character of atomic power dawned on even those privy to the experiments. Yet as the end of the war brought one era to a close and foreshadowed the start of another, Churchill undoubtedly grasped from an early point not only that possession of 'the Air' was to be far more important in contemporary strategy than overseas lodgements[86], but that the special attributes of 'Tube Alloys' fitted Britain's needs like a glove. Thus whereas for many years the advantage in world politics had seemed to lie with the great continental nations, endowed with almost limitless resources of manpower and materials, the Atom Bomb presaged a form of dominion in which the territorial size of the homeland counted for less, in which scientists (of which Britain had a great supply) were worth more than foreign exchange reserves (of which Britain had none at all), and which was based on 'armies' of heavy metal rather than conscripted hordes. Gaining a stake in this most convenient innovation, therefore, provided the key to allowing Britain to defy the odds once more, or, as Churchill had once expressed his fundamental goal, to get the old dog 'to sit up and wag its tail'.

The problem was that British claims to an effective stake in 'Tube Alloys' (or the Manhattan Programme as the Americans called it, after the enterprise was transferred wholesale from British to American laboratories after the end of 1942) became increasingly exiguous as time had gone on.[87] Roosevelt had responded to Churchill's pleas for guarantees in this branch of the allied effort by giving him a series of verbal assurances, most notably at the Quebec Conference during August 1943, but the President's 'minders' had made sure that nothing solid was put down on paper, so that when Roosevelt died from cancer in April 1945 these promises died with him. It is not too much to say that the British were to spend the best part of twenty years (up to the Polaris Agreement of December 1962) trying to retrieve this position. The high significance of the issues involved induced in Churchill a certain diffidence in his exchanges with Roosevelt's successor in the White House, Harry Truman, making him deaf to the many urgent calls on him to intervene with the new President to forestall the awful precedent which would be set by any use of the novel device against Japan.[88] On balance, it is difficult to see that any efforts along these lines by the British leadership could have been other than fruitless in the circumstances, and might easily have damaged much of the fabric of the Anglo-American relationship: once the final trials in the Nevada Desert proved that the innovation was, in the language of the cypher, a 'plop' not a 'flop', it was inevitable that it should be plopped sooner rather than later. On 6 August 1945 two atom bombs were dropped on the cities of Hiroshima and Nagasaki, and the last curtain fell on the Second World War.

In fact by this juncture Winston Churchill was no longer the occupant of No. 10 Downing Street. Midway through the Potsdam Conference, convened to explore a formal settlement in Europe, the Conservative and Labour leaderships (both of which were in attendance) returned home for the climax of the British general election on 26 July, the result of which accorded the Labour Party, with Clement Attlee at its head, an outright majority over all the other parties for the first time in its history. The final irony in what was for Britain a war of excruciating ironies, therefore, is that whilst it did indeed represent 'the last great achievement of an imperial ruling class', the immediate legacy of that achievement was immediately transferred into the hands of British Socialism. The latter's administration of its trust is the subject of our next chapter.

Labour's Bulldog Breed

The Labour Government of 1945–51 almost invariably attracts a good press. Clement Attlee has often been claimed as one of the most effective, if also self-effacing, of modern Prime Ministers; whilst few Foreign Secretaries are reckoned to have 'stood up' for Britain with the aplomb of Ernest Bevin. The ministry presided over radical achievements at home and abroad: in the latter sphere these included the beginnings of a wise and pragmatic decolonization (embracing the independence of India and the invention of the multi-racial Commonwealth), the playing of a leading role in European economic recovery, and, perhaps above all, the championing of the idea of the Western Alliance, culminating in the signature of the North Atlantic Treaty on 4 April 1949. With this in mind, one scholar, for example, has detected a 'rough strength' in the England of Attlee and Bevin which has not been seen since[1]; whilst the political reputations of the latter have gained in direct proportion to the disparagements very generally heaped upon the Labour leaderships of a later day.

Predictably, less benevolent interpretations of the Labour Government's record have also been put forward, based on party and ideological differences. Some have felt that the continuation of wartime *dirigisme* in economic life – and its expansion through the nationalization of industries – was a drastic misreading of the needs of British society when her competitors were wasting no time returning to free-market principles.[2] On the overseas side, the ministry has been less vulnerable to the usual revisionist barbs. Even here, however, one commentator has pointed out that perhaps the most remarkable thing about Britain's evacuation from India in 1947 was not the fact of her departure (which could no longer be delayed) but that in doing so Labour ministers managed to avoid drawing any of the lessons as to the United Kingdom's true position in the world which, in retrospect at least, appear glaringly obvious.[3] The logging of debits and credits along these lines is ultimately futile, but they at least constitute a *point d'appui* for an analysis of the bind (closely entwined as it was with matters of foreign policy and defence) which afflicted British public affairs virtually from the start of the post-war era.

Inevitably Ernest Bevin occupies the centre-stage of this saga, since even more than Attlee he epitomized the spirit which infused the government. His appointment as Foreign Secretary surprised many, since others had been tipped more widely for the job, and apparently it was only a last-minute 'suggestion' emanating from Buckingham Palace which dispatched Bevin, with his dropped vowels and carter's manners, to the dignified splendours of Carlton House Terrace.[4] Nevertheless, it was an appointment which would not have amazed those who had noticed how, as a member of the War Cabinet after 1940, Bevin had married his Trade Union pugnacity as the founder of the Transport and General Workers' Union to a strikingly bulldog patriotism – being the only speaker, as we have already observed, at the Labour Party Conference in 1944 prepared to approve Churchill's controversial initiative in Greece. This record certainly fitted him to accommodate the contradictions bedevilling any socialist presiding over the Foreign Office, that residual lodgement of the aristocratic principle in modern British administration. The key to the ministerial dispensation in 1945 was, then, exactly this: Bevin delivered to the Foreign Office and the 'overseas' establishment a pliable intellect and acquiescent Trade Unions, whilst the Foreign Office provided Bevin with the ideal platform to develop the composite image of the working-man's Churchill on which his appeal to the political nation was largely founded. Nothing summed this up more characteristically than when the new Foreign Secretary arrived back at the Potsdam Conference in Berlin with the rousing admonition (designed as much for the audience at home as the one abroad) that 'I'm not going to have Britain barged about', though it should be added that during the next few years a number of his counterparts in other countries were to differ as to who was doing most of the barging.

The manner in which British overseas policy was subsequently conducted within the Labour ministry requires early emphasis. Alan Bullock, in his massive official biography of Bevin, has noted that whilst a permanent structure of Cabinet committees was set up to supervise civil matters, no such system was created with respect to foreign affairs. 'Every Monday when he was in London', Bullock relates, 'Bevin gave a report to the Cabinet and this was placed at the head of the agenda, but it was primarily intended for information, and neither Bevin's nor Attlee's attitude encouraged extended discussion. . .'.[5] This rigid distinction between home and overseas policy merely replicated, and adapted, the demarcation within the wartime Coalition, whereby the Tories had run the war and the Socialists (along with a Liberal 'tail') had been allowed to dominate domestic issues. The nub of this formula was to yoke together and reconcile the twin goals of 'Welfare' and 'Greatness' within the British government, ensuring that neither of the two halves of national policy-making encroached on the other's patch, lest home priorities get in the way of overseas, or vice versa. Bevin was the crucial link between the separate administrative and political fiefs which were thereby kept in motion, since on the one hand he had the Trade Union bosses in his pocket, and on the other he presided over the making of foreign policy. It was therefore natural that, at least until very late in the day, Attlee invariably followed in the wake of Bevin, not the other way around.

Keeping Welfarism and Greatness going simultaneously when the country was facing an 'economic Dunkirk' was, however, a forbidding prospect. The scale of the commercial challenge was summed up in the Treasury's estimate towards the end of the war that the United Kingdom would have to increase her exports by a staggering *75% just in order to regain the standard of living enjoyed in 1938*. Part of the problem, of course, was that the politicians had promised the British people not merely a return to the halcyon days of 1938, but something far more wonderful still – a 'New Jerusalem'. Yet similar promises ('Homes Fit for Heroes') made between 1914 and 1918 had not prevented the political nation afterwards from squeezing accumulated inflation out of the system, and ensuring a transfer of resources out of consumption and into exports and investment by a painful process of deflationary adjustment. In many ways the most striking facet of British affairs after 1945 was that a comparable process was avoided, precisely because to have done so would have infringed the political and social 'ground rules' on which the war had been conducted, and which long afterwards remained entrenched in national political culture.

In retrospect it is easy to see that from the beginning the fiscal and political sums simply did not add up. But then the wartime sums had not added up either, and the system had none the less scraped by. The war itself showed how the vehicle of British government had a remarkable facility for keeping going even when the petrol gauge was pointing unmistakably to 'Empty'. One of the most important methods by which this perpetual motion was sustained was by pipetting supplies from the great tank across the Atlantic; consequently the appeal of getting 'mixed up' with the Americans (mixed up, that is, with their money) was as pervasive among the leading Labour politicians in 1945 as it was among their Conservative counterparts – indeed, perhaps more so. The initial effect of President Truman's abrupt cancellation of Lend-Lease arrangements in July 1945, extending even to materials and foodstuffs currently in the pipeline, was therefore shattering. The only alternative to such free aid was an outright loan, which could only be forthcoming from the United States. Lord Keynes was entrusted with the ensuing negotiations in Washington. Later he was to be criticized for fostering illusions as to the ease with which the Americans could continue to be parted from their dollars.[6] This was unfair in so far as the whole meaning of Keynes in British public life was based on the conception (which his purely academic works may or may not have validated) that the money-sign could always be fudged. The unfortunate fact remained that in 1945 the great economist exercised far less of a fascination over American bankers than he did over his own countrymen, and although the United Kingdom was duly offered a loan of $3.75 billions, the latter carried a coupon of interest at the going rate and was coupled with an important proviso: that within one year of the Agreement being ratified by the United States Congress, pound sterling had to be made convertible with the dollar. In effect, finance was made available, but only on condition that the British shortly dismantled the currency and trade controls which after 1939 had been part and parcel of the war effort against Hitler, but which now ran counter to American plans for a multilateral world system.

Some Britons, on both Right and Left (but mainly the former), opposed acceptance of these terms. They did so partly on the grounds of preserving national independence – this being the first time that the issue of British national autonomy was held to be at stake under peacetime conditions. The anti-Loan faction also contended that United Kingdom interests would best be met by returning to the 'sterling float' successfully introduced by Neville Chamberlain at the Exchequer during the 1930s.[7] According to this argument, for the pound to be fixed on the dollar following the Second World War was to replicate the error made between 1925 and 1931 in adhering too rigidly to the Gold Standard. Suggestively, this case for a flexible exchange rate was allied to the thesis that British industry would be better off making a clean and rapid adjustment to post-war markets rather than going in search of subsidies which would only make the process more protracted and ultimately less efficient. Such advocacy of a 'bracing shower' was to reoccur sporadically (and abortively) in British economic debates in 1951, 1957 and 1970, before finally sweeping all before it after 1979 (by which time it had crystallized into something called 'Thatcherism'). In 1945, meanwhile, the opposition to the United States Loan remained essentially vestigial. As Keynes pointed out, refusal of the deal would lead straight to what he termed, rather dramatically, 'Starvation Corner'[8], and since this dismal destination had not appeared on the map of 'New Jerusalem' unfurled at the recent general election there was never really any likelihood that the Labour Cabinet would forgo the greenbacks lying invitingly on the table.

More intriguing than the Labour Government's agreement to a deadline for convertibility at a fixed rate, however, was the omission in the intervening period to take the remedial measures which might have allowed sterling to 'look the dollar in the face' when the moment of reckoning duly arrived. One corrective action which the Americans themselves proposed was that the United Kingdom should unilaterally write-down the debts she owed to fellow sterling (mostly Empire-Commonwealth) partners, not least since the liabilities concerned had been incurred defending those same countries from invasion by the enemy. Why, it was argued, should India, for instance, receive a premium for the honour of having been defended against the incursions of Japan? Yet the authorities in London refused to contemplate an initiative which would have been immensely corrosive across the broad face of sterling-imperial relations. One relatively clear-cut method of improving the scope for domestic financial equilibrium was therefore ruled out. The manner in which the Labour Government drifted into the great convertibility crisis of the summer of 1947 was also partly due to the fact that neither in Whitehall nor in the City was a mass flight from the pound actually anticipated. Various transitional arrangements with overseas sterling-holders had been negotiated by the Treasury, and it was expected that these would help to 'hold the line' against the speculators.[9] In the event, only the depth of the crisis itself – when the currency slumped on the ropes, and British officials and ministers had to rush to Washington to get permission to reimpose those very controls outlawed under the terms of the 1945 Loan – revealed just how fragile international confidence in Britain had already become. Lack of foresight alone is not an entirely convincing explanation for the posture struck by the Labour ministry during this sequence of events. A more profound reason for the paralysis afflicting Attlee and his colleagues as they were caught in the glare of convertibility was that any preventive action (necessarily involving substantial cuts in public expenditure, particularly on the military) was incompatible with the institutional and political compromises on which their authority rested. Like most governments in such a quandary, this one waited to be engulfed by the inevitable débâcle, in the hope that amidst the resulting confusion something would turn up. As we shall see, this expectation was not to be entirely disappointed.

It is against this background that we may set Attlee's telling if short-lived attempt during the early phases of the ministry to circumscribe the overseas ambitions of the government over which he presided.[10] Thus he began to talk ominously of 'deficit areas' overseas, and in early 1946 produced a memorandum which has been portrayed as 'amongst the most radical [ever] produced by a British Prime Minister'.[11] In it he called for a comprehensive evacuation from the Middle East, including Egypt and Greece, thus establishing 'a wide glacis of desert and Arabs between ourselves and the Russians'.[12] Behind such prescriptions lay a broad vision of the United Kingdom's place in the world as, in Attlee's incisive interpretation, 'the easterly extension of a strategic area the centre of which is the American Continent rather than as a power looking eastwards through the Mediterranean to India and the East.' In essence, here was an updated and Atlanticized model of Bonar Law's plea of 1922 that 'We cannot act alone as the Policeman of the World', and the Labour Prime Minister's arguments in 1946 were undoubtedly coloured by memories of the prudent retrenchments which had helped to stabilize the British position in the aftermath of the war of 1914–18.

Stuffing the genie of British *imperium* in the Middle East back into its bottle after 1919, however, had proved feasible (within limits) because the phenomenon itself was a novel one; whilst the cut-backs had then been catalysed by a series of outright revolts, most devastatingly that in Iraq during 1920. Circumstances in 1946 made any repeat of this process unlikely. Not only were the Middle Eastern networks of the metropolitan overseas establishment more securely entrenched, but they enjoyed the moral imprimatur of the Mediterranean Strategy pursued between 1939 and 1945. The greater scale of the British military presence in the area temporarily helped to damp down incipient local threats, though, as we shall see, it failed to stifle the determined urban terrorism of the Jewish Haganah in Palestine. Most fundamentally, the absolute priority of domestic stabilization which marked British affairs during the first half of the 1920s could not be replicated under the schizoid arrangements within British administration after 1945. Thus to Hugh Dalton (who shared much of Attlee's scepticism in these regards) Bevin's overwhelming 'fascination' with the Middle East was evident in every Cabinet discussion of foreign policy.[13] As soon as the premier showed signs of wobbling on this central commitment, the Foreign Secretary lined up with the Chiefs of Staff to point out that it was inconceivable for Britain to retreat from the region 'through which we bring influence to bear on the soft underbelly of France, Italy, Yugoslavia, Greece and Turkey'.[14] Faced with this invincible opposition, Attlee quickly backed down, and as far as foreign policy was concerned the latter retreated into that enigmatic shell which subsequently became the hallmark of his official temperament. In effect, if rational discourse could not reshape British policy-making according to post-war realities, the Labour premier's response was to sit back and wait upon events to impose their own inexorable curtailments, as they soon did in Greece, Palestine and, most signally of all, India. Unfortunately, such *attentisme* was by its very nature slow, messy and prone to easy circumvention by vested interests with their propensity to slip from one jerry-built redoubt to another, like Victorian redcoats wheeling between their square formations to fend off the assaults of the Dervish horde. By the time the process had fully worked itself out according to this pattern – which meant by the later 1960s – the damage had been done, and not only to the Dervishes.

In speaking of the 'soft underbelly of Europe' Bevin was, of course, browbeating his chief with the Churchillian baton that always lay ready to hand, and the shadow of the Conservative leader may be said to have overcast the Labour ministry in matters of external policy throughout its life. A striking instance of what this meant came in the House of Commons on 7 May 1946, when Attlee announced his government's willingness in principle to scale down the British military presence in Egypt on the precondition that the latter agreed to cast-iron guarantees being afforded to British and imperial interests. Churchill immediately rose to intone that this was 'a very grave statement, one of the most momentous I have ever heard in this House'[15], whilst Anthony Eden instantly followed in his wake to declare that the Suez Canal was sacrosanct as the 'swing door to the Middle East'. By such interventions the Conservative Opposition made it crystal clear that it regarded the Middle East in general, and Egypt in particular, as the litmus test of the bipartisan consensus in foreign and imperial policy handed on from the wartime Coalition of 1940–45. Consequently not long passed before the talks between London and Cairo (probably always doomed to failure) were gradually run down on the grounds of 'the future of the Sudan', that hoary old Foreign Office chestnut when it came to putting Egyptians in their place. It was therefore at this early juncture after the Second World War that the attitudes struck by individuals and parties on Egyptian issues were defined as a pre-eminent measure of 'soundness' within contemporary British politics. The lesson this held for a Labour ministry, in particular, was too obvious to need explicit spelling-out.

The Middle-Eastern bias in British policy was further buttressed at this stage by the preoccupation with the fate of the ex-Italian Empire, particularly Cyrenaica. As Wm. Roger Louis has shown[16], one reason why the Labour Government coveted the latter territory was because its spaciousness and low density of population promised to provide excellent facilities for the independent British atomic programme, finally authorized by the Cabinet in January 1947 but anticipated for some time before. As Bevin said of the Bomb, 'We've got to have the bloody Union Jack flying over it'.[17] Even without this consideration, Cyrenaica was essential to what British military and diplomatic circles – characterized as always by a remarkable fertility in the matter of cultural and geographical concepts – began to refer to as the 'Central Arab World'. It is noteworthy that in this setting Anglo-Soviet relations first took a turn for the worse. Thus the wry disdain with which the Soviet Foreign Minister, V.M. Molotov, treated the United Kingdom's claims from the Potsdam talks onwards, including a sarcastic Soviet counter-bid for 'a corner of Tripolitania', raised anew the traditional bogey of a Russian barrier to English supremacy in the Near East. 'It was clear', Molotov baited Bevin in the Council of Foreign Ministers, 'that the [British] Secretary of State did not want to come to terms with anybody about anything. He was claiming everything, even [Italian] Somaliland.'[18] Since, among the Big Three Powers at the time, the United Kingdom indeed appeared as the only one making old-fashioned territorial demands, such remarks came painfully close to home. Bevin, the Titan of the TGWU, renowned for his own strong-arming of opponents, was not used to negotiating from weakness, let alone ridicule, and his hatred for Molotov never flagged for the remainder of his life.

One disturbing aspect of the international discussions on the distribution of ex-Italian booty was that it revealed (shades of Tehran in 1943!) a continuing American tendency to lean towards Moscow rather than London. James Byrnes, the American Secretary of State, made little attempt to conceal his dislike of Bevin, considering him disorganized and unintelligent.[19] Whatever the accuracy of such a judgement – in most British narratives Bevin tends to emerge as an untutored genius – the main threat to the United Kingdom was patently that of a Soviet-American condominium constructed over their heads. It was entirely logical, therefore, that it was an Englishman who fortuitously discovered the existence of an 'Iron Curtain' between East and West before any Americans had thought of it – the phrase was coined by Winston Churchill in a speech delivered in Fulton, Missouri on 5 March 1946[20], and immediately integrated into the British policy consensus. In fact an endemic rivalry between the United States and the Soviet Union as competing superpowers was probably inevitable without the encouragement of outsiders, but for the United Kingdom, quite understandably in the circumstances, it could not come quickly enough. Hence

Bevin took every opportunity to stoke up Soviet anxieties as to what Western intentions might be, telling Molotov to his face that the Soviet Union (with over twenty million war dead) was no better than Hitler's Germany. Gaucheness to this degree had to be rationed, but Bevin with an impishness which was partly natural to him but which was also a pale imitation of the Churchillian brand of humour, could not resist the occasional coy display of the cards he held in his hand. Hence on one occasion on the way into a conference banquet, Hugh Dalton, the Chancellor of the Exchequer, anxiously quizzed Bevin as to how close the world leaders were to a compromise. 'Like the strike leader said', came the whiplash reply, '"Thank God there's no chance of a settlement".'[21] The rising tensions between the other Great Powers was indeed grist to the Bevinite mill, even if not all of his colleagues shared the expansive vision of British interests which the Foreign Secretary enjoyed wearing so prominently on his sleeve.

The continued cultivation of 'prestige' as the quintessence of British diplomacy would have been all very well if its economic foundations had been secure. As it was, at the heart of British dilemmas after 1945 lay the temptation for its leaders to 'bid up' the overseas and foreign policy stakes, only to find repeatedly that the ground gave way beneath them at home. The classic pattern was set, as we have already seen, by the sterling débâcle during the summer of 1947. That currency collapse was itself only the climax of a protracted economic crisis whose immediate origins were climatic. The winter of 1946–7 had proved the worst in living memory, when the Thames unprecedentedly iced-over; the railway tracks froze in sympathy: coal distribution became chaotic; soon light and power began to fail; finally, the factories started to close. Much of this plight was blamed on the responsible Minister, Emmanuel Shinwell, who fed the Cabinet with optimistic reports on fuel supplies until the dismal truth dawned – 'bone-headed perversity' is a typical assessment of his performance by one of his colleagues in the dignified calm of forty years after.[22] Yet in truth the culpability may be more equally shared. At a time when coal was the life-blood of reconstruction, ministers and officials expected the undermanned and undercapitalized mines to go on meeting the escalating demands of both domestic demand *and* the export trade. The arithmetic simply did not work, and Shinwell, rather than be the bearer of bad news, acted perfectly rationally in keeping mum until the dam burst, and the waters of public odium covered his colleagues as well as himself. The coal shortage thereafter acted not only as a long-term constraint on recovery at home, but also on British influence abroad, especially in Europe. Yet the impasse in the mines was symptomatic, too, of something more profound: after a sustained period in which the role of the economy had been above all to shore up the national effort in other directions – in which resources were always squeezed *out*, but never put back *in* – the system itself began to go on strike. If it was part of the natural flow in British social history that the northern coal operatives should be the first to show signs of incipient revolt, other parts of the labour force were sure to follow. Thus it was that the 'English disease' first appeared on the public stage.

The uniqueness of the British malady, however, remained for some while obscured by its relationship to the more vivid dislocations in Europe as a whole. It was with the latter principally in mind that the new American Secretary of State, General George C. Marshall, made a speech at Harvard University on 5 June 1947 in the course of which he offered large-scale dollar aid if the European countries came up with a co-ordinated and practical programme for reconstruction to justify the investment. There followed what Bevin's biographer regards as the turning point of his career as Foreign Secretary, when, whilst his Continental counterparts dithered, he leapt from the grid and assumed the putative leadership of the European nations.[23] From that point on, Alan Bullock contends, Bevin's diplomacy, so often fumbling and unsure hitherto, attained an intellectual coherence and courage of which the signing of the North Atlantic Treaty was the logical culmination in the field of political security. According to this interpretation, whilst acknowledgement is given to the fact that the Labour Government's (and, above all, the Foreign Secretary's) initial enthusiasm for Marshall Aid did not afterwards translate into support for the wider ideal of west European integration under the aegis of the Organization for European Economic Co-ordination [OEEC], the blame for the United Kingdom's alleged 'missing of the bus' in post-war Europe is laid squarely at the feet, not of Attlee's ministry, but of successive Conservative Governments after October 1951 who, by implication, should by then have known better.

In our next chapter we shall see that such an assertion does not lack for evidence to support it. Nevertheless, Bevin's motives, and the limitations inherent in them, with respect to the 'Marshall process' from 1947 onwards bear closer examination. The real key to his thinking was reflected in his exchanges with two of the American Secretary of State's assistants sent to London immediately following the Harvard speech, during which the Foreign Secretary stressed that the British priority was to be accorded the primacy 'which we held in 1923–4 in [European] economic reconstruction after the last war'.[24] That Britain *had* enjoyed any such preponderance *vis-à-vis* Europe in the 1920s was itself a contentious proposition. The accuracy of the historical analogue, however, was irrelevant. At bottom, no British Government after 1945 (Socialist or Tory) was prepared to enter into a multilateral European process in which they were put on a conventional negotiating basis ('lumped in', as Stafford Cripps later put it when he went to the Exchequer) with other Europeans. The roots of this sentiment went deep. After all, Neville Chamberlain had tried to negotiate in Europe, and everybody knew what had happened to him. Instead, the United Kingdom sought to elevate itself above the Continental morass, offering itself as the filter through which Anglo-American largesse might be distributed and its authority transmitted. Once it became transparently clear, as it soon did, that the Americans harboured very different ideas as to how the Marshall Aid programme should function, and that their actions were guided by economic rather than purely power-political criteria, Bevin's sentiments, and those of British officialdom generally, towards Europe cooled very rapidly indeed.

Meanwhile, however, the connection forged in the official Whitehall mind between Marshall Aid and British primacy in Europe also cut across what was becoming known as 'East-West Relations'. In particular, it gave a considerable fillip to the anti-Sovietism in London which renewed fears of a Russian forced entry into the Middle East in 1945–6 had done so much to stir up. Quite obviously, the United Kingdom – which at that moment was having considerable difficulty even keeping its own electric lights operating – could not hope to *lead* any European grouping of which the Soviet Union was a part. What the British could aspire to preponderate over was a strictly west European rump, and the smaller the rump, in many ways, the better (a feeling which, as we shall note later, underlay distinct equivocations regarding the 'acceptability' of Western Germany which continued well into the next decade). Hence at the crucial meeting in Paris during July 1947 on the ambit of American financial assistance, Bevin – immensely highly strung, according to a key aide[25] – made no secret of his eagerness to see a wedge driven between the Soviets and the Americans. 'This is the birth of the Western bloc', he whispered excitedly at the moment when a final break was perceived to be inevitable. Behind this apotheosis lay the answer to a conundrum which went back to the seminal divide over Appeasement ten years before. Then it had been axiomatic to some sceptics that it was nonsensical to go to war with Germany when the only certain result would be to let Stalin in 'though the back door'. The birth of the Western bloc over which Bevin waxed lyrical in 1947 solved the puzzle by isolating Russia and its *de facto* satellites behind a *cordon sanitaire*. In short, far from the division of postwar Europe being a political disaster for British policy-makers, it was, in fact, the best of all possible worlds. This, perhaps, helps to explain why it was that when the Cold War finally thawed out years later, the British showed more hesitation in embracing the fact than most.

If the summer and autumn of 1947 was indeed the juncture at which Bevin and the Labour Government got into a purposeful stride on foreign policy, it did not seem like it to those ministers responsible for other areas of public administration. Dalton thus identified the same transition as one in which 'our self-confidence [as Ministers] weakened individually and collectively', and felt that the Labour Government never fully recovered its nerve.[26] Afterwards, Attlee retreated more and more into himself; whilst it is difficult to identify any economic strategy between 1947 and 1951 unless tinkering with controls and the publication of voluminous statistical charts be so considered. The essential bind within 'modern' British government – decisive and confident when dealing with what in German political science is called *Aussenpolitik*, but reduced to nervous exhaustion and intellectual bankruptcy whenever events forced an emphasis on *Innenpolitik* – is strikingly displayed by such a paradigm. We shall shortly turn, in this regard, to the disturbing signs of fragmentation which attended the final phases of the Labour ministry. Before doing so, however, we must look at imperial issues, since these intruded powerfully on its experience, and in one instance – that of India's independence – afforded it (and above all Attlee) a success as unsullied as such things are ever likely to be in the generally dismal field of public affairs.

Between 1939 and 1945, for the second time in less than thirty years, the British had squeezed another great war effort out of India. This was quite an achievement in the light of the apparent weakness of the Raj during the 1920s and 1930s. The methods employed, however, though effective in the short term, were bound to be deleterious in the longer term. After the Quit India rebellion of August 1942, for example, the Congress party had been swept off the streets, and the bulk of its leadership incarcerated.[27] Not without a good deal of tacit encouragement from the Viceregal regime, the resulting void in Indian politics had been filled by the rapid growth of the Muslim League, led by Ali Jinnah. It was under these wartime conditions that the cry for a separate Muslim state called 'Pakistan' became a staple element in the political life of the northern provinces of the Sub-Continent, where the Muslim population was concentrated. Overall, by confronting Hindu nationalism head-on the Imperial

Government in London succeeded in one last big heave to bend India to metropolitan purposes, but in so doing broke many of the old balances and compromises on which the British presence had long been based. By the end of the Second World War, as Churchill himself wryly admitted[28], the chief imponderable was not whether British rule in India would survive, but under what circumstances – and to whose benefit among the local elements struggling for the reversion – it would be brought to an end.

As Viceroy the Labour Government inherited Lord Wavell, at heart a bluff and conscientious soldier-administrator who despised political sophistication in a situation where tactical subtlety had become the essence of the matter. Much to Wavell's chagrin, the new ministry in London had dispatched a Cabinet Mission to look over his shoulder whilst negotiations got under way with the nationalist politicians (the Congress leaders having finally been released from prison for the purpose). Even more than the residual bitterness between Congress and the British, it was the deteriorating relations between Congress and the Muslim League which underpinned the deadlock at the Simla Conference in the spring of 1946, after which the Cabinet Mission returned dispiritedly to London. In the wake of this fresh blockage, Wavell, perhaps motivated by a desire to impress upon the Home Government the risks being run by those who were carrying responsibility on the spot, forwarded to the Labour Government for its approval a contingency 'Breakdown Plan' for operation during an emergency.[29] Under this gloomy scenario, the evacuation of British personnel would begin in the south and progressively roll up into the more violent and communally-riven north. It was this Plan which earned Wavell a second spectacular dismissal to match his earlier departure from North Africa, and served as the immediate trigger for the decisive governmental decisions which ensued.

The reason for this outcome is not hard to seek. Any 'breakdown' of the sort unhappily envisaged, in which British lives (quite likely involving women and children) would be lost, threatened to hoist the Labour Government on the old petard of its 'fitness to govern'. The mere indication of willingness to plan for such invidious circumstances was enough to seal Wavell's fate. Above all, his memorandum implicitly underlined the fact that there were now more risks in *staying* in India, politically-speaking, than there were in *going*. Consequently a policy of last resort – that of the 'imposed solution' – which had circulated for several years in informed circles suddenly moved into the foreground of British thinking. According to this formula, the United Kingdom authorities had only to announce unilaterally that they would leave India by a specified date in order to regain the initiative into their own hands. The local politicians, deprived of their traditional referee, would thus be automatically forced to thrash out a workable agreement amongst themselves, since the alternative would be civil war. The 'imposed solution', in other words, promised to solve the Indian problem in one fell swoop by throwing the problem at the Indians. This was the policy Attlee now adopted.

The Labour premier's trickiest problem was not so much to find an appropriate policy, since there was one available on the shelf to be taken down and dusted off, as to find the right man to carry it out. The executant of an 'imposed solution' required nerve, brashness, theatricality and stubborn singlemindedness. Here, too, Attlee was lucky in the person of Lord Louis Mountbatten. At the time Mountbatten's appointment was a surprise, since his career to date had not always been characterized by steady courses or sound judgement, as Philip Ziegler's absorbing biography has shown.[30] What had been faults in other places and at other times, however, including a pronounced streak of deviousness, became for Mountbatten a virtue in India after he took up his post on 22 March 1947. He enjoyed, in addition, one special advantage which recommended him to Attlee: his familial relation to the British monarchy. 'We want something royal in a spiritual and temporal sense for the abject subjects of this great eastern empire'[31] one Englishman had remarked in the spacious days when the Raj was being cobbled together at the end of the eighteenth century. In 1947 'something royal' was required to bestow a measure of legitimacy on the going out of empire, just as it had once eased the coming in. For these reasons Mountbatten was an inspired appointment, and nothing conjures up the spirit of Britain's departure from the Sub-Continent better than the press photographs of the last Viceroy's shimmeringly elegant presence surrounded by the beaming brown beauty of Indian children. Thus was afforded a celebration of India's future which succeeded in being at the same time a tribute to England's mannered superiority.

With the smooth manners went the hard knocks. Mountbatten came armed with the British Cabinet's statement of 20 February 1947 that India would move to independence, come what may, in July 1948, a target soon shunted forward, as the problem of maintaining law and order mounted, to 15 August 1947. At the same time, in one of his first meetings with the Indian party leaders, the Viceroy tabled a document entitled *The Administrative Consequences of Partition*.[32] By telling the politicians how to carve up the Sub-Continent, Mountbatten flagged that the threat of partition was no longer a weapon that could be used *against* the British. Indeed, once the latter had embraced the feasibility of division, there arose the prospect that a British Viceroy might choose as his legatees not merely two parties (Congress and the Muslim League) but some other multiple, since there was no lack of exotic partitioners in the region to choose from. That the rival factions began dutifully to feed from Mountbatten's hand was a feat, then, which required tact and insight, but no great skill. The transport of even the most exotic oriental ware loses half its care once it is assumed that a crack along the way is not an unthinkable mishap.

Inevitably the United Kingdom's mode of departure from India, and in particular Mountbatten's part in it, has not lacked for critics.[33] By concentrating his attention so exclusively on the two main parties, and the respective religious communities preponderantly associated with them, Mountbatten undoubtedly made himself deaf to the imprecations of others. Not all of the excluded were prepared merely to gaze upon other people's good fortune. Principal among these were the martial Sikhs, spread so awkwardly across the Punjab. Before the 'freedom hour' of midnight struck on 15 August 1947, and even more drastically afterwards, this section took to the sword in large numbers, with consequences that are well known.[34] Those narrators who dwell upon these localized horrors have often contended that Mountbatten was guilty of having inadequately listened to Sikh protestations, and thus helped to drive them to extremities. Yet such criticisms are ultimately beside the point. The last Viceroy – like most last viceroys – was appointed, not to solve indigenous problems, but to simplify them sufficiently to allow the expatriate Army and administration to get out with dignity – and their skins. This is what Mountbatten did with the glamorous panache that was the length and breadth of his public personality. If flaws there were, they lay not in his conduct, but in his remit[35].

The remit, of course, came from Attlee. One of his aides noted that despite (or arguably because of) all the travails of his government nearer home, the premier was 'really more interested in the Indian problem than anything else'.[36] This curious fact reflected not only his close association with Indian policy going back to his participation on the Simon Commission in the later 1920s. The harsh reality was that India was the only aspect of overseas policy – almost the only aspect of national policy as a whole – upon which Attlee as Prime Minister was able to put the mark of his own distinctive Radicalism (nationalization of domestic industry, for example, meaning little or nothing to him). Bevin, who came from an entirely different tradition of essentially proletarian chauvinism, showed early signs of baulking at the great Indian decision, but allowed himself for once to be overruled by his chief. Attlee's leverage in this matter stemmed from Indian realities which no amount of rhetorical emotion could obscure. But Bevin's unusual pusillanimity (starkly contrasting with his attitude to developments in the Middle East) was in part also the natural counterpart of the silence on the benches opposite in the House of Commons. One of the striking facets of the passage of the Indian Independence Bill through the British Parliament, indeed, were the dogs that did not bark, Churchill's absences from these debates constituting one of the most notable diplomatic illnesses in British history.[37] For those who remembered the bruising contest over much more modest

Indian Reform in the thirties there was a degree of irony about this situation. The key to the difference lay in a general, if veiled, consensus within the British legislature which had come into being by the latter date. India had become, in effect, an incubus which the Conservatives did not want on the agenda when their time to form a new government arrived; they were happy to look discreetly the other way whilst the Socialists did a scuppering job that would have been infinitely more embarrassing for them to perform. Meanwhile the Labour Government was happy to rid itself of one unsustainable liability without running the gauntlet of an Opposition screaming 'surrender' in the division lobbies. On this basis the British nation slid off the Indian hook a good deal more easily than anybody would have anticipated even a couple of years earlier.

So mellifluous was this process, in fact, that one observer has even concluded that it was *too* easy for the British good. Thus Enoch Powell has compared the demise of the British Raj in India and the later experience of France in its hallmark-decolonization in Algeria, pointing out that the latter was a traumatizing sequence which, as it were, 'cleansed' the metropole of imperial psychology and drove its cadres to apply a ruthlessly clinical intelligence to the *real* national interest, which now lay in different directions altogether.[38] By contrast, the British serenaded themselves out of India in such a way that the metropolitan elites concerned permitted themselves to carry on as if nothing had really happened that need affect their fundamental assumptions about their role as a class, or the United Kingdom's role in the world. One need not share Enoch Powell's maverick lament that India did not become Britain's Algeria to agree that there is more than a grain of truth in this analysis. What is so striking about the demission of 1947, from the United Kingdom's perspective, was the studied avoidance of a defence review which might logically be thought to spring from the evacuation of Britain's largest and traditionally most pivotal imperial possession.[39] The fact was that, regardless of alterations in objective conditions, the 'global role' remained too critical to the British identity of themselves, and in particular to the make-up of social and political power within the metropole, for the cat of any such 'review' to be let out of the bag. Subsequent experience was to prove the delicacy of this point, since there was nothing so certain in the 1950s and 1960s (not to mention later) to unsettle the high political world than the rumour that a defence assessment was on the way.

Such carpings apart, the granting of independence to India, albeit at the cost of partition, was indubitably a considerable achievement by the Labour Government for which historians have usually awarded it an alpha rating. Judgements of its handling of Palestine have tended to be more severe. Yet the latter problem had long threatened to be more awkward than the former. Palestine's place within Mediterranean strategy meant that the territory could not be shrugged off in the half-blasé style that was applied in the Sub-Continent, whose role as a 'barrack in the eastern seas' had long been in decline; nor was it rare in imperial experience for small possessions to pose even more intractable issues than their bigger brethren. Above all, the crucial fact was that by 1945 the excruciating balancing act between Arab and Jewish interests which the British had maintained throughout the history of the Mandate had broken down. Thus the more extreme Zionists – believing, not altogether mistakenly, that the British had covertly decided to break faith with the Balfour Declaration of 1917 – had taken to guns and gangs, and on 6 November 1944 they assassinated in Cairo the British Minister Resident in the Middle East, Lord Moyne.[40] This was the psychological moment when the Anglo-Zionist tie began to unravel; and when Churchill subsequently heard that the convicted terrorists had yet to meet the gallows, he saw to it that they did not tarry long.[41] Later depredations by the 'men of violence' such as the famous blowing-up of the King David Hotel (housing British Military Headquarters) in July 1946 only made this chasm wider. Against such a grim background, and without the legacy of a clear and effective policy bequeathed by its predecessors in office, it followed that the Labour team never succeeded in inventing one for themselves – except, in the end, that of evacuation, literally 'bag and baggage'.

Palestine (because it was a Mandate, not a colony) came under the aegis of the Foreign Office, and therefore fell to Bevin's rumbustious supervision. The policy, or rather the posture, he developed won him at the time and since a reputation for anti-Semitism. His assertion that pressure from the United States after the war to speed up Jewish immigration into Palestine arose from the fact that the Americans did not want 'too many of them [the Jews] in New York' was indiscreet, if not entirely devoid of truth. More tasteless was Bevin's quip, in the context of Displaced Persons' Camps in Europe, about Jews 'wanting to get to the head of the queue'.[42] Nevertheless, his anti-Semitism, if such it can be called, was not autonomous; it was wrapped up in the 'pure Englishry' and dislike of all foreigners which Trade Union leaders and the British Foreign Office alike in this era wore on their sleeves as a form of democratic insignia. Much more important in predetermining Bevin's approach to Palestine was the fact that he became Foreign Secretary just at the juncture when the long-argued case of the diplomatic professionals that British interests in the Middle East were best pursued through the vehicle of an Anglo-Arab 'commonwealth' finally triumphed over the quintessentially strategic romanticism which had always constituted the essence of Anglo-Zionism. *Realpolitik*, not racism, was Bevin's guiding star.

The crux of British policy in the Mandate after 1945, therefore, was to cap the influx of Jews and to focus on the objective of a bi-national Palestinian state, within which the Arabs might remain the largest and most influential community. *Ipso facto*, of course, this ruled out partition and scaled down the historic, but always ambiguous, commitment to a Jewish 'Homeland' in the area. The problem was that to a great many people (though not to Arabs) the revelations of Nazi genocide in Europe legitimated and even necessitated a great *increase* in Jewish entries into Palestine. This caused the British grave difficulties in public relations, as the sad tale of the refugee hulk *Exodus* exemplified. It also caused the British increasing problems in their relations with the United States. The motives behind the Truman Administration's move towards Zionism, just when the British were trying to back away, is not our concern, except to say that the emphasis on 'votes in New York' has almost certainly been overdone. Hitherto American access to the Middle East had largely depended on the thin wedge of oil developers and missionaries; in 1946–7 United States' expansionists desired a bigger slice of the action, and the Zionists came to their hand, just as they had to those of the British (above all to Lloyd George) in 1917–18. President Truman, therefore, used the rabbis just as much as they used him.[43] Either way, the British (not to mention the indigenous Palestinians) could never win.

There followed a curious process in which British attempts to wriggle off Balfour's hook were consistently frustrated by American actions. The climax of these 'misunderstandings' came with Truman's Yom Kippur statement of 4 October 1946, in which he effectively came out in favour of a Jewish state in Palestine. It was a moment when the Anglo-American relationship seemingly hung in the balance. 'I have received with great regret', Attlee wrote acidly to Truman, to whom, on previously hearing of the draft statement, he had telegraphed for discussions prior to its release, 'your letter refusing even a few hours' grace to the Prime Minister of the country which has the actual responsibility for the government of Palestine in order that he might acquaint you with the actual situation and probable results of your action . . . I shall await with interest to learn what were the imperative reasons which compelled this precipitancy'.[44] Yet beyond the cryptic Attlee did not go. Not only had London come to depend too heavily on the assistance of the United States in Europe to risk a transatlantic breakdown over Palestine, she was also looking hopefully to the Americans to share the burden of security elsewhere, especially in Greece. During early February 1947 the British pushed the ball firmly into the Americans' court by announcing unilaterally that their troops would soon be withdrawing from that country (though, in the event, the British military presence continued in truncated form until 1950). The decision in Washington to respond to this *de facto* British invitation to assume the slack of western authority over a large part of the eastern Mediterranean theatre was forcibly expressed in the Truman Doctrine of March 1947, laying down that henceforth the United States would 'support free peoples who are resisting subjugation by armed minorities or by outside pressure'.[45] It was as part of these broader accommodations, rationalized by the thesis of a new struggle for 'world freedom', that the Anglo-American difficulty over Palestine was necessarily subordinated.

Abdication, hopefully graceful, from the Mandate was increasingly the only course thus left open to Britain. The first major shift in this direction came when the Labour Government announced in mid-February 1947 that the future of Palestine would be referred to the United Nations. If, as has been suggested, it was hoped in Whitehall that the result of this action would be to mire the United Nations itself in disagreement, such that the latter would eventually be forced to hand full responsibility for Palestine back to the long-suffering Mandatory, only disappointment awaited. The Special Committee which visited Palestine recommended partition, and on 29 November 1947 the United Nations Assembly (amidst a veritable tidal wave of humanitarianism and kick-backs to Latin American delegates) proceeded to a historic vote which put its imprimatur upon two new states, one Jewish and one Arab, each consisting of three discrete segments. By this time the British had already made clear that they would have no part in imposing such a solution at bayonet-point on the Arabs, and that the Mandate would end *regardless of local circumstances* on 15 May 1948, a time-limit carefully calculated to allow the retrieval of the valuable stores and equipment which had accumulated in the territory. Afterwards the British Army proceeded to gradually draw in its perimeter and cut its way to the coast, making no attempt to police the vicious battle for land and power which broke out in its wake. This was an ignominious end to the British presence in Palestine (the most ignominious, indeed, of *all* modern British decolonizations), but it is doubtful whether efforts whilst on the retreat to pacify the surrounding country would have had any other effect than that of costing the lives of British personnel.[46] For the United Kingdom, there were no longer friends to be cultivated in the territory, but it was hoped to avoid making more enemies than those which already existed. Such a cast of mind was not conducive to vigorous action or broad human sympathy.

It is, however, virtually a law of all major decolonizations that the departing power seeks, *en passant*, to identify a new or enlarged grapple-hold in a region adjacent to the one being vacated. Hence in this case every step trodden by the British Army on the way to its disembarkation point at Haifa increased the value ascribed in London to the satellite-kingdom of Jordan and, in particular, to the British-led Arab Legion on which King Abdullah's authority in that country heavily depended. The more important Jordan became in British eyes, the more attractive became the prospect of its territorial aggrandizement amidst the upheavals of the time. The evidence suggests that Bevin and the Foreign Office encouraged Abdullah ('Mr Bevin's Little King', as he was called) to join the other Arab nations in their invasion of Israel in May 1948, but with more than half an eye on the loot which might be extracted for himself should the general campaign fall apart at the seams.[47] This was for the United Kingdom another moment of extreme delicacy, since if the Jewish armies had turned their full weight on the Jordanians, pressure on Britain to intervene on behalf of the latter might well have proved irresistible, with grave consequences not least for Anglo-American relations. Although the unvarnished truth of these passages can probably never be known, it was perhaps not entirely coincidental that whilst the Jews comprehensively defeated Egypt and Syria, they did not similarly throw the Arab Legion with its British officers out of the West Bank (including East Jerusalem) which the latter had occupied at the outset of the fighting. The putative Arab-Palestinian entity decreed in Manhattan, therefore, never saw the light of day, since part of it disappeared into the maw of Greater Israel, and part of it went into the maw of Greater Jordan.

Overall, whilst the dénouement in Palestine was hardly a triumph for British arms or diplomacy, it was hoped in Whitehall that as a damage-limitation exercise things had not turned out too catastrophically. Another unsustainable commitment had been liquidated. Anglo-American relations had been preserved. Jordan had been padded out as a potentially stronger bastion of British influence in the region. Discontented Palestinian refugees – refused access to Egypt – had been bottled up in the Gaza camps where, it was assumed, they could do little damage to anybody other than themselves. Finally, the Egyptians, though smarting from their own humiliation, were hardly in a position to kick the British out of Suez, their own Army having just been evicted from the Levant by the new Jewish state. From Britain's vantage-point, this was obviously not a perfect outcome, but it could at least be credibly presented as the best of all possible worlds that remained viable in the troubled Middle East.

Unfortunately this expectation was to be belied. Far from the emergence of Israel cowing Arab political civilization and making it more pliable in those venues where the British sought to retain their existing stake, it fanned the flames of an intense anti-westernism. The British presence was first in line of the fireball. Over some thirty years the United Kingdom had hawked its friendship around from one Arab country to another, extolling the benefits of security which their goodwill could provide. When in the Arab-Israeli War of 1948–9 these guarantees of support were put to the test, they were found to be practically worthless. Even in Iraq, where British bribes could still keep an old hand like Nuri-es-Said clinging to power, it only required the announcement of a new draft treaty with Britain to bring riots to the streets of Baghdad.[48] In Jordan alone – the model Anglo-Arab polity – did time seem to stand still, until Abdullah himself was gunned down in Jerusalem on his way to Friday Prayers on 20 July 1951. A few weeks before, the Iranian Government had appropriated the British-owned Anglo-Iranian Oil Company. This action (to which we shall return later) heralded a long-drawn-out crisis for British prestige in the Middle East which bedevilled not only the final phases of the Labour Government but successive Conservative ministries thereafter.

Whilst Britain's informal empire in the Middle East was

entering a tail-spin, her formal empire in Africa was, paradoxically, enjoying something of a boom. At a time of grave
food and raw material shortages, resource-rich Africa was thought
to offer a way out of the metropole's economic embarrassment.
Thus Bevin latched on to the opportunity, as he put it, 'to
organize the middle part of the planet – western Europe,
the Middle East, the Mediterranean, the Commonwealth', but
especially emphasizing that if the United Kingdom 'pushed on
and developed Africa we could have the United States dependent
on us and eating out of our hands in five years'.[49] Such reveries
– in which the French franc zone was also conceived as an
appendage of a consolidated and enlarged sterling area – typify
how Bevin, in contrast to Attlee, consistently sought to promote
the formula of a Third Force in world affairs managed from
London. Along the way, not only did Black Africa enjoy one
of its transient moments in the forefront of the British political
imagination, but the Labour Government came to wax more
lyrically about the extractive possibilities of colonial empire than
any administration since the days of Joseph Chamberlain.[50]

This vision, however, was already fading fast by the end of
the decade, and disappeared altogether, as we shall see, during
the early fifties. Certainly the massive sterling devaluation of
September 1949 proved that ideas of having the *Americans*
eating out of *British* hands were, to put it mildly, optimistic;
ebullient chatter about 'organizing the middle of the planet' was
not to be heard again. Subsequently the French, for their part,
decided not to amalgamate their colonial assets with the United
Kingdom but to combine their coal and steel production with
Western Germany[51] – a very different way of approaching the
future. Perhaps even more fundamentally, hopes of showering an
African cornucopia upon the housewives of a rationed metropole
evaporated at source: the local peasantries involved started to
go on strike, and even began to do what they had hitherto
neglected and rally around the banners of trouble-making urban
politicians[52]. Africa, in short, was the last frontier of British
imperial economy in the twentieth century; once its essential
aridity was grasped anew the resistance in London to political

change – at least where there were few white settlers to complicate the issue, as in west Africa – was commensurately eroded. By the time the Labour Government left office, the Gold Coast, for example, was already well on its way to a measure of self-government. This was less a reflection of any fundamental diminution of Britain's overall colonial commitment than of 'Native' Africa's enduring marginality to the imperial heartland.

There is a final aspect of the Labour Government's approach to imperial issues after 1945 which requires mention: the emergence of a new, multi-racial 'Commonwealth'. After 1926 this appellation had been used to describe an intimate group of 'British' nations whose common characteristics included not only self-governing status, but also the fact that they were (or were regarded, since South Africa clearly posed certain anomalies) as 'white' nations. Already during the late thirties, primarily as a response to the veiled republicanism of Eamon de Valera's government in the Irish Free State, some officials in Whitehall began to toy with the possibilities of a constitutionally eclectic, no-rule-book Commonwealth capable of providing berths for a more diverse group of countries, speculation on this matter including future independent regimes in India and Egypt.[53] The Second World War froze this potentially innovative tendency, as it froze much else besides. It resurfaced after August 1947, when it became obvious that (despite Mountbatten's imprecations to Nehru as the first Prime Minister of independent India) the latter country would not long be satisfied with the Dominion Status, carrying with it allegiance to a foreign throne, on which the recent transfer of power – if only for reasons of haste – had been based.[54] Pakistan equally made plain in a style of reluctant blackmail that if nothing less than a republic would do for India, then nothing less would do for her either.

The issue of republicanism, of course, touched a sensitive nerve, since as we have previously noted the monarchical tie had for some while become central to imperial thinking. Nevertheless, pragmatism was the order of the day, and in this respect the mind was wonderfully concentrated by the jolt administered when Burma, on becoming independent in 1948, refused to have anything to do with Commonwealth membership. The message that some suitably sartorial alteration was called for was heightened by the great value ascribed in Whitehall to reinforcing the Anglo-Indian connection for the shared tasks and interests that hopefully lay ahead. The self-governing entities of what some still quaintly called the 'British Empire' were thus convened in London during April 1949, at which meeting India and Pakistan together received the go-ahead to don the mantle of republican virtue. As a necessary consequence, the erstwhile idea of an indivisible, Imperial monarchy (within whose sacramental and mysterious person, as it were, unity and diversity could be endlessly reconciled with each other) was transmuted into a less exotic, earthy proposition whereby King George VI and his heirs became Head of a plural Commonwealth, this headship being acknowledged even by those members who happened themselves to be republics. It was, we may note in passing, dedication to this updated ideal of Crown and Overseas Realm which became the most distinctive hallmark of the reign of Queen Elizabeth II after she succeeded to the throne on the sudden death of her father in February 1952.

The 'New' Commonwealth of 1949, however, remained at bottom very much a metropolitan inspiration. 'Its members', John Darwin has written in a neat summary, 'had little in common with each other apart from the strength of their *bilateral* ties with Britain. New members were admitted not by the choice of existing members but, in effect, at the discretion of the British Government. The post-war Commonwealth was a British creation, constructed for British purposes.'[55] These purposes led the British to be more sympathetic towards some of their traditional satellite-partners than others. Thus one aspect of these developments which stands out in relief against the backdrop of later history is the very considerable effort that British ministers and officials put into persuading India to remain in the Commonwealth, and how little concern (not to say some scarcely-concealed pleasure) was felt at the departure from it of the Irish Free State (the newly-styled Eire).[56] This can hardly be a matter of criticism, in so far as the Second

World War – when the Irish had been neutral – drove such a gulf between the two peoples that almost no concessions would have been sufficient to tempt the Dublin government to remain in an organization with even a tincture of loyalty to English royals. Even so, in this bias of the United Kingdom to rate fellow-feeling with India so high, and fellow-feeling with Ireland so low, there was an inversion of geographical, let alone political, logic which in the end was to carry a hefty price-tag. Perhaps the most subtle effect of the Commonwealth-mindedness inaugurated in 1949, however, was that it further deflected the British official mind from those courses of convergence and integration which were simultaneously getting under way amongst her Continental neighbours. The problem of the United Kingdom's relationship to this last phenomenon, at first no bigger than one man's hand, was soon to become a large cloud overhanging the final phases of Clement Attlee's Labour Government.

'On merits', a high-level, inter-departmental meeting of officials in Whitehall recorded their agreement in January 1949, 'there is no attraction for us in long-term economic co-operation with Europe. At best it will be a drain on our resources. At worst it can seriously damage our economy.'[57] Explanations for this attitude – which shifted only gradually and grudgingly thereafter – have conventionally been attributed to an insularity bred of an instinctively imperial psychology and past. This is true only in part. British officialdom had remained aloof from European economic reconstruction in the early thirties, for example, not primarily because of its prior affection for an Empire-Commonwealth, but because it was reckoned that the United Kingdom would be expected to stump up most of the money for making it a success. The British response once Marshall Aid got into its stride was predicated on much the same ground. In the late forties, as in the early thirties, complex feelings about German revival were at the root of the matter. This complexity was summed up by one leading Foreign Office official, Oliver Harvey, when he remarked as early as 1946 that 'we do not want an efficient Germany, but one with strong local vested interests'.[58] Since the bulk of the industrial plant of that devastated country fell within the zone of British occupation, the United Kingdom authorities appeared to be in a good position to see that German 'efficiency' did not get out of hand. The transplantation of a powerful trade union structure under the supervision of relevant British personnel also helped in this respect. The ideal of a low-level equilibrium in an incipient 'western' Germany, however, depended on American willingness to continue picking up the tab. Contrarywise, United States policy soon began to swing behind the goal of an 'efficient', and therefore productive, unit which could pay its own way in the world. The Rubicon was crossed in June 1948 when, under irresistible American pressure, it was decided to create a federal West German state and to institute a currency reform. The fact that United Kingdom opposition to further west European integration subsequently increased *pari passu* was no coincidence, since British hesitations about unbridled European reconstruction were organically connected to fears of renewal in Germany. It was not, therefore, pure chance that it was a noted British Germanophobe, Hugh Dalton, who dictated the spirit of the Labour Party official statement, *European Unity*, in May 1950, a publication which made little attempt to hide hostility to the enterprise.[59] The result of these vibrations was an uneasiness between London and the infant German Federal Republic which was to play a significant, if not always publicly visible, role in subsequent developments.[60]

Economic anxiety principally lay behind these responses, which may help to explain the paradox that British equivocations towards Germany continued even when those of France (whose own neuroses had always been linked to military and strategic vulnerability) were beginning to subside. Thus in the immediate aftermath of 1945 a sellers' market had prevailed, such that anything which fell off a production line could find a vent. This suited the United Kingdom, whose industrial infrastructure, being less damaged than most other ex-belligerent countries, could pretty much have European export markets to itself. But sellers' markets never last, and the supply-side effects of the Marshall process progressively curtailed this one by reviving genuine competition between European producers. As a result, the United Kingdom after 1948 was starting to feel the bracing wind of normal competition for the first time since 1939 (and in some senses since 1931); one of its harbingers was the appearance of German consumer articles in English shops. Strikingly, British manufacturers began to collectively inveigh against 'unfair' German trade practices in 1949, *before* the latter's vaunted economic 'miracle' got under way in the middle of 1950. If the first job-lots of a new stream of German manufactures could trigger such British *Angst*, it followed that the broader ideal of European economic co-operation evoked feelings that were at best neutral, and at times plainly inimical.

The progressive slide into a state of structural sterling weakness, climaxing in the devaluation of the pound by a massive thirty per cent in September 1949, served to entrench these negative sentiments. It was at this stage, too, that the attitude towards Britain of international opinion took a critical and often patronizing turn. 'The United Kingdom is finished', Louis Johnson, the United States Secretary of Defence, declared with relish[61], and although Johnson was renowned for having no love for his racial cousins, comments along these lines became a staple of cosmopolitan gatherings whenever British backs were turned, even among those not ill-disposed on principle. The echo of such tittle-tattle inevitably resounded in London, and swiftly fed into party politics, where it helped to begin the unravelling of the threads of consensus which had been tightly held together since 1940. The politics of modern British decline may be said to have begun in this lowering milieu.

The speed and tenacity, even desperation, with which the Labour ministry now tried to plug itself into an American support system can only be understood in this context. Diplomatically the crisis over the Soviet blockade of Berlin in late 1948, and the subsequent signature of the North Atlantic Treaty in Washington on 4 April 1949, had established the framework for this effort. Its more complicated genesis in British social and economic flaccidity, refracted through the continuing weakness of sterling, however, has been underestimated. 'Tell workers they can't have increased wages now', Bevin told his worried Cabinet colleagues in June 1949 as they pondered the growing obstreperousness of the trade unions. 'This can't be settled on financial level. Must be taken to higher level. Try for temporary tide-over with Snyder [United States Treasury Secretary]'.[62] Taking things to a higher level meant going to Washington and soliciting a preferential position for Britain within the Bretton Woods system of fixed exchange rates. When the British negotiators, led by Bevin and Stafford Cripps as Chancellor of the Exchequer, arrived in the United States capital under the duress of the markets in the following September, they did not find their hosts uniformly sensitive to their plight. 'Get off your butt'[63] was the sage advice proffered to them by the Administration's Treasury Secretary. Fortunately for the British team, however, Snyder's disparagement was offset in other quarters, and following extensive bilateral talks the United Kingdom was allowed to devalue the pound – thus securing a large competitive advantage – and granted assurances that ways would be found to continue American aid to her even after November 1951, the dread date on which Marshall subsidies to Western Europe as a whole were to come to an end. As a leading British Treasury official afterwards remarked of continuing American aid to Britain, 'In fact our whole economic life has been propped up in this way.'[64]

The British success in securing an extended economic guarantee from the United States was itself only a by-blow of a much larger development: America's sudden decision, after a great deal of havering, to convert her latent power into global authority.[65] Amidst this evolution, the United Kingdom's implicit offer of her services as a diplomatic and military co-adjutant took on a new sheen. 'An attempt should [now] be made', a State Department memorandum drew one implication, 'to link the U.K. more closely with the U.S. and Canada and get the U.K. to disengage itself as much as possible from Continental European problems.'[66] Any euphoria in London that in thus deflecting the danger of their being 'lumped in' with the other Europeans, they had at the same time managed to put a brake on the process of Continental convergence itself, soon faded. Indeed, amongst American officials at the top of the European Recovery Administration disbursing Marshall funds the buzz-word was now 'integration', with all its radical overtones. In leading the French to drink at the pool of the German Federal Republic, these administrators were helped by the intense irritation, even anger, of the authorities in Paris that the British Government, in the recent devaluation of sterling, had made not even the pretence of consultation with themselves. Significantly, then, it was the United States who played broker – much to Britain's renewed discomfiture – in securing the announcement of the Schumann Plan in May 1950, by which France and Germany agreed to pool their coal and steel industries, so establishing the outlines of an axis on which much of Western Europe's later development was to turn.[67] Rather pointedly, whilst an invitation to join in this exercise was forwarded to London, it was couched in the spirit that a sombre third party might be asked to join a romancing couple in a visit to the cinema. The announcement of the Schumann initiative, in short, put the British off their balance in European politics; in large part they never afterwards recovered it.

The strategic understanding with the United States had a slippery dimension outside, as well as inside, Europe. Attlee's Atlanticism sprang from his conviction that Britain's place in a security system with its centre of gravity in North America would prove a source of longed-for tranquillity. But was tranquillity the likely consequence of close association with a superpower whose foreign policy was subject to the open-endedness now adumbrated, for example, in National Security Paper 68, the foundation-charter of America's own putative role as a new 'Policeman of the World'? With so many eggs in one basket, would not the United Kingdom in any future crisis be driven pell-mell to assume burdens regardless both of the cost and of the vagueness with which her own *national* interest might be involved? As British luck had it in this era, the difficulty, far from remaining hypothetical, soon became all too practical when in June 1950 war broke out between North and South Korea, the former (Communist) country launching a sudden attack on its neighbour. It was argued in the West that the grab by North Korea had been orchestrated by the Kremlin, and that it might only be a 'feint' before the real move was made in Europe or the Middle East. The fact that we know such apprehensions to have been baseless does not invalidate the prudence displayed at the time by policymakers in the West. A degree of British rearmament was therefore inevitable. That the Labour Government rearmed on a massive scale, far beyond the efforts of other European nations who might reasonably be considered even more at risk

  hiking defence expenditure from approximately £830 millions in 1950–1 to a proposed £4,700 millions over the following three years – stemmed, not so much from any rational evaluation of the way that aggressions in the Korean peninsula might impinge on the security of the United Kingdom, than from the fact that the Labour Government knew itself to be 'on trial' as America's senior ally and felt bound to act accordingly.

The economic consequences of Korean rearmament for the United Kingdom were damaging over and above the actual sums involved. The timing, especially, was unfortunate in several critical senses. Thus just when the sterling devaluation of September 1949 looked set to put post-war British reconstruction on a competitive basis, the steam was cut off from behind by a rearmament programme dramatically reversing the progress which had been made in shifting resources out of the military sector and into civilian-cum-consumer industries. On the principle of the economists' beloved J-Curve, by which the deleterious effects of currency devaluation in raising the prices of imports are off-set over time by improved sales abroad, Britain ended up incurring the costs of sterling depreciation without securing many of the benefits. Timing was crucial in another respect as well: the British economy was 'wired up' for the Korean Emergency to such a great extent that it was inevitably diverted from the great European export boom just then taking shape. Experience showed that, as at the dogs, the last one out of this trap was also sure to be the last one going round the track.

But the most important economic legacy of the Korean War for Britain lay in the structural boost it gave to inflation. All countries were affected to some extent by the inflationary stimulus flowing from the new mobilization; but the fact that the United Kingdom rearmed more completely, relative to her GNP, than any other western country made her vulnerability in this respect more acute than ever. Getting a grip on inflation was peculiarly difficult for the British political order before 1950/1; afterwards it was to prove almost impossible to staunch a haemorrhage which, whilst slow by later standards, was fatal to her competitive standing for all that.

Quite apart from economic considerations, the course of the fighting in Korea provided a bumpy ride.[68] Briefly, after substantial losses in the first wave of North Korea's assault, a 'United Nations' force under the colourful American supremo in Asia, General Douglas MacArthur, landed at Inchon and soon retook the southern capital of Seoul. Instead of stopping, however, MacArthur shortly pressed on beyond the *status quo ante* of the 38th Parallel, and by November 1950 had arrived at the Yalu River bordering Communist China. Whether, as his radical critics alleged[69], the United Nations commander actually *intended* to force China into the war, thus creating the circumstances in which Mao Tse-Tung's revolution might be reversed, cannot be commented on here. The massive intervention by hordes of Chinese infantry sent MacArthur's army reeling back down the peninsula, until it was boxed into a narrow perimeter in the south. At this point, not without encouragement from MacArthur, the United States' Joint Chiefs of Staff began to consider the possibility of using their atomic weaponry to save a dire situation.

The prospect of atomic intervention galvanized Attlee into an action which Churchill had avoided in a roughly comparable situation during 1945: he rushed to Washington in December 1950 and lobbied the President against resort to the Bomb.[70] This was the most striking personal contribution of the British premier in the sphere of diplomacy during the course of his government. The reason for such unaccustomed decisiveness was simple: by this juncture the Soviet Union had (admittedly crude) atomic devices of her own, and if the Americans launched an all-out attack on Russia's senior proxy (that is, China), it was highly likely that the Soviets would feel honour-bound to do the same *vis-à-vis* the United States' chief lieutenant, the United Kingdom. It was a measure of panic at thus being caught up in the proxy-logic of superpower conflict which had a dampening effect on Britain's Cold War enthusiasm. Whether Attlee's pleas were effective in dissuading Truman from the use of atomic weapons may be doubted; after a discreet interval – in which a conventional counter-attack had salvaged the United Nations' position in Korea – the President courageously lanced the boil by flying to Guam where he personally dismissed MacArthur from his post. The legend nevertheless grew amongst American officials, and especially in Republican political circles, that it was the pusillanimous and 'pro-Red' British who had jogged the President's elbow at the critical moment and thus snatched a muddled and unsatisfactory compromise from the jaws of potential victory.[71] For their part, the British extracted from the experience a certain suspicion of American *ultra* methods (soon to be called 'brinkmanship') which gave ammunition to those elements, on both the Right and Left, whose sentiments towards the transatlantic connection were ambiguous. In the end the war in Korea fizzled out, the status quo of June 1950 having been restored, from whence things have not shifted since. The seeds of a certain mistrust in Anglo-American relations had been sown, however, and ripened during the first half of the decade, before being painfully resolved amidst the Suez imbroglio of 1956.

One aspect of this 'misunderstanding' was the different weights which the British and Americans respectively accorded to the Far and Middle East. This, of course, was not entirely novel in relations between the two countries; but the contradictions became more distinct as the Cold War cut across the emergence of anti-western nationalism from the late 1940s onwards. Hence the United States often felt that Britain fell short of their expectations in East Asia (a tendency later to climax during the

Vietnam War); whilst the United Kingdom harboured a scarcely-concealed grudge that the Americans not only failed to support them adequately amidst their Middle Eastern embarrassments, but actually sought to profit from them. This latter theme was highlighted by the Iranian crisis which erupted in May 1951. For some years the Iranian Government had resented the low revenues earned from the British-owned Anglo-Persian Oil Company (AIOC). The position of the company was gravely undermined when in December 1950 Aramco, the American oil consortium, set a new precedent by splitting revenues on a fifty/fifty basis with Saudi Arabia, a settlement said by one historian to constitute 'as great a revolution in the economic affairs of the Middle East . . . as the transfer of power in India in 1947'.[72] Certainly one effect was to stimulate nationalist sentiment in Persia, and when an extremist premier, Mohammed Mosadeqq, shortly came to power, one of his first acts was to appropriate AIOC. It was this setback, even more than the conflict in Korea, which hung like a pall over the final months of the Labour Government, and was to have powerful reverberations in British politics generally.

To grasp the effect of this departure on much British opinion it must be set against the backdrop of a long tradition in which Islamic challengers had pitted themselves against British interests and prestige. All these opponents (from Arabi Pasha in Egypt during the early 1880s, the notorious Mahdi in the Sudan soon afterwards, the infamous 'Mad Mullah' of Somaliland, through to Mosadeqq himself) had been tainted with religious as well as political fanaticism; all, hitherto at least, had been extinguished in the end. The appropriation of the Anglo-Iranian Company, therefore, quite apart from the commercial loss involved, posed very directly the question of Britain's capacity and 'will' (a word coming very much into vogue) to go on meeting such recurrent threats. The point was rammed home all the more as the situation took on highly ironic overtones, Mosadeqq choosing to play the role of 'lunatic' ascribed to him by British propaganda, giving interviews to the Western press from beneath a rimy set of bedclothes as he lay in a darkened room in the bazaar quarter of Tehran. As A.P. Thornton has remarked more widely of the demise of British imperial authority, there was no surer dissolvent of power than well-aimed barbs of ridicule.[73]

The dilemma as Foreign Secretary was not to be faced by Ernest Bevin who, struck by cancer, clung tenaciously to his post before Attlee finally succeeded in easing him out in March 1951 (he died one month later). His successor was Herbert Morrison, whose first action on being elevated to a job he had long coveted was to send a clerk to the House of Commons to fetch a biography of Lord Palmerston, that earlier scourge of the unprincipled foreigner.[74] This, possibly apocryphal, story is often repeated in disparagement of Morrison, but it is worth noting that very similar anecdotes are told of his predecessor in a style designed to flatter the latter's bulldog qualities. The truth was that Morrison was unfortunate in taking on the job when, at least within his own party, the bottom was falling out of the market in *machismo* along whose crest Bevin had ridden since the end of the war. Despite all the new Foreign Secretary's rather lacklustre pleas for military intervention in Iran, Attlee and his other colleagues in the Government finally decided against the use of force. 'The bitter word "humiliation" ran through these [Cabinet] discussions', Wm. Roger Louis tells us[75], but in the circumstances imprecations of honour were outweighed by more practical considerations. One such consideration was that, bereft of the assistance of the Indian Army in Gulf operations, the British Chiefs of Staff were not at all confident of their ability to successfully reoccupy the Persian oil-fields (a hesitation well borne out when five years later a logistical mess attended Britain's attempt to regain the more proximate locus of Suez). The clinching argument against intervention, however, was Attlee's wider thesis that Britain could no longer afford 'to break with the United States on an issue of this kind'[76], by which he meant a matter involving large-scale military operations in a region of great strategic significance. The Labour Government's punishment of the recalcitrant Persians, therefore, did not go beyond a withdrawal of all British technical personnel from the refineries of Abadan, and nobody was under any illusion that this would be enough to bring the heirs of Cyrus to heel.[77]

Arguably, the most significant effects of the Iranian crisis within British politics were visited not upon the Government of the day, but the Opposition. The nature of these convolutions may be deduced from a perfervid note in the diary of Harold Macmillan. 'In all the years I have been in the House', he exploded after hearing Morrison give a statement of the Government's policy, 'I have heard nothing like it from a Foreign Secretary at such a moment. This dirty little cockney guttersnipe has at least revealed himself for what he is . . . Even the impenetrable Rab [Butler] was white and quivering with rage.'[78] The florid and emotive echo of Appeasement in this outburst was not accidental, and before long analogous references to the demonology of the 1930s – Munich, Hitler, Neville Chamberlain et al. – were to become endemic in Conservative politics. Meanwhile Macmillan's social critique of the 'Cockney guttersnipe' Morrison indicated that the 'warmth pervading England' (as Churchill had once referred to the wartime apotheosis) had at last taken a distinctly cool turn. This fragmentation of the consensual ethic was soon also to be exemplified by electoral mud-slinging in which the Labour Party sought to label Churchill a 'warmonger' whose finger could not be trusted anywhere near the atomic trigger, whilst Churchill, in revenge, tried to identify the Left once more with the pacifism it had followed in the years prior to 1938.[79]

The tensions between the main political parties as previous understandings broke apart was mirrored by differences *within* the parties themselves: thus Macmillan, in his feline manner, remarked that *even* 'Rab' Butler was dismayed by Morrison's performance over Iran, whilst (more spectacularly) the Labour Cabinet had already been split in April 1951 by the resignations of Aneurin Bevan, John Freeman and Harold Wilson over cuts in the new National Health Service designed to free resources for rearmament. The Bevanite controversy, which bedevilled Labour politics for much of the decade ahead, typified the corrosion of the Second World War order in British life. That order had come to hinge on an equipoise between the provision of full (or, as some saw it, over-full) employment and state welfare at home, and a matching commitment to British Great Power status and 'prestige' overseas. By 1951, however, the fiscal arithmetic underpinning this delicate political economy was fast coming unstuck. An American observer gave a lucid diagnosis of what was really happening:

> Having gone through another economic crisis . . . British leaders feel that they are now fighting a last-stand battle for survival as a world power. They see themselves confronted by a host of life and death problems. They are trying simultaneously to maintain their Commonwealth and Empire and military commitments, balance their trade, modernize their industry, balance their budget, fight off inflation, and prevent a fall in their standard of living.
>
> Since there are no margins, even trivial things such as a battalion despatched to Eritrea; a million pounds expenditure on this or that item; a million gained or lost in overseas trade; a penny rise in [the] price of bread or a dime on the price of domestic coal become critical problems of major dimension that require Cabinet attention.[80]

That the lineaments of the 'British disease' – which in essence consisted of trying to do so much that even the basics were botched – could be so starkly identified by a foreigner at the outset of the 1950s makes it all the more piquant that it took well into the next decade before the difficult issues began to be confronted head-on rather than on the flanks. All sorts of culpabilities are pointed to as explanations for this failure, perhaps the most fashionable being the alleged missing of the European bus by successive governments. The fundamental problem, as always, however, concerned governing psychology rather than specific policies, and applied to the system rather than the erring individuals in it. Thus the British political class, across the party spectrum, had striven so hard in recent years to write itself *up*, that it was well-nigh impossible to implicitly write itself *down* again by constructing a narrower and more sustainable set of goals. We shall argue later that only extraneous forces could eventually enforce a transition that the politicians were incapable of bringing about of their own intelligent volition. The insolubility of the dilemma was evidenced by the nature of the election campaigns fought in quick succession during May 1950 and October 1951, after which the Conservatives finally regained office under the continuing leadership of Winston Churchill. 'And England will start on her long journey back to greatness . . . That's what counts' was how one of Churchill's principal advisers defined the task which lay ahead.[81] Our next chapter will deal with this 'journey' which preoccupied Conservative governments until it had to be abandoned (at least in its more extravagant itinerary) along the sandbanks of the Nile at the end of 1956.

Into The Tunnel

The problem with the Conservative Government which Churchill led from October 1951 to April 1955, when Anthony Eden at last succeeded to the mantle, was implicit in its formation. Thus 'Jock' Colville, when asked by Churchill to return as his Principal Private Secretary, objected that he knew a good deal about foreign affairs, defence and colonial matters, but was 'abysmally ignorant of the Treasury, of economics generally, of Housing, Local Government, Transport, Pensions, Industry and Agriculture'.[1] He was nevertheless persuaded to serve. Similarly Churchill's favourite Second World War commander, Lord Alexander of Tunis, became Minister of Defence, whilst Lord Ismay went to the Commonwealth Relations Office (CRO). The former of these was arguably one of the weakest senior Cabinet appointments of the century, whilst Ismay was a failure at the CRO before moving on to a more congenial role as the first Secretary-General of NATO. Yet in these cases (as in some others) it was not that the appointees badgered their old chief for jobs, since none needed the salary, but that Churchill came into office determined to recreate the 'happy days' of 1940–45. The trait did not slacken over time. 'The present Cabinet does *not* represent the party', Harold Macmillan, who served in the Cabinet throughout, lamented in July 1954, 'it is a Churchill creation, and based on the practice of war, not of peace'.[2] It would have been truer to say that it was based on the habit of thinking about war, rather than its practice, but either way it was not, in its heart of hearts, a ministry whose authentic aims and goals were civilian in nature. Not surprisingly, then, its achievements in this sphere, despite a rhetorical emphasis during the elections on the abandonment of socialist controls and the renewal of personal freedoms, were to be slight.

In so far as the new Prime Minister did have a peace policy, or rather a domestic economic strategy, it was summed up in his own words as 'Houses and meat and not being scuppered', or, even more picturesquely, as 'let pork rip'.[3] Churchill has often been depicted as an eighteenth-century Whig who strayed by chance into the twentieth century Tory party, and to the extent that one of his instinctive beliefs was that 'The People' could always be satiated by a few more roasted joints, the description has a lot of merit. Letting pork rip, metaphorically, however, was not a substitute after 1951 for the sort of commercial and institutional modernization which began to characterize many peer nations, both inside and outside Europe. Furthermore, combined with the continuing (if slightly attenuated) pace of rearmament,[4] this emphasis on unleashing demand for consumer and capital goods which had in effect been repressed for some thirty years through depression, war and reconstruction, without engaging frontally with the capacity of the economy to improve supply, was bound to end in tears. There was an element of Greek tragedy in the way that British public life began slowly but surely in these years to be crucified on the cross of sterling, not merely as a trauma which came and went every couple of years, but as a constant blight on the process of policy-making.

On sterling, the Churchill Cabinet took a fateful decision during its first days in office: not to go ahead with Plan ROBOT. This scheme, hatched during the run-up to the October 1951 election, envisaged an accelerated restoration of the free market by abolishing exchange controls and letting the currency 'find its own level'.[5] ROBOT's proponents contended that ultimately the United Kingdom would have little real choice but to follow such a course, since if the Government did not adopt it as a matter of policy, the markets would impose it as a painful necessity. As an argument this did not appeal to the Prime Minister or the majority of his Cabinet. 'This goes ill', Lyttelton remarked to 'Rab' Butler in a note tossed across the Cabinet table during the discussion, 'the water looks cold to some of them. They prefer a genteel bankruptcy, *force majeure* being the plea.'[6] This was prophetic, though it took a long while for the logic to unravel in its extremity, and by then the plea indeed proved to be that 'there is no alternative'. Whilst some commentators always remained convinced that the implementation of ROBOT would have been overwhelmed by market forces just as convertibility under a Labour Government had been in 1947,[7] for others this drawing-back almost at the last moment by its Conservative successor constituted one of the most serious errors in British policy-making during the postwar era.

Although ROBOT was thus passed over, the doctrinal sensitivities which it touched upon could not be expunged. One of the intriguing aspects of Conservative politics in this period arose from the fact that the civil, economistic wing of the party, associated as it was with the old-fashioned orthodoxy of Baldwin and Chamberlain, always maintained a toe-hold, most prominently in the person of R.A. Butler, whom Churchill appointed Chancellor of the Exchequer in October 1951 somewhat in the spirit that a less favoured member of the household might be left to cope with the dirty laundry. It was around Butler's inscrutable personality through the early 1950s that there began to crystallize a growing sentiment amongst many younger Tories as to the need for fresh ideas directed more towards the internal needs of the United Kingdom than the prevailing concentration on foreign policy and defence. The Chancellor was not, of course, a threat to Churchill personally, who liked to have him around if only to expend upon him his more mordant wit. But as the whispers grew that Butler represented the wave of the future, he became a very real threat to those whose claims to preferment hinged on their association with the Churchillian formula. Almost despite his rather feline and yielding character, therefore, Butler progressively found himself at the centre of a revived Conservative *Schadenfreude*. Intense struggles of succession – surrounding in turn the protracted run-up to Churchill's retirement, the débâcle of Eden's premiership in early 1957, and finally the machinations attendant on the resignation of Harold Macmillan in 1963 – explain these surfeits of ill-will. Implicit in them, too, was a deep divide as to the ideals and goals which should inspire the Party and the nation during the latter half of the twentieth century.

While economics was not the centre-piece of Conservative administration after 1951, the subject requires some further comment before passing on. There is an inherent problem in writing of an era as one of material failure when living-standards started to rise consistently; towards the end of the decade Harold Macmillan was able to admonish the electorate that it 'had never had it so good' (though the euphoria on that occasion, it must be said, was decidedly transient). Butler's Chancellorship between 1951 and 1954 enjoyed successes which were incremental if not spectacular. Controls were lifted; subsidies kept in check, and sometimes reduced; commodity exchanges were 'freed'; and the pound nudged towards partial convertibility – all of which amounted to at least the outline of a mini-ROBOT.[8] One portrait of the period has even taken as its headline *The Age of Affluence*.[9] A later trade minister who served under Harold Wilson has caustically pointed out that a good deal of this new prosperity reflected nothing more than the lucky chance of greatly improved terms of trade once commodity prices slumped with the easing of the inflationary surge induced by the Korean War.[10] None the less, the fact remains that if this record may be counted a failure, some later British Governments would have been happy to emulate it.

Yet such a critique is not all sour grapes. Overseas holders of sterling, for example, were not so much interested in the British digestion of bread and pork as in the overall balance and trajectory of the economy, and here in a very distinct sense things were getting worse, not better. This was especially the case *relative* to the performance of other West European countries. Self-criticism regarding differential rates of growth – above all, the tendency whereby Britain came to be seen as a less successful country than either France or Western Germany – was destined to become part of the contemporary pattern of British political culture, such that before long citizens and interest groups began to point the finger of culpability at each other. In fact a fair portion of this material adjustment was almost certainly inevitable. Thus the size of the 'growth lag' between the United Kingdom and France was to some extent the product of a once-for-all shake-out of the French peasantry into urban employments which had been enforced in the United Kingdom a century before with the repeal of the Corn Laws. It was not easy, and in some degree impossible, for public policy in Britain after 1951 to get to grips with these structural developments. The fact remains that the marginal easements in the United Kingdom's condition during the decade were due to the way in which the country was able to coast along on the crest of a boom whose centre of gravity remained elsewhere. As such, outsiders noticed not the success this registered in parochial terms of 'houses and meat and not being scuppered', but the fundamentally halting nature of British economic advance when other nations were apparently bounding ahead. The resulting nervousness was communicated through the position of sterling and the Bank of England's vulnerable reserves on which the currency depended. 'We are dealing here with confidence . . . an incalculable factor', the Permanent Secretary of the Treasury warned his Chancellor in September 1955. 'We cannot predict how it will act, but we know that it tends to extremes.'[11]

Within the Treasury some of the blame for these grim constraints was attributed to social spending. To a much greater extent, however, it was credited to what became known euphemistically as 'overseas expenditure'. 'We . . . know that it is defence expenditure which has broken our backs', Harold Macmillan, having looked at the books, noted in 1955 during his brief spell as Butler's successor at the Exchequer. 'We also know that we get no defence from the defence expenditure. The only way I can see by which we could restore our economy is by getting down to the defence problem.'[12] This was easier said than done. One aspect of the predicament was nicely illustrated when Churchill visited Washington early on during his new government and rashly agreed to speak to the staff of the British Embassy and their families. Expecting to have some fifty or sixty auditors, when he appeared on the Embassy lawn he found himself confronted by a thousand people. A subsequent check revealed that the military establishment of the mission had swelled to include forty-seven lieutenant-colonels and forty-three wing-commanders.[13] The truth was one which ramified far beyond the single posting; and ultimately it was the aggregates which counted. Thus in 1955–6 the United Kingdom was devoting over nine per cent of Gross National Product to defence, a figure which showed every sign of settling rigidly at that level, whereas in other major Continental countries the comparable statistic was half the amount *and falling*. Burdened with this handicap, it was no wonder that British businessmen forfeited their entrepreneurial spirits, and settled for whatever comfortable niches in home and foreign markets they could lay their hands on.

External constraints on British welfare, broadly conceived, were of course matched by bottle-necks of an increasingly complex kind at home. As we have previously remarked, the trade unions had shown signs of seceding from the Second World War concordat during the later years of the Labour Government. It was from the early fifties, and especially from the middle of the decade, that the problem of militancy among Union negotiators, and – perhaps even more significantly – in the work-place itself, began to assume a shape later to become all too familiar. In this regard Churchill has been criticized for keeping as his Minister of Labour a lawyer, Sir Walter Monckton, professionally adept at arranging settlements 'out of court', with a quite explicit remit to deliver whatever concessions were required to keep the Home Front quiet.[14] Taken in isolation, criticism along these lines is largely pointless. An increasingly *ancien régime* society whose elite career structure was so bound up with a surplus of lieutenant-colonels and wing-commanders had, as a matter of social necessity, to keep topping up with excess bus-drivers, print-workers and factory labour generally, since this was the unwritten contract which kept the political order together. Amidst such a setting rationalization and technology could only be looked at askance. Caught in the resulting impasse, the Prime Minister's sole recourse was lamentation. 'Tragic indeed', he commiserated with the House of Commons, 'is the spectacle of the might, majesty, dominion and power of the once magnificent and still considerable British Empire having to worry and wonder how we can pay our monthly bills.'[15] Grandiloquent self-pity of this sort increasingly failed to satisfy the sentiments of certain Tories with a radical disposition, who were apt to revert to an alternative orthodoxy couched in the language of cutting coats according to the cloth available. As yet, however, this school of domestic thrift (with its Little England overtones) remained a marginal, if increasingly acidic, presence in the party.

After October 1951, as before, it was the Americans who were looked to for help in plugging the all-too-material gap. How this aid came to be rationalized on the British side can be gauged from the case which Churchill put to the American President when visiting Washington, to the effect that the United Kingdom was determined to maintain her 'internal independence' economically, but that she would not be 'abashed' to become wholly dependent on the United States for assistance in the external sphere.[16] It is, indeed, highly ironic that this dichotomy between internal autonomy and external dependence, so frequently applied by Great Britain to her own overseas possessions in the past, should ultimately have become applicable to the straitened metropole itself. In the event, the British never quite succeeded in gaining the same privileged position *vis-à-vis* the Mutual Security Act, passed by the United States Congress at the very time that the Conservatives returned to office in the United Kingdom, that they had once possessed in respect of Marshall Aid. The resentment this generated overlapped with a wider disillusionment that Britain's efforts during the Korean conflict had not only met with little reward, but that the very understandings on which that effort had been made had been flouted. 'Our whole experience since . . . July 1950 has been unfortunate', a leading Treasury official went so far as to say by 1954. 'Indeed, the results of the United States' actions – stoppage of Marshall Aid, tin and rubber policy, virtual abandonment of burden-sharing [and the] failure to find means to finance U.K. defence production . . . would be more readily understandable if their [the Americans'] purpose was to weaken the United Kingdom, rather than to strengthen it.'[17] The ascription of bad faith here reflected more than anything else the febrile mood beginning to grip Whitehall. Yet the disturbing sense of being cut adrift, even with a degree of disdain, was not wholly imaginary. The new Republican Administration in America after November 1952, with President Eisenhower at its head, is well known to have been elected on a Communist-bashing ticket. Less remembered is the fact that it also gained office on a budget-balancing ticket; as such, it did not feel a keen obligation to keep the British in the state to which the latter had become accustomed. Butler, for instance, got the message when he visited Washington in March 1953 and found the reception less than wholly welcoming. 'I sat on President Eisenhower's left . . . but was unable to elicit a single constructive comment', the Chancellor of the Exchequer later related his experience at a White House dinner. 'When I mentioned our desire to bring the economic links between our two countries together he gazed at me in silence . . . to me he always remained an enigma.'[18] The anecdote, indeed, could almost stand as a parable for Anglo-American relations more generally during the first half of the fifties. The political, rather than financial, meanings behind the enigma demand some further attention, since they went to the heart of the Churchill Government's experience.

It is deeply ironic that Dwight D. Eisenhower, the most Anglophile of American military commanders during the Second World War, should later have been at the helm as President when relations with the United Kingdom were often strained, and finally came (as they did over Suez) within a hair's breadth of shearing apart altogether. Had he lent his name and fame to the Democratic Party ticket in the race for the Presidency (as at one time seemed possible), the end-result in this respect would probably have been more muted, if not wholly different. In teaming up with the Republicans, however, Eisenhower immediately came under the imposing influence of that party's foreign policy expert, John Foster Dulles. The latter's lack of affection for the Anglo-Saxon connection was well known;

he was instrumental, for example, in fending off Churchill's desire to attend the inaugural celebrations in Washington on the grounds that the American public would suspect that the English maestro was once again weaving spells on its leaders. Annoyed and disappointed at this rebuff, the Prime Minister vowed never to have anything to do with Dulles whose 'great slab of a face he distrusted and detested'[19], but this was not possible after the latter had been confirmed as Secretary of State under the Eisenhower dispensation. In the light of later developments it is noteworthy that the British antipathy to Dulles was by no means the monopoly of Anthony Eden, either as Foreign Secretary in Churchill's team or subsequently as Prime Minister himself.

What was it, then, about Dullesian Republicanism which at the outset of the new (if not yet quite imperial) Presidency made it deeply suspicious of the British — so much so that during his period of office, as one of the Secretary of State's biographers has put it, they 'were apt to be the last people whose views he wished to hear'.[20] The Grand Old Party in American politics had finally regained office after an excruciatingly long interval. Its cadres needed to make a big mark to ensure that such a protracted exclusion was never repeated; they looked to success in the foreign policy field ('liberating' the countries under Communist domination), and in particular to exploiting their monopoly of inter-continental atomic power, to secure their position. Herein lay the roots of that diplomacy — with its echoes of 'Teddy' Roosevelt and his big Republican stick in the early 1900s — which came to be known generally in the 1950s as 'brinkmanship', and with which Dulles' own name was closely associated. Experience at the height of the Korean War had shown, in American eyes, how the British, whilst staunch in conventional wars being carried on at a suitable distance, tended to lose their nerve when the atomic stakes were driven up. The United Kingdom indubitably lay athwart that 'atomic nationalism' which one commentator has seen as constituting the hallmark of Eisenhower's America[21]; and there were soon signs that in regional diplomacy United States policy-makers began to write their unreliable and increasingly fragile British confrères out of the script.[22] This could hardly go unnoticed for long in London, and when it was, even the English champions of political Anglo-Saxonism were given pause for thought. 'He [Churchill] thought that the hydrogen bomb accounted for a certain arrogance in the Americans', Lord Moran, the premier's physician, recounted in his diary. 'He did not want them to be arrogant.'[23] It was in this unstable and dangerous milieu that Anglo-American 'misunderstanding' developed a propensity to come to the surface all too swiftly.

This background explains in large part why, whereas Churchill set out to base his ministry on the 'restoration' of the wartime transatlantic alliance, its theme-song turned out to be rather different: the quest for a Three Power 'Summit' between the United States, Britain and the Soviet Union. The death of Stalin in March 1953 provided just such an opportunity, and in the following May Churchill delivered in Parliament a foreign policy address in which he called for a meeting along these lines 'without officials and without agenda'. Afterwards some of his closest colleagues in Cabinet explained the premier's constant advocacy of a summit as an excuse for clinging to office even when his first stroke was seen manifestly to have curtailed his physical and, alas, his mental powers. The feelings which flowed from this situation reached dismal depths; one who saw both Churchill and Eden close-up in this period testified to the 'cold hatred' which finally came to subsist between them.[24] Certainly it was telling that whenever the gossip about Churchill's fitness for office reached a new crescendo, and a visitation by 'senior Conservatives' to the great man's bedside seemed imminent, a fresh hare was let loose by 'Downing Street sources' in the form of a renewed call for a summit at which Churchill himself would clearly be the United Kingdom's ideal representative. To this extent the question of the succession (or putting off the succession) cut across this aspect of national policy, as it cut across most others.

Nevertheless, there was more to Churchill's erstwhile summitry than a continuing hunger for place. Above all, the proposal sprang from the desire for a suitably graphic method of proving that Britain still *counted*. Even Churchill's advisers observed that in his personal dealings with the United States leadership, many of them wartime comrades, the personal respect and affection of the latter was mixed up with a good deal of patronizing impatience with the Englishman's overblown claims on their attention[25]; and if his aides felt it so, one can be assured that Churchill – not slow in such matters – did as well. The Prime Minister had once 'dragged in' the Americans to off-set the preponderance of Germany; now he sought, in a somewhat different sense, to 'drag in' the Soviets to dilute American supremacy. This, of course, did not at all mean that Churchill wished to end the Cold War itself; but he did wish, by firing a covert shot across the bows of the United States, to see that the United Kingdom was not deprived of her rightful prominence in the contest of nations. It was a shot fired in a spirit of exhausted irascibility. 'The P.M. is depressed and bewildered', Colville wrote in his diary at this time, 'he said to me this evening: "the zest is diminished". I think it is that he cannot see the light at the end of the tunnel.'[26]

For the Republican Administration in the United States, British-inspired summitry merely confirmed many suspicions. In so far as United Kingdom ministers and officials failed to grasp the risks they were running in this respect, their experience at the Bermuda Conference of December 1953 put them right. At that meeting Eisenhower reportedly came down on Churchill 'like a ton of bricks'[27] and buried any possibility of a thaw with the Soviets. Even a British team not famous for its fastidious discourse was taken aback at the ferocity with which the Americans expressed their intentions towards the Russians, Stalin's death notwithstanding.[28] Whether the failure to exploit this juncture in international affairs represented a lost opportunity is not our concern. What does seem certain is that the grilling the British received caused a reaction (admittedly more so among some than others) which was later to surface under Eden's premiership. As for Churchill, Bermuda marked the effective end of his career as a world statesman; subsequently he returned to the summit theme, but with growing feebleness and lack of reality. In terms of British policy, perhaps the most important effect of the transparent failure of British *diplomacy* to make the national voice heard sufficiently loudly at the highest level was the determination to put even more emphasis on the *military* alternative: that is, the evolution of a credible British nuclear deterrent.

After 1945 the United Kingdom had pushed ahead with its own atomic programme, not as its preferred option, since an Anglo-American condominium always remained its most cost-effective ideal, but as a matter of necessity. When in 1950 the British research programme approached the testing stage, access to the existing facilities in the Nevada Desert was requested, but this application to the United States was refused.[29] As a result, an appropriate stretch of Australian outback was leased, the first British device being exploded at Monte Bello in October 1952. Amidst this sequence it was the *independence* of the British deterrent which became integral to the rationale enshrined, for example, in the Chiefs of Staff's seminal 'Global Strategy Paper' of mid-1952. The critical gloss in this document was that only the acquisition of a unilateral deterrent could ensure that London's voice would be heard in American counsels. Anthony Verrier has summed up what this 'voice' implied by explaining that it involved a capacity to 'force America to support Britain in a crisis in order to pre-empt the risk of American cities being the target of a [Soviet] retaliatory strike. This was nothing less than a blackmailing argument . . .'.[30] The blackmail, in effect, was that the United States would not be able to stay out of a nuclear war arising elsewhere even if she wished to do so. The depth of the British commitment to this inherently political gambit was shown when in June 1954 Churchill informed Eisenhower that the United Kingdom, far from being knocked out of the deterrent stakes by the development of the Hydrogen Bomb (or 'Super' as it was colloquially known), was already making progress towards acquiring this new and even more devastating form of power.

Henceforth the essence of Britain's relationship with the United States was defined in terms of the deterrent, later to culminate in the Polaris Agreement of 1962; the Soviet Union, as one noted commentator in this field has pointed out, being little more than the 'ideal-type aggressor' which the sketching of such scenarios necessitated.[31] From the perspective of the current discussion, however, the most striking facet here is how the precise conception of British nuclear force came to define (more strikingly, for example, than the possession of an empire) the prevailing image of the nation as a Great Power. This definition was characterized by Oliver Franks, a paragon of the post-war diplomatic establishment and ex-Ambassador to Washington, when in his 1954 Reith Lectures for the BBC he stated categorically that the United Kingdom 'is going to continue to be what she has been', and specified that he meant by that a nation whose 'action . . . can decisively affect the fate of other Great Powers in the world'.[32] Such a rendering of British 'greatness' was significant for a genuine modesty – abandoning the illusions of 'equality' with the superpowers which had always lingered in Bevin's mind, as it did to some extent in Churchill's – without abdicating from the claim to be an independent factor in world affairs, *of whom even the most powerful among other nations had to take account*. Persuasive and intelligent though this interpretation of British goals might be, the problem remained that such a construction all too easily clashed with the Dulles-Eisenhower conviction that in the universal struggle between the Free World and Communism there was no room for junior allies, however dignified their history, to pursue courses of their own outside the framework of a NATO entity whose proper command-centre lay in the United States.

In fact the crucial test of loyalty to NATO after 1951 as it appeared to Washington was the acceptance by other West European powers of German rearmament. This emphasis even shunted into the background (albeit temporarily) the strategy of European economic integration, which had been such a feature of American desiderata since the original unveiling of Marshall Aid. The whole purpose of the plan for a European Defence Community (EDC) was to accommodate German rearmament within some kind of supranational European Army, so making it acceptable to French opinion, for whom fears of German *military* revival remained strong; indeed, EDC itself was originally the brainchild of a French premier, René Pleven.[33] Almost from the start, however, the EDC's most pressing advocate was the United States, since every German facing eastwards with a rifle represented an accretion of force which could otherwise come from only one source – herself. It was, more than anything else, Churchill's distaste for EDC – a 'sludgy amalgam', as he famously deprecated it – which came to disturb his Government's relations with the Eisenhower administration.[34]

It also disturbed relations between London and Paris. The French (for whom memories of 1940 were scarcely dimmed) were not reassured by British promises that, whilst they could not themselves join EDC, they would be staunch in any crisis; whilst the British were outraged at the deftness with which their closest neighbour argued that, if the United Kingdom did not commit itself to the proposal, nor could they, thereby succeeding in the deflection of American criticisms on to 'perfidious Albion' – 'in his [Dulles'] desperate pursuit of the vanishing shadow of EDC', one historian has concluded, 'Britain . . . was the whipping boy'.[35] Thus alienated, Churchill, *en route* to the Bermuda Conference, made great play with the fact that his leisure reading for the journey consisted of C.S. Forester's adventure novel set in the Napoleonic era, *Death to the French*; and during the ensuing Conference he treated the delegates from Paris with a disdain that was disapproved of even among his own advisers, if only to compensate for his own discomfiture at the hands of Eisenhower.[36] It was on these military issues, then, rather than with respect to the economic questions which later treatments have tended to emphasize, that Britain's relations with France and with Western Europe generally took a turn for the worse over the first half of the 1950s.

Furious at the impasse over German rearmament, after late 1953 Dulles brandished the threat of an 'agonizing reappraisal' in American policy; and it was Britain, more than any other major NATO ally, who appeared in danger of being reappraised. For this reason, when the French Chamber finally threw out EDC altogether in August 1954, triggering a crisis which Dulles described with calculated melodrama as one of 'almost terrifying proportions'[37], the British Government, and Eden as Foreign

Secretary, were propelled into frantic action to ward off the evil eye. Eden shuttled between West European capitals, and hit upon the idea of reviving the Anglo-French-Benelux Brussels Treaty of 1948, to which Italy and – the whole point of the exercise – Western Germany might be added.[38] The climax of this sequence was the London Conference of 28 September–3 October 1954, at which Britain agreed (under the umbrella of a new organization called the Western European Union) to contribute four divisions on a permanent basis to the defence of Europe. This was the price the United Kingdom paid – and Dulles and Eisenhower expected her to pay – in order to coax France not only into accepting German rearmament, but the status of the Federal Republic as a fully-fledged sovereign member of NATO. By thus bidding up her military commitment to NATO-in-Europe, Britain had managed almost at the last moment to stuff the genie of 'agonizing reappraisal' back into its bottle. Whether it would stay there remained problematical.

Churchill's attitude to EDC, of course, merely reflected the wider disparagement in London of the general movement towards European consolidation and unity. When the Conservative Government had first come back to office, it had been widely forecast that it would prove more sympathetic than its predecessor to the European movement, if only because Churchill himself had been the latter's foremost rhetorical progenitor in the immediate aftermath of 1945. That this did not prove to be the case has been laid, not so much at Churchill's door ('sludgy amalgam' notwithstanding), as at Anthony Eden's. 'What you've got to remember', one official recalled the latter saying on one occasion, 'is that, if you looked at the postbag of any English village and examined the letters coming in from abroad to the whole population, ninety per cent of them come from beyond Europe . . .'.[39] The key to Eden's thinking here lay in the reference to 'the whole population'. In his estimation, the European idea propagandized by such continental *savants* as Jean Monnet was essentially a social expression whose British 'type' was the self-conscious Hampstead intelligentsia who spent their leisure hours engrossed in the novels of Balzac.

To this extent Eden's anti-Europeanism was merely a branch of the village-populism which ran so deeply in twentieth-century Toryism, and which the Foreign Secretary clung to all the more tenaciously because it represented one of his few points of genuine contact with domestic British affairs. Yet to highlight the negative stance of Eden alone in all this is to gloss over the fact that the prejudice involved was virtually universal among his generation of practising politicians – irrespective, indeed, of party. As even such an ardent later advocate of Britain's 'place in Europe' as Gladwyn Jebb has had the grace to admit, his own views prior to the Suez crisis of 1956 were very different from what they became thereafter.[40] Not all were to be so honest in their retrospectives.

The EDC débâcle, in fact, had the effect of confirming British expectations that real integration in Europe was not a practical proposition, if only because French fears of Germany remained as tangible as ever. In retrospect we can see that it actually led to the successful *relance* of the European movement by shifting its axis from military affairs (where a Franco-German merger remained impossible) to economic matters (on which Paris and Bonn soon found much to talk about). Since the contemporary revolution in French life and institutions which underlay this transition is of the sort that historians have called 'silent'[41], the failure in Whitehall to detect its vibrations at the time is not so surprising. Thus the British Government dispatched a mere Board of Trade 'observer' to the Messina Conference of June 1955, confident that such diffidence on their part would block any further progress, as it had done under comparable circumstances some twenty years before.[42] In the event the other delegations present at that meeting proceeded none the less to appoint a powerful committee under the chairmanship of the Belgian politician, M. Paul Henri Spaak, charged with mapping a course towards customs unity. At this juncture the British subsequently claimed to have withdrawn. The truth was otherwise. 'It wasn't a decision to withdraw', the British civil servant concerned, who was presumably best placed to know, recalled much later. 'We were thrown out.'[43] Certainly the adhesion of Italy and the Benelux Powers to the process of unification added a momentum to affairs which Franco-German action alone at this stage could not have done. The emergence of the 'Messina Powers' (soon to be known as 'The Six') represented a consolidation of West European opinion against which Britain – with its gathering inflation and slithering balance of payments – suddenly looked a lot less imposing.

It was this sense of being 'brought up short', an apprehension of national diminution, which explains the heightened tension in British public life from 1955 onwards, and which came to affect the gamut of national policy. Thus Spaak himself noted as his committee set about its task how the British mood shifted 'from one of mildly disdainful scepticism to growing fear'.[44] Anxiety drove successive British Governments to seek to trip up the moves which led to the signature of the Treaty of Rome in January 1957, and afterwards to try to guide the European Economic Community (or Common Market) into some convenient cul-de-sac. Condemnation of these tactics has become almost *de rigueur* with much later British political opinion. These criticisms have gained credence, it might be said, by the rationales which were used at the time to promote Whitehall's case. 'The main reason why we dislike the Common Market', wrote one official tentatively, '. . . is its effect on the Commonwealth'[45], and it is arguments such as this which from the vantage-point of a later day appear to exhibit a crushing bathos. Yet for many years the Commonwealth tie had constituted a convenient excuse for not doing something which the British authorities did not wish to do anyway, for reasons that were either not so respectable or were too complex to be reduced to a neat formula. That this was so in this instance may be evidenced by the fact that when the United Kingdom's attitude to the EEC underwent a transformation after 1960, the 'kith and kin' overseas were soon dropped with an aplomb which belied previous protestations of affection.

What, then, was the *real* reason which dictated the equivocal, and sometimes plainly hostile, reaction by Conservative governments in this period to the Common Market? The truth was that the unification of Europe after 1945 could only be pioneered from *within* the Continental heartland; whilst, by the same token, the

British could never be more than a subsidiary, and dispensable, factor within the overall process. Here is the lie to that hoary old chestnut of recent British history and a good deal of contemporary opinion generally: to wit, that the United Kingdom was 'offered' the leadership of Europe after the Second World War, but turned it down in a fit of almost wilful blindness. No such leadership was on offer, if only because English hegemony in Europe was not exactly a traditional principle of French statecraft. At the heart of British Conservatism in the mid-fifties lay a desire, muddled but powerful, to get a grip on the nation's ebbing fortunes, and to maintain its room for independent manoeuvre, neither of which aims seemed likely to be secured by being press-ganged into a strategy whose centre of gravity inevitably lay elsewhere. Whether or not, in the light of later events, this approach is to be deprecated for the *economic* penalties incurred, it was wholly logical according to the more deep-seated instincts of an entire generation of British political leadership. Nor were the genuine dilemmas involved to be reduced when the issue of Britain's relationship to a coalescent Europe subsequently assumed more advanced but perhaps equally intractable forms.

By 1955 this question of Britain's independent status as a Great Power, and her residual right to pursue her own interests according to her own lights, had become inextricably mixed up with the accumulating tensions in the Middle East. Harassed by Dulles, boxed-in by the Europeans, it was in this region of the world that Eden, first as Foreign Secretary, then as Prime Minister, came to stake his claims on the future. Egypt was the crux of this nervous but single-minded tendency. Before relating these latter events which were to culminate so disastrously, however, we must first take a convenient opportunity to say something about the nature of imperial developments proper between 1951 and 1956.

In the political mythology of British decolonization, the early and mid-fifties constitutes the era when, amidst the after-glow of Indian independence, Britain's colonies elsewhere took their place on the conveyor-belt which propelled them, albeit at varying speeds, towards self-government. Naturally there were problems to be overcome along the way (which in the most acute form necessitated the declaration of 'Emergencies' in Malaya, Kenya, British Guiana and Cyprus), and eventually the transition was to be accelerated far faster than the responsible authorities in London anticipated. Nevertheless, about the ultimate destination implicit in British colonial policy after 1950–1, it has often been claimed, there was never any doubt. Hence the United Kingdom's conduct during the era leading up to the climax of the 'end of Empire' has been portrayed (most classically in the memoirs of Harold Macmillan) as clear and consistent throughout. As with all myths, there are in this account some elements which are true, and some which at the least are very misleading.

Whilst the crux of this subject matter was political, there is an economic dimension which merits a preliminary gloss. Colonial Development in general, and African development in particular, we have seen, had for a brief period after 1947 appeared as a key factor in metropolitan calculations. By the end of the Labour Government, however, what one Colonial Office official has retrospectively described as Ernest Bevin's belief that all that was required to boost African production was to 'drive Africans into the bush and leave them there'[46] had already lost much of its credibility. The rather lamentable record of such costly projects as the Ground Nut Scheme in East Africa hastened the disillusionment; it was the latter botch which gave birth to the noted aphorism 'Give us the job and we will finish the tools'. Yet more fundamental factors were also at work. As the sense of metropolitan economic crisis deepened after 1950, a Treasury critique emerged in which Britain's obligation to develop overseas possessions, far from seeming to be part of the solution, now appeared to be part of the problem, not least because desperately needed capital was thereby diverted from home industry.[47] In short, Britain could not rearm, renovate her domestic infra-structure *and* play fairy-godmother to a gaggle of poor colonial societies; predictably it was the latter commitment which began to break up under the strain. Sceptics subsequently painted a picture of Colonial Development and Welfare as a bottomless pit down which British taxpayers' money was being sunk, with no apparent benefit to themselves. It was an indication of the curtailment of the *mise-en-valeur* ascribed to dependent territories that when Harold Macmillan became Prime Minister in January 1957, one of his first acts was to order a profit and loss account for the residual Colonial Empire to be drawn up; and although, as has been pointed out[48], no practical implications automatically sprang from this action, it was the asking of the question in such a quarter that was important. Consequently when the political floodgates to decolonization opened wide after 1959, there were, significantly, to be no *economic* constraints or vested interests to keep the process from unwinding very quickly indeed.

The downgrading of colonial development was only part of a progressive erosion of the wider Sterling Area (including as it did many independent Commonwealth countries). Again, in the later forties the Sterling Area in a dollar-hungry world had blossomed in British eyes as providing a fresh basis for her most cherished role – the leader of a coherent and loyal bloc. The trouble was that the loyalties involved were all too easily worn through, first by the misery of collective import-cuts associated with the crisis leading to sterling devaluation in September 1949, and then with the belt-tightening arising from the difficulties of 1950/1.[49] It gradually became evident that independent countries such as Australia[50], India and Pakistan, for example, were increasingly bent on pursuing their own development strategies without allowing themselves to be diverted by the needs of co-operation in the Area as a whole, or by the spectre of inflation. What was more, it began to be realized in London that those colonies who were on their way to some form of self-government were not likely to act any more 'responsibly' when power was in local hands than in the case of those territories which had gone before. Sterling solidarity and collective discipline, in brief, were fast disappearing by 1955–6, and it was in this context that many British commentators started to blame the imperial-cum-currency connection for all sorts of pernicious side-effects, principal among which was the way that such 'soft' markets helped to cushion British managements and workers from world competition.[51] The Sterling Area thus continued to have a shadowy existence into the 1960s, but as a framework for United Kingdom policy-formation it was already disintegrating when Macmillan succeeded Eden to the premiership. The secular economic significance of the Empire-Commonwealth was therefore being continuously undermined from 1950–1 onwards, and later events cannot be fully explained without reference to such structural shifts, invisible though they may have been to many contemporaries.

Economics and politics, however, are rarely finely calibrated together, and it was of the essence in the United Kingdom's post-war psychology that they were at constant odds with each other. Hence a government consciously engaged after 1951 on a 'journey back to greatness' was not likely to draw any neat conclusions from the trends (not always transparent at the time) which we have just described – at least not until the logic became absolutely compelling. One historian has recently encapsulated Conservative colonial policy between 1951 and 1957 in the phrase 'keeping change within bounds'.[52] In so far as all imperial polities are by their nature engaged in fending off perennial threats to their existence, this description is not to be disputed. Yet the portrayal conjures up an impression of prevailing liberal, Canningite Toryism (seeking to balance new and old worlds under contemporary conditions) which bears little relationship to the gritty, defensive emotions running forcefully through Conservative parliamentary ranks during the period, and of which the Suez adventure was only the climax. Rather, the moving spirit of the metropolitan times might be said to have lain in a distinction between those territories and regions now largely irrelevant to British needs, and where as a consequence change could be hurried on as rapidly as local circumstances allowed (which was often not all that rapid anyway), and those instances where change was to be firmly suppressed. This *modus operandi* was not so much a manifestation of liberal colonialism of the sort that could cut an acceptable figure at the United Nations, as of a finely-honed strategic conception in which it was not the control of large, unwieldy land-masses which mattered, but the mapping out of what Enoch Powell has defined as a new 'empire of points'.[53] It is in this sense that a vein of realistic adjustment ran increasingly close to the surface of British official thinking, since although the United Kingdom could clearly no longer hold down sub-continents, she was – and intended to remain – quite capable of retaining critical stations on the compass of world affairs. How large and how numerous these residual lodgements might be was one of the main underlying issues in British overseas policy.

What this model of colonial adaptation meant in Africa was that the 'native' states of West Africa were indeed put on a political transmission-belt which carried them through to what one senior Colonial Office official later typified as the 'black majority thing'.[54] Specifically, no attempt was made after October 1951 to reverse the constitutional reforms already under way in the Gold Coast, under the rubric of which the nationalist leader, Kwame Nkrumah, was invested with the sonorous title of 'Prime Minister' in mid-1952; Churchill evinced a reluctant and even disdainful air over this departure, as he had as Opposition leader at the time of Indian independence, but there was never any question of more forceful opposition on his part.[55] Henceforth the checks to the Gold Coast's advancement were internal, rather than external, in nature, since not all Gold Coasters were as enthusiastic about Nkrumah as his British promoters. The decolonization show was kept successfully on the road until an independent Ghana finally emerged in March 1957.[56] Nor was there any attempt to foist on to Nigeria something less than was already being granted to her much smaller Anglophone neighbour, although the sheer scale and complexity of Nigerian affairs was to add a couple of years to the schedule. Indeed, when full self-government finally arrived in Nigeria during 1960, it was leading Nigerian politicians, not their British counterparts, who felt that the pace had been dangerously fast.[57]

In those British African dependencies where white settlers remained a leading factor – indeed, *the* leading factor, as it still appeared to many in Whitehall – the anticipated pattern was very different. In these instances the relevant model was summed up in the slogan of 'multi-racialism'. According to this ideal the interests and identities of the various racial groups – Africans, Europeans and Asians – would mingle as sustained economic growth generated a native bourgeoisie whose sympathies gelled with expatriate privilege rather than with the raw new proletariat bottled up in the expanding shantytowns of the cities, or with the sharecroppers and landless labourers of the rural districts. The evolutionary principle enshrined in this approach fitted with the pseudo-Whig reading of English social and constitutional history which formed such a tangible part of the intellectual luggage of British official classes in this era. Fortuitously, also, the long-established mechanics of British colonial polities – with their executive and legislative councils, and delicate balances struck between nominated officials and elected unofficials, the latter often on communal 'rolls' – provided an almost unlimited prospect for fine gradations in the devolution of power leading to local (but not necessarily majority) self-government. In this burgeoning era of colonial fancy-franchises, the constitutional time-tables in 'settler' Africa trailed off as far as the eye could see.

The most outstanding practical embodiment of the multi-racial idea was the establishment of the Central African Federation (CAF) in 1953, a composite entity made up of Northern Rhodesia, Southern Rhodesia and Nyasaland.[58] The ambiguity surrounding colonial policy-making during this period is summed up in the fact that the cobbling-together of this 'closer union' on the basis of white supremacy, an enterprise which had been consistently baulked at by British Governments *before* 1939 on the grounds that it was a settler-ramp, should have been enacted at a time when liberal ideas concerning colonies were supposedly coming to the fore. The new Federation was rationalized as constituting a bulwark against the creeping segregationism stemming from the Union of South Africa, where an Afrikaner-Nationalist regime had been installed in power since 1948. The most authentic test of this argument lay in the response of the local African populations, who would most certainly have welcomed the innovation with open arms if it had indeed savoured of salvation from South African embraces; as it was, in so far as their opinions were sought in a shotgun consultation, blacks were anti-Federation from the start on the ground that it was more likely to let segregation *in* than to keep it *out*. African opposition was nevertheless ridden over rough-shod in London, with the argument that it insufficiently appreciated what was in the best interests of everybody, majorities and minorities alike. Amidst these barely-suppressed differences the Central African Federation came into existence essentially under the inspiration of the metropole's need for a 'model' case of multi-racial development, just as the Gold Coast was being simultaneously promoted as a model of political change within a Native State.

Multi-racialism in British Central Africa was fully consonant with (and to some extent required) a reinforcement of the whites in demographic and commercial terms. After 1953 United Kingdom migrants began to arrive in the CAF in large numbers, happy to leave behind them the deprivations of English life for the sun-dappled verandas and family swimming-pools of an African paradise. Unfortunately, whilst the economic development side of multi-racialism undoubtedly occurred, racial mixing did not; the new settlers, with their futures still to make, being less disposed in this regard, it was often remarked, than the more established European cadres. In brief, the logic of multi-racialism broke up – as it was probably bound to do – on the rocks of racial exclusivity.[59] As we shall see in the next chapter, the knock-on effects of this particular impasse were to play a catalytic role in bringing about the 'end of empire' more or less throughout British Africa. As long as multi-racialism remained politically and, as it were, morally credible, the notion that the United Kingdom was in firm control of a colonial schema in large parts of that continent remained durable.

The role of multi-racialism in prospectively adding to, rather than curtailing, the African colonial agenda may be seen in conjunction with another principle which began to stir after 1951: that there were some territories for whom self-determination was not a permissible destiny at all. These instances essentially concerned so-called 'fortress colonies' – small, strategically-situated possessions, self-evidently not the hubs of a grand formal empire on the old lines, but offering bases from which British power and influence could be projected in a flexible, cheap and modern manner within their various regional habitats. Cyprus – Disraeli's original *'place d'armes'* of 1878 – provided a test-case for the metropole's determination to uphold a selective (or exceptionalist) theory along these lines. For some while the authorities in London had reiterated that the reason for denying self-determination to that island, when it was already being handed out to Africans in the Gold Coast, was that the disturbed international conditions of the day ruled out any relaxation of control in such a vital strategic location. As this argument wore thin after early 1953, the pressure built up for a frank statement of Britain's intention to stay put, come what may. This was the background to the episode in the House of Commons on 28 July 1954 when a British colonial minister, cleverly harassed at the despatch-box by his Labour 'shadow', used the word 'never' to apparently describe the possibility of self-determination being applied to Cyprus.[60] Rather unfairly (since this more or less accurately reflected underlying policy) such indelicacy soon led to the eclipse of the minister's career; less illogically, some Greek Cypriots (whose goal for themselves was not independence, but union with what they regarded as their Hellenic motherland) turned to bombs and assassinations as an expression of their views, since ballots were clearly to be denied them.[61]

This was the start of a trauma in which the sporadic atrocities of Nicosia's 'Murder Mile' became a stock feature of British media reporting on the dark forces at large in the outside world. Yet Cyprus was not the only colony to which the word 'never' was applied on such convenient occasions as parliamentary question-time. As John Darwin has remarked, Malta was also subsequently put in such an exceptional category.[62] But the most pregnant example – barely-noticed at the time – was Aden. 'Her Majesty's Government', another Colonial Office spokesman declared in a parliamentary statement on 18 May 1956, 'wish to make it clear that the importance of Aden both strategically and economically within the Commonwealth is such that they cannot foresee the possibility of any fundamental relaxation of their responsibility for the Colony.' Herein was to be found the immediate origins of the East of Suez policy which was to be the hallmark of the United Kingdom's conventional defence posture during the decade after 1957. Whatever their future significances may have been, Cyprus, Malta, Aden and, indeed, Gibraltar (with respect to the last of which Francoist irredentism now began to raise its head) evoked with varying degrees of warmth a sentiment which ran close to the surface of British politics as the 1950s reached their mid-point: that there were places and circumstances in which the United Kingdom could be pushed so far *and no further*.

To a later generation such strong reactive impulses may well appear, in the context, contrary to the true proportion of affairs as they stood in 1955–6. Yet the dominant mentality in British politics at this time remained that forged out of the Appeasement controversy and the war which had followed; its cast of mind was naturally *resistant*, prone to kicking against the pricks rather than running with the grain. Where Britons continued to differ, as in the 1930s, was quite where the line lay between necessary accommodations with reality and unseemly surrender. It was above all around the point of Egypt, and the Suez Base in particular, that this fundamental issue had come to revolve. The crisis to which it gave rise was to be one of the major watersheds in modern British history. The final section of this chapter will therefore deal with this saga, and in doing so with the Prime Minister after April 1955, Anthony Eden, whose public destruction it encompassed.

The British position in Egypt had paradoxically taken a turn for the worse almost as soon as the Conservatives had returned to power in 1951. Whether coincidentally or not, *fedayeen* (or terrorist) harassment of British camps, installations and personnel was stepped up within the Suez area; probably also

the British forces involved felt freer to react once Churchill
had replaced Attlee in Downing Street. Whatever the nuances
in these respects, in January 1952 the British Army moved
to disarm the unreliable auxiliary Egyptian police, killing
forty-one; the following day anti-foreign riots surged through
Cairo, claiming lives of their own. In Egyptian politics forces
were unleashed which led in July of that year to a revolution
exiling King Farouk to the deprivations of the Côte d'Azur,
whilst establishing in power a regime of junior army officers
led by General Neguib and Colonel Nasser. Simultaneously
more covert, if not necessarily more subtle, currents began
to course with renewed vigour through British politics which
ultimately led to the invasion of 1956.

The pace and texture of these currents may be gauged from
an incident early on in the new British ministry when Churchill,
for whom Egypt-bashing had come to play the same role that
India-bashing had done in the thirties, clashed with Eden (the
latter restored once more to his Foreign Office patrimony) over
attitudes to that country. 'He [Churchill] made a tremendous
attack on the Egyptians', a third party recorded the occasion.
'Rising from his chair, the old man advanced on Anthony [Eden],
saying with his indomitable Churchill growl, "Tell them that if
we have any more of their cheek we will set the Jews on them
and drive them back into the gutter, from which they should
never have emerged".'[63] The force of such language was not
merely gratuitous; it was the premier's way of putting down a
'marker' with a colleague suspected in some quarters of relying
on diplomacy where only force could meet the exigencies of
the situation. Churchill's weakening grip on the premiership
depended more than anything else on the support he could
muster on the Conservative backbenches; and playing on the
'Egyptian' emotions of the latter was one of the main ways
that this support was kept alive in the face of gossip about
the great man's declining physical and mental condition. When
Eden nevertheless insisted on starting negotiations with the new
regime in Cairo, it followed naturally that he became the butt of
all sorts of Appeasement jokes among a section of his colleagues,

the Prime Minister giving the lead in remarking that he 'never knew before that Munich was on the Nile'.[64] Later Eden himself was to make much use of pejorative references to Appeasement in his campaign against Nasser, likening him repeatedly to Hitler, a habit usually ascribed to his overheated imagination. The fact that the logic of such comparisons arose from more complex currents in Tory partisanship is less frequently noticed.

The nature of this difference over Egypt between Churchill and Eden, however, also reflected something deeper. Whilst invoking a tough line on the issue, Churchill always anticipated doing so either in harness with the Americans or with their tacit acquiescence. One of his constant themes in negotiating with the United States was thus for joint action over Middle Eastern affairs in general, and Egypt in particular. In contrast, it was Eden's proclivity to do without American assistance which inclined him at the same time to compromise with Nasser, if an appropriate deal could be made to stick. By taking so largely on himself the burden of concluding a treaty with Nasser's Egypt in September 1954, the Foreign Secretary was thus pointing up subtly different emphases where the United States was concerned even before the course of the Suez crisis in 1956 brought this factor to the forefront. These contrasting emphases, furthermore, had a history behind them. Of all the major British statesmen of the Second World War generation, Eden had been the one least integrated into the machinery of the Anglo-American alliance.[65] He was serious when he once remarked that he always felt more comfortable when visiting Moscow than Washington. His wartime relations with American representatives had been frequently volatile; on one occasion he had to leave the dining-table at Chequers to cool down after a clash with General George C. Marshall. The fundamental point here is not that Eden disliked Americans but that he, more than any other leading Englishman, was committed to the ideal of an independent, unilateral and above all national identity mediated quintessentially through the conduct of foreign policy. Where Churchill was prepared to trade-in a large measure of autonomy if it meant an accretion of real power, for Eden the only power worth having was that which was authentically national in its derivation. Thus summit gestures apart, the former never tired of reiterating his conviction that for the United Kingdom the goodwill of the United States was an absolute necessity which, by implication, could not command too high a price, whereas by 1954 the latter was expostulating to his intimates that 'all the Americans want to do is to replace the French in Indo-China. They want to replace us in Egypt too. They want to run the world.'[66] The questions this implicitly posed were never put on the public agenda, if only because they were too important, but they remained amongst the most powerful in 'high' British politics.

It was, indeed, the frictions generated between Eden and Dulles over the crisis in Indo-China during 1954 which overhung later developments with respect to Egypt. Very briefly, when the French garrison at Dien Bien Phu seemed about to fall to its Communist besiegers, the United States Government looked to Britain for support in military action to avert a catastrophe.[67] The response in London was that no involvement in the use of force would be acceptable to them until negotiation had been exhausted, and at the Geneva Conference of 26 April–21 July 1954 (partially boycotted by the Americans) the British Foreign Secretary closeted himself with the Russian and Chinese delegations in their respective lakeside villas, the end-result being a settlement in which Indo-China was divided into two, the northern half being handed to Ho Chi Minh's Communists. The collapse of French resolve in the area left Dulles with little option but to swallow the pill which others had thrust upon him, but 'pathological rage' was one contemporary description of his feelings towards his United Kingdom counterpart when it was all over[68]. Suspicion that something was afoot in the British camp was not, in fact, entirely mistaken. Eden's aides, for example, had noticed how their chief's mood throughout the Geneva proceedings had been positively *'exalté'*, with the 'look of 1940' coming into his eyes at significant moments.[69] For the Foreign Secretary, the true spirit of 1940 lay in Britain's ability and will to shape her own destiny, and make her own friends – in short, to be nobody's cat's-paw. Above all, it was a spirit which promised to provide an inspiring and historic theme for the looming premiership which Eden had spent so long awaiting in Churchill's shadow.

Of course, if the British did not fall in with American policy in South East Asia, it followed that the Americans would not add power to the British elbow in the Middle East. This was the logic (allied to the Chiefs of Staff's advice that the stake in Suez was now practically useless) which made up Eden's mind to 'settle' with Nasser in the treaty already referred to, under the terms of which British troops were to be progressively evacuated from the Base and its facilities put into 'mothballs'. In return, the United Kingdom was accorded a vague 'right of re-entry' in the event of any external threat to Egyptian sovereignty. By adopting this tack (which Churchill himself only went along with most reluctantly), Eden automatically put himself at odds with those within his own party for whom any settlement with the Egyptians was a euphemism for surrender.[70] Virtually from the moment that he succeeded to the premiership in April 1955, criticism began to be put about that inside this Prime Minister's velvet glove there was a velvet fist. Developments in the eastern Mediterranean consequently soon emerged as the litmus-test of Eden's reputation and the prospects for his continued leadership.

Eden instinctively looked to astute diplomacy to guarantee the satisfactory working of the treaty with Egypt, and the British position in the Middle East at large. The crux of this diplomacy was the Baghdad Pact which Britain joined – alongside Turkey, Iraq and Pakistan – in March 1955. In essence, the Pact was designed to prove that the most powerful countries in the region remained those who worked *with*, not *against*, the British; as Macmillan summed it up, 'So it comes to a mild squeeze on Egypt, and benefits to the loyal Arabs . . . Let unpleasant things happen to Nasser, and pleasant things to others.'[71] For this approach to work, and to confound French warnings that its only effect would be to further alienate the feelings of something called 'the Arab nation', it was essential that Jordan should be integrated into the Baghdad Pact. At the outset London was confident that the young Jordanian monarch, Hussein, could be coaxed into playing his prescribed part. The Chief of the Imperial General Staff was packed off to Amman where he lectured the young King that 'the smart thing was to wear the new kind of hat'[72], the hat in question being a regional alliance to keep Egypt in check. Hussein, however, was canny beyond his years; he decided that the smart thing to do was to avoid ending up like his grandfather, which meant neglecting any action which bore the imprint of subservience to Britain. He therefore abjured the Pact and, when riots broke out in Amman during January 1956, he went further and shortly cast a sop to the largely Palestinian crowds by dismissing General Glubb as British Commander-in-Chief of the Jordanian Arab Legion. Given the gruesome fate which awaited his Hashemite relatives during the Iraq Revolution two years later[73], we can see now how sage Hussein's actions were. For the United Kingdom at the time, however, the failure to 'turn' the small Kingdom which it had itself carved out of the sand was a moment of truth for its position throughout the Levant. Afterwards Eden, not least with an eye on his own party, was driven by necessity 'to strike some blow, somewhere, to counterbalance'.[74] The only blow which could really count in the circumstances was against Nasser himself, newly-framed in the role of the evil genius of Middle Eastern politics. By nationalizing the Suez Canal Company on 27 July 1956, therefore, the Egyptian leader was only precipitating, on legal and moral grounds of his own choosing, a showdown with Britain which, had it not occurred on this matter, would most certainly have broken out on another.

We now know that, to all intents and purposes, Eden was bent on using force against Nasser from the moment the Canal was nationalized. The real political problem thereafter was how to present such an intervention to United Kingdom and world 'opinion' when the crunch came. 'If we lose out in the Middle East', Macmillan, the most hawkish of all the Prime Minister's colleagues, thus mused, 'we lose the oil. If we lose the oil, we cannot live.'[75] This argumentation was to be prominent throughout the ensuing crisis. Yet if the supply of oil *had* been considered vital for British survival, the obvious occasion for intervention was surely not against Egypt in 1956, but against Iran in 1950; such intervention had not supervened, and the British people did not starve as a consequence. Fundamentally, then, the oil argument with respect to Suez – like the 'defence of trade' rationale later tacked on to the Indian Ocean strategy of the 1960s – was an attempt to promote as a material necessity (with the man-in-the-street in mind) a policy which in truth was rooted in preoccupations with 'prestige': it not only had no relation to economic concerns, but by 1956 was desperately at odds with them (as the outcome of the crisis all too plainly showed). Arguably the deepest paradox of the Suez affair in British political terms was that it was Eden who got caught up in this contradictory spiral, when he had previously sought to get the United Kingdom off the Egyptian hook which others had been intent on keeping in place.

The essentially covert nature of the policy process which led to Britain's participation in the Suez War of October/November 1956 means that the surface aspect of events – the telegrams, attempted mediations, offers and counter-offers which followed in such dramatic abundance – are even more illusory in their significance than is usually the case. The details will not be repeated here.[76] At bottom, the nationalization of the Suez Canal did not provide a principle for British action so much as a necessary pretext. Even so, it was a pretext in need of a bit of French dressing, since it was in Paris (where Nasser was made the scapegoat for the war going on in Algeria) that the plan for a Franco-British-Israeli assault on Egypt was secretly cobbled together during the late summer and early autumn. According to these arrangements, Israel, ostensibly in reply to terrorist incursions along the Gaza Strip, would invade Egypt and drive on to the Canal; Britain and France, with an affectation of studied impartiality, would declare the Canal endangered and issue an ultimatum for the belligerents to cease fire and withdraw ten miles from either side of the Canal; and when Egypt refused – as refuse she must such an injunction – the Anglo-French forces would invade on the grounds of 'putting out the fire', making sure that in liquidating the flames, they also liquidated Nasser.

There are two problematical aspects to this enterprise from the British vantage-point which require comment before turning to the aftermath following the Anglo-French attack upon Egypt which commenced on 31 October. First, why, as more and more individuals were brought within the planning process, was opposition to the plan so muted? Eden and his close associates proved adept at lulling 'sleeping partners' in the Cabinet and elsewhere by providing enough information to keep them compromised, but not enough to make them principals. Special care was taken to neutralize Butler in this way.[77] As the rumour-mills began to grind, the latter could have blown the whistle easily enough by asking a few probing supplementaries designed to bring the whole thing into the light of day. Other than uttering a few disclaimers about 'no use of force', later to cost him dear, he chose not to do so. Butler's passivity is explained not only by his oblique temperament, but by the chauvinist mood which had gripped the Conservative Party conference at Llandudno during the second week of October. As the crisis neared its climax thereafter, the spotlights were on to detect any party member exhibiting the tell-tale signs of the 'weak sister'. Harold Macmillan, for example, was prominent in raising the bogey of disloyal elements whom he did not fail to identify as 'mostly young and mostly the sons of "Munich-ites"'.[78] In short, this was a moment – like April 1940 – for paying one's respects to the Man of Providence. 'If our country realizes its soul and inspiration your courage will have achieved this miracle', Alec Douglas-Home, who had a Chamberlainite past to live down, wrote speedily to Eden[79]; and he was by no means alone in such missives of encouragement. In brief, the great majority of politicians, even among the ranks of the Opposition, lay low and waited to see how things would turn out, though when it was all over the air was rent with the cries of the innocent and undefiled.

The second underlying question is why the Edenites felt they could get away with an action likely to arouse intense displeasure in Washington? In answer to this conundrum Eden's apologists later claimed that Dulles betrayed the British by actually *encouraging* the adoption of aggression against Nasser, only to change his spots when the invasion actually occurred. It is also frequently stated in this context that the invasion was timed to coincide with the Presidential election in the United States at the beginning of November, on the assumption – mistaken as it turned out – that Eisenhower's response would be constrained by his sensitivity to Jewish opinion at home. Whilst these factors are not to be wholly discounted, their persuasiveness is limited. No British Government would ever have allowed its fate to hinge so centrally on the uncertain outcomes of electoral politics in another country, irrespective of that country's importance; the United Kingdom was not, after all, a banana republic. Much more important, because more deeply ingrained in British experience, was the continuing belief in London that the country retained a residual capacity to blackmail America *providing that the issue concerned was not considered vital to American security*. It was because the British still felt that this principle applied in the eastern Mediterranean that there arose what the United Kingdom's departing Ambassador from Washington described as 'the active deception of the United States; the rapid shelving of a decade and a half of joint consultations, sharing of intelligence, the pooling of resources against a common [Communist] enemy . . .'.[80] Only when this basic judgement was shown to have become disastrously flawed was Eden forced into a headlong and humiliating retreat.

The mechanism which brought about that retreat was a sterling crisis, which one recent narrator describes as having been 'viciously orchestrated' by the United States Treasury.[81] Certainly Dulles' withering censure of Anglo-French belligerency in the United Nations General Assembly on 2 November was aimed as much at the money-markets as at the court of world opinion. Why, then, did the United States react so divergently from British expectations? At the time the authorities in Washington emphasized that the use of force was no longer an acceptable method of conducting international affairs. This may reasonably be put to one side – before very long the United States was to show in the Far East that force was by no means an anachronism where it gelled with her own national interests.

What, above all, heightened genuine American disgust was the blithe disregard the British and French had shown towards her status as a superpower. Thus for some days these countries had presided over a news black-out in the Middle East, and reduced Washington to relying on press agencies for scraps of information as to what was happening in one of the strategic hubs of world affairs. This was not the stuff of superpowerdom; and the fact that the Anglo-French attack served to distract attention from events in Hungary, where the Soviet Union was simultaneously putting down an anti-Communist rising, only rubbed salt into the wound. The British miscalculation with respect to American psychology and priorities, then, was not just tactical, but touched upon what it actually meant to be a superpower in a world fundamentally different from that of the Second World War, when so many British preconceptions had been formed.

The idea of the United States being a superpower had by 1956 become inextricably linked with the mystique of the presidential office itself, which helps to explain the puzzle as to why it was that throughout this episode Eisenhower's anger exceeded that even of Dulles. From this fact also flowed the logic of the British Foreign Secretary, Selwyn Lloyd, when amidst the diplomatic carnage of Britain's withdrawal from the adventure he predicted that '. . . we have to purge our contempt of the President in some way'.[82] The only way to purge the contempt – having already put the invasion into reverse, much to French anger since Egyptian resistance to the attack had quickly crumpled – was to purge the Prime Minister. This aspect of the Suez end-game was first revealed in David Carlton's study of Eden[83], and has recently had further light shed on it by Alistair Horne's official biography of Harold Macmillan. Horne's volume includes a transcript by Macmillan of a crucial exchange he had with the United States Treasury Secretary, George Humphrey, regarding the way in which the damage to Britain's position might be repaired. It merits a full quotation:

> He [Humphrey] said that it was like a business
> deal. They [the Americans] were putting a lot of

money into the [future] reorganisation of Britain and they would hope very much that the business would be successful. But, of course, when you were reconstructing a business that was in difficulties, the personal problems could not be ruled out.

I [Macmillan] said: 'Don't you trust the board?' and he said: 'Well, since you ask me, I think it would be as well if we could deal as much as possible with the [other] directors.'[84]

Such signals helped seal Eden's fate and, with the Prime Minister convalescing in Jamaica from his liver disease, the rituals of succession were swiftly under way, from which Macmillan soon emerged victorious. Superficially, at least, it is odd that Macmillan was thus unscathed by the fact that, having been the most hawkish of ministers before things started to go wrong, he had overnight become the one most insistent on sounding the bugle of recall: as Harold Wilson icily put it from the sidelines, 'First in, first out.' Why, then, were Butler's undoubted claims to seniority brushed aside with relative ease?[85] American preferences, however discreetly communicated, affected – inevitably under such extraordinary circumstances – the outcome of what was a brief but incisive struggle for the reversion. Thus Butler, having been Minister for Education during the Second World War, hardly loomed large in the American imagination; we saw earlier the uninterest he had aroused in President Eisenhower when visiting Washington in his later capacity as Chancellor of the Exchequer.[86] Macmillan, by contrast, had spent much of his wartime career in North Africa plugging himself into the circuit of visiting Americans; Eisenhower had held him in high esteem ever since the day in Casablanca during 1943 when he tried to introduce his English subordinate to Franklin Roosevelt, only to find that the two hailed each other on first-name terms as old social acquaintances.[87] These things counted. But what signified more than any explicit indications of United States' opinion was the fact that Macmillan's political – and even his personal

– mentality had long been geared to the method, as it has been expressed, of making himself agreeable 'to men who are more powerful than he was'.[88] In January 1957 this quality was, to say the least, in considerable demand in British politics.

Nevertheless, pertinent though such considerations were, they were not the chief reason why Macmillan gained the palm over Butler. The essence of the matter was rather reflected in the proceedings of the crucial meeting of Conservative parliamentarians at which the two candidates paraded their wares. Butler, it appears, was strangely mute, whereas when Macmillan spoke he did so with great gusto, his arms waving so expressively that they all but shooed his opponent off the podium. Yet it was the words, even more than the body language, which swung the pendulum. 'It is our task', Macmillan intoned as to the reconstruction effort which lay ahead, 'to ensure that like the retreat from Mons and Dunkirk, it should prove the prelude to strategic victory. It can be done'.[89] No words could better convey, according to the labels commonly circulating in the party at the time, that Macmillan espoused to be a Warrior, whilst Butler was a Cardinal; nor could they fail to bring to the forefront of the minds of his auditors that Macmillan was a veteran of the war of 1914–18, whilst not only had Butler fought in neither conflict, but he had been an Appeaser up to, and some said beyond, September 1939. Macmillan, in short, spoke to the mass of Tory backbenchers in terms of the symbols that they cherished most dearly, and offered them implicit assurances that the 'journey back to greatness' embarked upon only a few years before had been interrupted rather than abandoned; in contrast, Butler had found such promises impossible to give, and so in his enigmatic way had said nothing at all, before reassuming his accustomed position in the semi-shadow. But what, in truth, could 'strategic victory' mean in the circumstances of 1957, with the nation now poised on top of the 'knife-edged economy'? For all the brave talk of modernization, the most telling fact was that Macmillan gained the highest place by defining his goals in terms of the past, rather than of the present. Here was the fatal conundrum which ensured that his leadership, whilst it had its successes, was to seem increasingly out of touch with the needs of the times, and was destined to end, if in a less spectacular fashion than that of his immediate predecessor, then with a degree of ignominy only a shade less harsh.

The Modernization of Britain?

The four dominant motifs in Harold Macmillan's premiership from January 1957 to October 1963 were the quest for a national nuclear deterrent, the changing stance towards Europe, the East of Suez defence policy and the 'end of Empire'. Our analysis shall deal with each of these in turn. But the sum of any premiership is always greater than its parts; and its essence is usually to be found in the assumptions and prejudices which an individual brings with him (or her) to the job. What fundamental conception, then, of the 'needs of the moment' did Macmillan have when he first took up the burdens of leadership? The answer to this may be gleaned from a remark he made to Winston Churchill, and which he often repeated in one form or another. 'It is no longer the case', he had said to his mentor, 'of choosing between the policies of Marlborough and Bolingbroke, but of combining them.'[1] In other words, it was necessary to mellow an essentially war-minded regime (in which the critical imperatives were instinctively *external*) with effective priorities geared to the internal condition of the nation. Like Churchill himself, Macmillan was stronger on the details of the history of the eighteenth century than the one in which he lived. Had it been otherwise, he might have caught at least the echo in his own words of Bonar Law's classic dictum stretching back to the 1920s: 'We cannot act alone as the Policeman of the World.' Indeed, it is in precisely this context of a clash of values and aims between a doctrine of the United Kingdom as on the one hand a Great Power and, on the other hand, as a truly modern and smoothly functioning domestic society, that the real continuities in British history during the century may be found.

Yet the most telling aspect of Macmillan's observation was that he thought of combining the two forms of *staatspolitik,* rather than deciding between them. Afterwards he struggled valiantly as Prime Minister to find ways of harnessing the two together, an ideal which sat comfortably with the Middle Way philosophy which he espoused in his rhetorical efforts. Perhaps, too, given the mould of national and even more of party, opinion, this was the maximum which it was open to Macmillan to attempt. Nevertheless, the failure to define goals more clearly (or rather, the propensity to let various conflicting goals run side by side) was to lead to the progressive bankruptcy of his ministry after 1960. What laid Macmillan low in the end was not the Profumo affair (with which we are not concerned), but the more profound problem that English Toryism had lost the art of discoursing with itself or the nation on how best to administer a capitalist, free-flowing society in time of peace. Nor was this surprising, since the last Conservative leader to ponder these problems seriously was the one whose memory was most uniformly despised, umbrella and all. The somewhat dim charade surrounding Macmillan's eventual retirement only served to highlight how binding the paralysis remained.

The most consistent and compelling concern of Macmillan's years in power was the nuclear deterrent, and in this respect the benchmarks were established early on with the Defence White Paper of April 1957. The 'Sandys Doctrine' (named after the responsible minister) of nuclear primacy within the United Kingdom's defence policy which this introduced was the new government's answer to the problem Macmillan himself had once defined as how to get the maximum return on inflated defence spending.[2] Nevertheless, as an arch political tactician, the Prime Minister was not insensible to the more intangible benefits which sprang from the nuclear source. These benefits were exemplified during Macmillan's first really major challenge in the House of Commons, when he had the awkward task of conveying the terms of a settlement with Egypt. Rumour was rife that the 'new boy' might trip up with respect to one side of the House or the other. Accidentally (or otherwise), however, the debate coincided with news of the successful British hydrogen 'test', and by turning the debate towards the deterrent as a fresh symbol of British prestige and influence, Macmillan triumphed over his detractors. The lesson was one he did not forget.

In fact, as one commentator has pointed out, the main thrust of the Defence White Paper in readjusting the balance between nuclear and conventional arms was not original; it simply consolidated doctrine concerning British military organization which had taken shape earlier in the decade.[3] The doctrine, however, took on an extra allure in the aftermath of Suez. Firstly, there was the argument that once the United Kingdom possessed a credible deterrent 'small fry' such as Nasser would never again try to interfere with her interests. In this sense, it was assumed, the deterrent would restore the natural order, not least in the Middle East, which had gone so badly askew in recent times. Experience was to prove that nuclear capability was not of any real efficacy in policing what was becoming generically known as the Third World[4], but in 1957 the assumption had an understandable resonance in Britain. The second, and main, attraction of the heightened nuclear emphasis concerned relations with the two superpowers, especially the United States. The recent crisis had shown how singularly difficult it was for Britain to make her voice heard in Washington or Moscow, and from it was derived the related lesson that her desiderata would continue to be ignored until she could 'rattle her rockets' in the manner approved by the superpowers when their interests were held to be stake. This logic was neither entirely novel, nor of the sort which could be aired in White Papers, but it was to prove the most enduring rationale of that will-o'-the-wisp of the early 1960s – the truly *independent* British deterrent.

The nuclear impulse had a special significance for the bulk of the Right wing of the Conservative party, whose core belief in the United Kingdom's Great Power status had been so defiled in the course of recent events. Thus it was suggestive that younger Tories of a strategic disposition began making speeches in which the Hydrogen Bomb was hailed as giving Britain the opportunity to recover lost ground.[5] A stock element in these perorations was that the enhanced scale of 'terror' in nuclear scenarios, and particularly the capacity for extensive as well as intensive damage, had fortuitously truncated the advantages which for decades had accrued to the great continental nations. Julian Amery, for example, stressed these points with a zeal which his father, Leopold, had for many years devoted to the ideal of Imperial Economic Unity. For the son, as for the father before him, the vision was never quite to come off. Nevertheless, it was to prove highly significant that after Suez the cauterized emotions of many Britons, especially amongst Tories of the 'overseas' type such as Amery, were canalized into (and thus mitigated by) an intensified brand of nuclear patriotism. As we shall argue later on, this was a phenomenon which, however much it distorted technological and political reality, was to make Macmillan's task of modulating his party's grievances in the Age of Decolonization more manageable than it might otherwise have been.

Even in 1957 it was transparent that the United Kingdom would need American co-operation to fulfil its aims in this sphere, although only time was to show the extent of that reliance. Anxiety as to whether or not such assistance would be forthcoming was alleviated by the eagerness of the United States to propitiate for the knuckle-rapping of 1956, and to strike anew the note of a 'special relationship'. President Eisenhower met with Macmillan in Bermuda during March 1957 and afterwards referred to that occasion as '. . . by far the most successful international conference that I have attended since the close of World War Two'.[6] Cynics might reflect that this was not saying a great deal. Nevertheless, there followed a renewed phase of intense military and intelligence co-operation between Britain and America, culminating during 1958 in the amendment by Congress of the Atomic Energy Act. One of the distinguishing marks of this new legislation was that it was patently designed to apply only to the United Kingdom. Other countries, especially in Western Europe, were quick to spot the discriminatory pattern which United States policy took on thereafter regarding military matters in general, and nuclear matters in particular. Naturally the resulting jealousies (especially, as we shall see, in France) were visited upon the recipient, rather than the donor, of such favours; and ultimately the coherence of Macmillan's policies were to founder in large part on the contradictions to which these developments gave rise. Meanwhile the glossy image of 'Supermac', whilst primarily based on a fleeting sense of domestic economic contentment which paved the way for the election victory of October 1959, was reinforced by the imprimatur afforded by such tokens of Eisenhower's approval.

The British Prime Minister's hopes of building on that approval – and, as he liked to formulate the United Kingdom's role *vis-à-vis* the United States, of 'playing Greeks to their Romans'[7] – was considerably facilitated during the first year of his premiership by the Soviet Union's launch of Sputnik, the first space satellite. Sputnik undermined the American public's sense of invulnerability to nuclear attack, and helped to create the impression of a Soviet lead in missile technology; as Macmillan himself put it, 'The American cocksure-ness is shaken'.[8] The breezy days of Dullesian 'brinkmanship' disappeared overnight, and in this less congenial climate the need for an affectionate and consistent embrace with another friendly Power (over and above the cold functionalism of the NATO alliance) became pronounced. As one United States diplomat recalled, at the top of the Washington hierarchy the feeling grew that 'we must have someone to talk to in the world'[9]; and during the next few years the increasingly maverick tendencies in French diplomacy, and apprehensions that Western Europe was no longer quite so responsive to the coaxings and occasional dictates of American policy as it had once been, boosted appreciation in the United States of what the British (for all their irritating ways) had to offer. To this extent the assertions at the time and since that the so-called 'Special Relationship' between Britain and America was always in reality a 'one-way street' are not strictly true, even if they evoke something of its spirit.

Circumstances during the initial phases of Macmillan's tenure, therefore, afforded him somewhat more leverage over American policy than might have been anticipated in January 1957. In seeking to define a foreign policy which was unquestionably loyal to NATO precepts, and yet which provided scope for distinctively British actions, Macmillan reverted, as was his wont, to a Churchillian gambit: the idea of an East-West Summit. His so-called 'voyage of discovery' to the Soviet Union in February 1959 may have been, as his critics alleged, designed to cull the 'peace vote' at the general election then looming, but the trip undoubtedly also held a larger significance in Macmillan's political conceptions. After his return he pressed NATO partners, and above all the United States, for their agreement to a summit initiative, arousing suspicions, not wholly unfounded, in Bonn that the British were susceptible to 'selling out' the interests of the Federal Republic over the running crisis in Berlin if they could make a profit by so doing.[10] Despite German hesitations, however, Eisenhower gave his approval for a Four-Power conference to be held during May 1960 in Paris (the venue being the usual Anglo-American sop to the French). Quite why he did so is not clear. 'I had no intention of bickering with my best friend' was how Eisenhower explained his reasons in his memoirs[11], although one suspects that like Churchill before him (and like President Reagan in a later day) the logic was also that of an ageing statesman who wished to leave office wreathed in the laurels of peace rather than surrounded by the odour of war.[12] Whatever factors broke up the log-jam in the White House, Macmillan was accorded the prize of a summit which would evoke rich memories of the wartime conferences in which the British leader sat, for all the world to see, as an equal alongside the other great powers in the world; Paris, in short, was to be his Casablanca.

As Eisenhower reached the end of his second term, however, his ability (always problematical) to shape underlying administration policy was on the wane, and Macmillan expressed the premonitory fear to his Foreign Secretary, Selwyn Lloyd, that the Pentagon 'might do everything in their power to make the disarmament conference [in Paris] fail'.[13] To what extent this provides a key to the amazing saga surrounding the authorization of United States' 'spyflights' over the Soviet Union during the run-up to the summit naturally remains obscure. It appears that the U-2 aircraft concerned were assumed in Washington to be invulnerable to interception; and that even if 'downed', the unfortunate pilot would swallow the appropriate cyanide pill. Alas, not only was one such machine shot down, but the pilot, Gary Powers, did his duty to himself rather than to his employer. Scarcely had the Big-Power delegations met in the French capital than the conference was overwhelmed by a deluge of Soviet-American bickering, with General Secretary Khrushchev refusing to turn a blind eye to the U-2 affair, and Eisenhower adamant against anything that smacked of an apology. At first Macmillan and the British officials present tried to shuttle between the two main antagonists with various bits of paper, but gave up once they realized that the only result was to make them appear patently irrelevant, and even ridiculous. 'It is impossible to describe this day', the Prime Minister wrote in his diary of the eventual break-up. 'It is ignominious; it is tragic; it is almost incredible.'[14] One of his closest advisers was of the opinion that he never saw Macmillan so exhausted and depressed than he was at this juncture, noting further that '[it] was the moment that he suddenly realized that Britain counted for nothing. . . I think this represented a real watershed in his life.'[15]

It also represented a watershed for the United Kingdom: the abortive summit of 1960 was the last time that a British Government appeared on the international stage as a great and independent power in the traditional sense of this description. Afterwards, the aims with which Macmillan had set out on his premiership had to be drastically curtailed and amended, and it will be essential to our argument that he was never able to define in his own mind just what the new fall-back position should consist of (other than the acquisition of an up-to-date nuclear deterrent). It is clear that the Conservative Government's change of course towards Europe in 1960–61 bore a direct relationship to the evaporation of those long-harboured hopes that the United Kingdom might succeed in carving out a comfortable and prestigious niche for itself in the realm of superpower politics. For there was one lesson of political life which Macmillan understood very well: if one door slams shut, another one must be kicked open as soon as possible. Hence in July 1961 the United Kingdom Government officially requested to begin negotiations concerning entry into the European Economic Community – though time was to show that the obliqueness of this approach was the most telling thing about it.

The Conservative Government's conversion to Common Market membership appeared unlikely at any time prior to 1960. Disgust in Paris at what was regarded as British pusillanimity in backing down over the Suez campaign in 1956 had been particularly significant in driving a final nail in the coffin of Anglo-French relations, and confirmed the tendency to look to Germany instead.[16] In this political sense the EEC (minus the United Kingdom) got under way with a head wind already behind it. The chasm represented by the English Channel got wider following the British initiatives which led to the emergence of the European Free Trade Association (EFTA) in November 1959. In effect an alternative caucus to the EEC, consisting of the United Kingdom, Sweden, Norway, Denmark, Switzerland, Austria and Portugal, EFTA appeared to the Treaty of Rome powers as a crude 'spoiling' tactic on the part of the authorities in London designed to sabotage the *relance* of the European movement. In fact the British case – that ultimately Europe could only be truly unified through Free Trade, and that the 'Six' would surely revert to it once experience proved the point – was not without cogency, and may even be seen as validated by the European Single Market of the 1990s.[17] None of this, however, can altogether obscure the blunt truth that at the time EFTA constituted a threat to divide Europe against the infant EEC. It reflected, too, the United Kingdom's besetting desire only to join associations in Europe which she could lead from the front, rather than those in which her status was that of a common-or-garden member. The very peripheral character (in the geographical sense) of EFTA was reminiscent, indeed, of the 'soft underbelly of Europe' which was the overripe fruit of

Churchill's strategic imagination; and like the latter's wartime campaigns in the Mediterranean, it was capable of being seen by sceptics as inherently evasive about the dominant issues of the day.

The difficulty which Britain faced with respect to Europe was greatly enhanced at this time by an event which had nothing to do with supra-national clubs or associations: the return to power of General de Gaulle in France during June 1958 amidst circumstances which, if not precisely those of a coup, bore close similarities to the type. The constitution of the Fifth Republic which was swiftly draped over the new policy was subsequently characterized by a leader of the opposition, François Mitterand, as 'the revenge of the executive over the legislature' for the erratic behaviour of the latter in recent times. Its remarkable success in underpinning a stable and prosperous France was not, of course, fully anticipated from the outset. None the less, one thing was clear: henceforth France was to be governed by a strong man. Up to this point the United Kingdom had no wish to see France embroiled in the civil conflict which her Algerian entanglements had threatened; yet there was a tangible sense in which Whitehall's gamble on the unworkability of the Treaty of Rome hinged, more than anything else, on the persistence of a weak and nervous Fourth Republic.[18] The sight of de Gaulle settling magnificently – if reluctantly, since he hated the building – into the Elysée Palace, taking all his prickly and even frankly hostile sentiments towards *les Anglo-Saxons* with him, understandably aroused fresh uncertainties in London. Subsequently Anglo-French rivalry became a distinct element in European affairs, adding momentum, as we shall see, to the scramble *out* of redundant colonial empires and *into* the more glamorous and pertinent game of nuclear deterrence. The skill with which the French executed this transition was shown by the way that, whilst all the world was watching the 'Battle of Algiers', where old-fashioned French paratroopers played hide-and-seek with Muslim rebels, out in the desert French military scientists were making the most of their last opportunity to test nuclear devices in wide open spaces. In short, in 1958

Macmillan had been able to sweep aside French claims to equality with the United States and the United Kingdom within the Western Alliance as 'absurd'[19]; during 1960–1 the French came to appear well on their way to establishing hegemony in Western Europe, based on military as well as economic revival. This alone was enough to induce the sense of confused and even frightened helplessness which settled over the British government by the latter date.

An essential aspect of this burgeoning French leadership was the acquiescence of the German Federal Republic. One retired British diplomat has ventured the opinion that in these years Konrad Adenauer's dislike of the British was insufficiently appreciated. The German Chancellor, according to this account, 'regarded us (the British) as some kind of maritime pirates, jolly good at swiping chunks of Africa and looking after our own interests, but not very reliable in a European context'[20]; and if such was his prejudice, British policy since the war had done little to sway him from it. Nevertheless, such a gloss understates the subtlety of Adenauer's beliefs, and especially his conviction that the real purpose of the European Community was the assuagement of Franco-German hatreds, to which end British participation was not only marginal but an actual hindrance. It also leaves discreetly shrouded the fact that ever since its establishment, the British had shown themselves to be equivocal as to the place that the Federal Republic should occupy within the Western system. By 1957 it was too late for Macmillan (pronounced though his dislike of all Germans was) to cavil at the integration of the *Bundesrepublik* within alliance institutions; but from the moment that a new crisis in East-West relations over Berlin began to boil up after the middle of 1958, the British Prime Minister exhibited what appeared in Bonn as distinctly shifty signs, contrasting starkly with the firm posture adopted by de Gaulle.[21] It is against this background that we may understand the basis of German pliancy which allowed the French leader to progressively shape the EEC in his own image, not least through the 'acceleration' after 1960 towards a unified external tariff and a Common Agricultural Policy. It was this acceleration – its early impulse coinciding fortuitously with the collapse of the Paris Summit – which assisted in persuading Macmillan that it was imperative to get a foot in the door before it was banged and bolted for good.

Amidst all these changes and shifts, then, how important was the Macmillan Government's vaunted emphasis on *economic* modernization in bringing about the 'turn to Europe'? Most commentators have concluded that strictly political considerations were always paramount, and there seems no reason to disagree with this. Indeed, those economic factors which did surface were often not of a sort which had much to do with modernization as the term is conventionally understood. Some British industries, for example, appeared principally drawn to the EEC because it offered fresh opportunities for protection to replace the Imperial Preferences which the tightening bands of the General Agreement on Tariffs and Trade had outlawed.[22] The same inspiration was even more starkly apparent among the agriculturalists. 'Rab' Butler later confessed how responsive he was to the National Farmers' Union in all matters that touched the interests of its constituency.[23] Why, then, did the farmers take their tractors off the lawn of 10 Downing Street after 1960, and accept – as Butler never thought they would – that their own farm price reviews should be mixed up with those of French and German peasants? Lord Soames, Macmillan's Minister of Agriculture, has helped to explain this puzzle by indicating how the farming lobby came to grasp that a progressively increasing level of subsidy could no longer be squeezed out of the straitened and increasingly obstreperous British Treasury. In short, the logic apparently went, '. . . the [Agricultural] policy would have to be changed anyway because the level of support . . . necessary was beyond the ability of the country to carry'.[24] What Britain's sturdy rural population needed was a new public trough in which to immerse itself; hence a political problem miraculously disappeared – though, of course, years were to pass before the dream of cornucopia (all too briefly) was to be fulfilled. Whether this had much to do with modernization depended on whether you could see hay-stacks from the bay-window.

Still, the decision to apply to join the Common Market did have a relevance to British political economy in a sense which requires further elucidation. By the later fifties the problem of national economic discipline had moved – despite, as it were, the politicians – into the foreground of public consciousness. These matters always made Macmillan deeply uncomfortable. He had invested far too much personal political capital in retrospective anguish at the unemployment in his old constituency of Stockton-on-Tees during the Depression to adopt the strict anti-inflationary stance which an influential minority of Conservative politicians, following in the abortive tradition of ROBOT, were once again advocating. Macmillan had even been prepared to accept the resignations of his entire Treasury Front Bench team in January 1958 rather than adopt a modest tranche of what were coming to be called 'monetarist' policies.[25] Yet if 'discipline' could not be applied directly by fiscal and monetary methods to workers and managements for fear of the political reverberations, the Common Market offered a method of doing so *indirectly* by shackling the British economy to that of the more competitive Europeans, and above all to the industrious Germans. This would inevitably lead to rationalization and higher unemployment, but the shock would be more gradual, and even more important, less attributable to the action of the government of the day. It was, again, an American analyst who recorded the British dilemma most clearly. 'I had a very strong belief during the whole of this period', George Ball wrote, 'that Britain was going to have a very hard time resolving the problem of industrialization if they [sic] were left within a strictly national context, but that in a broader context many things would have been possible.'[26] The Common Market, therefore, provided a framework within which the British Government could hope to engage with problems which, on its own, it lacked the confidence and internal cohesion to tackle.

The reasoning which lay behind the United Kingdom's re-orientation towards Europe after 1960 was, therefore, varied in its derivation. But how deep did this Damascene conversion go, especially when measured, as it was bound to be over time, by other currents and temptations in British life? In Western

Europe strong doubts existed on this score, not least owing to the very speed with which attitudes in London had appeared to change. Such suspicions were further augmented by the curious tendency of the British Government, just when it was expressing its new-found desire to play the part of a good 'European', to adopt decisions in the field of defence which implied that its instinct to look *outside* Europe for its major role in the world was undiminished. These decisions all related to the equally rapid emergence of the defence strategy which came to sport the grand title of 'East of Suez'. This theme was to prove so central to British developments during the decade of the sixties that its background must be briefly sketched.

Phillip Darby, the historian of the East of Suez policy, has observed how in the 1950s the military Services had continued to regard the government's job as primarily that of providing the funds they required, a role not meant to extend to prescribing the strategic purposes to which such monies should be devoted.[27] It was because the Sandys reforms referred to earlier, with the doctrine of nuclear primacy as their centre-piece, were geared to the related criteria of cheapness and closer ministerial control that they triggered such powerful eruptions in military circles. So deeply were emotions stirred that the incumbent Chief of the Imperial General Staff, Field Marshal Sir Gerald Templer, rowed with the Minister of Defence every time they met – including social occasions.[28] The outcome of this controversy was that the Chiefs of Staff – exploiting their ultimate threat of resignation – succeeded in establishing that the government could spend *more* on nuclear hardware, but not *less* on conventional manpower and equipment. In particular, the decision to abandon the aircraft-carrier role was reversed, despite Sandys' conviction that such an investment was 'expensive, vulnerable and irrelevant to national needs'.[29] 'We failed, yes. The Services were too strong. . .' was Macmillan's summing up of this episode, and after Sandys moved on to the Commonwealth Relations Office in 1960 the Defence portfolio was put in the hands of a businessman,

Harold Watkinson, who, as the euphemism has it, 'believed in letting professionals run things'.[30] What the military professionals wanted more than anything else at this time was a 'world of their own', one whose conventional (as opposed to nuclear) contours were familiar and amiable, and at the entrance to which – lest any meddling civilians should fail to notice – a large sign might be hung forbidding trespass to the unauthorized. East of Suez, aircraft carriers and all, provided just such a timely ideal; and some of the most intense divisions in British politics during the coming years were to be generated when financial necessity drove ministers (mainly Labour ones after 1964, since it was much too explosive for their Conservative counterparts) to lay their hands on this Ark of the Covenant.

The East of Suez phenomenon did not only reflect vested interest. The loss of guaranteed access to Egypt and its through-way after 1956 accorded a genuine intellectual persuasiveness to treating the Indian Ocean as a self-contained, closed-off theatre of operations. In addition, the accent on efficient and clinical mobility, allowing friendly regimes to be dependably insured by British arms against occasional threats of radical subversion, jelled with the post-Suez world, providing that the pretexts of interference were always carefully chosen. Experience proved the point. The successful intervention in Oman during 1957, when a rebellion against the pro-British Sultan was snuffed out, set the tone. According to Alistair Horne, this was 'an operation which [Macmillan] regarded with considerable personal pride to the end of his days'[31], and it is easy to grasp why; Oman was to the Prime Minister in that post-Suez year what intervention in Greece had once been for Churchill – proof that the United Kingdom *could* act on its own if it set its mind to it, and that there was 'life in the old dog yet'. Perhaps the most perfect example of an East of Suez campaign was that in Kuwait during 1960, when a massive, and very expensive, British campaign was set in motion to pre-empt an attack by revolutionary Iraq (which never came, and according to some incorrigible sceptics, had never been imminent in the first place).[32] All in all, such minor but deeply satisfying triumphs of conventional overseas arms contrasted starkly with the increasing technical difficulties attending Britain's nuclear deterrent programme, serving to underline the argument that the United Kingdom should stick to a role at which it indubitably remained a dab hand. Darby remarks on the chronology of this tendency as follows:

> If anything, 1960 saw an *increasing* emphasis on Britain's role East of Suez. It is difficult to document the slight sharpening of focus, as it rested more on decisions taken regarding hardware and force structures than on any changed appreciation of the risks of conflict in the Indian Ocean area vis-à-vis Europe. However, the gist of military thinking, the strengthening of Britain's strategically mobile capacity, the movement of some additional forces into the region, all indicate the government's tendency to *upgrade* the East of Suez role [Italics added].[33]

As part of this process huge sums of money were expended, only to be lost as the policy was forced to jump from one expedient to another. Thus in late 1957 the decision was taken to establish a strategic reserve in Kenya. This was soon expanded into plans for a major new base, complete with air-conditioned married quarters at a cost of £7.5 millions (it was a period when the recruitment problems of the Services appeared in the press as an issue of first-rank importance). The cheques for this facility were still being signed when Iain Macleod, the Colonial Secretary, announced in August 1961 that the prospective independence of Kenya would preclude any such military presence. The strategists were as a result driven not to a change of mind, but to a change of venue: construction began in Aden of the biggest single garrison ever undertaken by a British Government. There, too, as we shall see, local complications were to mar the planners' ideals. The pattern in these years was invariably the same, with the British military authorities edging their way into one base area after another, followed – after much disputation at Parliamentary Question Times – by a precipitate withdrawal under financial and (in the unhappy case of Aden) military duress.

This sorry spectacle is often said to have resulted from a chronic lack of co-ordination in Whitehall which came to a head in the early sixties. No doubt there is something in this. It is, nevertheless, a strange phenomenon on the part of the country which prided itself on having (and was said by others to possess) the finest civil service in the world. Indeed, at least part of the problem was probably attributable, not to the right arm not knowing what the left arm was doing, but to each arm knowing very well what the other was up to, and seeking to frustrate it. Amidst this muddle and intrigue the civilian politicians and the military, the cutters and the spenders, sought to work out a compromise in which East of Suez was accorded its place among the nation's priorities, only to find that financial crisis and shifts in the territories concerned kept moving the benchmarks. As Darby points out, the fact that the strategy survived for so long, and in so many different versions, 'was less of a tribute to the willingness of the nation to bear the costs of empire without the dividends, than a consequence of the fact that the issue never saw the light of political day'.[34] That this was the case may be said to reflect the larger reality that the British system of government, particularly as it affected overseas matters, was, more than most of its counterparts among the advanced countries, a form of iceberg in which the critical mass was permanently out of sight.

These covert tendencies were particularly evident in the case of the 'light soil' of South Arabia and the Colony of Aden. Indeed, it was in this land of warring sheikhs and inveterate tribal hatreds that the British turn to East of Suez had its chief centre of emotional as well as strategic gravity. The logic of the policy as it developed after 1956 was predicated on the need for a stronghold in the Middle Eastern world which was beyond the reach of the long arm of Nasserite propaganda. The southern littoral of Arabia seemed to meet these criteria in ideal fashion, since it appeared almost inconceivable, providing the proper precautions were taken, that the modern virus of nationalism could infect such a feudal milieu.[35] Hence there emerged in 1959, under formal British protection, the

Federation of South Arabia, to which Aden Colony adhered shortly afterwards. Here was a classic marriage of landed and autocratic magnates, native merchants and British oversight which could be relied upon to last far into the future. The polity was even provided with a brand new administrative headquarters of its own, built out in the sand at Al Ittihad – perhaps the only capital in the world without permanent inhabitants. Unfortunately the preconceptions infusing this enterprise proved far from watertight, since the subsequent revolution in South Yemen, and the trade union militancy in Aden port itself, soon began to undermine the federal structure. Later on the fate of Aden and the Federation was to play a signal part in the final unravelling of the East of Suez policy after 1967–8, in which context we shall return to the theme. Meanwhile we may note that the Conservative Government's fixed gaze on the translucent distances of Arabia, whatever its merits in strategic terms, had the advantage that it provided a sop to those of its supporters whose loyalty was at the same time being sorely tried by the dismantling of the colonial empire, primarily in Africa.

The relationship between the Suez crisis of 1956 and the sub-sequent winding-up of the British colonial empire which was set in motion after 1959 has become a cause of controversy amongst historians. Some commentators have claimed that the former was a seminal cause of the latter, pointing, for example, to the fact (remarked upon in the previous chapter) that as soon as Harold Macmillan arrived in 10 Downing Street he ordered the Treasury to draw up a net profit and loss account for the remaining colonies. Subsequently, it has been contended, the pace and nice tactics of Macmillan's colonial policy reflected the kaleidoscopic conditions prevailing in the various dependencies, but the nub of policy in this respect was implicit in the agenda of 'reorganization' laid down at the outset of his term.[36] Indeed, decolonization was arguably the *only* part of this agenda which was subsequently carried through with a concentrated purpose. In contrast to this approach, other historians have demurred from regarding Suez as the tap-root of later departures from Africa or elsewhere.[37] They point to subsequent events (such as the Belgian decision to quit the Congo in 1960, with its bloody aftermath) as having been instrumental in wrenching British thinking along new lines. Above all, they accord a more pronounced weight to a bevy of territorial nationalisms in *evicting* the United Kingdom from possessions it otherwise had no relatively proximate intention of relinquishing.

These two schools of thought are not necessarily incompatible: in many ways they merely focus on different parts of the anatomy of decolonization. Macmillan's retrospective claim that on assuming office he was unsure whether he was 'destined to be the remodeller or liquidator of Empire' may, or may not, amount to more than what two commentators have described as a 'stylish conceit'.[38] The linkage between Suez and later territorial retreats, however, may most profitably be explored, not at the level of individual inclinations and insights, but rather in terms of a broader transition in British politics which the events of 1956–7 set in motion, and which gathered pace, albeit fitfully, over the decade following. In this respect it must be said that in reflecting the 'new Britain' of the late 1950s, Macmillan himself was always a bit awkward; understandably so, since the most effective part of his appeal lay in the guise he consciously assumed as The Last Edwardian.[39] More suggestive of underlying trends as they impinged upon the governing party of the day were the persona and convictions of Iain Macleod, whom Macmillan appointed Colonial Secretary in late 1959, and who was to preside over the crucial decision to accelerate political development in British Africa. As his biographer, Nigel Fisher, has pointed out, Macleod lacked the traditional profile of a senior Tory politician: he was the son of a doctor rather than of a landowner; he had been to Fettes, not to Eton; and during the war he had been in a line regiment, not the Brigade of Guards.[40] One need not agree with Fisher that this made him a new kind of 'classless politician'[41] to appreciate that it differentiated him from the grandee wing of the party. Yet what is most significant is not who Macleod was, but the political vision which he, and other Tories like him, had come to possess by the election year of 1959. In a speech he gave on the hustings Macleod evocatively described the cadre whom he conceived to be central to up-dated Conservative doctrine. It is worth quoting at some length:

> They are as surely men of property as if they held broad acres or led great corporations. Perhaps they own a house or, more probably, they are buying one through a building society. They have a car and a television set – perhaps a refrigerator and a washing machine. They are beginning to invest in stocks and shares, either directly or through unit trusts. At this time of year you will find them looking at gaily coloured travel brochures and planning their summer holiday. But now they do not only think of the English seaside resorts – the pamphlets that they study are of the Costa Brava, the Rhineland, the Italian cities. . . . They are for the most part employees drawing high wages in a prosperous and commanding economy. . . . We can give them the opportunity they long for instead of the equality they despise.[42]

Here was a cohort whose conception of an overseas mission lay in Lloret de Mar, not in the Tropics; and in retrospect we can see that the constituent elements in what later came together in the phenomenon of 'Thatcherism' were already making their initial presence felt (although Macleod's use of language evinced a condescension which was wholly alien to Margaret Thatcher, who first entered Parliament as the representative of Finchley following the 1959 poll). As yet this social grouping remained too inchoate a force to transform the political landscape; but it was none the less a factor helping to underpin a bias towards the concentration of public expenditure at home (on financing mortgage tax relief, for example, as a great house inflation got under way) rather than seeping 'overseas' under one label or another. The petty bourgeoisie was never Macmillan's favourite class, but he saw the drift well enough. In appointing Macleod to the Colonial Office, the Prime Minister was 'in effect, issuing a general directive to "get a move on in Africa" '.[43]

This is not to say that all the roots of British decolonization were to be found, as it were, in Surbiton. The need for a 'move on' was also closely related to the crisis which had unfolded in the Central African Federation, whose earlier establishment we have already recounted. By 1958 the metropolitan liberal ideal of 'multi-racialism' in that gimcrack polity had been confounded by the stark reality of racial ill-feeling. Then, in January 1959, following riots in Blantyre township in Nyasaland, interpreted by the local authorities as stemming from an organized conspiracy to murder all the whites in the colony, the settler-dominated Federal Government exploited the opportunity to crack down on African nationalists not only in Nyasaland itself – where the black leader Hastings Banda was imprisoned along with many others – but throughout the region.[44] A perturbing feature of this sequence of events, viewed from London, was that the Southern Rhodesia-based Federal Government, led by the pugnacious Polish emigré, Roy Welensky, was remarkably successful at dragging in its wake the Colonial Governors of the Crown Colonies of Northern Rhodesia and Nyasaland, thereby tarring the British Government with the brush of repression. The dangers this presented were intensified when an official judicial enquiry headed by Judge Devlin, whilst passing with understandable discretion over the causes of the Blantyre disturbances, concluded bluntly that the apparatus which had emerged in its wake was that of a 'police state'. The very speed with which the incidents in question had unravelled illustrated clearly how a government in London could end up becoming the prisoner of its 'kith and kin' in settler-Africa, just as France had become trapped in Algeria. From this moment on, Macmillan's priority was to make sure that *he* controlled the pace and direction of affairs in British colonial Africa, rather than the intransigent European communities and their frequently die-hard leaders – 'Africans are not the problem in Africa; it is the Europeans' was the way Macmillan tellingly described the contemporary dilemma by the end of 1959.[45]

The only way to get a grip on these affairs, as the Prime Minister fully appreciated, was to act quickly and decisively to regain the initiative and keep the enemy (many of whom now had a white face) off-balance. Here was the tactical inspiration behind Macmillan's epochal tour of Africa in early 1960 during which, after a brief stopover in Ghana, and a few days spent with Welensky in Salisbury during which controversy was discreetly avoided, the British leader moved on to the Union of South Africa in whose legislature he delivered his most famous utterance that a 'wind of change' was blowing through the African continent. It was typical of Macmillan's oblique tactics in political life that it was on his way back from the Union by ship, rather than during his tour of the area, that he issued the order for the release of Hastings Banda from gaol in Nyasaland. Such releases of black radicals (from that of Kwame Nkrumah in the Gold Coast in 1951, through to Jomo Kenyatta in Kenya in 1962, and, it might be added, Nelson Mandela in South Africa during 1990) have played an intriguing role in the management of change in English-speaking Africa during the late colonial era. Of all these, however, that of Hastings Banda was arguably the most important, not because of his own intrinsic significance, but because the decision by Macmillan to sanction his political activities effectively turned the odds drastically against the survival of the Central African Federation[46], and by the same token helped at a crucial moment to set British policy firmly in a decolonizing mould.

The tenacity with which Macmillan afterwards cleaved to his controversial course was accentuated by the British habit in this period of looking over their shoulder at de Gaulle. Had the latter, after coming to power in France, remained wedded to the Algerian *colons* who had helped to put him where he was, British policy might well have taken a more ambiguous air. But de Gaulle moved rapidly to grant independence to French possessions in West Africa; and although Algeria presented bigger problems (including the threat of his own assassination at the hands of the OAS), his determination to cut himself free from the problem became transparent in 1960–1.[47] The nub of the Gaullist strategy evolved, in short, into the restoration of the metropole's own freedom of manoeuvre; the securing of the *force de frappe* – not of the casbah – the fresh essence of French grandeur. In London the awful prospect loomed of France smoothly disengaged from its colonial trauma, whilst the United Kingdom was sucked deeper and deeper into its morass of African encumbrances. Affrighted at this dreadful prospect, Macmillan had little choice but to steal the Gaullist *Zeitgeist* which sums up, indeed, the true cause of the end of modern European empire: 'Decolonization is not only our policy, it is our interest.' What happened in the Belgian Congo at this time may have been made much of in the British tabloids, now discovering a marked taste for atrocities, but it was the fate of French Algeria which had a far more direct impact upon strategic British decisions.

The application of this British interest in its multiple settings we cannot dwell upon, but the technique may be glossed over. 'In the end, as often happened at these constitutional conferences', one writer, for example, has described the proceedings of the Round Table Conference on Kenya in 1960, 'Macleod produced a document and said, in effect: "This is my plan which you must accept or reject".'[48] The resemblence which these tactics bore to the *diktat* exercised by Mountbatten over Indian politicians in 1947 is striking; and indeed it was natural that in casting about for an appropriate method of decolonization British ministers should have lighted upon the obvious precedent. The greater formlessness of African politics, compared to those of India during its run-up to independence, did make things less predictable, so that in Kenya – to give one instance – local conditions (shaped especially by acute land-hunger) did not become sufficiently stable for self-government to be finally granted until December 1963. In 1947 the British decision to get out of India had not been complicated by the threat of external competitors moving in to fill the vacuum, whereas in leaving Africa the possibility of Soviet penetration had continually to be borne in mind. Yet whatever the difficulties and sleights of hand involved, the latter process was not marred by the partition and massacres which had earlier blighted the South Asian experience of decolonization. Overall, the Conservative

Government's record in the climax of the end of empire might be said to have exhibited – as was once said of Macleod's skills at bridge – '. . . good card sense . . . efficient [but] not inspired'.[49]

In relating the saga of decolonization, however, it is easy to underestimate the controversy aroused in British politics at the time, and specifically the risk of an internal explosion within the Conservative Party. How did Macmillan pull it off? One percipient Tory backbencher recalled how, at those dangerous moments when bogey figures such as Archbishop Makarios of Cyprus, Hastings Banda in Nyasaland and Jomo Kenyatta in Kenya were released from detention, Macmillan would flit '. . . from group to group in the [House of Commons] Smoking Room with chatty observations that X's son had been commissioned in the Coldstream Guards, had he, how splendid!, or that Y had become Lord Lieutenant of Leicestershire, how well deserved', thus sending the traditionalists home to dinner 'in the comfortable knowledge that their world had not really been disturbed'.[50] Such assurance that the sum total of patronage was little affected by sloughing off the small change of colonies might appear a minor touch, but Macmillan knew it to be close to the heart of the matter.

In presiding over such a welter of territorial transitions, the Prime Minister was also plainly fortunate that things did not go badly wrong in several places at once, so giving an opportunity to his critics to pull him down. The moment when serious trouble briefly loomed came at the end of 1961, when intense unhappiness felt by a good many Conservatives over the extension of black majority rule to Northern Rhodesia overlapped with the warm passions generated by the United Nations' intervention against the secession of Katanga from the strife-torn Congolese Republic. Katanga, where the breakaway leader Moise Tshombe was propped up by Belgian mercenaries and mining capital[51], lay adjacent to Northern Rhodesia; and this sudden configuration appeared for a brief while capable of changing the regional odds in the contest for mastery between black nationalism and white power. When, therefore, the UN sent in troops to stuff the

Katangan genie back in its Congolese bottle, and Macmillan (under American pressure) was constrained into supporting these actions, the disgust in many quarters of his own party threatened to get out of hand. 'All the same forces are being mobilized as were at Suez', Macmillan sinisterly noted[52], and his anxiety at the reappearance of the chemistry which had destroyed his predecessor may readily be understood. Nevertheless, for all the threatening gossip, including references to a possible 'Curragh-style' mutiny among British troops in East Africa, the logic of decolonization had become too compelling for the machine to be put into reverse at such a late stage. Rightly or wrongly, in an earlier period the great British democracy could easily be persuaded that Egypt had something to do with its own welfare; in 1961–2 (with the corrosive cult of television satire under way) any pretension that the fate of Central Africa mattered deeply in Orpington or Oldham would have wilted in the heightened glare of the studio arc-lights. True Die-Hards like Lord Salisbury retired to their estates and wrote letters to their friends about the world, and Britain especially, 'going to the dogs'. The minds of others moved on, so that for all the continued rumblings emanating from the Congolese tragedy this most intense of the 'inner crises' of British decolonization had spent itself almost as soon as it had erupted.

One 'hidden' cost of decolonization for the United Kingdom was that the Conservative Government expended so much of its political capital in the endeavour that it had precious little left over with which to tackle economic problems. Arguably the most decisive decision by the Conservative Government in the economic field occurred early on when the Cabinet, and in particular the Prime Minister, resisted the pressure emanating from the Treasury to limit the growth of public expenditure in the 1958 Budget to £50 millions, leading to the resignations of all three Treasury ministers (Peter Thorneycroft, Enoch Powell and Nigel Birch)[53]. 'That is not the path to greatness', Thorneycroft, reverting to the central code of his party, said of inflation fuelled by public deficits when he defended his resignation in the Commons, 'it is the road to ruin.'[54] Retrospectively (though not, of course, without being *parti pris* himself), Powell has identified this juncture as marking the end of a brief spurt in which a serious attempt had been made to rein in public spending, and the beginning of an era when the state's fiscal claims were ratchetted progressively upwards.[55] By 1960, public expenditure had grown not by £50 millions, but by the very considerable figure of £750 millions (East of Suez contributing prominently to these sums). The unhappy rumblings at the Treasury naturally continued against this background, but Thorneycroft's successor, Derick Heathcoat Amory, did not have the temperament to make too much of a fuss. "What's wrong with a bit of inflation, Derry?" was the syrup administered by Macmillan whenever Amory ventured a protest[56], and when the patient none the less showed signs of revolt, he was swiftly eased out and replaced by Selwyn Lloyd, whose penchant for playing the monkey to Macmillan's organ-grinder had already been amply demonstrated by his previous record at the Foreign Office.

Macmillan's innate inflationism has made his record something of a butt for the Conservative New Right of a later day, who often hold him only marginally less culpable of the country's subsequent woes than Harold Wilson. Adding, or subtracting, merit-points along these lines are not our concern. The essential observation is that the politics for which Macmillan stood – and which underpinned the post-1940 consensus as a whole, fragile though it had become in the course of time – actually *required* the administration of recurrent doses of inflation. To this extent Macmillan was entirely consistent. In retirement the ex-premier sought an intellectual rationalization for the bias of his economic policies. 'So Keynes always said', he remarked of the assumptions which governed his age, 'between $2\frac{1}{2}$ and 3 per cent [inflation per annum] then nobody would notice. . . And this we achieved.'[57] Anything less than such an increment would indeed have necessitated the unscrambling of the fiscal and political accounts on which the dominant orthodoxy depended for its stability; and when it came to the crunch Macmillan was not prepared to break with the One Nation, Great Power faith which distilled the essence of British political philosophy, and with the propagation of which his own career had been closely entwined. Many of his later Right-wing detractors, moreover, caught by the principle of Vilfredo Pareto's 'circulation of elites', would – had they been active at the time rather than later, when Conservative values had undergone a revolution – almost certaintly have been among the first to cry 'foul' if Macmillan had adopted any other tack than the one he did.

But behind Macmillan's attitude to inflation lay something even more basic: a distaste for the whole subject of economic administration. When his official biographer, having talked to Macmillan exhaustively of the foreign policy record of his Government, raised the matter of domestic and economic affairs, he thus received the dismissive reply 'I left all that to Rab [Butler]'. Of course, this was not strictly true, if only because fine-tuning the economic cycle had become critical to winning elections, as the outcomes in 1955 and 1959 had illustrated; but the spirit of the remark was authentic. In the same vein one reviewer of Macmillan's hefty memoirs noted that the boredom the author felt with respect to anything other than external issues showed through on almost every page.[58] Interestingly, it had not always been so. During the early thirties, Macmillan had been prominent among a group of young Turks who consistently flagged their modern-mindedness by giving speeches larded with matter on such fashionable subjects as currencies, commodity controls and import quotas. All this has changed after 1939: the discourse which paid dividends from then on was one which was predicated in terms of platoons, not of pound sterling. In all this Macmillan was no different from the bulk of his party, his class or (come to that) his generation. In sticking rigidly to the priorities of greatness, rather than engaging with the messy and (it was often felt) insoluble problems presented by a complex commercial and industrial society, the Conservative governmental machine after 1957 stuck to what it knew best, and abjured entering territory a map of which they were no more in possession of than their opponents – and perhaps less so.

The problem was that after 1960 people, both citizens at home and speculators abroad, *did* begin to notice 2% to 3% inflation, especially as the real trend was above these figures; trade unions started insisting more rigidly on recouping the margins in their wage rounds (plus a bit extra); whilst the British electorate as a whole, and especially the consuming-classes, became irritably conscious that, whilst their counterparts in other countries were enjoying an 'economic miracle', the United Kingdom was for some reason missing out on the boom (1960 was the year when German living-standards outstripped those in Britain). For Macmillan the most tangible indication that economic pressures were getting to the parts they had long failed to reach was that Selwyn Lloyd at the Exchequer – perhaps out of a desire to belie his reputation for pliancy – surprised all his colleagues by digging in a new pair of anti-inflationary heels. As the Prime Minister's mind turned towards the next election, a complication of this sort had to be avoided at all costs; it was, therefore, his determination to sack Lloyd which, by a kind of multiplier effect, led to the famous 'Night of the Long Knives' on 13 July 1961 when Macmillan dismissed one-third of his Cabinet at a stroke (after all, one way of getting rid of a Chancellor without anybody noticing unduly was to sack a lot of other people at the same time). Ironically, although the purpose of this bloodletting was to promote the Prime Minister as a decisive and omnipotent figure, it succeeded only in attaching to the ministry and its chief a taint of ridicule which never afterwards left it; in the immortal tag which the Liberal politician, Jeremy Thorpe, put on these *contre-temps,* 'Greater love hath no man than he lay down his friends for his life'. In the judgement of one dispassionate commentator, the method of Selwyn Lloyd's disappearance marked the beginning of the end of Macmillan's authority as a leader.[59]

Attempting to ride out the growing instability of his government, Macmillan sought, in collaboration with his new Chancellor, Reginald Maudling, to stimulate a mini-boom which could at least carry the party and the country through to the next set of polls. Ultimately it was the backwash of the 'Maudling boom', not least as it spilled over into international speculation against the pound, which was to box in successive British governments after the middle sixties. That Macmillan himself had become painfully aware of the brink the United Kingdom was fast approaching may be said to have been reflected in his authorship of a memorandum entitled 'Modernization of Britain' which was forwarded from 10 Downing Street for the perusal of Butler (though one can only imagine what wry humour the receipt of such a document in this case must have occasioned). 'We have now reached a stage in our post-war history', the premier wrote in a classic exposition of shutting the stable door when the horse had long since bolted, 'when some more radical attack must be made upon the weakness of our economy, both productive and structural.'[60] No Prime Minister had written or spoken in this vein for a quarter of a century. Yet since the document in question relied exclusively on geeing-up the trade unions and an extra layer of regional policy, the actual form that any 'radicalism' might take in correcting current economic tendencies remained decidedly obscure. Anyway, no conceivable programme of reform in this area could be relevant to the electoral time-table which now began to dominate all considerations. In this context it was not the modernization of the British economy, but the modernization of the British nuclear deterrent, with its clear connotations of 'strategic victory', which came to preoccupy Macmillan's mind to the exclusion of virtually everything else. The 'Skybolt Crisis' with the Americans, and the repercussions that the eventual Polaris deal had in Europe, during December 1962–January 1963 were in many ways to constitute the true climax of the Macmillan premiership.

The grail-like quest for a national nuclear deterrent ran throughout the Macmillan years, though its rationale was to change with political and (just as importantly) technological realities. During the late fifties the *independence* of the national capacity to deter remained central to British atomic doctrine. The launch of Sputnik by the Soviet Union inaugurated a fresh arms race based on the development of missiles and rocketry in which 'keeping up with the Joneses' became increasingly difficult. To begin with, the Ministry of Defence in Britain had devised a 'guided bomb' (named Blue Steel), only for this expensive project to be dropped in favour of a surface-to-surface missile called experimentally 'Blue Streak'. The ideal of the all-British deterrent, however, foundered when it was revealed that, in addition to the £65 millions which had already been invested, another £650 millions would be required to see it through to completion. In February 1960 Blue Streak was cancelled[61], and with it the full flush of Bevin's original ambition in the atomic sphere ('We've got to have the bloody Union Jack flying over it') became subject to dilution. It was the superadded effect of the failed Summit in Paris coming on top of this setback which marked the first half of 1960 as a watershed in the history of British Conservatism during the aftermath of Suez.

According to one lucid analyst of the United Kingdom's nuclear policies, Macmillan's failure to exploit the opportunity presented by Blue Streak's cancellation to 'educate' the British public in nuclear affairs was a sad mistake.[62] Yet whatever the true credibility of deterrence in the hands of second-tier Powers, it would have been extraordinarily difficult for any British leader in the circumstances to dismantle the colonial empire at the same time as liquidating Britain's nuclear ambitions; in short, it was practicable to do one of these things, but not both. Ruling out the non-nuclear option, therefore, there were two routes open to the British after 1960: to go into harness with either the French or the Americans. There was, indeed, some support at this time for an *entente nucleaire,* but it was largely to be found amongst a school of Conservatives for whom anti-Americanism had always constituted a great temptation (including a number who, in their hearts, had not forgiven the United States for Suez).[63] Yet at bottom the choice was not really much of a choice at all. In any scenario involving nuclear co-operation, the critical element was trust; and the quality most conspicuously missing in Anglo-French relations over many years had been precisely this elusive quantity in human affairs. Getting 'mixed up' with the Americans, not with the French, had been the instinctive fall-back position of the British ever since 1940, and this was the tack Macmillan inevitably adopted after the Blue Streak débâcle curtailed the United Kingdom's horizons in the sphere of deterrence. In crude terms, this meant getting a missile 'off-the-peg' from the United States – and getting it quick.

Of the two main United States nuclear development projects, the submarine-launched Polaris rocket and the Skybolt missile, it was the latter upon which the British Government sought to affix its claim (being able to be fired from an aircraft, Skybolt had the advantage that the United Kingdom's existing V-Bomber fleet could be kept operational). These hopes cut across the election to the United States Presidency of John F. Kennedy in November 1960. In predicting whether this result was good or bad from London's vantage-point, the fact that the winner was not a Republican vied with the more gloomy remembrance that the family stock from which he came had a history of Anglophobia, as befitted an Irish-American dynasty. Macmillan's hopes of turning the balance in the right direction hinged on presenting the new Administration with some big 'Idea' which in its evolution would reinforce the Anglo-American tie – a variant on the theme of 'playing Greeks to their Romans' which, as a phrase at least, was now distinctly unconvincing and outdated. The idea which Macmillan invented for the purpose was that of a 'Grand Design' (with its nice echo of the wartime Grand Alliance), based on a potted version of the recent presidential election in which Kennedy had exploited the image of a 'missile gap' to dish his opponent, Richard Nixon; as the Prime Minister expressed it in his master-document, there was now a burning need 'to organize the great forces of the Free World – economically, politically and militarily – in a coherent effort to withstand the Communist tide all over the world'.[64] With this flourish, the old actor-manager cast aside the mantle of Bolingbroke and revealed himself anew in his Marlborough costume, hoping thereby that the classical attributes of the warrior would jell with the sub-Churchillian rhetoric so characteristic of Kennedy's own political persona.

The credence given by the Americans at first to this fresh ploy from Downing Street is indicated by the anecdote that when Kennedy and his advisors got around to discussing Macmillan's draft, it could not be located, and was eventually tracked down in the bedroom of the President's young daughter.[65] Like most political anecdotes, this one is more interesting for the spirit in which it was told than its literal accuracy, but is no less revealing for that. Yet in the event Kennedy during his brief presidency *did* respond to the siren-call of Macmillan's friendship, such that in the saga of the Anglo-American 'Special Relationship' the unlikely rapport between the ageing, rather fusty British leader and the youthful hero of a new American 'Camelot' may be seen as the second of a trio of very personal engagements between the leaders of the two countries (Roosevelt-Churchill, Kennedy-Macmillan, Reagan-Thatcher). This outcome is, perhaps, pre-eminently to be explained by the accident that very early in his own tenure Kennedy suffered a political reverse of humiliating dimensions: the attempt to displace Fidel Castro's regime in Cuba which came to grief during April 1961 in the Bay of Pigs; it was, in a sense, his Pearl Harbor, and it propelled Kennedy, as Roosevelt had once been catapulted, into a closer tie with the British than would otherwise have occurred. After the Bay of Pigs fiasco, therefore, the young's President's taste for adventurous unilateral action was diluted, and the value put upon keeping the British 'in play' rose accordingly. This was to pay off during the second (and far more serious) Cuban crisis in October-November 1962, when Macmillan's support at a time when the world seemingly teetered on the brink of nuclear war played some small part in strengthening Kennedy's negotiating hand with Khrushchev, and allowed the former to win back the hand he had previously lost.

Whether Kennedy's leaning towards his British ally would extend to bestowing upon it the desired nuclear gift remained problematical. This was especially so because a parallel theme within American policy after 1960 was a reassessment of European realities, in which a closer understanding with Western Germany tended to be rated more highly than banking on the increasingly unbankable British. Mixed up with this thinking, furthermore, were the crucial implications arising from a managerial revolution carried out at the Pentagon by Robert McNamara in his role as Defense

Secretary which, in its war-gaming dimension, was summed up in the doctrine of 'Flexible Response'. Because the nub of this flexibility was to make 'controlled' nuclear confrontation more credible as a real-life scenario, it became all the more vital to ensure that there was only one Western command-centre doing the controlling. Here again the non-nuclear Germans tended to be looked upon more fondly than the British, with their half-baked and dangerous ideas of junior (and, in American eyes, therefore maverick) deterrents. In this way there commenced a campaign which the authorities in London were quick to discern was geared to running them – as arch-proliferators – out of the nuclear business altogether.[66]

The high point of this campaign was the American decision on 7 November 1962 (when the Cuban crisis was still in progress) to cancel the Skybolt programme, and with it the British claims which had become attached. At the time intense controversy raged across the Atlantic as to whether or not London had been forewarned as to the impending departure. Perhaps the wisest conclusion in an inevitably confused affair is that the broad hints emanating from Washington over a long period as to Skybolt's likely fate were sufficiently broad for the British to have grasped them had it been convenient to do so. Very suggestive here is the incident in January 1962 when Julian Amery, the United Kingdom Minister responsible, visited Washington and was granted an interview with the President; during the course of this meeting Kennedy began to touch on Skybolt's technical inadequacies, only to have his discourse interrupted when Amery 'fell off his chair in shock'.[67] Whether this report may be taken literally is a matter for conjecture, but it was clearly the reaction of a man who did not wish to receive the information being proffered. By thus shutting their ears, and aping reactions of mingled shock and horror to the slightest suggestion of any hold-up to Skybolt, the British undoubtedly calculated that the Americans would be forced to go on with developing the weapon even if their own interest in it had lapsed. When the axe none the less fell, the British Defence Minister, Lord Thorneycroft, hurried to

Washington where he indulged in what was openly flagged as 'one of the bluntest talks ever within the Anglo-American alliance'.[68]

The fact was that although, in the words of Robert McNamara, Skybolt was 'proven to be a pile of junk'[69] it was 'our' junk and as such capable of exercising talismanic powers in British politics. But what gave the cancellation by the United States especial force was that it overlapped with transparent signs that the Americans had decided to 'pull the plug' on British claims to Great Power status, even of the second-order kind into which they had of late been transmuted. Indeed, the acid comment by the doyen of American foreign policy, Dean Acheson, during a speech to the West Point Military Academy on 5 December 1962 that 'Great Britain had lost an Empire and has not yet found a role' entered the lexicon of British political discourse almost as soon as it had been uttered. The crisis these various tendencies engendered came to a head when Macmillan met with Kennedy at Nassau in the Bahamas on 19 December for a four-day conference. The tactics adopted by the former consisted of a mixture of sentiment and blackmail – that is, the same tactics as the British had sought to use with their transatlantic ally ever since the Second World War, only tuned up a bit to meet the exigencies of the moment. Thus whilst Macmillan indulged in an emotional account of British sacrifices in two world wars, and her 'due' as a consequence, he also threatened that unless a substitute for Skybolt was found immediately the Americans would find themselves before long dealing with a British Conservative leadership far less well disposed towards them than he was – the threat, in other words, of a second Eden. It was striking, as Alistair Horne remarks in dealing with this episode[70], that the same sort of rather maudlin rhetoric which in other negotiations left de Gaulle and Adenauer cold, now worked like a charm with Kennedy, who, faced with the Prime Minister's urgent pleas, agreed that Britain's equity in Skybolt should be transferred to Polaris. In thus obtaining virtually at the last gasp an up-to-date nuclear deterrent, with a life-expectancy stretching many years ahead, Macmillan pulled off the kind of coup which mattered most in British political life.

What explains this, in many ways, startling success? Horne attributes it to the 'magic' of the friendship between Kennedy and Macmillan, at the same time quoting the more down-to-earth remark by the American leader that the whole thing was a 'political necessity but [also] a piece of military foolishness'.[71] Certainly if the matter had been left to the respective delegations, it is quite likely that the Nassau conference would have broken up in disarray: on the British side Thorneycroft was all for walking out on the United States, whilst most of the American experts present apparently advised that the British should get the thumbs-down. The reason for the outcome cannot be known (if ever) until more time has passed. But it may be noted that in nuclear questions the reactions of those holding the highest posts in the countries concerned are often at odds with those beneath and around them; it is they, after all, who carry an awesome responsibility with no parallel in other branches of policy. Hence whilst the President's subordinates might, in this case, contemplate with equanimity the British going off on their own, for Kennedy the prospect of 'having nobody to talk to' in some future crisis was more forbidding. The very *personal* nature of this success from the British point of view, and the fact that it was so tied up with presidential psychology, made it all the more liable to rapid erosion. That the agreement meant something very different on the two sides of the Atlantic is reflected in the nuances of a telephone conversation between the two leaders on 19 January 1963. The excerpt runs as follows:

> *Prime Minister*: I say, did you enjoy Nassau? I loved it, didn't you? I thought it was awfully good.
> *President Kennedy*: Oh, which is that?
> *Prime Minister*: The Nassau Meeting.
> *President Kennedy*: Oh, yes – very good, very good.[72]

Macmillan's attempt to put on a brave face ('awfully good') and Kennedy's plain indifference is easily explained: five days before, and as a direct counter to the Nassau Agreement, President de Gaulle had assembled an impromptu press conference in Paris which brought negotiations regarding the United Kingdom's entry into the EEC grinding to a halt. Why did the mercurial Frenchman do it? One version emanating from the Elysée Palace was that when Macmillan had met de Gaulle at Rambouillet on 15–16 December 1962, he pledged himself to nuclear co-operation with France, only to defect at the first opportunity into an exclusive (and, in Gaullist eyes, abject) dependence on the United States.[73] At Rambouillet the British premier must certainly have been under a great temptation to line up an escape-route just in case things went badly wrong at Nassau. Nevertheless, it is highly probable that even if the subsequent Anglo-American Polaris deal had not provided the French leader with one excuse for barring the United Kingdom from Europe, another one would have been found. At bottom, for the sake of a replacement for Skybolt, it may be said that Macmillan was prepared to play directly into de Gaulle's hands by allowing him to depict the United Kingdom as a country permanently anchored, not to the adjoining Continent, but to North America. In doing so he merely made crystal clear the real priorities of the Government he led.

De Gaulle's action was none the less a bitter and indeed shattering blow. 'All our policies at home and abroad are in ruins', Macmillan confided privately, though, as the spirit of Mons came upon him once more, he did not forget to add, 'except our courage and determination.'[74] What made the Paris press conference of 14 January so seminal an event was its very publicity, with a battery of television cameras to beam the occasion into millions of British homes. Macmillan had often previously expressed to his aides the opinion that de Gaulle would try to sabotage British access to the EEC, but that he would shrink from doing so *openly*. When the latter did precisely this, with what has been described as an 'insulting condescension' to Macmillan himself[75], the corrosive force of humiliation was once more felt in British politics. All in all, by early 1963 the post-Suez reorganization of the United Kingdom had, after six years, only one concrete achievement to its credit: the 'independent' (or at least quasi-independent) nuclear deterrent, and the place at the Top Table of Nations which it was alleged to secure. For the incumbent administration it was not much with which to face an electorate whose own culture and tastes were being shaped by The Beatles rather than the echo of distant battles.

In fact for most of 1963 British public opinion was too consumed by its interest in the salacious aspects of the scandal surrounding the Minister of War, John Profumo, to think about much else. Undoubtedly this *cause celèbre* took its toll on the Prime Minister physically as well as politically; the sudden deterioration in his health during early October made up his mind to leave office, leading to the remarkable saga of his hospitalization on the eve of the Conservative Party Conference in Blackpool, and the intriguing which immediately engulfed the 'magic circle' of inner Cabinet members and Tory grandees. The passage of time and the publication of myriad accounts have only served to give weight to the interpretation that from the moment Macmillan decided to go, the whole purpose of the exercise was to deny the reversion to Butler: in short, the blood-lines of this succession battle, as that of 1957, went back a long way. It seemed for a while that the palm might go to Quintin Hogg, but the very brashness of his lobbying (complete with 'I Love Quintin' buttons and rent-a-crowd supporters in the streets of Blackpool) only exposed him to the ridicule of the media. Meanwhile the convolutions of Cabinet consultation and the transmission of the Royal Advice – the latter subject, it was alleged in some quarters, to some unseemly 'massaging'[76] – led to the palm passing instead into the hands of Alec Douglas-Home who, although once tarred with the brush of Munich, had since succeeded in rehabilitating himself in a way that Butler – for all his 'service to the state' – had never quite managed to do.

Iain Macleod's response on hearing that a Douglas-Home bandwagon was rolling was allegedly to ungraciously exclaim 'Don't be bloody ridiculous'.[77] From the vantage-point of nearly thirty years later it may indeed seem amazing that under the pressing circumstances which existed the Conservative Party could entrust itself, and the nation, to the leadership of an Anglo-Scottish magnate who made the fatal error once in the job of admitting in a press interview that his knowledge of economics was of the 'matchstick variety'. Yet the logic is not far to seek. Macmillan's appointment of Home to the Foreign Secretaryship in 1960, for example, was said by the then Conservative Chief Whip to be the one 'which gave him [Macmillan] most pleasure', because it 'appealed both to his sense of history . . . and . . . his love of Trollope'[78]; even more telling in this respect was Macmillan's own advocacy at the height of the succession crisis to the effect that Home represented 'the best of the governing class'.[79] There is another factor not to be wholly discounted as having played a part in proceedings: that in pushing Home's claims as a stopgap Macmillan was attempting to keep open the chances of his own future return to office – a possibility which apparently he still cherished during the 1970s.[80] Be this as it may, the succession to the Prime Ministership of a veritable Duke of Omnium, for whom economics was a dismal and unregarded science, was fully in accordance with the dominant mode of 'modern' Conservative statecraft: it marked yet another affirmation that the old dog, and the old class, could still wag its tail when it really mattered.

In marked contrast, the Labour Party since January 1963 (following the death of Hugh Gaitskell) had possessed a leader in Harold Wilson who, having been an economics don at Oxford University, was presumed to be expert on the subject; and although his own theme-song during the general election of October 1964 ('the white heat of the technological revolution') has itself in retrospect been widely condescended to, compared to his main opponent addressing the problem of sterling the effect was positively electrifying. The remarkable inversion at the heart of British political culture during the present century was reflected further in the way that during this contest the supposed party of free enterprise and capitalism addressed itself to the subject of economics as little as decency allowed, leaving its Socialist opponents in effective possession of the field. Instead, the constant – virtually the only – refrain of Alec Douglas-Home's speeches was the patriotic thesis that the independent British deterrent guaranteed the United Kingdom's place at the Top Table, and that the reservation could only be safe henceforth in Conservative hands.[81] For all its tinny ring as a 'call to the nation' when real power and success in the outside world was fast becoming defined in very different (and overwhelmingly material) terms, its continuing echo in British affairs was illustrated by the resilience of the Conservative vote when the results came through (it was the first professional 'TV election', with the ubiquitous swingometer presaging much gadgetry to come). Henceforth the nuclear 'card' was to be a prominent feature of the political market-place. Nevertheless, the Labour Party obtained a wafer-thin majority of three seats in the new House of Commons, and proceeded to form its first ministry since 1951. Experience was to show that ultimately only the inexorable necessities of the financial crisis itself – rather than the intelligent pre-emption of the domestic political process – was able to enforce an alignment of British priorities and attitudes with the post-war world system as it had now taken shape. Our final chapter, therefore, will deal with the period from October 1964 to the great sterling devaluation of November 1967 and its immediate aftermath, which brought about this long-delayed apotheosis.

Off the Perch

One weekend in June 1966 Harold Wilson entertained at Chequers his predecessor as Labour premier, Clement Attlee, who had recently suffered a mild stroke. In his memoirs Wilson records the following responses which the latter made to questions put to him by the present incumbent:

> Q: Clem, yourself excluded, and politics apart, who of all the Prime Ministers Britain has had since you became old enough to take an interest, do you consider the best, as Prime Minister?
> A: Salisbury.
> Q: If you were in this chair, again, and apart from all the day-to-day problems that press upon a Prime Minister, where would you throw your weight? What subject would you give a higher priority than it is getting?
> A: Transport.[1]

That Attlee should give his compliments to Lord Salisbury in this manner is not particularly surprising – he could hardly have responded to Wilson's prompting by quoting the socialist merits of Ramsay MacDonald, the renegade of 1931. But the main interest in Attlee's replies lies rather in their implied critique that other British leaders during the course of the century had set themselves too disparate a range of tasks, too many of which were tangential to the actual lives of the majority of the citizens of the country. Wilson evidently approved of Attlee's wisdom by the time he wrote his account. Yet up to the time of that sunny Chequers weekend the Labour Government had been organized according to a different formula. 'I want to make it quite clear', the new Labour Prime Minister had instructed the House of Commons on 16 December 1964, 'that . . . we cannot afford to relinquish the world role', and as we shall see, the point was frequently reiterated in the months ahead. It was only after mid-1966, and only wholeheartedly with the cataclysm of sterling's devaluation in the autumn of 1967, that the world role was finally liquidated, and what Attlee might have called the 'Transport Principle' came to emerge as the touchstone of a new (if still highly contentious) dispensation in United Kingdom affairs. In relating how this came about we are, of course, encroaching very much on the terrain of contemporary history, and for that reason we shall be necessarily brief and tentative in our treatment. Nevertheless, the political and psychological adjustment touched off by devaluation constitutes the logical climax for the themes we have pursued in these pages. We shall begin, then, by looking at the central decisions taken at the outset of the Labour Government's term in the areas of sterling, the deterrent, East of Suez and Europe.

It has become virtually an orthodoxy that the Wilson Government's basic error was not to devalue the currency within the first week of office. The existing £800 millions deficit in the balance of payments would have provided an adequate excuse; the Tories could have been blamed to the hilt ('thirteen wasted years', as the campaign slogan had it); and precious freedom of manoeuvre thereby gained. The later course of events certainly lends cogency to the argument. In self-exculpation, Wilson afterwards claimed that such a devaluation would have been exploited by his opponents as 'selling the country short', and its benefits quickly eroded by competitive depreciations abroad.[2] There is, as usual, force on both sides of the debate. The fundamental cause of the new premier's gut instinct against an early adjustment of sterling's value, however, lay not in any precise economic judgement, but in the broad strategy which Wilson envisioned for his government. That strategy was, essentially, to emulate the 'rough strength' conventionally reckoned to have been the successful hallmark of the last socialist ministry under Clement Attlee, expressed in current circumstances by a call to the country to unite in a crusade to 'save the pound'. To have devalued in October 1964 would have immediately tarred the Labour Government with the brush of Little Englandism, and thus have deprived it of what promised to be a central purpose at once tangible, patriotic and capable of engaging broad-bottomed support in the country. If later developments showed this to be a mistake, it certainly made sense both in terms of the situation Wilson occupied at the time, and, perhaps even more strikingly, the reference-models on which his own tradition and experience turned.

The second major strategic decision taken alongside sterling was that to maintain the nuclear deterrent. In recent times the Labour Party had been bitterly divided over the issue, and these fractures had widened as the broader national consensus showed signs of breaking up after 1960 (the latter year witnessing the high-tide of the Campaign for Nuclear Disarmament). Wilson himself, in opposition, had showed open sympathy with the emotions, if not always with the exact aims, of CND. Nevertheless, the decision to maintain Polaris once Labour got into power was predictable. The possession of a nuclear arm had for some years been a key to Downing Street's leverage in the slippery, not to say anarchic, field of defence, and no holder of that office could then, or indeed later, lightly give it up for that reason alone. The announcement that Labour Britain would remain a member of the atomic club also helped to evoke the same forthright image that Ernest Bevin had created when he declared at Potsdam in July 1945 that, as a socialist, he was no more willing to see his country 'barged about' than the Tories.[3] The advent of the deterrent had reformulated the hardy old chestnut of Socialism's 'fitness to govern'; it was not a test Wilson could afford to fail. At the same time the latter clearly had to introduce some radical twist to satisfy his Left-wing critics. This was achieved by the frank admission that his government would not delude itself (or allow the country to be deluded) into thinking that in keeping Polaris it was the proud possessor of an *independent* deterrent. 'The fact is that there is no independent deterrent', Wilson declared in the

Commons whilst the benches opposite, stimulated by the frail majority enjoyed by the government, bayed for parliamentary blood, 'because we are dependent on the Americans.' By firmly announcing that the Polaris deal would be honoured, whilst deftly pricking the bubble of national 'independence', Wilson successfully deflected the only real weapon which his opponents, in the aftermath of their own defeat, had in their hands. This was the sort of tactical master-stroke for which Wilson was shortly to be famous.

It was the East of Suez policy which proved the chief bane of the Labour Government after 1964, although this was by no means predictable at the outset. For some while prior to the 1964 election the leaders in the party had been distancing themselves from the commitment to Europe (with which, by a curious osmosis, they had come to be associated more closely than their opponents), and emphasized instead more traditional commitments. As Phillip Darby has put it, the Labour Party had 're-examined Britain's position . . . and saw a mission in *staying* in Asia where before it had seen a mission in *going*. Thus the shadow Cabinet adopted the world role, injected it with a stronger moral content, and the scene was set for the empire's swansong.'[4] After gaining office, it was instantly noticeable that in making speeches on external affairs Wilson's references to the East of Suez policy were more roseate than those he accorded to Europe or the nuclear deterrent. His extravagant tendency in this respect may be said to have climaxed in New Delhi during June 1965, when he announced – to the consternation as well as the education of his auditors – that 'Britain's frontiers are on the Himalayas'.[5] As one historian has caustically observed, this was followed by one of the fastest strategic withdrawals in modern times.[6] The joke is a good one, but at the same time it is not difficult to appreciate why for Wilson, predominantly a man of the 1940s, the 'world role' (in which the determination to stay East of Suez was complementary to the fight to save the pound) continued until very late in the day to seem part of the necessary glue which could help British Socialism stick together as a credible instrument of government. After all, if the

Conservatives had in their time got away with playing Britain's cards up to (and often considerably beyond) their face value in world diplomacy, there was no reason why a Labour ministry need be bashful about doing the same.

The Labour Government's refusal to tamper with the East of Suez strategy merits a few further reflections. Thus it is suggestive that in the period running up to October 1964 the Conservative Cabinet had dispatched a stream of officials to such venues as the Federation of South Arabia and Malaysia, who on arrival repeated old promises and even made new ones. The East of Suez policy, therefore, was effectually 'mined' for in-coming Labour politicians; survival alone necessitated that the terrain where the devices were laid be left undisturbed. By the same token, Wilson and his senior colleagues could not but be conscious that in this sphere every action was being watched by the respective Chiefs of the military staffs lest 'the tail wagged the dog'. Even the previous Conservative administration had enjoyed a stormy relationship with the Services, until they had effectively lifted the pressure for economy and control; nods and winks were enough to signify that if the new lot took the same tack, trouble (and resignations) would fly. Such considerations helped to underpin the Labour Government's proclivity to repeat the essence of 1945–51: that is, to maintain a strict bipartisanship in the field of foreign and defence policy, whilst emphasizing differences in those matters of internal affairs where their opponents held the low and vulnerable ground. All in all, the East of Suez policy was driven after October 1964 by a heady mixture of romanticism and ministerial self-interest that was not likely to be easily reversed even if contrary courses made themselves felt, as they were bound to do.

As for Europe, the evidence suggests that on entering office the Labour Government had no intention whatsoever of renewing the previous application to join the organization of the 'Six'. On the Left of the party the EEC stood condemned as a 'Black International' of conservative Catholics, industrial magnates and peasant chieftains; as such (before Vietnam transformed the demonological order) it was decidedly more disreputable in

ideological terms than the United States.[7] Quite apart from
attitudes to the EEC proper, however, it is noteworthy that anti-
Europeanism was always more strongly entrenched in Labour's
ranks than was generally true of their opponents, even if it had
at times suited the party's elders to foster a different impression.
The reasons for this went back a long way. It had been a
commonplace during the Second World War and its aftermath
that figures such as Bevin and Dalton hated the Germans far more
acutely than did their Conservative counterparts[8]; much of this
hostility simply got transposed on to the 'European movement'
during the post-war era. Whatever the personal and psychological
tendencies infusing this bias, a brand of proletarian chauvinism
continued to be prominent in the party during the 1960s, which
the contemporary imagery of the 'Gnomes of Zurich' only
encouraged. Playing to this gallery provides the only explanation
for the early and remarkable decision by the Wilson Cabinet to
trim the trade deficit by imposing import surcharges against
European goods *without* any attempt to discriminate between the
Common Market countries and the United Kingdom's erstwhile
partners in EFTA.[9] Arguably no single decision by a British
Government since the end of the Second World War has been so
universally condemned in Western Europe than this controversial
and inept venture into trade diplomacy.

At the same time it may be observed that the Labour Government's calculations *vis-à-vis* Europe appeared cogent enough in
the circumstances. Ever since the London Conference accords
of 1954, it had been an axiom of British policy that her influence
on the mainland of Europe was secured above all by her military
presence, and thus was independent of whether the United
Kingdom did, or did not, belong to what was, after all, only
a local customs union. This assumption, by no means without
substance when America's own commitment sometimes appeared
to be draining off in other directions, remained persuasive in
the mid-sixties. Furthermore, it was the Labour Government
after 1964, far more than their Conservative predecessors, who
sought to use their military leverage to gain advantages in other
areas of policy by threatening 'the Continentals' – often rather

heavy-handedly – that the strength of the British Army on the Rhine might be *reduced*. Even in strictly economic terms the boot was not all on one foot in the sphere of Anglo-European relations. Hence if London lived in fear of the roller-coaster of currency speculation, so did some of the nations across the water; if sterling was pushed down, the franc and the mark would be revalued permanently upwards, potentially bringing the export-led 'miracles' of the French and German economies to a stop. There was, finally, an intangible consideration arising from the ambivalent character of United States policy. The Americans had long shown a propensity to nudge the United Kingdom into the integrating institutions of Western Europe. This theme did not disappear altogether after the early 1960s, but as the maverick foreign policy of de Gaulle (summed up in his vision of a 'Europe from the Atlantic to the Urals') began to irritate Washington, there was a tendency for United States pressure on Britain in this regard to become distinctly less pressing. As the sheen went off the 'Rome Powers', who even started squabbling in a rather unseemly way among themselves[10], there were solid grounds for believing that the Labour Government could avoid travelling on the road to Canossa which the Conservatives had unavailingly traversed after July 1961.

It was indicative of just how deeply the Atlanticist current ran in the new government that Harold Wilson's first trip abroad was to Washington, where he arrived less than two months after taking office. Like other British premiers before him, his first concern was to establish rapport with the president of the day, in this case (following the tragic assassination of John Kennedy in November 1963) with Lyndon B. Johnson. The relations between Wilson and Johnson make an interesting enigma. In his memoirs Wilson portrays them as intimate and frank. Frankness, certainly, was a cardinal virtue of the panhandle-politician from Texas; whether any intimacy between the two survived later disagreements is more doubtful. In late 1964, however, the escalation of the American presence in Vietnam had yet to occur.

British assurances that their commitments East of Suez were unsullied by a mere change of party government earned much American goodwill, since the latter had enough worries without filling yet another vacuum. Wilson's evident determination to avoid a devaluation of sterling also met American desiderata, since the dollar was itself in a fragile condition, and thus vulnerable to an international crisis which the fall of sterling might precipitate. 'Holding the line' against the threat of Communism in Afro-Asia, and containing threats to the existing monetary order (not least those stemming from gold-hoarding France), together underpinned a formula in which American power and purposes could become once more 'mixed up' with the United Kingdom. 'We are now built into the American system', Richard Crossman unhappily recorded in his diary.[11] The phrase 'built into' was especially apposite here, since Wilson's vision of the United Kingdom's relationship with her main ally and patron resembled not so much Macmillan's loose rendering of 'playing Greeks to their Romans', as Clement Attlee's ideal (equally based on wartime experience) whereby Britain could guarantee herself a stable and prosperous future as '. . . an easterly extension of a strategic area the centre of which is the American continent'.[12] The manner in which Atlanticism overlapped with the pacific impulses of 'socialist foreign policy' dated back, indeed, to the era of the 1920s; and whatever the grumblings this caused on the Bevanite Left, for the bulk of Labour parliamentarians following the 1964 election the logic appeared as appealing as ever.

The problem was that being 'built into' the imperial presidency which had come into being at some indefinite point during Kennedy's charismatic incumbency and which Johnson, in his more rustic way, inherited, was a different proposition from being built into, say, the America of Harry Truman. In February 1965 American bombers launched their first major assault on North Vietnam from aircraft-carriers concentrated in the Gulf of Tonkin. The escalation of the Johnson Administration was under way; it passed its Rubicon later in the year when the bombing was extended to Hanoi and Haiphong (with their civilian populations). Faced with these developments, analogies between

Attlee's premiership and the situation confronted by Wilson began to break down. In 1950, it was true, the former had been faced with an emergency in Korea, and had accepted the burden of rearmament as the price of an American alliance. But at that time Korea appeared to have a salience for British interests which justified the cost, even if in retrospect the effort was generally seen to have been overdone. Vietnam more than a decade later was, from a United Kingdom vantage-point, altogether less compelling. Putting Britain in the Age of Carnaby Street back into dull-grey uniforms (even just psychologically) was not something Wilson could contemplate. Indeed, the early years of the Labour Government coincided with generational and cultural shifts for which the issue of Vietnam provided a coping-stone in Britain as it did in many other countries (including the United States itself). In this respect the 'snap' general election which Wilson called in March 1966 – resulting in a greatly enlarged Labour majority in the Commons – had the subterranean and accidental significance that the new parliamentary cohort was one which, in its cast of mind and experience, marked a sharp break with the past. In the sphere of foreign policy, as in other branches of public as well as private life, the old landmarks were evidently breaking up, even if it was not yet clear what the new ones were going to be.

As the American build-up in Vietnam proceeded, therefore, the Wilson Cabinet's stance was to afford general support for Washington's goals in the region, but to eschew its own closer involvement by stressing the United Kingdom's dormant status as co-chairman (alongside the Soviet Union) of the Geneva Conference on Indo-China. After the United States' bombing campaign intensified, a more overt dissociation of Britain from American policy ensued. Propelled not least by the need to damp down a situation in which the intimacy of the Anglo-American tie was at risk, Wilson made two attempts at mediation. The first of these – through a proposed Commonwealth peace mission – was ephemeral (and probably unwise, since the involvement of some of the countries concerned made it smack of Third World neutralism which could only serve to cause irritation across the

Atlantic). The second attempt came when the Soviet premier, Alexei Kosygin, visited London in February 1967, and an initiative was planned to convert the Tet (or Chinese New Year) 'pause' in the fighting into an effective truce. This was much more serious, if only because the situation had itself gravely deteriorated; it appears to have foundered largely in Washington. Wilson's abortive interventions are often quoted as examples of his greatly exaggerated ideas of the United Kingdom's diplomatic weight. That his actions were mostly bluster cannot be denied. Nevertheless, given what we now know of the Soviets' fears at the time that the Vietnam War could easily have ignited a nuclear confrontation between the superpowers, there is some reason for toning down the sarcasm. With so much at stake, a little bluster in the cause of peace is, perhaps, no great failing.

Inevitably, the effects of these equivocations and mediations were damaging to the 'Special Relationship', if only because events highlighted that the specialness was fading away – British students took to their anti-Vietnam 'demos' with as much gusto as their West European peers. At first, it is true, any resentment in the United States was mild, since the war in Asia was not expected to stretch American resources unduly, nor to hold dangers on the same general scale as Korea had before it. But this altered as the quagmire deepened, and British pusillanimity contrasted with the solidarity shown by some, at least, of the other allies (especially Australia and New Zealand). What the Americans came to cherish was not British military assistance, but some token of political endorsement. As Johnson typically put it, 'a platoon of bagpipers' was all that was required.[13] After mid-1966, it was clear that not even such a Scottish bauble would be forthcoming; and before long (for reasons which necessarily extend far beyond the subject of this study) the Johnson Presidency entered the slough of despond, climaxing in the incumbent's dramatic announcement in March 1968 that he would not be putting himself forward for re-election. This is to jump briefly ahead of our narrative; yet at some imprecise point during these developments the attempt to reconstruct a unique tie between Socialist Britain and a Democratic administration in the

United States undoubtedly came unstuck. When the Republicans under Richard Nixon finally regained office in November 1968, the United Kingdom featured small on the new administration's map of world affairs; indeed, during the overlapping era of Nixon's occupation of the White House in the United States, and that of Edward Heath's tenure of 10 Downing Street after June 1970, exchanges between the two countries were to be colder than at any point since the post-Suez 'healing'.[14] Meanwhile, we may note that by 1967 the main plank of Wilson's foreign policy had, to all intents and purposes, already been kicked by events from underneath his government.

This cooling of the Anglo-American spirit could not be without implications for the position of sterling, especially as the political uncertainties and inflationary pressures associated with Vietnam further unsettled the money-markets. Wilson always denied that President Johnson or any of his go-betweens ever made co-operation on currency matters dependent on a quid pro quo in South-East Asia.[15] This is no doubt true in the letter; whether it is true in spirit – especially in relation to the phase which began in the early summer of 1966, when the currency markets began to seriously gyrate – is more problematical. The lengthening lines of 'swap' credits which European financiers had for some while afforded the Bank of England, for example, had hitherto been secured with the help of the influence brought to bear by the United States Treasury Secretary, Joe Fowler, as he trawled the counting-houses of Basle; it was a form of assistance which became less visible over time.[16] This is not to say that when the British currency finally broke under the pressure in November 1967 the Americans were implicated (as they had been during 1956) in a run on sterling. Nevertheless, by then the waves of speculation were such that something was clearly going to give somewhere in the creaking edifice of the Bretton Woods monetary system; and on the other side of the Atlantic the sentiment was understandably one of 'better sterling than the dollar'. The snapping of the dollar-sterling 'special relationship' – to be subsequently capped by the liquidation of fixed exchange rates – marked the break-up of an Anglo-American economic concordat which (albeit with many ups and downs) had prevailed ever since 1947, and in many senses since the Mutual Aid Agreement of 1941. Not only, therefore, did these events mark a watershed in the life of the Labour Government, but they amounted to a more profound 'parting of the ways' in recent British history. Henceforth the British and Americans were to share many goals in common, but their intersection was to take place in a far more shifting, multilateral and diffuse context.

Indeed 1966 was the year when the United Kingdom's internal and external dilemmas at last jammed solidly up against each other, so that during the summer run on the pound (accentuated by a seamen's strike) the Prime Minister was reduced to propagandizing England's footballing victory in the World Cup as if it had been won on the beaches of Dunkirk. Wilson's retrospective account hinges on the argument that the surge of speculation which set in at this point, and which subsequently undermined the gamut of the government's policies, bore no relationship to 'real' economic conditions. He has attributed the phenomenon to the irrationality and selfishness of the speculators themselves, and (by direct implication at least) to political prejudice in the Bank of England, where the arch Lord Cromer reigned supreme. The latter suspicion illustrates how, for British Socialism, the shadow of 1931 stretched into the decade of the 1960s. It is true that the average rate of economic growth which prevailed during the six years after 1964 was greater than that later enjoyed, for example, during the decade of the 1980s, when many Britons prided themselves on having had a belated 'miracle' of their own. It was precisely this growth in the general level of economic activity which led the Prime Minister and his Chancellor of the Exchequer, James Callaghan, to continue to believe, almost until the water closed over their heads, that they could repeat the trick of previous Conservative governments, and float along on the crest of buoyant world trade until calmer waters were reached. Indeed this scenario might conceivably have worked out if the almighty dollar had provided the same powerful anchor that it had during the previous decade; as it was, the Labour Cabinet's parochial calculations got trampled underfoot in the gadarene rush which ultimately led to the complete collapse of Bretton Woods. To this extent Wilson and Callaghan were simply unlucky that as financial markets began to discount a fundamental change in the international system of money, they fixed upon sterling as the weakest link in the fragile chain of fixed rates. To sustain the comparison we have previously made, where Attlee's government had been able to plug itself into an American-led world that was fortuitously taking shape, and gained what coherence it had from this central fact, Wilson's government was inextricably bound up with a world, and its related assumptions, that was beginning to fall apart.

Yet if the scapegoating of Wilson on both Right and Left in British politics has subsequently been overdone, the government he led remained supine as it got carried away on the tide of a society which wanted more universities, more deterrence, a sustained and even expanded world role, better pensions, and higher wages and salaries – all at once. As technology and capitalism entered a new competitive phase in the outside world, and Japan stopped making transistor radios and started making cars, British political economy was confronted with painful choices as to its critical priorities and values. Choosing between roles, however, was precisely what the dominant ethos of British government found it most difficult to do; so that the gut response to any assertion that the nation could no longer carry the full range of its burdens continued to be a gritty and even hostile 'Can't we?'. What the foreign speculators, for all their profiteering, quite rationally deduced from this paralysis – thrown into high relief by the gyrations of the reserves – was what the egregious Richard Crossman saw inside the Cabinet staring him in the face: a political leadership presiding over one hike in Bank Rate after another without any apparent intention of resolving the contradictions becoming daily more ineluctable.[17]

In fact the triumvirate of Wilson, Callaghan and Denis Healey (at the Ministry of Defence) did try to chuck excess ballast over the side of the keeling ship of state, only to find that every time more water came back over the gunwales. Thus in the Budget for 1965 a limit of £2,000 millions was put on defence spending – the first time such an arbitrary 'cap' had been established, suggestively, since 1938. An early and spectacular victim was the TSR2 reconnaissance airplane, specially designed for East of Suez operations. It was the Royal Navy, however, which had been the happy recipient of the bulk of increased 'overseas' expenditures since 1957. The Defence White Paper of February 1966 sought to make inroads in this area, announcing that a new generation of aircraft-carriers would not be built, and that the United Kingdom would withdraw from Aden Colony and the South Arabian Federation, *regardless of local circumstances,* in 1967 or 1968.[18] Even this hacking at the margins of the East of Suez policy brought about the immediate resignation not only of the Navy Minister[19], but of the First Sea Lord as well. This (with its shades of old Jacky Fisher many years before) was testimony to the brittleness of feeling at the heart of the British establishment as the financial crisis began to work its way through the system. The 1966 White Paper, indeed, was to begin a gossiping campaign against Wilson as the source of the decline of 'Queen and Country' which was later (as evidence now makes incontrovertible) to get seriously out of hand, not least among the Secret Service.

To understand how deep these passions went it is necessary to recall how the very visibility and traditional 'feel' of the East of Suez policy had become almost synonymous with the nation's determination to maintain its prestige in the world generally; a sensation all the more powerful since the claims of Polaris to genuine *Britishness* were distinctly exiguous. It may even be contended that the problem of scaling down the East of Suez strategy which faced Wilson was politically a more slippery matter than dismantling the bulk of the residual Colonial Empire after 1959 had been for Macmillan, since only a small and diminishing minority had believed that, say, Nigeria or Nyasaland still redounded in any meaningful way to British interests, whereas the numbers who thought that bases and ships in the Indian Ocean remained strategically vital were large and, with some hype from the *Daily Express,* actually growing. The atmosphere of profound alienation which therefore developed when the Labour Government started to renege on its commitments in this area, and in particular when it announced the imminent end of the British presence in Aden and the surrounding Federation, is conveyed by Sir Kennedy Trevaskis, one of the originators of the South Arabian polity, who as soon as he heard of the White Paper recommendations turned up at Denis Healey's office at the Defence Ministry 'incoherent with emotion'.[20] Healey calmly pointed out that it had become impossible to impose a military base on a local population clearly bent on making it unviable. 'Surely I must see', Trevaskis' account of his interview goes on, 'that to undertake a defence commitment to the Federation which had only been proposed by Sandys as a complement to a [now defunct] defence base would be nonsensical? I did not. I saw only a long line of Arab friends whom I, and others, had led up the garden path.'[21] Here, threatening to break out anew, with consequences nobody could foretell, was the old doctrinal conflict: on the one hand arguments of a reasoned and prudential kind as to what was feasible in the real world, and on the other a fundamentally moral critique imbued with the belief that the United Kingdom could meet its commitments overseas if it would only find the requisite courage and self-belief. Power and 'will', reality and honour – these were the motifs which ran from Czechoslovakia in the 1930s to South Arabia thirty years later, not exactly as the crow flies, but unerringly straight for all that. When Trevaskis rushed into controversial print with his version of recent events in 1968, the record of the Labour Government bore the predictable headlines of 'An essay in Appeasement' and 'Surrender to Anarchy'.

In these sensitive circumstances, to have liquidated the East of Suez policy in one go would have risked a political explosion of major dimensions. The Labour Government's stance after the furore over the 1966 White Paper, therefore, was to delicately taper its focus towards the Gulf – it was announced, for example, that another new base would be built in Bahrain whilst diluting the overall strategic rationale with the statement that henceforth

the United Kingdom would only participate in large-scale operations in the region alongside an ally (presumably the United
States). Typical of the plunging situation in which the Wilson
government now found itself, no sooner had the retreat been
sounded into this new redoubt, than further detonations – in the
form of the Arab-Israeli War of June 1967 – caused the earthworks
to collapse once more. The Six Day War – during which American
policy was made with what seemed a very public neglect of any
co-ordination with European partners, including Britain – marked
the end of the phase since 1956 when the United States had been
concerned to let the United Kingdom's (admittedly drastically
curtailed) interests in the Middle East down gently; if the
Europeans were so unhelpful towards America's predicament
in Vietnam, there was no reason why America should strive to
take account of their views with respect to other major issues
on the international stage. Of even more immediate concern in
London than these diplomatic implications, however, was the
fact that the Arab-Israeli conflict triggered waves of speculation
in the world money markets which continued throughout the
summer, and which ultimately compelled the British authorities
on 18 November to take the action they had so long resisted –
the devaluation of the pound sterling.

As with any large devaluation of a major currency, it was
the political decisions which flowed from the British action,
rather than the specific alteration in the currency's value, which
was most important for the future. John Darwin's analysis
of this sequence neatly pinpoints the dissolution of the old
Labour dispensation under which Wilson had played Attlee
to the Bevinite grouping of James Callaghan, Denis Healey,
George Brown and Michael Stewart.[22] Roy Jenkins was elevated
to the Treasury, taking with him, as befitted a biographer
of Asquith, proclivities which were domestic and European,
rather than strategic, in nature. Tensions remained high during
the ensuing debate over the basic thrust of policy, but with
the International Monetary Fund lurking in the background,
sweeping retrenchments could not be avoided. In mid-January
1968 it was announced that the British military presence would

be withdrawn from Malaysia, Singapore *and* the Gulf by the end of 1971; and the same unfortunate junior minister who, only months before, had toured the Gulf sheikhdoms giving resolute assurances that the British determination to guarantee these Kingdoms was both solemn and permanent, now returned with the sheepish message that the commitment was null and void. Such a wholesale swallowing of national pride, in a region where the British had long been intent on preserving their 'face', could only be effected as part of a major upheaval in which a conception of British statecraft which was, in John Darwin's words, 'emotional and romantic' was finally replaced by an alternative governing ideology which was 'coldly rational and cost-effective'.[23]

An historic British transition which embraced a less concentrated relationship with the United States, and the gutting of the world role, could not but have consequences for the United Kingdom's approach to Europe as well. On this front Wilson had been engaged since the middle of 1966 in a delicate shift of gear. Crossman explained this in his diary by arguing that the Prime Minister, like Macmillan before him, was seeking to use Europe as an escape from his problems at home[24], and although Crossman's daily effusions had in them the spirit of a kangaroo-court, there was probably some truth in the criticism. Whatever the motive, in May 1967 the British Government lodged its second application to join the Common Market, a request stripped of the oblique phraseology which had accompanied its predecessor in 1961. That the context had very significantly changed in the interval was evoked by the exchanges which Wilson had with President de Gaulle in Paris shortly afterwards, when the fighting in the Middle East had barely stopped, and the two leaders were just returned from attending the funeral of Konrad Adenauer. Both the American and German factors were central to their discussions. Thus whereas de Gaulle chided the British for taking so long to learn the inevitable truth that the United States would only look to its own interests in a major international crisis, the British premier exploited renewed French fears that the Germans were on their way once again to a commercial and political mastery in Europe. 'Indeed, he [de Gaulle] and we had to face the possibility', Wilson argued in appropriately sombre tones, 'that a time might come, perhaps quite soon, when the US and Germany would be linked more closely together in political matters. He could surely see the dangers if France and the US were engaged . . . in a struggle for the soul of Germany'.[25] The conference ended with the leaders of this putative new entente – delicious humour! – pouring gentle scorn on the Atlanticism of 'les Hollandais', 'les Allemands' and 'les pauvres Italiens'. This vision was not to be entirely accurate (though the European *bouleversement* in 1989–90 may be said to accord it a fresh coat of prophetic paint); and a good deal of tribulation lay ahead before the British were finally able to sign on the dotted line of the Treaty of Rome in 1972. Even after that moment of destiny there was a long interim of re-negotiations and, to coin a phrase, much beating of handbags before the United Kingdom's fate within an integrated Europe was to be sealed. Nevertheless, it was the interaction between the acute internal reassessments springing from the devaluation of sterling in November 1967 with the first major shift in the log-jam of an enlarged EEC which constituted nothing less than a *rite de passage* in British public affairs.

There was, alongside these travails, one other running sore in United Kingdom policy we have yet to mention: the crisis which broke out over Rhodesia (as Southern Rhodesia came to be called in this period). Following the break-up of the Central African Federation in January 1964, the white-dominated regime in this latter territory demanded independence on the basis of the 1961 constitution. According to Rhodesian sources which have emerged, Alec Douglas-Home as Prime Minister was 'quite cynical' in asking for purely cosmetic concessions in order to allow him to hand over sovereignty promptly to Rhodesia's existing rulers.[26] The local whites, however, belonged to the no-nonsense Die-Hard school which believed that the cosmetics really mattered, and that appearances and reality could not be separated along the lines of such typical English convenience. With the coming to power of the extreme Rhodesia

Front under Ian Smith in April 1964, and the formation of
a British Socialist government seven months later, the gap
between London and Salisbury became unbridgeable. Although
Wilson sought feverishly for a way out of the impasse, on
11 November 1965 the Southern Rhodesians finally issued a
Unilateral Declaration of Independence. Here was a Labour
premier's nightmare: a rebellion against the Crown which he
did not have the capacity to put down.

After November 1965 the Labour Government was caught
between the Scylla of a disintegrated Commonwealth and the
Charybdis of criticism emanating from his Conservative (and
other) domestic opponents. Sanctions – which it was claimed
would bring down the illegal Rhodesian regime 'in days and weeks
rather than months' – were designed to help the government
navigate speedily around the first of these obstacles, whilst
adoption of the 'no use of force' principle (force, that is,
that would have to be used against 'kith and kin') assisted the
avoidance of the second. Having got over the difficult early hump,
Wilson tried on two occasions to negotiate a solution directly with
Smith: talks were held on board HMS *Tiger* in December 1966,
and on board HMS *Fearless* in October 1968 (venues presumably
chosen to shroud in naval braggadocio a situation which was
deeply humiliating for the United Kingdom, whose Governor
remained under 'house arrest' in Salisbury throughout). Both
conferences broke down on points of detail which need not
detain us.[27] Undoubtedly Wilson's chief aim throughout this
saga was to get his government through to the next election
without slipping irretrievably over the banana-skin of UDI; nor
was any subsequent British leader able to do any better until
purely extraneous factors gradually brought Smith to heel after
the mid-1970s. Wilson's success in jumping the Rhodesian hurdle
without coming completely a cropper was something of a virtuoso
performance, galling through it was to extremists on all sides.

Yet although the Labour Government was not undone over
Rhodesia, it was certainly damaged. The bile it generated within
British political life spilt over after the general election of March
1966 into a nascent 'stop Wilson' movement. This sentiment

remained tentative and inchoate, nevertheless, until the devaluation of November 1967 whipped up feelings to a new peak, in which the apprehensions of an old order being put to the knife (exaggerated though such fears usually are) was tangible. The remarkable hubbub surrounding regimental reform in the British Army (with much emotion concerning the loss of great names and 'colours') was only one peg on which this controversy was hung – especially since one of the units involved, the Argyll and Sutherland Highlanders, was hailed virtually throughout the British media for the 'retaking' of the infamous Crater District in central Aden in May 1968. This latter action, indeed, under the exotic leadership of Lieutenant-Colonel 'Mad' Mitchell, may be said to go down in history as the last 'imperial' action by the British Army in an overseas theatre.[28] Before long, amidst these brittle emotions, in proverbial 'high places' rumbling talk was to be heard of the need for an emergency coalition government, and even more sinister whisperings as to the possibility of a coup. Fired by such possibilities, not a few eminent persons began to hold themselves in readiness for their country's call.[29] Murky though this subject naturally remains, sporadic interest has since focused on the meeting held at the London home of Lord Mountbatten on 8 May 1968 when the Press baron, Cecil King, expounded the need for intervention against the Wilson government. 'The only doubt was whether the new regime would send for . . . King', wrote one observer of these curious goings-on, 'or King send for the new regime.'[30] 1968 was a year of cathartic and often disoriented feelings in many countries other than Britain, and historians are ill-advised to take *opera bouffe* too seriously. At the very least, however, these signals indicated the chasm which divided off a traditional, legitimist cadre which felt its identity and achievements to be at stake, and a burgeoning post-devaluation order which some feared could only be kept at bay by a man (a woman being as yet unimaginable) on a white horse.

Such extreme vibrations within the body politic were to lead in a few years to the belief that the United Kingdom had become 'ungovernable'. What seemed at the time to be a plight of ungovernability, however, was simply in large measure the confused heat and noise accompanying the emergence of a new political discourse to replace the One Nation, Great Power method which endured a lingering death after the hammer-blows of 1967–8. One aspect of this redefinition within the mainstream of national politics was the regroupings among Labour politicians to which we have already referred (though later accidents ensured that it was not the last upset on the Left which the process enforced). Another, ultimately more important, dimension was evident at the Conservative Party Conference in October 1968, when at a fringe meeting the little-known Member of Parliament for Finchley, Margaret Thatcher, made a speech which has been identified as the original enunciation of the doctrine later to be associated with her own prolonged premiership. 'There are dangers in consensus', Thatcher declared on this occasion. 'It could be an attempt to satisfy people holding no particular views about anything. . . What is needed now is a far greater independence from the Government and a comparative reduction in the role of government.'[31] A reworking of Tory orthodoxy along these lines was wholly natural, since once the grail of 'prestige' (with its interventionist apparatus) receded into the background, a purist vision of free markets automatically came to fill the ideological and moral vacuum. Ever since the Edwardians defined for themselves a threat of national decay, the quest for 'greatness' had been at the heart of the politicians' attempts to hold together English urban civilization, and to imbue it with common purposes and values which otherwise seemed liable to disintegrate in a welter of class and sectional animosity. The liquidation of greatness (which in the interval had come to permeate all the principal factions in the state) was bound to push British politics out towards the extremes once more, and indeed civil society after 1968 was shortly to throw up commotions on a scale last seen in the syndicalist hey-day of 1911. Unfamiliar and shot through with disloyalties though this appeared to many observers, it may best be regarded as the inevitable trauma of a polity at last adapting to the problem of efficiently governing itself, rather than other people. It was unfortunate that this seminal transformation occurred just when international economic conditions, triggered by the oil-price hikes of yet another Middle Eastern war in 1973, made the task more difficult than ever. The success with which the underlying problems were eventually tackled is a question relating to a very different phase of British development than the one we have been concerned with in this book, and which only a later generation will be able to examine dispassionately. When the storm-clouds of these various struggles have finally abated, however, historical judgements may properly reflect the wisdom regarding his native land which Disraeli wryly dispensed to one who visited him in old age. 'It is a very difficult country to move', the great man sadly remarked, '. . . and one in which there is more disappointment than success.'[32]

Epilogue
Greatness and the Nation

Napoleon said that the English were a nation of
shopkeepers, and it is for them to show that in
the middle of the twentieth century they have not
forgotten how to keep shop

Sir Charles Petrie, *The Liverpool Post*
3 September 1954

One who knew both Lloyd George and Winston Churchill
well once asked them on the eve of the Great War what was
the most impressive sight they had ever seen. Lloyd George's
answer was 'the march past Gladstone's body as it lay in
Westminster Hall'; Churchill's response was 'without a doubt,
the advance of the Dervishes at the Battle of Omdurman'.[1] In
its anecdotal fashion this epitomized – which was doubtless
why its author recorded the exchange – two distinct versions
of British statesmanship: one redolent of a dignified order,
marked though it was by many bitter past controversies, of
an essentially self-contained polity; the other evoking a spirited
engagement with opportunities and commotions abroad. Both
politicians, in fact, were subsequently to switch between these
contrary ideals as professional circumstances demanded. In the
long-term, however, it was the image of Omdurman, not of
Gladstone's lying-in-state, which impressed itself most forcefully
upon British political culture, until it became difficult to conceive
of the United Kingdom's interests apart from its destiny overseas.
The strains eventually culminating in the Suez crisis of 1956
derived precisely from the irresistible pressures working against

the geographical bias deeply embedded in the mentality of British elites over such a long period of time. 'International law and the temper of international opinion' one leading British official thus fearfully derided the constraining tendencies at this point, 'is all set against the things which made us a great nation in our activities *outside our own territory*. Bit by bit we shall be driven back into our island where we shall starve.'[2] Clearly the tasks of domestic government could not easily provide consolations or alternative values for those whose preconceptions had been moulded into more exotic – or at least more distended – shapes.

Yet if this external bias worked itself out according to twentieth-century imperatives, its roots stretched back to the climax of mid-Victorian Britain, and to the seminal rivalry between the two greatest leaders of that age. Thus of Disraeli it was said by Walter Bagehot that he was at heart a political romantic, preferring to deal with 'ideal measures' and 'ideal heroes' instead of exploring 'the heart of a deep national conviction'.[3] The mock-Disraelian spirit came to permeate much of the modern body politic in England, when the 'ideal measures' came to reside in the orchestration of the nation's war powers, and the 'ideal heroes' those who formed themselves in their image. 'I don't care twopence about the ballot', the combative Violet Effingham summed up this evolving philosophy in Anthony Trollope's *Phineas Finn*. 'Are we going to have a new iron fleet? That's the question', and this tendency of thought progressively infiltrated British culture for the century after the 1860s, until by the end of the period the question which appeared to move many people more than any other was whether the nation was going to acquire a new iron weapon in the form of a credible nuclear deterrent. The problem was that along the way a 'deep national conviction' – one, that is, which related to the internal development of domestic society over and beyond the febrile substitute of 'public welfare' – did indeed become obscured. Furthermore, it became increasingly difficult in the interregnums between compelling (and self-legitimizing) emergencies abroad to identify a set of administrative-political signals by which the nation's course might be charted in times of tranquillity. Instead, the supervening periods came to be

tarred with the brush of mediocrity (*pace* the 1920s) or with a
crushing burden of guilt (*pace* the 'dull and dishonest' decade of
the 1930s) which contrasted so transparently with heroic struggles
against successive foreign tyrannies in the outside world. When
the necessity eventually arose – as sooner or later it must – to
rediscover some deep national conviction capable of directing
collective and individual energies to the struggle against internal
decay, the process was inevitably one of very considerable social
and psychological strain.

In seeking out such continuities in nineteenth and twentieth
century British politics, Gladstone provides at least as vital a
key as Disraeli. The essence of Gladstone's position, as H.
C. G. Mathew has put it in a brilliant essay, 'implied that
a peacetime equilibrium of the state and its finances could be
achieved. The rest of the [nineteenth] century was to be the
battleground on which he fought the forces which prevented
it.'[4] It is intrinsic to our interpretation that the same issue
carried over with an equivalent centrality to the battleground
of the twentieth century as well. One of the tell-tale mechanisms
of this transfer was the distaste felt amongst certain sections
of the political class for the variety of language and expertise
to which such a peacetime equilibrium appeared inexorably to
lead. Nor is it without significance that this particular offence
was manifested as much by Joseph Chamberlain, fresh from
his municipal triumphs as Mayor of Birmingham, as by the
Grand Old Man himself. 'They', J. L. Hammond once wrote,
referring to the aristocratic Whig nobles in the Liberal cabinet
of the early 1880s, 'were in deadly fear of Chamberlain, with his
crude courage, his dislike of their class, *his special knowledge of
questions in which they had never interested themselves* . . . and
his command of forces which they thought irresponsible and
revolutionary.'[5] Joseph Chamberlain was soon catapulted by his
Irish passions into an alliance with the Unionists, and after the
South African War of 1899–1902 he sought to fuse the themes
of political greatness and economic growth within the test-tube
of Imperial Protection; but his dislike of the landed oligarchs,
whatever their party hue, and their aversion for his interests and

methods, never fully dissipated. These mutual contempts were grafted upon the course of later British affairs by the immutable ties of blood and familial devotion, for Winston Churchill was above all things an unruly scion of the great ducal house of Blenheim, striving to evolve a brand of twentieth-century Whiggism, whilst Neville Chamberlain was at bottom an heir of a Midlands dynasty seeking to put the Civic Radicalism of his father on a national footing. The latter values enjoyed only a vicarious existence after June 1940, and only gradually revived in the course of the 1950s and 1960s. Meanwhile there continued to exist at the heart of British government an uneasy sense that a peacetime equilibrium of the state and its finances was beyond reach, and a related aversion among much of the political and administrative elite for the sort of vocabulary and mental concepts which such an ideal involved. The language of greatness was one which everybody could understand and which made the practice of mass democratic politics, once so feared, really rather easy; the language of national modernization, in contrast, strained not only people's intellects, but undermined the unity of the people under its accustomed leaders.

What we may label a modern and militant Whiggery, however, was not simply the reflection of a patrician disdain for the messy and baffling problems of domestic society. It was closely related, as well, to a genuine belief that internal conflicts within Britain were bound to end either in the triumph of social barbarians or in outright civil disorder. This sense of fatalism was discernible from the 1890s onwards, but it gained real momentum during the Edwardian era: as Charles Masterman, the Liberal politician, put it in 1911, 'We are all talking as people must have talked before the French Revolution.'[6] For a generation which believed that 'a class war . . . is the most insidious form of national disintegration'[7], one of the advantages of the German 'threat' was that it provided a focus for broadly-based loyalties which contemporary society otherwise seemed incapable of providing (a phenomenon which Maurice Cowling has aptly referred to as 'synthetic Jacobinism'). As a disillusioned commentator, writing in 1922, remarked, what had sent so many thousands of recruits rushing with wild joy to the recruiting stations in August 1914 was relief at having their lives touched by 'an immense simplification'.[8] It was a simplification which could only be defined in terms of external goals and challenges, and which for a later generation of Britons came to be mediated through the mythology of 1940 and the 'spirit of Dunkirk'. 'Come then', Churchill broadcast to the nation at this juncture, 'let us to the task, to the battle, to the toil – each to our part, each to our station.' Herein lay the enduring imagery and appeal of international struggle for the English (especially upper-class) mind: it created and legitimated a framework within which everything seemed to happen, and yet everything stayed the same; and in which each individual could claim an expanded and dignified role in the community without altering its delicate gradations. The tenacious longevity of the 'world role' after 1945, expressed both through the commitment to an 'independent' nuclear deterrent and the 'East of Suez' strategy, equally derived from the sense that in the effort to assert Britain's right to sit at the 'Top Table of nations', the ship of state could secure a political ballast which appeared to be available from no other source.

The orthodoxy we have described did not, of course, have it all its own way; Britain's civic traditions and the impulses of *homus economicus* were too strong for that. It was the recrudescence of old-fashioned fiscal preoccupations, rooted in a distaste for ill-advised adventure, which led to the terminal explosions within the Lloyd George coalition during the early 1920s, and which underpinned the tranquil Toryism of the Law-Baldwin regime which followed. *The Times* played a leading role at that time in calling for a return to quieter, or at least more mundane, concerns at home. Indeed, of that newspaper's proprietor, Lord Rothermere, it has been noted that he 'was not demanding a Businessman's government. Rather he was making a statement of belief that Britain was an economic rather than a military or administrative nation and that this was the most important fact about her.'[9] A great deal of British politics in the inter-war years came to revolve around this desire on the part of leading sections in the state to reconstruct national virtue along the lines of the Napoleonic adage, despised by some but worn as a badge of honour by others, that the United Kingdom was a 'nation of shopkeepers'. At Baldwin's canny (perhaps too canny) invitation even Churchill for a while adapted himself to this shift in the mental landscape, devoting himself to what he described on attaining the Treasury Board as 'the great social issues of the day'; his rhetorical method was quite simply to apply to economics the identical gloss which he had hitherto put upon martial endeavour, introducing his crucial Budget in 1925 to Parliament as 'national, and not class or party, in its extent or intention'.[10] But already by the end of the decade Churchill had given up the struggle, telling Leopold Amery in historical code that the Victorians, after all, had been 'small men making a lot of to do about . . . small matters'.[11] The 1930s subsequently produced the most intense strains because whereas one set of economic pressures produced a National Government determined to subordinate all else to material stabilization and renewal, a competing pattern of priorities soon took shape under the impact of external crisis tending instead to reassert the prerogatives of the military-administrative state. The argument over Appeasement, furthermore, waxed all the more luxuriantly because it was able to draw upon the ancestral passions generated by the Little Englandism of an earlier day. A nation, after all, is never happier than when cleaving to its habitual discontents; and when Neville Chamberlain's critics denounced the 'betrayal' of Czechoslovakia, and a year later acted to avert the betrayal of Poland, the ghost of General Gordon could be seen once more stalking the corridors of the Palace of Westminster.[12]

These subjects cannot be dilated upon without some parallel reference to ethical considerations, even if historians do generally make poor philosophers. Since Appeasement has been so much the touchstone of our story, is not the dominant fact, then, that Churchill was right, Chamberlain wrong and Adolf Hitler the most evil man in history? As far as the struggle against Hitlerism is concerned, the most balanced conclusion in a very slippery area appears to be that of an American historian, Eleanor Gates, who has written as follows:

That there were profound moral issues at stake in the war is almost beside the point. Few countries, not exclusively Britain and France, act primarily on behalf of moral principles unless, of course, their survival or well-being appear to depend on it. And this remains true even where moral considerations *have* played a lively part, as they did with Churchill and the men around him (and as they had . . . with the appeasers before them), and even where 'survival' ultimately turns out to be considerably less than what its stubborn sponsors had hoped from it. From the point of view of his reputation in history, it was Mr. Churchill's good fortune that the survival of England *could* be linked to the survival of freedom, decency and democratic institutions elsewhere. But the role of David to Hitler's Goliath was a role England might well have played regardless of the character of its formidable opponent.[13]

The moral legend of Appeasement distorting the relationship between image and reality in British life inevitably got caught up in the war which followed. The British propaganda machine at the time, and the folk memory to which it gave rise, clung to the idea that the conflict was 'another round' between the United Kingdom and Germany, the one side (reinforced after December 1941 by its larger Anglo-Saxon ally) standing for Freedom and Democracy, the other for Fascist dictatorship. In fact anything resembling an Anglo-German rivalry in Europe was resolved once and for all in 1940; subsequently the *real* question to be settled lay between Hitler and Stalin – between, that is, two dictatorships of which, in so far as these things can be judged, the latter was arguably the more vicious. The necessity to reconcile this alignment with the morality play as it was subsumed into British public affairs meant, for example, that long after the war, the Katyn Massacre, in which the entire Polish officer corps was wiped out, continued to be ascribed to German actions, when it had transparently taken place at Stalin's express command. For much of the war the Americans, in their earthy way, poked fun at the British tendency to deny that what was at stake was merely an old-fashioned fight for supremacy, and certainly Roosevelt was congenitally averse to the kind of ruby rhetoric that was meat and drink to Churchill. Towards the end of the Second World War, however, United States officials, especially on the military side, adopted the style and vocabulary of what came to be vaguely but heart-warmingly referred to as 'The Cause', before it eventually crystallized anew around the ethic of the Cold War in 1948/9. Meanwhile the British idea of themselves became widely rooted in certain preconceptions – correlated only very loosely with economic weight or efficiency – as to what was their 'due' in the international pecking order. Our argument, then, is that it was these moral tensions, always liable to high political manipulation through the resurrected symbols from the era of Appeasement, with their supple application one moment to the Cold War front in Europe and the next to the extra-NATO sphere where Arab Hitlers quickly multiplied, which bedevilled the evolution of practical statesmanship under the circumstances of the 1950s and, indeed, later. Embedded in this problematic, too, is the conundrum somewhat indiscreetly pointed out in the mid-1970s by the West German Chancellor, Helmut Schmidt, when he remarked that the problem with the British was that they had never been able to rid themselves of the illusion that they had emerged victorious from the war of 1939–45.

None of this is to say that in attempting to meet its distinctive goals, and in responding to the inevitable hiccups along the way, British policy lacked deftness or imagination; of the latter quality there was, perhaps, a surfeit. Defeated in Europe in 1940, Churchillian war strategy had reverted – as Lloyd George's had done before – to a 'Mediterranean Strategy' in which victory might be gauged by arrival at the gates of Tripoli, rather than at the gates of Berlin or Vienna. Hence arose the irony that between 1940 and 1945 Churchill fought, not the 'ideal' war he had envisaged at the outset of the struggle with Hitler, but very much the sort of limited, insular and broken-backed engagement which Chamberlain might have chosen to conduct had he stayed in power – a 'mild Colonial war' as one sceptic had forecast as early as 1936.[14] Above all, this was a theatre and a strategy in which the British war leadership could appear to be fighting successful campaigns on its own terms and in a clear *national* interest. By the same token, after 1945 it was the central and eastern Mediterranean which became the hub of much British diplomacy and emotion, the one major zone of the world where the Americans, it was fondly supposed, could be manoeuvred, and if necessary blackmailed, into following in the British wake, rather than *vice versa*. When, in the Suez crisis of 1956, this theory came unstuck, by which time even docile Greek Cypriot villagers were up in arms, the search for some residual British overseas primacy simply shifted to South Arabia (including Aden) and the Gulf states. The practical issue involved in these various convolutions was whether it was any longer feasible for the United Kingdom to sustain a major military base surrounded by a hostile population. In the end, it was not the policy-makers in London who settled this matter once and for all, but the financial markets and the 'Gnomes of Zurich', since only the collapse of sterling in November 1967 succeeded in eventually cutting off the 'East of Suez' strategy at its root. Looking broadly at the development of British policy during the twentieth century, one of its most striking traits was the search both at the state-directed economic level (mediated through 'Empire Trade' and a sterling monetary bloc) and in the sphere of strategy, for some modified version of 'Pax Britannica', one whose geographical application was necessarily more circumscribed, and whose methods were more discreet, but which might still constitute a regional British hegemony giving credence to those notions of 'Prestige' on which politics in the United Kingdom depended for so much of its content. What is to be questioned is not the skill and perseverence which went into these efforts on the part of a governing elite whose forte they were, but the degree to which they were congruent with the real nature of power in the 'modern' world.

Against the background of this analysis, much of the discussion which has taken place as to the United Kingdom's economic performance, whether measured from 1880 or over the shorter

haul since 1945, seems curiously beside the point. Such analyses
have invariably concentrated on some concrete error of policy
within government, be it to do with the principles and organization of national education, the management of the currency or the
nature of industrial relations. Treatments of this kind, breeding
off the fetid preoccupation with 'decline', all too often have
filtered through to contemporary party and sectional polemics
with rival groups accusing each other of responsibility for the
nation's gathering difficulties; the intelligentsia have been many
people's favourite scapegoat in this regard. But for most of the
period covered by this book the essence of British public affairs
– its central thrust – simply did not relate to the nurturing
of commercial or productive efficiency. What economic policy
was meant to do was prop up the structure of Welfare at
home and Greatness abroad which gave both the Right and
Left a stake (though not necessarily an equal stake) in the
political consensus of the day. Most practising politicians, and the
different components of social leadership, took their customary
place in this network of priorities – the priorities not of an
expanding and flexible society, but of a country marked by
many of the characteristics of an *ancien régime*. As time went
by this top-heavy polity became increasingly unstable, since the
workers began to jib at being told to 'pull up their socks' not for
themselves but for the more nebulous (and thus less compelling)
goal of 'keeping Britain great', whilst, even more significantly
for the final outcome, an enlarged and more *arriviste* middle
class rebelled against the financial imposts it involved. In short,
there is not much to be gained from delving into the minutiae
of economic 'failure', since the question cuts across much more
fundamental questions as to the complexion and aims of the ruling
regime itself. Overall, in what it set out to do as a nation, the
United Kingdom was rather more successful than many might
have predicted, whilst the record of the physical economy proper
in these decades – its managers, investors, industrial infantry,
and even its trade unions – at meeting the welter of conflicting
demands imposed upon it might even be described as a 'miracle'
in its own right, although of a rather different variety from the

more bourgeois sort enjoyed elsewhere in Western Europe and Japan after 1945.

Concentration on national decline has naturally become deeply entangled with the issue of Europe in British politics. It has become almost axiomatic, for example, that successive British Governments 'missed the bus' of Continental integration from the late 1940s onwards, rejecting the leadership of the neighbouring countries when it was offered to her 'on a plate' and fatally standing aloof when the Treaty of Rome establishing the EEC was signed in January 1957. This is misleading. On a higher plane, the most historic achievement of that process was the assuagement of Franco-German hatreds, and this positively *required* that the United Kingdom remain on the sidelines, since full participation by a third major party would have complicated and probably destabilized the dynamic of reconciliation (as the débâcle over the putative European Defence Community vividly illustrated). More practically, too, the United Kingdom never spurned the leadership of Europe for the very simple reason that she was never offered it; any rendering to the contrary is oblivious to the transformation of French political psychology after the destruction of the Entente Cordiale in 1940. Afterwards no French government was to look to Britain for help in securing her European objectives. The truly critical issues in British political economy during the post-war era had no necessary connection with whether the United Kingdom did, or did not, join an entity which, apart from its key role as the vehicle for Franco-German diplomacy, was to remain for so many years a limited commercial-agricultural alliance. Significantly, when Harold Macmillan 'turned' to Europe in 1962, and when Harold Wilson did the same (though not definitively) in 1967, they did so, not as a 'solution' to British problems, but as a protective façade behind which *real* solutions might begin to be sought.

Here, one suspects, was another 'immense simplification' in the sense that the difficulties of modernization and reform might only be surmounted if they could be externalized, and the sting of change thereby removed. Even the language of greatness (with its definition of opponents as 'Little Englanders') became curiously transposed onto the rhetorical corpus of Britain-in-Europe, a kind of refurbished Continental Commitment, so that in the late sixties and early seventies the thesis of British entry into the EEC was founded not on its practical implications for economic and social policy, but on the heightened influence and prestige it would bring in the chancelleries of the world. To these motivations was added, however, a grimmer apprehension that without some quick-fix diversion the nation itself was sliding rapidly out of control. As Lord Gladwyn, a leading 'pro-European' of the era, put it, amidst widespread talk of the United Kingdom's endemic 'ungovernability', since the end of the Second World War no Prime Minister had been able to articulate a sustainable national policy; he added darkly that 'should the European idea really collapse, there is indeed good reason to suppose that some "providential man" will pull all these [economic] skeletons out of the cupboard. If by any chance . . . the economic situation gets any worse than it now is, I have little doubt of his eventual emergence.'[15] It may be said that this proved a wise prediction, with the qualification that it got wrong the gender in which providentialism soon made its presence felt on the British stage. In sum, by the end of the period covered in this volume there were already, in embryo, only two viable options in national affairs, one of which involved locking the country into the institutional network based on the amorphous but magnetic power-house in Brussels, and the other of which involved a high-risk, 'white horse' politics in which a dynamic and inevitably abrasive leader should charge hither and thither in the quest to put the country 'back on its own feet'.

Increasingly discernible in these controversies was the under-lying question of British sovereignty. That sovereignty, filtered through the medium of national greatness, had become so mixed up with conceptions of international and imperial leadership that when these prerogatives began to be diluted the baby of national integrity was apt to be thrown out with the bathwater of a faded and unsustainable grandeur. This effect was compounded by a widely-felt pessimism that the United Kingdom's problems were now too deep-seated to be susceptible to merely national correctives. 'The plain fact is', a leading financial expert remarked in the early 1960s when the gyrations of sterling were underscoring these dilemmas, 'that economically, just as politically and militarily, we have not been sovereign since the war'.[16] This uneasy awareness made it all the more difficult to mobilize the nation behind the goal of economic renewal which the events of 1967–8 established once again as the touchstone of political life; for how could a democratic people be roused to a great effort of reconstruction when its very nationhood was being exposed to equivocation? In response to such confusions some politicians were drawn to visions of Europe which they had hitherto abjured; some on the Left championed a militant and besieged Socialism; whilst on the Right a tendency arose to move towards a creed of Adam Smith-style free markets all the more intellectually appealing for being associated with a restored national autonomy. These differences – like other fractures of thought and feeling during the century – ran most deeply of all within the Conservative party; and the splits within that organ as manifested after 1968, culminating in a change of leadership during 1975, conformed to the envenomed traditions of 1922 and 1940.

What, fundamentally, began to take shape in the 1970s was a revived version of a bourgeois civic radicalism which in recent times had occupied only a subordinate place within the state; the roller-coaster of inflation and industrial troubles ensured that this revival had a strong messianic strain. But after an interval in which British greatness had been expressed in military and administrative, rather than economic, terms, was it feasible to rediscover the instincts of an essentially commercial and shop-keeping citizenry? 'Supposing I put the ball at their feet and they don't kick it? That was the nightmare' was how Margaret Thatcher later evoked her basic misgiving when, having triumphed at the polls, she set out after May 1979 on a 'revolution from above' designed to apply Victorian values to the very different society of late twentieth-century Britain.[17] The successes and failures of the prolonged premiership which followed cannot concern us. Its dénouement, however, confirmed that, although British society was certainly capable of closing the competitive gap which in recent years had opened up with many of its peer countries, its capacity and preparedness to transform itself in the *laissez-faire* and distinctively national image of Thatcherite politics remained problematical. What made the issue of European union, both monetary and legislative, increasingly relevant in domestic British politics, to the extent that it eventually contributed directly to Mrs Thatcher's own departure from office in November 1990, was that it came to offer a convenient shorthand for defining anew the perennial battle-lines between moderation and radicalism, individualism and collectivism, nationalism and supranationalism. It is ironic that a century in which the United Kingdom exhausted so much physical and moral energy ordering the affairs of other societies should move towards its close with British opinion acutely at odds over the virtues and credibility of her own national competence in significant areas of public policy. Nevertheless, the fact that Britons, whatever their continuing internal disputes, had succeeded in tracing the lineaments of a new equipoise, one element of which was that they were content to see themselves as they were rather than as they wanted others to see them, was a matter for satisfaction and some practical comfort for the future.

Appendix
British Monarchs, Prime Ministers and Foreign Secretaries, 1900–70

MONARCHS

June 1837–Jan. 1901	Victoria
Jan. 1901–May 1910	Edward VII
May 1910–Jan. 1936	George V
Jan. 1936–Dec. 1936	Edward VIII (Abd.)
Dec. 1936–Feb. 1952	George VI
Feb. 1952–	Elizabeth II

PRIME MINISTERS

June 1895–July 1902	Marquess of Salisbury (Con.)
July 1902–Dec. 1905	A. J. Balfour (Con.)
Dec. 1905–Apr. 1908	Sir Henry Campbell-Bannerman (Lib.)
Apr. 1908–May 1915	H. H. Asquith (Lib.)
May 1915–Dec. 1916	H. H. Asquith (Coal.)
Dec. 1916–Oct. 1922	David Lloyd George (Coal.)
Oct. 1922–May 1923	Andrew Bonar Law (Con.)
May 1923–Jan. 1924	Stanley Baldwin (Con.)
Jan. 1924–Nov. 1924	Ramsay MacDonald (Lab.)
Nov. 1924–June 1929	Stanley Baldwin (Con.)
June 1929–Aug. 1931	Ramsay MacDonald (Lab.)
Aug. 1931–June 1935	Ramsay MacDonald (Nat.)
June 1935–May 1937	Stanley Baldwin (Nat.)
May 1937–May 1940	Neville Chamberlain (Nat.)
May 1940–Aug. 1945	Winston Churchill (Coal.)
Aug. 1945–Oct. 1951	Clement Attlee (Lab.)
Oct. 1951–Apr. 1955	Winston Churchill (Con.)

Apr. 1955–Jan. 1957	Sir Anthony Eden (Con.)
Jan. 1957–Oct. 1963	Harold Macmillan (Con.)
Oct. 1963–Oct. 1964	Sir Alec Douglas-Home (Con.)
Oct. 1964–June 1970	Harold Wilson (Lab.)
June 1970–Mar. 1974	Edward Heath (Con.)

FOREIGN SECRETARIES

June 1895–Oct. 1900	Marquess of Salisbury (Con.)
Oct. 1900–Dec. 1905	Marquess of Lansdowne (Con.)
Dec. 1905–May 1915	Sir Edward Grey (Lib.)
May 1915–Dec. 1916	Sir Edward Grey (Coal.)
Dec. 1916–Oct. 1919	A. J. Balfour (Coal.)
Oct. 1919–Oct. 1922	Marquess of Curzon (Coal.)
Oct. 1922–Jan. 1924	Marquess of Curzon (Con.)
Jan. 1924–Nov. 1924	Ramsay MacDonald (Lab.)
Nov. 1924–June 1929	Austen Chamberlain (Con.)
June 1929–Aug. 1931	Arthur Henderson (Lab.)
Aug. 1931–Nov. 1931	Marquess of Reading (Nat.)
Nov. 1931–June 1935	Sir John Simon (Nat.)
June 1935–Dec. 1935	Sir Samuel Hoare (Nat.)
Dec. 1935–Mar. 1938	Anthony Eden (Nat.)
Mar. 1938–May 1940	Viscount Halifax (Nat.)
May 1940–Dec. 1940	Viscount Halifax (Coal.)
Dec. 1940–Aug. 1945	Anthony Eden (Coal.)
Aug. 1945–Mar. 1951	Ernest Bevin (Lab.)
Mar. 1951–Oct. 1951	Herbert Morrison (Lab.)
Oct. 1951–Apr. 1955	Anthony Eden (Con.)
Apr. 1955–Dec. 1955	Harold Macmillan (Con.)
Dec. 1955–July 1960	Selwyn Lloyd (Con.)
July 1960–Oct. 1963	Earl of Home (Con.)
Oct. 1963–Oct. 1964	R. A. Butler (Con.)
Oct. 1964–Jan. 1965	Patrick Gordon Walker (Lab.)
Jan. 1965–Aug. 1967	Michael Stewart (Lab.)
Aug. 1967–Apr. 1968	George Brown (Lab.)
Apr. 1968–June 1970	Michael Stewart (Lab.)
June 1970–Mar. 1974	Sir Alec Douglas-Home (Con.)

Abd.	=	Abdicated
Con.	=	Conservative
Lab.	=	Labour
Lib.	=	Liberal
Coal.	=	Coalition
Nat.	=	National

Notes

Place of publication is London unless otherwise noted.

PROLOGUE
1. Paul Kennedy, *The Rise and Fall of the Great Powers: Economic Change and Military Conflict from 1500 to 2000* (1988).
2. Paul Kennedy, *The Rise and Fall of British Naval Mastery* (1976).
3. Robert Blake, *The Decline of Power: Britain, 1915–64* (1986).
4. In *King Lear*, Act IV, Sc. VI Gloucester, blinded by his enemies, is under the mistaken impression that he has jumped from the precipice. The lines which follow, for those who like to mix history and literature, nicely mirror the paradox of British political psychology: 'Edgar: . . . but thou dost breathe,/Hast heavy substance, bleed'st not, speak'st, art sound./Ten masts at each make not the altitude/ Which thou hast perpendicularly fell:/Thy life's a miracle. Speak yet again?/Gloucester: But have I fall'n or no?'
5. Sir Lionel Cust, *King Edward VII and His Court: Some Reminiscences* (1930), 15.
6. Christopher Thorne, *The Issue of War: States, Societies and the Far Eastern Conflict of 1941–5* (1985), 134. Also see David Dilks (ed.), *The Diaries of Alexander Cadogan, 1938–45* (1971), 571. Such prognostications may be seen as in part a residue of Churchill's suggestion in June 1940 for a 'union' of Britain and France. Certainly the drift of the Benelux countries away from a British orientation after

1945 was coloured by the sense of having been so roughly discounted in London as independent factors during the Second World War.

7. Sir Frederick Ponsonby, *Recollections of Three Reigns* (1951), 82–3.

8. As other departments of state began to require specialized forms of competence or experience, it was very noticeable that the peerage looked to the Foreign Office as a special preserve of their own. This right was to continue through the century when Conservative governments were in office, so that even Margaret Thatcher, not noted for her love of the landed aristocracy, threw them the prescribed sop when making Lord Carrington Foreign Secretary in her first Cabinet.

9. Kersaudy, *Churchill and de Gaulle* (1981), 362.

10. Thorne, *The Issue of War*, 242–3.

11. Anthony Howard, 'In with the in-crowd', *The Sunday Times*, 23 September 1990.

CHAPTER ONE   GREATNESS AND THE EDWARDIANS

1. S. Marks and S. Trapido, 'Lord Milner and the South African State', *History Workshop*, VIII (1979), 50–81.

2. A. N. Porter, 'The South African War (1899–1902): Context and Motive Reconsidered', *Journal of African History*, 31 (1990), 43–57.

3. The military events of the war may be followed in Rayne Kruger, *Good Bye Dolly Gray* (1959); a more recent account is Thomas Pakenham, *The Boer War* (1979).

4. J. A. Smith, *John Buchan* (1965), 97.

5. The work of Milner's 'kindergarten' is the subject of Donald Denoon, *A Grand Illusion: the failure of imperial policy in the Transvaal colony during the period of reconstruction, 1905–1910* (1973).

6. A. M. Gollin, *Proconsul in Politics: a study of Lord Milner in power and in opposition* (1964), 599–607.

7. Ibid., 48.

8. Kipling's ambivalent feelings towards the metropole are

described in Charles Carrington, *Rudyard Kipling: His Life and Work* (1955), 172–212; also see Angus Wilson, *The Strange Ride of Rudyard Kipling: His Life and Works* (1977), 191–266.

9. Carrington, *Rudyard Kipling*, 123–4.
10. Quoted in Aaron L. Friedberg, *The Weary Titan: Britain and the Experience of Relative Decline, 1895–1905* (Princeton, 1988), 72.
11. Leopold Amery, *The Sunday Times*, 7 February 1932 quoted in Julian Amery, *Joseph Chamberlain and the Tariff Reform Campaign* (1969), 194.
12. Quoted in Friedberg, *The Weary Titan*, 114.
13. Quoted in Julian Amery, *Joseph Chamberlain and the Tariff Reform Campaign*, 319–20.
14. Balfour's gyrations on the tariff issue are reconstructed in Alan Sykes, *Tariff Reform in British Politics, 1903–1913* (Oxford, 1979).
15. A. L. Kennedy, *Salisbury, 1830–1903: Portrait of a Statesman* (1953), 268.
16. Ibid., 335.
17. For the Prime Minister's enigmatic gloom in the final stages of his career see J. A. S. Grenville, *Lord Salisbury and Foreign Policy: The Close of the Nineteenth Century* (1964).
18. See Ian Nish, *The Anglo-Japanese Alliance* (1966).
19. A. J. Marder, *From Dreadnought to Scapa Flow. Volume 1* (1961), 456.
20. E. J. Hobsbawm, *The Age of Empire, 1875–1914* (1987), 318–19.
21. Nicholas d'Ombrain, *War Machinery and High Policy: Defence Administration in Peacetime Britain, 1902–14* (1973), 146–7.
22. Fisher's reforms are detailed in Marder, *Dreadnought*, 14–207.
23. Quoted in Friedberg, *The Weary Titan*, 154.
24. For the truncated role of the Committee of Imperial Defence see d'Ombrain, *War Machinery and High Policy*, 44–73, 92–114.

25. Keith Wilson, *The Policy of the Entente: Essays on the Determinants of British Foreign Policy, 1904–14* (Cambridge, 1985), 20.

26. Lord Haldane, *Autobiography* (1929), 191; also Keith Robbins, *Sir Edward Grey* (1971), 145–9.

27. Wilson, *The Policy of the Entente*, 17.

28. Quoted in Randolph Churchill, *Winston S. Churchill. Volume II: The Young Statesman, 1901–14* (1967), 316.

29. Gollin, *Proconsul in Politics*, 99.

30. Ronald Hyam, 'The myth of the "Magnanimous Gesture": the Liberal government, Smuts and conciliation, 1906' in Ronald Hyam and Ged Martin, *Reappraisals in British Imperial History* (1975), 167–87.

31. A parallel may be drawn between Campbell-Bannerman's commitment, both radical and personal, on the issue of self-government in the Transvaal at the outset of the century and that of Attlee to Indian independence later on.

32. Quoted in Ronald Hyam, *Elgin and Churchill at the Colonial Office* (1968), 119.

33. For an elegant definition of this view in the broad perspective of late nineteenth-century development see A. F. Madden, 'Changing Attitudes and Widening Responsibilities, 1895–1914' in E. A. Benians and others (eds.), *The Cambridge History of the British Empire. Volume III: The Empire-Commonwealth* (Cambridge, 1935), 338–404.

34. Shula Marks, 'Southern and Central Africa, 1886–1910' in J. D. Fage and R. Oliver, *Cambridge History of Africa. Volume 6: from 1870 to 1905*, (1985) 481–92.

35. For a survey of the Cromer era see Robert Tignor, *Modernization and British Colonial Rule in Egypt, 1881–1914* (Princeton, 1966).

36. Quoted in Richard Symonds, *Oxford and Empire: The Last Lost Cause?* (1986), 12.

37. Peter Mellini, *Sir Eldon Gorst: The Overshadowed Proconsul* (Stanford, 1977), 133.

38. Ibid., 151.

39. Ibid., 207.

40. Stephen E. Koss, *John Morley at the India Office, 1905–1910* (Berkeley, 1967), 55.

41. Stanley A. Wolpert, *Morley and India, 1906–1910* (1967), 103–4.

42. Ibid., 109. This situation echoed that of Gladstone's agonizings over the application of Coercion Acts to Ireland some twenty years before.

43. Ibid., 61; also see Koss, *Morley*, 118.

44. Quoted in Wilson, *The Policy of the Entente*, 77.

45. The journalist was J. A. Spender, quoted in Robbins, *Grey*, 134.

46. Paul Kennedy, *The Realities Behind Diplomacy: Background Influences on British External Policy, 1865–1980* (1981), 127–8.

47. John Grigg, *Lloyd George: The People's Champion, 1902–1911* (1978), 243–76.

48. Randolph Churchill, *Churchill*, II, 360.

49. Norman Stone, *Europe Transformed, 1878–1919* (Glasgow, 1983), 153.

50. John Grigg, *Lloyd George: The People's Champion*, 308–9.

51. D'Ombrain, *War Machinery*, 161–2.

52. For Churchill's rumbustious tenure at the pre-war Admiralty see Randolph Churchill, *Churchill*, II, 658–65 and Richard Hough, *The Great War at Sea, 1914–18* (Oxford, 1983), 22–36.

53. D'Ombrain, *War Machinery*, 259.

54. Winston S. Churchill, *The World Crisis, 1911–14* (1923), 193.

55. John Morley, *Memorandum on Resignation: August 1914* (1928), 5.

56. Randolph Churchill, *Churchill*, II, 718.

57. Peter Rowland, *The Last Liberal Governments: The Promised Land, 1905–10* (1968), 211.

58. Wilson, *The Policy of the Entente*, 245.

59. Ibid., 79.

60. This mode of presentation, for example, was to be characteristic of anti-Appeasers during and after the Munich

crisis of September 1938. See above 154.

61.   Wilson, *The Policy of the Entente*, 141.

62.   Lord Riddell, *War Diary, 1914–18* (1933), 12.

CHAPTER TWO   THE KNOCK-OUT WAR

 1.   The classic one-volume account is Sir Llewellyn Woodward, *Great Britain and the War of 1914–18* (1967). A more recent attempt to cover the ground is Trevor Wilson, *The Myriad Faces of War: Britain and the Great War, 1914–18* (Cambridge, 1986).

 2.   The 'radical' credentials of the Great War are to the fore in Arthur Marwick, *The Deluge: British Society and the Great War* (1969).

 3.   An instance of this genre of breast-beating is Correlli Barnett, *The Collapse of British Power* (1968).

 4.   George H. Cassar, *Kitchener: Architect of Victory* (1977), 286; and John Terraine, *Douglas Haig: The Educated Soldier* (1966), 127–8.

 5.   Terraine, *Haig*, 128.

 6.   H. Montgomery Hyde, *Carson* (1960), 378. The famous recruiting poster to which this refers, featuring Kitchener sternly beckoning his countrymen to take up arms, was to be revived as a cult image during the 1960s.

 7.   The most recent instalment in this controversy is Trevor Royle, *The Kitchener Enigma* (1985).

 8.   Riddell, *War Diary*, 10.

 9.   Cassar, *Architect of Victory*, 268.

10.   Martin Gilbert, *Winston S. Churchill. Volume III: 1914–16* (1971), 571.

11.   Richard Holmes, *The Little Field Marshal: Sir John French* (1982), 292; also see Wilson, *Myriad Faces of War*, 202–3.

12.   Earl of Oxford and Asquith, *Memories and Reflections, 1852–1927. Volume 2* (1928), 100.

13.   Gilbert, *Churchill*, III, 32–95 describes the difficult start to the war experienced by Churchill and the Admiralty.

14.   Ibid., 126–39.

15.   Ibid., 355.

16. Ibid., 357–8.
17. Hough, *The Great War at Sea*, 144–68.
18. Gilbert, *Churchill*, III, 442.
19. See above 163–4.
20. Hankey, *The Supreme Command. Volume Two* (1961), 570.
21. John Grigg, *Lloyd George: From Peace to War, 1912–16*, 161–7.
22. See above 47.
23. Stephen McKenna, *McKenna* (1933), 299.
24. Gilbert. *Churchill*, III, 693–4.
25. David Lloyd George, *War Memoirs. Volume II* (1933), 755; for a recent assessment of the impact of the war on Irish life see R. F. Foster, *Modern Ireland, 1600–1972* (1988), 461–94.
26. F. S. L. Lyons, *Ireland Since the Famine* (1971), 368.
27. Riddell, *War Diary*, 184.
28. Robert Blake, *The Unknown Prime Minister: The Life and Times of Andrew Bonar Law, 1858–1923* (1955), 290.
29. This correspondence has now been published. See Michael and Eleanor Brock (eds), *H. H. Asquith: Letters to Venetia Stanley* (Oxford, 1982).
30. Terraine, *Haig*, 230; also see Hankey, *Supreme Command*, 510–16 for the rationale in its fully-developed form.
31. B. H. Liddell Hart, *The Liddell Hart Memoirs. Volume 1* (1965), 75.
32. Lord Newton, *Lord Lansdowne: A Biography* (1929), 443.
33. F. W. Hirst, *The Consequences of the War to Great Britain* (1934), 73.
34. See 'Memorandum by Lord Crewe: The Break-Up of the First Coalition' in Lord Oxford and Asquith, *Memories and Reflections, 1852–1927. Volume 2*, 127; also see Newton, *Lansdowne*, 450–1.
35. Robbins, *Grey*, 342–6.
36. For a partisan view of the planning of the Flanders campaign see Lloyd George, *War Memoirs: Volume IV* (1934), 2167; also Terraine, *Haig*, 337.
37. Lord Riddell, *Intimate Diary of the Peace Conference and*

After, 1918–23 (1933), 297. Foch described Haig's plan as 'a duck's march . . . to Ostend and Zeebrugge' – see Lloyd George, *War Memoirs*, IV, 2143.

38. Bernard Montgomery – awarded the DSO for actions during the First Battle of Ypres in 1914– typified the revulsion of a younger generation of Army professionals to the fighting on the Western Front. See Carlo D'Este, *Bitter Victory: The Battle For Sicily, 1943* (1988), 94–5. Not all, however, were to feel quite the same way. See above 85.

39. Paul Kennedy, *Realities Behind Diplomacy*, 211.

40. Despite the emphasis critical contemporaries put on an alleged 'loss of nerve' on Lansdowne's part, the latter's biographer stressed that it is 'quite evident that the Peace Letter was not an act of sudden impulse but represented a reasoned conclusion which had been formed a year earlier'. See Newton, *Lansdowne*, 463.

41. As Leopold Amery expressed the dominant British interpretation, 'the Yanks are just waking up to the fact that there is a war on, and that they may miss the last call for the dining car'. See John Barnes and David Nicolson (eds), *The Leo Amery Diaries. Vol. 1: 1876–1927* (1980), 213.

42. Lord Riddell, *Intimate Diary of the Peace Conference and After*, 272.

43. Stuart MacIntyre, *The Oxford History of Australia. Volume IV, 1901–42* (Oxford, 1986), 139.

44. For the genesis of this phenomenon see Suzanne Buckley, 'The Colonial Office and the Origins of an Imperial Development Board: The Impact of World War One', *The Journal of Imperial and Commonwealth History*, II: 3 (May 1974), 308–17.

45. The best scholarly treatment of the Imperial War Cabinet is Philip Wigley's *Canada and the transition to Commonwealth: British-Canadian Relations*, 1917–26 (Cambridge, 1977), 27–67.

46. Very suggestive on this matter is Jeffrey Greenhut, 'The Imperial Reserve: The Indian Corps on the Western Front',

The Journal of Imperial and Commonwealth History, XII: 1 (October 1983), 54–74.

47. This episode is retold by R. W. E. Harper and Harry Miller, *Singapore Mutiny*, (Oxford, 1984).

48. Relations between the War and India Offices in London hit rock-bottom early on in the war and never recovered. See Cassar, *Kitchener*, 224.

49. The definitive account of this campaign is A. J. Barker, *The Neglected War; Mesopotamia, 1914–18* (1967). The fate of Townshend's force is described in Ronald Miller, *Kut: The Death of an Army* (1969).

50. Howard M. Sachar, *The Emergence of the Modern Middle East, 1914–18* (New York, 1969), 212.

51. Ibid., 43–4.

52. Lieut.-Col. P. G. Elgood, *Egypt and the Army* (1929), 254–6; also see Ronald Hyam, 'Empire and Sexual Opportunity', *The Journal of Imperial and Commonwealth History*, XIV: 2 (January 1986), 52.

53. Roger Adelsen, *Mark Sykes: Portrait of an Amateur* (1972), 180.

54. For this febrile atmosphere see Colin Forbes Adam, *The Life of Lord Lloyd* (1948), 87–8.

55. Richard Aldington, *Lawrence of Arabia* (1955) later gained notoriety as a new genre of debunking biography.

56. Sachar, *Emergence of the Modern Middle East*, 230.

57. Ibid., 243.

58. Leonard Stein, *The Balfour Declaration* (1961) provides definitive detail.

59. Wilson, *Myriad Faces of War*, 547–9.

60. Martin Middlebrook, *March 1918* (1984) provides a full narrative of the crisis.

61. See Riddell, *Intimate Diary of the Peace Conference and After*, 151, where the telegram is accorded the status of an 'historic document'.

62. For the influential Cabinet Secretary's views at this point see Lord Hankey, *The Supreme Command, 1914–18*, (1961), 852–63.

63. Stephen McKenna, *McKenna*, 314.
64. Nigel Nicolson, *Alex* (1973), 52.
65. Churchill's multi-volume work, *The World Crisis*, was completed and published in its entirety by the end of 1923.

CHAPTER THREE   POLICEMAN OF THE WORLD

1. Kenneth O. Morgan, *Consensus and Disunity: The Lloyd George Coalition, 1918–22* (Oxford, 1979), 31.
2. Robert Skidelsky, *John Maynard Keynes: Hope Betrayed, 1883–1920* (1984), 378.
3. Ibid., 356.
4. Dan P. Silverman, *Reconstructing Europe after the Great War* (1982), 117–18.
5. The most evocative account of the Conference – Keynes's apart – remains Harold Nicolson, *Peacemaking 1919* (1933).
6. Morgan, *Consensus and Disunity*, 139.
7. Martin Gilbert, *Winston S. Churchill. Volume IV: 1917–22* (1976), 63.
8. Barnes and Nicholson (eds), *The Leo Amery Diaries*, 257.
9. Riddell, *Intimate Diary*, 106. This idiom of the 'non-existence' of the defeated became widespread among the victor nations – Lloyd George, for example, went on to assure the House of Commons that 'Turkey is no more'. See Gilbert, *Churchill*, IV, 488
10. See Robert Machray, *The Struggle for the Danube and the Little Entente*, 1929–1938 (1938) for background.
11. Riddell, *Intimate Diary*, 15.
12. For Churchill's role in the origins of Intervention against the Bolsheviks see Gilbert, *Churchill*, IV, 320–49.
13. Ibid., 371–2.
14. Sachar, *Emergence of the Modern Middle East*, 369.
15. Ibid., 375.
16. G. C. Peden, *British Economic and Social Policy: From Lloyd George to Margaret Thatcher* (1982), 64.
17. For the domestic agricultural situation in the immediate post-war period see Andrew Fenton Cooper, *British Agricultural Policy: A Study in Conservative Politics*

(1987), 113–26.

18. Carole Fink, *The Genoa Conference: European Diplomacy 1921–2* (Chapel Hill, N.C., 1984), 136.
19. Riddell, *Intimate Diary*, 347.
20. Fink, *The Genoa Conference*, 258–80.
21. Keith Middlemass and John Barnes, *Baldwin: a biography* (1969), 122–4.
22. For the role of the Die Hards in undermining the Coalition see Morgan, *Consensus and Disunity*, 236–54.
23. Keith Jeffery, *The British Army and the Crisis of Empire, 1918–22* (Manchester, 1984), 104.
24. For the sad dénouement of Montagu's career see S. D. Waley, *Edwin Montagu* (1964), 268–75; also Maurice Cowling, *The Impact of Labour* (Cambridge, 1971), 158–61.
25. Jeffery, *Crisis of Empire*, 114. An excellent overview of the regional context is John Darwin, *Britain, Egypt and the Middle East: Imperial Policy in the Aftermath of War* (1984).
26. Jeffery, *Crisis of Empire*, 121.
27. For a full treatment of the military aspects of the insurgency see Charles Townshend, *The British Campaign in Ireland 1919–21* (Oxford, 1975).
28. Riddell, *Intimate Diary*, 290.
29. Gilbert, *Churchill*, IV, 460.
30. Frank Pakenham, *Peace by Ordeal* (1955), 342.
31. Jeffery, *Crisis of Empire*, 92.
32. This metaphor recurs at intervals in the five volumes of Harold Macmillan's memoirs.
33. Harold Nicolson, *Curzon: The Last Phase* (1934), 104.
34. The Earl of Ronaldshay, *The Life of Lord Curzon. Volume III* (1929), 298–9.
35. David Walder, *The Chanak Affair* (London, 1969).
36. For Curzon's position on Greek-Turkish policy see Morgan, *Consensus and Disunity*, 319–21, 324–6.
37. Tim Harington, *Tim Harington Looks Back* (1940), 126.
38. Morgan, *Consensus and Disunity*, 210.

39. See above 87.

40. Blake, *The Unknown Prime Minister*, 448.

41. Robert C. Self, *Tories and Tariffs: The Conservative Party and the Politics of Tariff Reform, 1922–32* (1986), 13.

42. John Campbell, *F. E. Smith: First Earl Birkenhead* (1983), 636–42.

43. Self, *Tories and Tariffs*, 13.

44. Middlemass and Barnes, *Baldwin*, 150.

45. G. M. Young, *Baldwin* (1955), 39.

46. Ibid., 77.

47. Robert Rhodes James (ed.), *Chips: The Diaries of Sir Henry Chips Channon* (1967), 117.

48. Much of this feeling was wrapped up in images of Great War France – as Lord Halifax later recalled the typically stirring vision, 'a French territorial battalion, moving up towards the front: an old curé with wide-brimmed hat and black soutane in front with an officer; the men marching at ease, badly turned out, but gay, laughing and singing; transport carts with rather shabby horses or mules and pretty dirty harness, piled high with regimental and personal baggage. To me it was the embodiment of the spirit of France . . .'. See the Earl of Halifax, *Fullness of Days* (1957), 81. But later on this affection was curiously inverted – see above 168.

49. Quoted in R. F. Holland, *Britain and the Commonwealth Alliance* (1981), 47.

50. Ibid., 47–52; also see Wigley, *Canada and the Transition to Commonwealth*, 240–47.

51. Middlemass and Barnes, *Baldwin*, 136–48.

52. For background to this relationship, see Sir Henry Clay, *Lord Norman* (1957), 134–71.

53. Stephen Roskill, *Naval Policy between the Wars. Vol. I: The Period of Anglo-American Antagonism, 1919–29* (1968).

54. See Stephen Roskill, *Admiral of the Fleet Earl Beatty. The Last Naval Hero* (1979).

55. For a full treatment of the origins of this departure see W. David McIntyre, *The Rise and Fall of the Singapore Base*

(1979), 53–68.

56. Roskill, *Naval Policy between the Wars*, I, 498–516.

57. David Marquand, *Ramsay MacDonald* (1977), 473.

58. Middlemass and Barnes, *Baldwin*, 375.

59. Michael Howard, *The Continental Commitment: The Dilemma of British Defence Policy in the Era of Two World Wars* (1971), 70.

60. Young, *Baldwin*, 88.

61. Martin Gilbert, *Winston S. Churchill. Volume V: 1922–39* (1976), 53–62 for Churchill's accession to the Chancellorship.

62. The best overview of the British economy in this period is Sydney Pollard, *The Development of the British Economy. Third Edition: 1914–80* (1983), 106–53.

63. For Churchill's role in the decision to return to the Gold Standard see Gilbert, *Churchill*, V, 92–100.

64. Robert Boothby, who served under Churchill at the Treasury, recalled him saying after one meeting of senior officials, bankers and economists, 'I wish they were admirals or generals. I speak their language, and can beat them. But after a while these fellows start talking Persian. And then I am lost.' See Robert Boothby, *Recollections of a Rebel* (1965), 46.

65. Donald Moggridge, *British Monetary Policy, 1924–31: The Norman Conquest of $4.86* (1975), 29.

66. Gilbert, *Churchill*, IV, 99–100.

67. Ibid.

68. Middlemass and Barnes, *Baldwin*, 327.

69. Gilbert, *Churchill*, V, 146–74 covers Churchill's controversial behaviour during the General Strike, including his energetic and sometimes bellicose editorship of the *British Gazette*.

70. Middlemass and Barnes, *Baldwin*, 444–53.

71. Martin Gilbert, *Churchill, V, 272*.

72. *Maurice Cowling, The Impact of Labour, 1920–24: The Beginnings of Modern British Politics* (Cambridge, 1971).

73. Quoted in E. A. Brett, *Colonialism and Underdevelopment*

in East Africa: the Politics of Change, 1919–39 (1973), 18.

74. For Amery's own interpretation of events at this juncture see his memoirs entitled *My Political Life. Volume 2: War and Peace, 1914–29* (1953), 371–99.

75. I. D. Drummond, *British Economic Policy and the Empire, 1919–39* (1972), 37–88.

76. R. F. Holland, *Britain and the Commonwealth Alliance*, 104–5.

77. Douglas Jay, *Change and Fortune: A Political Record* (1980), 364–5.

78. Middlemass and Barnes, *Baldwin*, 234–5.

79. Quoted in Holland, *Commonwealth Alliance*, 61.

80. Chris Bayly (General Editor), *Atlas of the British Empire* (1989), 182.

81. See Waley, *Edwin Montagu*, 197–9.

82. For Lloyd's career in Egypt see Colin Forbes Adam, *Lord Lloyd*, 191–227. A more recent treatment, but one marred by romantic excess, is John Charmley, *Lord Lloyd and the Decline of the British Empire* (1987), 126–62.

CHAPTER FOUR   REALITY AND HONOUR IN THE AGE OF APPEASEMENT

1. Marquand, *Ramsay MacDonald*, 508.

2. Ibid., 514.

3. Ibid.

4. This is the theme of Robert Skidelsky, *Politicians and the Slump* (London, 1967).

5. For Snowden's account see Philip, Viscount Snowden, *An Autobiography. Volume II: 1919–34* (1934), 890–944.

6. Holland, *Commonwealth Alliance*, 122.

7. Marquand, *Ramsay MacDonald*, 605.

8. The drama which ensued can be followed in R. Bassett, *Nineteen Thirty-One: Political Crisis* (1958).

9. Marquand, *Ramsay MacDonald*, 622.

10. A. J. P. Taylor, *Beaverbrook* (1972), 276–7.

11. Ibid., 277. The general context of rural pressures is

analysed in Andrew Fenton Cooper, *British Agricultural Policy, 1912–36*, 113–26.

12. Stuart Ball, *Baldwin and the Conservative Party. The Crisis of 1929–31* (1988), 169.

13. Adam, *Lord Lloyd*, 219.

14. Gilbert, *Churchill*, V, 355.

15. Ibid.

16. Ball, *Baldwin and the Conservative Party*, 115.

17. Ibid., 183.

18. Samuel Hoare's memoirs rank as one of the most interesting of those published by leading British statesmen involved in the diplomacy of the 1930s. For his account of the formation of the National Government see Lord Templewood, *Nine Troubled Years* (1954), 13–41.

19. It is relevant in this context that Keynes expressed the view *before* the break-up of the Labour Government that sterling would have to be devalued regardless of events on the political front.

20. As a peer (Lord Arnold) remarked in the House of Lords on 25 March 1936, Anglo-Dominion trade disputes in this era testified to the ancient truth that 'there is no quarrel like a family quarrel'. For an excellent analysis of the context see T. J. Rooth, 'British Commercial Policy in the 1930s, with special reference to overseas primary producers', Thesis submitted for the Doctorate of Philosophy, University of Hull, 1984.

21. The fullest treatment of the Ottawa Conference is I. D. Drummond, *Imperial Economic Policy, 1917–39. Studies in Expansion and Protection* (1974), 170–299.

22. Quoted in Holland, *Commonwealth Alliance*, 141–2.

23. The so-called 'economic war' between the United Kingdom and the Irish Free State arose from the refusal of the government of Eamon de Valera after its election in February 1932 to pay the annuities due to British ex-civil servants in Ireland. See Deidre McMahon, *Republicans and Imperialists: Anglo-Irish Relations in the 1930s* (1984), 28–72.

24. Drummond, *Imperial Economic Policy*, 67.
25. See, for example, Ruth Megaw, 'Australia and the Anglo-American Trade Agreement of 1938', *Journal of Imperial and Commonwealth History*, 3 (1975), 191–211; R. F. Holland, 'The End of an Imperial Economy: Anglo-Canadian Disengagement in the 1930s', *Journal of Imperial and Commonwealth History*, 2 (1983), 159–75.
26. See Frank Freidel, *Franklin D. Roosevelt: Launching the New Deal* (Boston, 1973).
27. Herbert Feis, *1933: Characters in a Crisis* (Boston, 1966), 165–82.
28. See Gilbert, *Churchill*, V, 736. The industrialist was Lord Weir, a prominent figure in (and erstwhile President of) the Federation of British Industries. For the development of the latter body's views see R. F. Holland, 'The Federation of British Industries and the International Economy, 1918–39', *Economic History Review*, 33 (1981), 38–72.
29. Gilbert, *Churchill*, V, 776.
30. A full treatment of the course of this legislation is Carl Bridge, *Holding India to the Empire: The Conservative Party and the Government of India Act, 1935* (Madras, 1988).
31. Ibid., 153.
32. John Darwin, 'Imperialism in Decline? Tendencies in British Imperial Policy Between the Wars', *Historical Journal*, 23: 3 (1980), 657–79.
33. Bridge, *Holding India to the Empire*, 70.
34. J. Gallagher, *The Decline, Revival and Fall of the British Empire: The Ford Lectures and other essays* (Cambridge, 1982), 137–9.
35. Gilbert, *Churchill*, V, 467–9.
36. Ibid., 596.
37. Ibid, 601. It was precisely the danger that India, like Ireland before her, might be 'pitchforked into the party warfare of England' which made Baldwin refer so often to the dangers indicated by the analogy – see Young, *Baldwin*, 186–7.
38. Gilbert, *Churchill*, V, 480.

39. Holland, *Commonwealth Alliance*, 169–70.
40. David Dilks (ed.), *The Diaries of Sir Alexander Cadogan, 1938–1945* (1971), 189–90.
41. A. J. P. Taylor, *The Origins of the Second World War* (1961), 107.
42. David Carlton, *Anthony Eden: A Political Biography* (1985), 51.
43. G. C. Peden, *British Rearmament and the Treasury: 1933–39* (Edinburgh, 1979) provides a full discussion of this theme.
44. Marquand, *Ramsay MacDonald*, 757.
45. Cowling, *Impact of Hitler: British Politics and British Policy, 1933–40* (1975), 5.
46. Templewood, *Nine Troubled Years*, 137.
47. The convolutions of British policy are outlined in Frank Hardie, *The Abyssinian Crisis* (1972).
48. Quoted in Holland, *Commonwealth Alliance*, 183.
49. Ibid., 185.
50. Cowling, *Impact of Hitler*, 165.
51. Carlton, *Eden*, 85.
52. Dilks (ed), *Diaries of Sir Alexander Cadogan*, 213.
53. Gilbert, *Churchill*, V, 785.
54. For Churchill and the Abdication crisis see Gilbert, *Churchill*, V, 809–31.
55. Keith Feiling, *The Life of Neville Chamberlain* (1955), 215–16.
56. J. L. Garvin, *The Life of Joseph Chamberlain. Volume 3: 1895–1900* (1934), 324–43.
57. See David Dilks, *Neville Chamberlain. Volume 1: Pioneering and Reform, 1836–1929* (Cambridge, 1984), 451–6.
58. Templewood, *Nine Troubled Years*, 212–3.
59. Cowling, *Impact of Hitler*, 281; also see Michael J. Cohen, *Palestine: Retreat from the Mandate. The making of British policy, 1936–1945* (1978), 1–9.
60. Howard, *Continental Commitment*, 117–18.
61. Brian Bond, 'Leslie Hore-Belisha at the War Office' in Ian Becket and John Gooch, *Politicians and Defence: Studies*

in the Formulation of British Defence Policy, 1845–1970 (Manchester, 1981)), 118.

62. Ian Colvin, *The Chamberlain Cabinet* (1971), 46.
63. Ibid., 95.
64. Cowling, *Impact of Hitler*, 289–90.
65. Malcolm Muggeridge (ed.), *Ciano's Diplomatic Papers* (1948), 182–4.
66. Gilbert, *Churchill*, V, 934.
67. Telford Taylor, *Munich: The Price of Peace* (1979) provides exhaustive detail.
68. Cowling, *Impact of Hitler*, 201.
69. Ibid., 280.
70. Dilks (ed.) *The Diaries of Sir Alexander Cadogan*, 103–4.
71. See above 50.
72. Gilbert, *Churchill*, V, 984.
73. Ibid., 978.
74. Templewood, *Nine Troubled Years*, 313–24.
75. Ibid., 310; also see the account in Colvin, *The Chamberlain Cabinet*, 165–6.
76. Lord Butler, *The Art of the Possible* (1971), 77–8; also see the discussion of Halifax's role in Cowling, *Impact of Hitler*, 257–91.
77. Taylor, *Origins*, 251.
78. Richard Lamb, *The Drift to War, 1922–1939* (1939), 298–324.
79. Taylor, *Origins*, 374.
80. Cowling, *Impact of Hitler*, 388.
81. Paul Addison, *The Road to 1945: British Politics and the Second World War*, (1978), 52.
82. Cowling, *Impact of Hitler*, 298.
83. Gilbert, *Churchill*, V, 1109.

CHAPTER FIVE   THE ELUSIVE TRIUMPH

1. John Vincent, *Sunday Times*, 29 September 1985.
2. Quoted in John Charmley, *Lord Lloyd and the decline of the British Empire*, 233.
3. Correlli Barnett, *The Audit of War: The Illusion and Reality of Britain as a Great Power* (1986).

4. Dilks (ed.), *The Diaries of Sir Alexander Cadogan*, 219.

5. Addison, *The Road to 1945*, 63.

6. Martin Gilbert, *Winston S. Churchill. Volume VI: The Finest Hour, 1939–41* (1983), 81.

7. Thomas Jones, *A Diary with Letters, 1931–1950* (1954), 440.

8. Arthur Bryant, *The Turn of the Tide. Based on the War Diaries of Field-Marshal Lord Alanbrooke* (1957), 28.

9. Paul Addison, *The Road to 1945*, 64.

10. Eire was a special target of Churchill's wartime slights. 'At war but skulking' was his definition of her psychological, as much as juridical, status – see Gilbert, *Churchill*, VI, 67.

11. Robert Rhodes James, *Chips: The Diaries of Sir Henry Channon* (1967), 243. This sense of stale fabrication made a forcible impression upon some observers. Charles Ritchie, a Canadian diplomat in London, for example, noted the attempt at this time to whip up all the enthusiasms of the early days of the Great War – 'It was like sitting in the dentist's waiting-room', he told one acquaintance, 'and turning over the pages of some twenty-five year old magazines'. See John Colville, *Fringes of Power. Diaries, 1939–55* (1985), 28.

12. Gilbert, *Churchill*, VI, 263.

13. Ibid., 298.

14. Cowling, *The Impact of Hitler*, 247.

15. Addison, *The Road to 1945*, 95–6.

16. Gilbert, *Churchill*, VI, 299.

17. Colville, *The Fringes of Power*, 129.

18. Addison, *Road to 1945*, 18.

19. Cowling, *Impact of Hitler*, 262.

20. Addison, *Road to 1945*, 83.

21. François Kersaudy, *Churchill and De Gaulle*, 30–1.

22. Alistair Horne, *To Lose a Battle* (1970) is an engaging narrative of the Fall of France.

23. For an excellent account of Anglo-French discord see Eleanor M. Gates, *The End of the Affair: The Collapse*

of the Anglo-French Alliance, 1939–40 (1981), 361–73.

24. Gilbert, *Churchill*, VI, 505.
25. Quoted in David Fraser, *Alanbrooke* (London, 1982), 137.
26. See footnote (48) on 368 above.
27. Gilbert, *Churchill*, VI, 457–8.
28. Lord Ismay, *The Memoirs of Lord Ismay* (1960), 139–40.
29. Ibid.
30. Gilbert, *Churchill*, VI, 413.
31. Ibid., 642.
32. One who sporadically had visions of himself displacing Churchill was the Australian politician, Robert Menzies. For the tangled relations of the two men see David Day, *Menzies and Churchill at War* (Sydney, 1988).
33. Gilbert, *Churchill*, VI, 358.
34. Churchill called the arrival of Hopkins in London 'a historic moment'. See Colville, *The Fringes of Power*, 331–48.
35. A. J. P. Taylor, *Churchill: Four Faces and the Man* (1965), 44.
36. Paul Kennedy, *The Rise and Fall of the Great Powers* 367.
37. R. S. Sayers, *Financial Policy, 1939–45* (1956), 58–90.
38. Michael Howard, *The Continental Commitment*, 143–4.
39. David Carlton, *Eden*, 180.
40. Artemis Cooper, *Cairo in the War* (1989).
41. This test was prescribed by Churchill precisely because it was one that his leadership could realistically expect to pass. Hence the premier's directive to the Cabinet on 28 April 1941 that 'It is to be impressed upon all ranks, especially the highest, that the life and honour of the country depends upon the successful defence of Egypt.'
42. Ronald Lewin, *The Chief: Field Marshal Lord Wavell, Commander-in-Chief and Viceroy, 1939–47* (1980), 117–46.
43. Gilbert, *Churchill*, VI, 1119.
44. Addison, *Road to 1945*, 134.
45. See 'A Pearl Harbor Bombshell', *The Independent*, 14 March 1989.
46. Gilbert, *Churchill*, VI, 941.

47. Ibid., 775.
48. Addison, *Road to 1945*, 276–7.
49. Gilbert, *Churchill*, VI, 829.
50. Virginia Thompson, *Post-Mortem on Malaya* (New York, 1943.
51. Fraser, *Alanbrooke*, 227.
52. Stuart MacIntyre, *Oxford History of Australia. Volume 4: 1901–42*, 325–76.
53. David Day, *The Great Betrayal: Britain, Australia and the Onset of the Pacific War, 1939–42* (1988).
54. W. David McIntyre, *The Rise and Fall of the Singapore Naval Base*, 222.
55. Difficulties with the United States are, for example, a consistent theme in S. J. Butlin and C. B. Schedvin, *Australia in the War of 1939–45. War Economy*, 1942–45 (1977).
56. John Robertson, 'Australia and the "Beat Hitler First" Strategy, 1941–2: A Problem in Wartime Consultation', *The Journal of Imperial and Commonwealth History*, XI: 3 (May 1983), 300–21.
57. American suspicions of British war thinking are evoked in Arthur Layton Funk, *The Politics of Torch: The Allied Landings and the Algiers Putsch, 1942* (New York, 1974) and Mark A. Stoler, *The Politics of the Second Front. American Military Planning and Diplomacy in Coalition Warfare, 1941–3* (1977).
58. Bryant, *The Turn of the Tide*, 282.
59. For a survey of the development of the Anglo-American Grand Alliance see David Reynolds, 'Roosevelt, Churchill, and the wartime Anglo-American Alliance, 1939–45: Towards a New Synthesis' in Wm. Roger Louis and Hedley Bull, *The 'Special Relationship': Anglo-American Relations Since 1945* (1986), 17–41.
60. Martin Gilbert, *Winston S. Churchill. Volume VII: Road to Victory, 1941–45* (1986), 128.
61. Apart from Paul Addison's survey highlighted elsewhere in these notes, there is a dearth of scholarly work on Britain's

wartime coalition government, as opposed to the war proper. A short but useful treatment is J. M. Lee, *The Churchill Coalition, 1940–45* (1980).

62. Philip Warner, *Auchinleck: The Lonely Soldier* (1981), 153–74.

63. Gilbert, *Churchill*, VII, 184–7.

64. Ibid., 179.

65. Ibid., 331.

66. Ibid., 335.

67. Fraser, *Alanbrooke*, 267–8.

68. For a recent and judicious assessment of a controversial subject in British military history see John Strawson, *The Italian Campaign* (1987).

69. Gilbert, *Churchill*, VII, 503.

70. Ismay to Eisenhower 14 May 1958, ISMAY IV/Eis/4a, Ismay papers, Liddell Hart Military Archive, King's College, London.

71. Gilbert, *Churchill*, VII, 530.

72. Ibid., 581.

73. In fact Churchill's instinctive hesitations about the re-invasion of Europe as a British interest continued more or less up to D-Day itself. 'The prospect of the Second Front worried him', Colville, his Private Secretary, wrote on 4 April 1944, 'though he says he is "hardening to it".' Churchill, whose native enthusiasms scarcely ever needed reinforcement, only 'hardened' to things he disliked under overwhelming *force majeure*. See Gilbert, *Churchill*, VII, 727.

74. Ian M. McLaine, *Ministry of Morale. Home Front Morale and the Ministry of Information in the Second World War* (1979), 274. Also see Basil Collier, *The War in the Far East, 1941–5* (1969).

75. Fraser, *Alanbrooke*, 337–9, 410–12.

76. Philip Ziegler, *Mountbatten: the official biography* (1985), 278–80.

77. Arthur Bryant, *Triumph in the West. Completing the War Diaries of Field-Marshal Viscount Alanbrooke* (1959), 166.

78. Winston Churchill, *The Second World War: Volume VI* (1954), 198.

79. Thomas B. Buell, *Master of Seapower: A Biography of Fleet Admiral Ernest J. King* (Boston, 1980), 459–62. 'In Churchill's view', David Carlton remarks, 'only one substantial prize could be secured by the exertions of Great Britain alone. This was Greece.' See Carlton, *Eden*, 248.

80. Alistair Horne, *Macmillan 1894–1956: Volume I of the Official Biography*, (1988) 397.

81. Dilks (ed.), *The Diaries of Alexander Cadogan*, 446.

82. Robert Rhodes James (ed), *Chips*, 398.

83. Gilbert, *Churchill*, VII, 1348.

84. Gilbert, *Churchill*, IV, 167.

85. Kersaudy, *Churchill and De Gaulle*, 328.

86. R. A. Butler, *The Art of the Possible*, 111. For Churchill's 'exultant' feelings towards the atomic bomb, and the more equivocal attitude of the professional soldiers, see Fraser, *Alanbrooke*, 490.

87. The official British history of 'Tube Alloys' is Margaret Gowing, *Britain and Atomic Energy, 1939–45* (1964).

88. For the desperate attempts of the Danish atomic scientist, Niels Bohr, to intercede with Churchill on the broad political and ethical implications of the Bomb see Gowing, *Atomic Energy*, 353–5, 371.

CHAPTER SIX   LABOUR'S BULLDOG BREED

1. Kenneth Morgan, *Labour in Power, 1945–51* (Oxford, 1981), 326–7.

2. A cryptic survey of the Government's record is T. E. B. Howarth, *Prospect and Reality: Great Britain, 1945–55* (1985).

3. See the chapter entitled 'The Failure to Reappraise' in Philip Darby, *British Defence Policy East of Suez, 1947–1968* (1973), 10–31.

4. Kenneth Harris, *Attlee* (1982) 264.

5. Alan Bullock, *Ernest Bevin: Foreign Secretary* (Oxford, 1985), 76.

6. Richard N. Gardner, *Sterling-Dollar Diplomacy: Anglo-American Collaboration in the Reconstruction of Multilateral Trade* (Oxford, 1956), 199–207.

7. See the critique in Leopold Amery, *The Washington Loan Agreement* (1946).

8. For the defence of the Agreement see Gardner, *Sterling-Dollar Diplomacy*, 232–6.

9. See Ben Pimlott, *Hugh Dalton* (1985), 476–94; also Harris, *Attlee*, 332–54.

10. Raymond Smith and John Zamatica, 'The Cold Warrior: Clement Attlee Reconsidered, 1945–7', *International Affairs* 61: 2 (Spring 1985), 237–52.

11. Bullock, *Bevin*, 242.

12. Harris, *Attlee*, 299.

13. Bullock, *Bevin*, 113.

14. Ibid., 242.

15. Wm. Roger Louis, *The British Empire in the Middle East, 1945–51: Arab Nationalism, the United States and Post-War Nationalism* (Oxford, 1984), 238.

16. Ibid., 105–7.

17. Bullock, *Bevin*, 352.

18. Ibid., 135.

19. The British Foreign Secretary at this time became something of a butt among American foreign policy figures. Sumner Welles – admittedly a misanthrope by nature – referred to 'Bevin-pox' as a 'plague in international affairs caused by postwar British imperialism'. See Louis, *The British Empire in the Middle East, 1945–51*, 488.

20. Martin Gilbert, *Never Despair. Winston S. Churchill: 1945–1965* (1988), 197–203.

21. Bullock, *Bevin*, 131.

22. Jay, *Change and Fortune: A Political Record*, 152.

23. See John Gimbel, *The Origins of the Marshall Plan* (Stanford, 1976).

24. Bullock, *Bevin*, 413.

25. Bullock, *Bevin*, 419–27; also see Piers Dixon, *Double Diploma* (1968), 207–30.

26. Bullock, *Bevin*, 393; also see Pimlott, *Hugh Dalton*, 494–521.
27. For a summary of the 1942 Rebellion and its aftermath see Sumit Sarkar, *Modern India, 1885–1947* (1983), 388–413.
28. See above, 196.
29. John Darwin, *Britain and Decolonisation: The Retreat from Empire in the Post-War World* (1988), 94.
30. Philip Ziegler, *Mountbatten: the official biography* (1985).
31. C. A. Bayly, *Imperial Meridian: The British Empire and the World, 1780–1830* (1989), 142.
32. Nicholas Mansergh and Penderel Moon (eds.), *Constitutional Relations Between Britain and India. The Transfer of Power, 1942–7. Volume XI: The Mountbatten Viceroyalty* (1973), 53–8.
33. An interesting summary by an eye-witness is W. H. Morris-Jones, 'The Transfer to Power, 1947: A View From the Sidelines', *Modern Asian Studies*, 16 (1982), 1–32.
34. The situation in the Punjab is tellingly described in Penderel Moon, *Divide and Quit* (1961).
35. Ziegler, *Mountbatten*, 437–41 gives a balanced judgement.
36. R. J. Moore, *Making the New Commonwealth* (Oxford, 1987), 193.
37. For Churchill's attitude to the coming of Indian Independence see Gilbert, *Never Despair*, 292–5, 298–302, 332–7.
38. 'Powell', a biographer has commented, 'came to envy France's constructive and creative agony in Algeria . . .'. See Roy Lewis, *Enoch Powell: Principle in Politics* (1979), 78–80.
39. See footnote (3) above.
40. Cohen, *Palestine. Retreat from the Mandate*, 186–91 summarizes wartime developments.
41. Gilbert, *Churchill*, VII, 1053.
42. Bullock, *Bevin*, 181.
43. For background see Zvi Ganin, *Truman, American Jewry and Israel* (New York, 1979).
44. Louis, *The British Empire in the Middle East, 1945–51*, 442.
45. See G. M. Alexander, *The Prelude to the Truman Doctrine:*

British Policy in Greece (1982).

46. General Sir William Jackson, *Withdrawal from Empire: A Military View* (1986), 58–67.

47. This episode has recently been studied in Avi Schlaim, *Collusion Across the Jordan. King Abdullah, the Zionist Movement and the Partition of Palestine* (Oxford, 1988).

48. Louis, *The British Empire in the Middle East, 1945–51*, 331–6.

49. Ben Pimlott (ed), *The Political Diary of Hugh Dalton, 1945–60*, 443.

50. See Ronald Hyam, 'Africa and the Labour Government', *The Journal of Imperial and Commonwealth History*, XVI:3 (May 1988), 148–72.

51. See above 232.

52. For the link between the drive towards agricultural improvement and African discontent in Kenya, see David Throup, *The Origins of Mau Mau* (1989).

53. R. F. Holland, *Commonwealth Alliance*, 164–6.

54. Nehru's role in this development is highlighted in R. J. Moore, *Making the New Commonwealth*, 121–60.

55. John Darwin, *Britain and Decolonisation: The Retreat from Empire in the Postwar World*, 153.

56. Moore, *Making the New Commonwealth*, 116–210.

57. Darwin, *Britain and Decolonisation*, 129.

58. Bullock, *Bevin*, 310.

59. Pimlott, *Hugh Dalton*, 580–2.

60. See above, 288.

61. Bullock, *Bevin*, 701.

62. Ibid., 704–6.

63. Michael Charlton, *The Price of Victory* (1983), 61.

64. Quoted in Alec Cairncross (ed.), *The Robert Hall Diaries, 1947–53* (1989), 57.

65. The literature on the external policies of the United States at this juncture is obviously immense. An excellent survey is J. L. Gaddis, *The U.S.A. and the Origins of the Cold War* (New York, 1972).

66. Bullock, *Bevin*, 722.

67. John W. Young, *The Foreign Policy of Churchill's Peacetime Administration, 1951–55* (Leicester, 1985), 117–21.
68. A recent account is Max Hastings, *The Korean War* (1982).
69. The doyen of American radical journalism in this period, I. F. Stone, gave MacArthur few benefits of the doubt in *The Hidden History of the Korean War* (New York, 1952).
70. Harris, *Attlee*, 461–7.
71. Differences between the western allies are revealingly traced in Robert O'Neill, *Australia in the Korean War, 1950–53: Vol. I, Strategy and Diplomacy* (Canberra, 1981), 272–300.
72. Louis, *The British Empire in the Middle East, 1945–51*, 595.
73. A. P. Thornton, *The Imperial Idea and Its Enemies* (1959), 313–15.
74. See Bernard Donoughue and G. W. Jones, *Herbert Morrison. Portrait of a Politician* (1973).
75. Louis, *The British Empire in the Middle East, 1945–51*, 688.
76. Ibid.
77. The withdrawal of personnel was to be repeated under the comparable circumstances of the nationalization of the Suez Canal Company by the Egyptian Government in 1956 – with no more effective results.
78. Alistair Horne, *Macmillan: 1894–1956*, 72.
79. Gilbert, *Never Despair*, 630–50.
80. John Darwin, *Britain and Decolonisation*, 163–4.
81. Gilbert, *Never Despair*, 650.

CHAPTER SEVEN   INTO THE TUNNEL

1. Colville, *Fringes of Power*, 632.
2. Horne, *Macmillan: 1894–1956*, 353.
3. Colville, *Fringes of Power*, 644.
4. The Churchill Government at first revised rearmament spending downwards, but the reductions were essentially notional and real spending subsequently increased further – peaking at approximately 12% of Gross National Product.

5. For ROBOT and its context see Alec Cairncross, *Years of Recovery: British Economic Policy, 1945–51* (1985), 286–310; also see Donald MacDougall, *Don and Mandarin: Memoirs of an Economist* (1988), 88–110.

6. Anthony Howard, *Rab: The Life of R. A. Butler* (1987), 187.

7. Douglas Jay, *Sterling* (1983), 130.

8. Samuel Brittan, *Steering the Economy: the role of the Treasury* (1971), discusses the substantive economic issues during the period.

9. Robert Skidelsky and Vernon Bogdanor (eds), *The Age of Affluence* (1970).

10. Jay, *Change and Fortune*, 213–14.

11. R. Lamb, *The Failure of the Eden Government* (1982), 47.

12. Ibid., 56.

13. Colville, *Fringes of Power*, 638.

14. Lord Birkenhead, *Walter Monckton: The Life of Viscount Monckton of Brenchley* (1969), 283–96; Monckton's favourite venue to negotiate with trade-union leaders was the Aperitif Grill in Jermyn Street – see Howarth, *Prospect and Reality*, 181.

15. Gilbert, *Never Despair*, 751.

16. Ibid., 678.

17. Cairncross, *Recovery*, 242.

18. Lord Butler, *The Art of the Possible*, 166–7.

19. Colville, *Fringes of Power*, 661–2.

20. For Dulles' equivocations towards the United Kingdom see Richard Goold-Adams, *The Time of Power: A Reappraisal of John Foster Dulles* (1962), 11–20.

21. R. B. Manderson-Jones, *The Special Relationship: Anglo-American Relations and Western European Unity, 1946–56* (1972), 110–11.

22. H. W. Brands, 'India and Pakistan in American Strategic Planning, 1947–54: Commonwealth as Collaborator', *The Journal of Imperial and Commonwealth History*, XV:I (October 1986), 41–54.

23. Lord Moran, *The Struggle for Survival* (1966), 445–6.

24. Colville, *Fringes of Power*, 706.
25. Gilbert, *Never Despair*, 677.
26. Colville, *Fringes of Power*, 650–51.
27. Evelyn Shuckburgh, *Descent to Suez: Diaries, 1951–56* (1986), 113.
28. Ibid.
29. John Baylis, *Anglo-American Defence Relations, 1939–84* (1984), 66.
30. Anthony Verrier, *Through the Looking-Glass: British Foreign Policy in the Age of Illusion* (1981), 218.
31. Lawrence Freedman, *The Evolution of Nuclear Strategy* (1974), 70.
32. Richard H. Ullman, 'America, Britain, and the Soviet Threat in Historical and Present Perspective' in Wm. Roger Louis and Hedley Bull, *The 'Special Relationship': Anglo-American Relations Since 1945*, 105.
33. Alfred Grosser, *The Western Alliance. European-American Relations Since 1945* (1980), 123–8.
34. Michael Charlton, *The Price of Victory*, 124–65.
35. Manderson-Jones, *The Special Relationship*, 120.
36. Gilbert, *Never Despair*, 916.
37. Richard Goold-Adams, *The Time of Power*, 155.
38. Carlton, *Eden*, 362–3.
39. Charlton, *The Price of Victory*, 61.
40. Lord Gladwyn, *Memoirs* (1972), 363.
41. The role of the Fourth Republic in laying the foundations of a French 'economic miracle' has been highlighted in John Ardagh, *The New French Revolution* (1968).
42. Suggestively, when the first major pan-European negotiations on economic issues had been held in 1931–2 – mainly with reference to agricultural production and exchange – the response of the British Government had been to send a Board of Trade 'observer' with a remit to take notes and say nothing. Then, as later, it was France and Germany who found that in *these* spheres they had interests in common.
43. Charlton, *The Price of Victory*, 191.
44. Ibid., 199.

45. Lamb, *The Failure of the Eden Government*, 79.

46. Sir Leslie Monson speaking at a symposium in London on 'Decolonisation and the Colonial Office' on 25 November 1988. This meeting was organized by the Institute of Contemporary History, which possesses a record of the meeting.

47. There is much evidence along these lines in D. J. Morgan, *The Official History of Colonial Development. Volume 3: A Reassessment of Aid Policy, 1951–65* (1980) and *Volume 4: Changes in British Aid Policy, 1951–70* (1980).

48. D. J. Morgan, *Reassessment of Aid Policy*, 13–17; but also see Darwin, *Britain and Decolonisation*, 230.

49. For tensions within the Sterling Area see Philip W. Bell, *The Sterling Area in the Postwar World: Internal Mechanism and Cohesion, 1946–52* (Oxford, 1956), 396–419; also Judd Polk, *Sterling: Its Meaning in World Finance* (1956), 103–45.

50. Australian economic policy was consistently the object of criticism in such British publications as *The Economist*, where that country was often compared to its detriment with the ever-virtuous (because non-inflationary) Canada.

51. This argument was prominent in Andrew Shonfield's influential work, *The British Economy Since the War*, published in 1958.

52. David Goldsworthy, 'Keeping Change Within Bounds: Aspects of Colonial Policy during the Churchill and Eden Governments, 1951–57', *The Journal of Imperial and Commonwealth History*, XVIII:I (January 1990), 81–108.

53. Lewis, *Enoch Powell: Principle in Politics*, 73–89.

54. The equivocal attitude of Colonial Office officials to African political advance is recaptured in the contributions by retired officers to the symposium detailed under fn. (46) above.

55. Goldsworthy, 'Keeping Change Within Bounds: Aspects of Colonial Policy during the Churchill and Eden Governments, 1951–57', 89.

56. This story is best retold in David Rooney, *Sir Charles Arden-Clarke* (1982).

57. Darwin, *Britain and Decolonisation*, 180–83.
58. The establishment and later course of the Federation's history can be followed in Robert Blake, *A History of Rhodesia* (1977).
59. The crucial moment here was the fall from power in Southern Rhodesia of the liberally-inclined premier, Garfield Todd, in 1957. See Blake, *Rhodesia*, 304–11.
60. A. N. Porter and A. J. Stockwell, *British Imperial Policy and Decolonization, 1938–64. Volume 2: 1951–64* (1989), 319–24.
61. A full political outline of what followed may be obtained in Nancy Crawshaw, *The Cyprus Revolt* (1978).
62. Darwin, *Britain and Decolonisation*, 279–90.
63. Shuckburgh, *Descent to Suez*, 29.
64. Ibid., 74.
65. Verrier, *Through the Looking Glass*, 79–159 is very revealing on this theme.
66. Shuckburgh, *Descent to Suez*, 187.
67. An excellent contemporary account is Ellen Hammer, *The Struggle for Indo-China* (Stanford, 1954).
68. Shuckburgh, *Descent to Suez*, 185.
69. Ibid., 193.
70. Wm. Roger Louis, 'The Tragedy of the Anglo-Egyptian Settlement of 1954' in Wm. Roger Louis and Roger Owen (eds), *Suez 1956: The Crisis and its Consequences* (Oxford, 1989), 43–71.
71. Horne, *Macmillan 1894–1956*, 369.
72. Shuckburgh, *Descent to Suez*, 308.
73. King Faisal II, together with some of his relatives and his longstanding Prime Minister, Nuri es Said, were murdered during the coup led by General Kassem on 14 July 1958.
74. Shuckburgh, *Descent to Suez*, 340.
75. Horne, *Macmillan: 1894–1956*, 388.
76. For a short and accessible narrative see David Carlton, *The Suez Crisis* (1988).
77. Howard, *Rab*, 229–42.
78. Horne, *Macmillan: 1894–1956*, 416.

79. For the role played by the incumbent Commonwealth Relations Secretary during the Suez crisis see Kenneth Young, *Sir Alec Douglas-Home* (1970), 85–100. Douglas-Home's main difference with Eden was that the former favoured a military operation carried out exclusively by British troops.

80. Horne, *Macmillan: 1894–1956*, 431.

81. Ibid. See especially Diane B. Kunz, 'The Importance of Having Money: The Economic Diplomacy of the Suez Crisis' in Louis and Owen (eds), *Suez 1956*, 215–32.

82. Lamb, *The Failure of the Eden Government*, 291.

83. Carlton, *Eden*, 455–65.

84. Horne, *Macmillan: 1894–1956*, 453.

85. For an account of this conjuncture from Butler's perspective see Howard, *Rab*, 241–8.

86. See above 248.

87. Horne, *Macmillan: 1894–1956*, 165–6.

88. Verrier, *Through the Looking Glass*, 91.

89. Lamb, *The Failure of the Eden Government*, 305.

CHAPTER EIGHT: THE MODERNIZATION OF BRITAIN?

1. Horne, *Macmillan 1894–56*, 350–1.

2. See above 245.

3. Andrew Pierre, *Nuclear Politics: The British Experience with an Independent Strategic Force, 1939–70* (Oxford, 1970), 95.

4. It is striking in this context that, as soon as the strategic role of nuclear deterrence among opposed alliances was undermined by the attenuation of the Cold War at the end of the 1980s, a new consensus showed signs of crystallizing around the need to counter such neo-Nasserite threats as those posed by régimes in Libya and Iraq.

5. Pierre, *Nuclear Politics*, 94.

6. Dwight D. Eisenhower, *The White House Years: Waging Peace, 1956–61* (1966), 289.

7. For the origins of this usage see Horne, *Macmillan 1894–1956*, 160.

8. Alistair Horne, *Macmillan: 1957–1986. Volume II of the*

Official Biography (1989), 55.

9. Charlton, *The Price of Victory*, 212–13.

10. Horne, *Macmillan: 1957–84*, 129–33.

11. Dwight D. Eisenhower, *Waging Peace*, 409.

12. It was at this time that a convention emerged whereby those who had built their careers as 'hawks' published memoirs with 'dovish' titles, thus covering all flanks. Examples of this were to abound over the following twenty years.

13. Horne, *Macmillan: 1957–1984*, 224.

14. 'To say that Macmillan was dismayed', the British Ambassador in Paris at the time has remarked, 'would be the greatest of understatements. He was shattered.' Gladwyn, *Memoirs*, 321.

15. Horne, *Macmillan: 1957–1984*, 224.

16. It was an accident of some moment that Chancellor Adenauer was closeted with Prime Minister Guy Mollet in Paris when the news came through of the British decision to withdraw. The German leader was quick to point out that the relationship he had to offer the French was more reliable.

17. The 'rediscovery' of EFTA as a significant part of the institutional fabric of Europe after the upheavals of 1989, and the importance ascribed to linking it more organically to the EEC, also suggests that the former organization was never the mere shell that some accounts imply.

18. British policy towards Europe in this period may be followed in Miriam Camps, *Britain and the European Community* (1964).

19. Horne, *Macmillan: 1957–1984*, 109.

20. Charlton, *The Price of Victory*, 207.

21. The German viewpoint may be gleaned from Terence Prittie, *Konrad Adenauer, 1876–1967* (1972), 210–15.

22. For the British economic debate over the Common Market see Camps, *Britain and the European Community*, 313–86.

23. Charlton, *The Price of Victory*, 245.

24. Ibid., 242.

25. See above 303.
26. Charlton, *The Price of Victory*, 273.
27. Darby, *British Defence Policy East of Suez, 1947–68*, 58, 114.
28. Templer's stormy relationship with Duncan Sandys is charted in Richard Cloake, *Templer: Tiger of Malaya* (1988), 358–83.
29. Horne, *Macmillan: 1957–84*, 49.
30. Ibid., 51.
31. Ibid., 43.
32. For the Kuwait operation see Darby, *British Defence Policy East of Suez*, 219–22, 244–50.
33. Ibid., 163.
34. Ibid., 329.
35. The atmosphere of the British presence in this region during the 1950s is conjured up in David Holden, *Farewell to Arabia* (1966).
36. See R. F. Holland, 'The Imperial Factor in British Strategies from Attlee to Macmillan, 1945–63', *The Journal of Imperial and Commonwealth History* XII:2 (January 1984), 165–86.
37. See John Darwin, *Britain and Decolonisation*, 224–5 and A. N. Porter and A. J. Stockwell, *British Imperial Policy and Decolonization*, II, 29–32.
38. Porter and Stockwell, *British Imperial Policy and Decolonization*, II, 31.
39. See George Hutchinson, *The Last Edwardian at No. 10* (1980).
40. Nigel Fisher, *Iain Macleod* (1973), 60.
41. Ibid.
42. Ibid., 136.
43. Iain Macleod, 'Trouble in Africa', *The Spectator*, 31 January 1964.
44. For an account of this episode see Clyde Sanger, *Central African Emergency* (1960), 227–75.
45. Horne, *Macmillan: 1957–84*, 188.
46. Blake, *Rhodesia*, 327.

47. For de Gaulle's Algerian policies see Alistair Horne, *A Savage War of Peace: Algeria, 1954–62* (1977), 373–97, 415–35, 480–504; French dilemmas in this setting, not least in their moral dimension, are also nicely captured in John Talbot, *The War Without a Name: France in Algeria, 1954–62* (1981), 216–49.

48. Fisher, *Iain Macleod*, 147.

49. Ibid., 41.

50. Nigel Fisher, *Harold Macmillan* (1982), 231.

51. A good coverage of the Congolese saga is Crawford Young, *Politics in the Congo: Decolonization and Independence* (Princeton, 1965).

52. Horne, *Macmillan: 1957–84*, 402; also see Fisher, *Macmillan*, 225.

53. It is suggestive that the critical choices on economic issues in virtually every British Government since the end of the Second World War – from the decision to seek an American loan in 1945, and the rejection of ROBOT in 1951, through to the abandonment of foreign exchange controls in 1979 – were made at the outset of administrations.

54. Horne, *Macmillan: 1957–84*, 77.

55. Roy Lewis, *Enoch Powell*, 50–57.

56. Horne, *Macmillan: 1957–84*, 140.

57. Ibid., 70.

58. Donald Gordon, *Baltimore Sun*, 21 November 1971.

59. Horne, *Macmillan: 1957–84*, 245.

60. Ibid., 469.

61. Lawrence Freedman, *Britain and Nuclear Weapons*, 8–9.

62. Pierre, *Nuclear Politics*, 196–201.

63. Ibid., 222–4.

64. Horne, *Macmillan: 1957–84*, 284.

65. Ibid., 286.

66. Pierre, *Nuclear Politics*, 230.

67. J. Baylis, *Anglo-American Defence Relations*, 101.

68. Ibid., 102.

69. Horne, *Macmillan: 1957–84*, 435.

70. Ibid., 438.

71. Ibid., 439.
72. Ibid., 443.
73. Baylis, *Anglo-American Defence Relations*, 104, 57.
74. Horne, *Macmillan: 1957–84*, 447.
75. Ibid., 446.
76. See Howard, *Rab*, 319.
77. Fisher, *Macmillan*, 342.
78. Horne, *Macmillan: 1957–84*, 242.
79. Ibid., 537.
80. Ibid., 613.
81. David Butler and Anthony King, *The British General Election of 1964* (1965), 130–1; also see Pierre, *Nuclear Politics*, 269–72.

CHAPTER NINE   OFF THE PERCH

1. Harold Wilson, *The Labour Government, 1964–1970: A Personal Record* (1971), 246.
2. Ibid., 6–7. It is noteworthy that whatever later divergences over economic policy developed between the Labour Government and the Bank of England, a prejudice against devaluation was something they held in common. '. . . I believe', wrote Christopher McMahon, expressing the demi-official Bank view, 'that as things are the United Kingdom should never devalue. She might be driven to it by an overwhelming crisis; but it would be an act of desperation carrying no assurance that it would improve her situation.' These were prophetic words. See Christopher McMahon, *Sterling in the Sixties* (1964), 58–9.
3. See above 201.
4. Darby, *British Defence Policy East of Suez*, 215.
5. Darwin, *Britain and Decolonisation*, 291.
6. John Darwin, 'British Decolonization since 1945: A Pattern or a Puzzle?' in R. Holland and G. Rizvi (eds), *Perspectives on Imperialism and Decolonization: Essays in Honour of A. F. Madden* (1984), 191.
7. Jay, *Change and Fortune*, 242–3 gives the anti-Common Market case as it appeared to a leading figure in the Labour

Party during the early sixties.

8. For the manner in which anti-Germanism blended smoothly with a wider anti-Europeanism on the Left of British politics after the Second World War, see Pimlott, *Hugh Dalton*, 567–9.

9. Jay, *Change and Fortune*, 297–300.

10. Miriam Camps, *European Unification in the Sixties* (1966), 81–124.

11. R. H. Crossman, *The Diaries of a Cabinet Minister. Volume 1: Minister of Housing, 1964–66* (1976), 94, 116–7.

12. See above 205.

13. Wilson, *The Labour Government, 1965 70*, 264; for a discussion of 'the American Connection' after October 1964 see Clive Ponting, *Breach of Promise: Labour in Power, 1964–70* (1988), 40–61.

14. It was the opinion of some commentators that as premier Heath deliberately allowed the 'Special Relationship' with the United States to wither in order to further the European dimension of British policy – in effect, to prove the United Kingdom's credentials as a 'good European'. His increasingly acidic tone towards America in later years adds credence to this view. See Baylis, *Anglo-American Defence Relations*, 174.

15. Wilson, *The Labour Government, 1964–70*, 187, 264.

16. The international economic and financial issues which came gradually to be so prominent are outlined in Alfred Grosser, *The Western Alliance: European-American Relations Since 1945*, 209–43.

17. Crossman, *Diaries of a Cabinet Minister. Volume 1*, 80.

18. Darwin, *Britain and Decolonisation*, 291–2; also Michael Dockrill, *British Defence Policy since 1945* (1988), 91–7.

19. The minister was Christopher Mayhew. See his chapter 'Why I Resigned' in *Britain's Role Tomorrow* (1967), 131–53.

20. Kennedy Trevaskis, *Shades of Amber: A South Arabian Episode* (1968), 237.

21. Ibid., 238. Denis Healey's somewhat bland reminiscences

of the East of Suez saga may be found in *The Time of My Life* (1989), 278–300. A study based on fresh research is Karl Pierogostini, *Abandoning Empire: Britain, Aden and South Arabia* (Washington, 1989).

22. Darwin, *Britain and Decolonisation*, 293.
23. Ibid., 294.
24. Crossman, *Diaries of a Cabinet Minister. Volume 2: Lord President of the Council and Leader of the House of Commons* (1976), 557.
25. Wilson, *The Labour Government, 1964–70*, 409.
26. Blake, *Rhodesia*, 356–7.
27. The laborious details of the *Tiger* and *Fearless* negotiations may be found in Kenneth Young, *Rhodesia and Independence* (1969).
28. Lt.-Col. Colin Mitchell, *Having Been A Soldier* (1969), 169–92.
29. For Macmillan's dismay in retirement at the dismantling of the East of Suez policy, for example, see Horne, *Macmillan: 1957–84*, 615.
30. See 'The Coup That Never Was', *The Times*, 7 August 1987; also Cecil King, *The Diary of Cecil King, 1965–70* (1972), 192–3.
31. Philip Goodhart, 'Woman at the Helm', *Financial Times*, 16 August 1989.
32. The visitor was the socialist intellectual and organizer H. M. Hyndman, who had described to Disraeli his vision of a great overhaul of national life. Within two weeks of this conversation, Disraeli was dead. See H. M. Hyndman, *The Record of an Adventurous Life* (1911), 244–5.

EPILOGUE   GREATNESS AND THE NATION
1. Riddell, *More Pages From My Diary*, 139.
2. Shuckburgh, *Descent to Suez*, 71.
3. Norman St John Stevas (ed.), *Walter Bagehot: Historical Essays* (New York, 1965), 230.
4. H. C. G. Mathew, *Gladstone, 1809–1876* (Oxford, 1988), 123–4.

5. J. L. Hammond, *Gladstone and the Irish Nation* (1938), 315.

6. Riddell, *More Pages From My Diary*, 39.

7. Cowling, *Impact of Labour*, 60.

8. C. E. Montagu, *Disenchantment* (1922), 5.

9. Cowling, *Impact of Labour*, 50.

10. Gilbert, *Churchill*, IV, 115. This theme of national unity unmitigated by party or sectional feeling was henceforth to be the basis for Churchill's addresses to foreign, as well as domestic, audiences. 'Let party hatreds die!' he told a crowd of 50,000 people gathered in Constitution Square in Athens during the remarkable events of December 1944. 'Let there be unity. Let there be resolute comradeship. Greece forever! Greece for all!' His famous speech on the unity of Europe delivered to the burghers of Zurich on 19 September 1946 was couched in the same vein. Where some commentators, and not a few historians afterwards, went wrong in this latter case was in supposing that Churchill's words meant something in terms of practical arrangements, and the United Kingdom's relationship to them.

11. Ibid., 339.

12. General Charles Gordon was the Victorian soldier and evangelizer who, having been dispatched to the Sudan by the Gladstone administration at the end of 1883 in order to save the Anglo-Egyptian garrisons in that territory during the revolt of the *Mahdi*, was widely considered to have been subsequently abandoned to a hero's death. He died in Khartoum in January 1885, a matter of hours before the expedition sent to relieve him arrived in the city.

13. Gates, *The End of an Affair*, 39.

14. Rhodes James, *The Diaries of Sir Henry Chips Channon*, 68.

15. Gladwyn, *Memoirs*, 412.

16. McMahon, *Sterling in the Sixties*, 112.

17. Antony Bevin, 'How Thatcher became a Thatcherite', *The Independent*, 1 May 1988.

Index